Collins
gem

Hockey Facts & Stats

2010–11

Andrew Podnieks

Collins Gem Hockey Facts & Stats, 2010–11
Copyright © 2010 by Andrew Podnieks.
All rights reserved.

First edition

Published by Collins, an imprint of HarperCollins Publishers Ltd.

HarperCollins books may be purchased for educational, business, or sales
promotional use through our Special Markets Department.

HarperCollins Publishers Ltd
2 Bloor Street East, 20th Floor
Toronto, Ontario, Canada
M4W 1A8

www.harpercollins.ca

ISBN: 978-1-55468-907-1

Library and Archives Canada Cataloguing in Publication data is available
upon request.

Printed and bound in Canada
9 8 7 6 5 4 3 2 1

Contents

INTERNATIONAL HOCKEY

Introduction

It wasn't long after the final game of the 2010 Stanley Cup playoffs that many in the hockey world started to call the 2009–10 season the greatest on record. And with so much compelling evidence, it's hard to argue.

The year began with first-overall draft choice John Tavares earning a spot in the lineup of the New York Islanders, joining a league that featured the rivalry of Sidney Crosby and Alexander Ovechkin. During the year, Martin Brodeur set all-time records for a goalie that might never be beaten, surpassing Terry Sawchuk's once-untouchable 103 career shutouts in the regular season and Patrick Roy's marks for wins and minutes played.

In January, 2010, Canada and the United States played a thrilling gold medal game to cap the World Junior (U20) Championship in Saskatoon, Saskatchewan, and during the event Steve Yzerman, Canada's executive director for the 2010 Olympic Winter Games in Vancouver, unveiled the Canadian lineup for the men's team.

The Winter Classic at Fenway Park in Boston between the Boston Bruins and Philadelphia Flyers was an unqualified success, and at game's end Team USA general manager Brian Burke unveiled his roster for the Olympics.

The Olympics themselves were simply the greatest ever. Canada won gold thanks to a thrilling overtime goal from, who else, Crosby, just days after Canada hammered the Russians, 7–3, in perhaps the fastest, most skilful hockey game ever played. The final game was watched by some 28 million Canadians, or 80 per cent of the country, making it by far the most watched broadcast in Canada's history.

The women's finals also featured a Canada–United States showdown, and, as in 2002, Canada won double gold. The heroes for the women were Marie-Philip Poulin and goalie Shannon

Szabados, the former for scoring the only two goals of the game, the latter for her brilliant play in shutting out the Americans in a 2–0 win.

The NHL season resumed, and the playoffs turned into one of the most exciting in recent memory, complete with upsets, dozens of playoff beards and only the occasional fight. The Montreal Canadiens thrilled fans across the country with their unexpected trip to the Eastern Conference final, and no one could have predicted Philadelphia's march to the finals.

Chicago, on the other hand, was one team expected to go far with a lineup full of youth and speed and talent, and the Hawks didn't disappoint. Led by their incredible captain and Conn Smythe Trophy winner, Jonathan Toews, the Hawks won the Cup for the first time since 1961. In the process, Toews joined the Triple Gold Club, having won the Olympic gold only months earlier and claiming gold from the World Championship in 2007. He joined Eric Staal and coach Mike Babcock as TGC members, these men having completed their trifectas in Vancouver in February 2010.

Indeed, it was a season to remember, one in which much went right and little went wrong (think head shots, the Phoenix Coyotes turmoil). As we head into the 2010–11 season, there is much to look forward to and much to enjoy, but last season will be a tough act to follow, that's for sure.

Andrew Podnieks
Toronto, August 2010

GLOSSARY OF ABBREVIATIONS

NHL Teams

ANA=Anaheim Ducks, ATL=Atlanta Thrashers, BOS=Boston Bruins, BUF=Buffalo Sabres, CAL=Calgary Flames, CAR=Carolina Hurricanes, CHI=Chicago Blackhawks, COL=Colorado Avalanche, CBJ=Columbus Blue Jackets, DAL=Dallas Stars, DET=Detroit Red Wings, EDM=Edmonton Oilers, FLO=Florida Panthers, LA=Los Angeles Kings, MIN=Minnesota Wild, MON=Montreal Canadiens, NAS=Nashville Predators, NJ=New Jersey Devils, NYI=New York Islanders, NYR=New York Rangers, OTT=Ottawa Senators, PHI=Philadelphia Flyers, PHO=Phoenix Coyotes, PIT=Pittsburgh Penguins, STL=St. Louis Blues, SJ=San Jose Sharks, TB=Tampa Bay Lightning, TOR=Toronto Maple Leafs, VAN=Vancouver Canucks, WAS=Washington Capitals

International

AUT	Austria	JPN	Japan
BLR	Belarus	KAZ	Kazakhstan
CAN	Canada	LAT	Latvia
CZE	Czech Republic	NOR	Norway
DEN	Denmark	RUS	Russia
FIN	Finland	SUI	Switzerland
FRA	France	SVK	Slovakia
GER	Germany	SWE	Sweden
ITA	Italy	USA	United States

THE TWENTY-FIRST OLYMPIC WINTER GAMES

VANCOUVER, CANADA, February 12–28, 2010

Results, Men

Final Placing

GOLD MEDAL	Canada
SILVER MEDAL	United States
BRONZE MEDAL	Finland
Fourth Place	Slovakia
Fifth Place	Sweden
Sixth Place	Russia
Seventh Place	Czech Republic
Eighth Place	Switzerland
Ninth Place	Belarus
Tenth Place	Norway
Eleventh Place	Germany
Twelfth Place	Latvia

All-Star Team

Goal	Ryan Miller (USA)
Defence	Shea Weber (CAN), Brian Rafalski (USA)
Forward	Jonathan Toews (CAN), Pavol Demitra (SVK), Zach Parise (USA)

Directorate Awards

Best Goalie	Ryan Miller (USA)
Best Defenceman	Brian Rafalski (USA)
Best Forward	Jonathan Toews (CAN)
Tournament MVP	Ryan Miller (USA)

TOURNAMENT FORMAT

The 12 teams were placed in three groups of four teams each and played a round-robin series of games within their group. The teams were then ranked according to their results, and the top four teams received byes to the quarterfinals. Teams 5 through 12 were re-seeded and played a single-game qualification round (5th vs. 12th, 6th vs. 11th, and so on). The winner of each game advanced to the quarterfinals, while the losers were eliminated. The quarterfinals and semifinals followed a single-game elimination format. The two semifinal winners met in the gold medal game, and the losers played for bronze.

FINAL STANDINGS

Group A	GP	W	OTW	OTL	L	GF	GA	P
United States	3	3	0	0	0	14	5	9
Canada	3	1	1	0	1	14	7	5
Switzerland	3	0	1	1	1	8	10	3
Norway	3	0	0	1	2	5	19	1

February 16	United States 3/Switzerland 1
February 16	Canada 8/Norway 0
February 18	United States 6/Norway 1
February 18	Canada 3/Switzerland 2 (SO)
February 20	Switzerland 5/Norway 4 (OT)
February 21	United States 5/Canada 3

Group B	GP	W	OTW	OTL	L	GF	GA	P
Russia	3	2	0	1	0	13	6	7
Czech Republic	3	2	0	0	1	10	7	6
Slovakia	3	1	1	0	1	9	4	5
Latvia	3	0	0	0	3	4	19	0

February 16	Russia 8/Latvia 2
February 17	Czech Republic 3/Slovakia 1

February 18	Slovakia 2/Russia 1 (SO)
February 19	Czech Republic 5/Latvia 2
February 20	Slovakia 6/Latvia 0
February 21	Russia 4/Czech Republic 2

Group C	GP	W	OTW	OTL	L	GF	GA	P
Sweden	3	3	0	0	0	9	2	9
Finland	3	2	0	0	1	10	4	6
Belarus	3	1	0	0	2	8	12	3
Germany	3	0	0	0	3	3	12	0

February 17	Finland 5/Belarus 1
February 17	Sweden 2/Germany 0
February 19	Sweden 4/Belarus 2
February 19	Finland 5/Germany 0
February 20	Belarus 5/Germany 3
February 21	Sweden 3/Finland 0

Qualification Playoff

February 23	Switzerland 3/Belarus 2
February 23	Canada 8/Germany 2
February 23	Czech Republic 3/Latvia 2 (OT)
February 23	Slovakia 4/Norway 3

Quarterfinals

February 24	United States 2/Switzerland 0
February 24	Canada 7/Russia 3
February 24	Finland 2/Czech Republic 0
February 24	Slovakia 4/Sweden 3

Semifinals

| February 26 | United States 6/Finland 1 |
| February 26 | Canada 3/Slovakia 2 |

Bronze Medal Game
February 27   Finland 5/Slovakia 3

Gold Medal Game
February 28   Canada 3/United States 2 (OT)

Team Canada Statistics
Mike Babcock, coach

#	Pos.		GP	G	A	P	Pim
16	F	Jonathan Toews	7	1	7	8	2
12	F	Jarome Iginla	7	5	2	7	0
87	F	Sidney Crosby	7	4	3	7	4
15	F	Dany Heatley	7	4	3	7	4
51	F	Ryan Getzlaf	7	3	4	7	2
6	D	Shea Weber	7	2	4	6	2
21	F	Eric Staal	7	1	5	6	6
22	D	Dan Boyle	7	1	5	6	2
2	D	Duncan Keith	7	0	6	6	2
24	F	Corey Perry	7	4	1	5	2
61	F	Rick Nash	7	2	3	5	0
18	F	Mike Richards	7	2	3	5	0
11	F	Patrick Marleau	7	2	3	5	0
20	D	Chris Pronger	7	0	5	5	2
10	F	Brenden Morrow	7	2	1	3	2
27	D	Scott Niedermayer	7	1	2	3	4
19	F	Joe Thornton	7	1	1	2	0
8	D	Drew Doughty	7	0	2	2	2
37	F	Patrice Bergeron	7	0	1	1	2
7	D	Brent Seabrook	7	0	1	1	2
1	GK	Roberto Luongo	5	0	0	0	0
30	GK	Martin Brodeur	2	0	0	0	0

In Goal	GP	W-L	Mins	GA	SO	GAA
Roberto Luongo	5	5–0	307:40	9	1	1.76
Martin Brodeur	2	1–1	124:18	6	0	2.90
Marc-Andre Fleury	DID NOT PLAY					

Results, Women

Final Placing

GOLD MEDAL	Canada
SILVER MEDAL	United States
BRONZE MEDAL	Finland
Fourth Place	Sweden
Fifth Place	Switzerland
Sixth Place	Russia
Seventh Place	China
Eighth Place	Slovakia

All-Star Team

Goal	Shannon Szabados (CAN)
Defence	Angela Ruggiero (USA), Molly Engstrom (USA)
Forward	Meghan Agosta (CAN), Jenny Potter (USA), Marie-Philip Poulin (CAN)

Directorate Awards

Best Goalie	Shannon Szabados (CAN)
Best Defenceman	Molly Engstrom (USA)
Best Forward	Meghan Agosta (CAN)
Tournament MVP	Meghan Agosta (CAN)

FINAL STANDINGS

Group A	GP	W	OTW	OTL	L	GF	GA	P
Canada	3	3	0	0	0	41	2	9
Sweden	3	2	0	0	1	10	15	6
Switzerland	3	1	0	0	2	6	15	3
Slovakia	3	0	0	0	3	4	29	0

February 13	Sweden 3/Switzerland 0
February 13	Canada 18/Slovakia 0
February 15	Canada 10/Switzerland 1
February 15	Sweden 6/Slovakia 2
February 17	Canada 13/Sweden 1
February 17	Switzerland 5/Slovakia 2

Group B	GP	W	OTW	OTL	L	GF	GA	P
United States	3	3	0	0	0	31	1	9
Finland	3	2	0	0	1	7	8	6
Russia	3	1	0	0	2	3	19	3
China	3	0	0	0	3	3	16	0

February 14	United States 12/China 1
February 14	Finland 5/Russia 1
February 16	United States 13/Russia 0
February 16	Finland 2/China 1
February 18	United States 6/Finland 0
February 18	Russia 2/China 1

Placement Games

February 20	Switzerland 6/China 0
February 20	Russia 4/Slovakia 2
February 22	China 3/Slovakia 1
February 22	Switzerland 2/Russia 1 (SO)

Semifinals

| February 22 | United States 9/Sweden 1 |
| February 22 | Canada 5/Finland 0 |

Bronze Medal Game

| February 25 | Finland 3/Sweden 2 (OT) |

Gold Medal Game

February 25   Canada 2/United States 0

Team Canada Statistics

Melody Davidson, coach

#	Pos.		GP	G	A	P	Pim
2	F	Meghan Agosta	5	9	6	15	2
16	F	Jayna Hefford	5	5	7	12	8
13	F	Caroline Ouellette	5	2	9	11	2
22	F	Hayley Wickenheiser	5	2	9	11	0
7	F	Cherie Piper	5	5	5	10	0
26	F	Sarah Vaillancourt	5	3	5	8	6
29	F	Marie-Philip Poulin	5	5	2	7	2
10	F	Gillian Apps	5	3	4	7	2
6	F	Rebecca Johnston	5	1	5	6	2
5	D	Colleen Sostorics	5	1	5	6	2
21	F	Haley Irwin	5	4	1	5	4
3	D	Carla MacLeod	5	2	3	5	2
4	D	Becky Kellar	5	0	4	4	6
18	D	Catherine Ward	5	2	2	4	4
25	D	Tessa Bonhomme	5	2	2	4	0
27	F	Gina Kingsbury	5	2	1	3	6
17	F	Jennifer Botterill	5	0	2	2	0
12	D	Meaghan Mikkelson	5	0	0	0	2
1	GK	Shannon Szabados	3	0	0	0	0
33	GK	Kim St. Pierre	2	0	0	0	0
32	GK	Charline Labonte	1	0	0	0	0

In Goal	GP	W-L	Mins	GA	SO	GAA
Kim St. Pierre	2	2–0	100:00	0	1	0.00
Shannon Szabados	3	3–0	180:00	1	2	0.33
Charline Labonte	1	0–0	20:00	1	0	3.00

Sledge Hockey

TENTH PARALYMPIC GAMES, March 13–20, 2010

Final Placing

GOLD MEDAL	United States
SILVER MEDAL	Japan
BRONZE MEDAL	Norway
Fourth Place	Canada
Fifth Place	Czech Republic
Sixth Place	Korea
Seventh Place	Italy
Eighth Place	Sweden

Final Standings

Group A	GP	W	OTW	OTL	L	GF	GA	P
United States	3	3	0	0	0	14	0	9
Japan	3	2	0	0	1	7	7	6
Czech Republic	3	1	0	0	2	5	7	3
Korea	3	0	0	0	3	2	14	0

March 13	United States 5/Korea 0
March 13	Japan 2/Czech Republic 1
March 14	United States 3/Czech Republic 0
March 14	Japan 5/Korea 0
March 16	Czech Republic 4/Korea 2
March 16	United States 6/Japan 0

Group B	GP	W	OTW	OTL	L	GF	GA	P
Canada	3	3	0	0	0	19	1	9
Norway	3	2	0	0	1	4	7	6
Sweden	3	1	0	0	2	3	12	3
Italy	3	0	0	0	3	1	7	0

March 13	Canada 4/Italy 0
March 13	Norway 2/Sweden 1
March 14	Norway 2/Italy 1
March 14	Canada 10/Sweden 1
March 16	Sweden 1/Italy 0
March 16	Canada 5/Norway 0

Placement Games

| March 17 | Czech Republic 3/Italy 2 |
| March 17 | Korea 2/Sweden 1 |

Seventh-Place Game

| March 19 | Italy 4/Sweden 0 |

Fifth-Place Game

| March 19 | Czech Republic 2/Korea 1 |

Semifinals

| March 18 | Japan 3/Canada 1 |
| March 18 | United States 3/Norway 0 |

Bronze Medal Game

| March 19 | Norway 2/Canada 1 |

Gold Medal Game

| March 20 | United States 2/Japan 0 |

Team Canada Statistics

Jeff Snyder, coach

#	Pos.		GP	G	A	P	Pim
12	F	Greg Westlake	5	7	3	10	4
27	F	Bradley Bowden	5	3	6	9	0
11	D	Adam Dixon	5	4	3	7	2
18	F	Billy Bridges	5	1	6	7	16
7	F	Marc Dorion	5	5	0	5	4
19	F	Todd Nicholson	5	0	4	4	4
17	D	Jean Labonte	5	1	1	2	2
8	F	Jeremy Booker	5	0	2	2	0
29	D	Graeme Murray	5	0	1	1	4
21	D	Ray Grassi	5	0	0	0	8
10	F	Shawn Matheson	5	0	0	0	2
4	F	Derek Whitson	5	0	0	0	2
3	F	Herve Lord	5	0	0	0	0
57	GK	Paul Rosen	4	0	0	0	0
22	GK	Benoit St. Amand	1	0	0	0	0

In Goal	GP	W-L	Mins	GA	SO	GAA
Paul Rosen	4	2–2	179:00	4	2	1.01
Benoit St. Amand	1	1–0	45:00	1	0	1.00

THE GAMES OF THE VII OLYMPIAD

ANTWERP, BELGIUM, April 23–September 12, 1920
(Winter Olympics held April 23–29, 1920)

FINAL PLACINGS

GOLD MEDAL	Canada
SILVER MEDAL	United States
BRONZE MEDAL	Czechoslovakia
Fourth Place	Sweden

THE FIRST OLYMPIC WINTER GAMES

CHAMONIX, FRANCE, January 25–February 5, 1924

FINAL PLACINGS

GOLD MEDAL	Canada
SILVER MEDAL	United States
BRONZE MEDAL	Great Britain
Fourth Place	Sweden
Fifth Place	Czechoslovakia
(tie)	France
Seventh Place	Belgium
(tie)	Switzerland

THE SECOND OLYMPIC WINTER GAMES

ST. MORITZ, SWITZERLAND, February 11–20, 1928

FINAL PLACINGS

GOLD MEDAL	Canada
SILVER MEDAL	Sweden
BRONZE MEDAL	Switzerland
Fourth Place	Great Britain
Fifth Place	France
Sixth Place	Czechoslovakia

Seventh Place	Belgium
(tie)	Austria
Ninth Place	Poland
Tenth Place	Germany
Eleventh Place	Hungary

THE THIRD OLYMPIC WINTER GAMES

LAKE PLACID, UNITED STATES, February 4–13, 1932

FINAL PLACINGS

GOLD MEDAL	Canada
SILVER MEDAL	United States
BRONZE MEDAL	Germany
Fourth Place	Poland

THE FOURTH OLYMPIC WINTER GAMES

GARMISCH–PARTENKIRCHEN, GERMANY, February 6–16, 1936

FINAL PLACINGS

GOLD MEDAL	Great Britain
SILVER MEDAL	Canada
BRONZE MEDAL	United States
Fourth Place	Czechoslovakia
Fifth Place	Germany
(tie)	Sweden
Seventh Place	Austria
(tie)	Hungary
Ninth Place	Italy
(tie)	France
(tie)	Japan
(tie)	Poland
Thirteenth Place	Belgium
(tie)	Latvia
(tie)	Switzerland

THE FIFTH OLYMPIC WINTER GAMES

ST. MORITZ, SWITZERLAND, January 30–February 8, 1948

FINAL PLACINGS

GOLD MEDAL	Canada
SILVER MEDAL	Czechoslovakia
BRONZE MEDAL	Switzerland
Fourth Place	United States
Fifth Place	Sweden
Sixth Place	Great Britain
Seventh Place	Poland
Eighth Place	Austria
Ninth Place	Italy

THE SIXTH OLYMPIC WINTER GAMES

OSLO, NORWAY, February 15–25, 1952

FINAL PLACINGS

GOLD MEDAL	Canada
SILVER MEDAL	United States
BRONZE MEDAL	Sweden
Fourth Place	Czechoslovakia
Fifth Place	Switzerland
Sixth Place	Poland
Seventh Place	Finland
Eighth Place	West Germany
Ninth Place	Norway

THE SEVENTH OLYMPIC WINTER GAMES

CORTINA d'AMPEZZO, ITALY, January 26–February 4, 1956

FINAL PLACINGS

GOLD MEDAL	Soviet Union
SILVER MEDAL	United States
BRONZE MEDAL	Canada
Fourth Place	Sweden

Fifth Place	Czechoslovakia
Sixth Place	Germany
Seventh Place	Italy
Eighth Place	Poland
Ninth Place	Switzerland
Tenth Place	Austria

THE EIGHTH OLYMPIC WINTER GAMES

SQUAW VALLEY, UNITED STATES, February 19–28, 1960

FINAL PLACINGS

GOLD MEDAL	United States
SILVER MEDAL	Canada
BRONZE MEDAL	Soviet Union
Fourth Place	Czechoslovakia
Fifth Place	Sweden
Sixth Place	Germany
Seventh Place	Finland
Eighth Place	Japan
Ninth Place	Australia

THE NINTH OLYMPIC WINTER GAMES

INNSBRUCK, AUSTRIA, January 29–February 9, 1964

FINAL PLACINGS

GOLD MEDAL	Soviet Union
SILVER MEDAL	Sweden
BRONZE MEDAL	Czechoslovakia
Fourth Place	Canada
Fifth Place	United States
Sixth Place	Finland
Seventh Place	Germany
Eighth Place	Switzerland
Ninth Place	Poland
Tenth Place	Norway

Eleventh Place	Japan
Twelfth Place	Romania
Thirteenth Place	Austria
Fourteenth Place	Yugoslavia
Fifteenth Place	Italy
Sixteenth Place	Hungary

THE TENTH OLYMPIC WINTER GAMES

GRENOBLE, FRANCE, February 6–17, 1968

FINAL PLACINGS

GOLD MEDAL	Soviet Union
SILVER MEDAL	Czechoslovakia
BRONZE MEDAL	Canada
Fourth Place	Sweden
Fifth Place	Finland
Sixth Place	United States
Seventh Place	West Germany
Eighth Place	East Germany
Ninth Place	Yugoslavia
Tenth Place	Japan
Eleventh Place	Norway
Twelfth Place	Romania
Thirteenth Place	Austria
Fourteenth Place	France

THE ELEVENTH OLYMPIC WINTER GAMES

SAPPORO, JAPAN, February 5–12, 1972

FINAL PLACINGS

GOLD MEDAL	Soviet Union
SILVER MEDAL	United States
BRONZE MEDAL	Czechoslovakia
Fourth Place	Sweden
Fifth Place	Finland

Sixth Place	Poland
Seventh Place	West Germany
Eighth Place	Norway
Ninth Place	Japan
Tenth Place	Switzerland
Eleventh Place	Yugoslavia

THE TWELFTH OLYMPIC WINTER GAMES

INNSBRUCK, AUSTRIA, February 4–13, 1976

FINAL PLACINGS

GOLD MEDAL	Soviet Union
SILVER MEDAL	Czechoslovakia
BRONZE MEDAL	West Germany
Fourth Place	Finland
Fifth Place	United States
Sixth Place	Poland
Seventh Place	Romania
Eighth Place	Austria
Ninth Place	Japan
Tenth Place	Yugoslavia
Eleventh Place	Switzerland
(tie)	Norway
Thirteenth Place	Bulgaria

THE THIRTEENTH OLYMPIC WINTER GAMES

LAKE PLACID, UNITED STATES, February 13–24, 1980

FINAL PLACINGS

GOLD MEDAL	United States
SILVER MEDAL	Soviet Union
BRONZE MEDAL	Sweden
Fourth Place	Finland
Fifth Place	Czechoslovakia
Sixth Place	Canada

Seventh Place	Poland
Eighth Place	Romania
Ninth Place	Netherlands
(tie)	Norway
Eleventh Place	West Germany
(tie)	Yugoslavia
Thirteenth Place	Japan

THE FOURTEENTH OLYMPIC WINTER GAMES

SARAJEVO, YUGOSLAVIA, February 7–19, 1984

FINAL PLACINGS

GOLD MEDAL	Soviet Union
SILVER MEDAL	Czechoslovakia
BRONZE MEDAL	Sweden
Fourth Place	Canada
Fifth Place	West Germany
Sixth Place	Finland
Seventh Place	United States
Eighth Place	Poland
Ninth Place	Italy
Tenth Place	Norway
Eleventh Place	Austria
(tie)	Yugoslavia

THE FIFTEENTH OLYMPIC WINTER GAMES

CALGARY, CANADA, February 13–28, 1988

FINAL PLACINGS

GOLD MEDAL	Soviet Union
SILVER MEDAL	Finland
BRONZE MEDAL	Sweden
Fourth Place	Canada
Fifth Place	West Germany
Sixth Place	Czechoslovakia

Seventh Place	United States
Eighth Place	Switzerland
Ninth Place	Austria
Tenth Place	Poland
Eleventh Place	France
Twelfth Place	Norway

THE SIXTEENTH OLYMPIC WINTER GAMES

ALBERTVILLE, FRANCE, February 8–23, 1992

FINAL PLACINGS

GOLD MEDAL	Unified Team
SILVER MEDAL	Canada
BRONZE MEDAL	Czechoslovakia
Fourth Place	United States
Fifth Place	Sweden
Sixth Place	Germany
Seventh Place	Finland
Eighth Place	France
Ninth Place	Norway
Tenth Place	Switzerland
Eleventh Place	Poland
Twelfth Place	Italy

THE SEVENTEENTH OLYMPIC WINTER GAMES

LILLEHAMMER, NORWAY, February 13–27, 1994

FINAL PLACINGS

GOLD MEDAL	Sweden
SILVER MEDAL	Canada
BRONZE MEDAL	Finland
Fourth Place	Russia
Fifth Place	Czech Republic
Sixth Place	Slovakia
Seventh Place	Germany

Eighth Place	United States
Ninth Place	Italy
Tenth Place	France
Eleventh Place	Norway
Twelfth Place	Austria

THE EIGHTEENTH OLYMPIC WINTER GAMES

NAGANO, JAPAN, February 7–22, 1998 (Men);
February 8–17, 1998 (Women)

FINAL PLACINGS: MEN

GOLD MEDAL	Czech Republic
SILVER MEDAL	Russia
BRONZE MEDAL	Finland
Fourth Place	Canada
Fifth Place (tie)	Sweden
	United States
	Belarus
	Kazakhstan
Ninth Place	Germany
Tenth Place	Slovakia
Eleventh Place	France
Twelfth Place	Italy
Thirteenth Place	Japan
Fourteenth Place	Austria

FINAL PLACINGS: WOMEN

GOLD MEDAL	United States
SILVER MEDAL	Canada
BRONZE MEDAL	Finland
Fourth Place	China
Fifth Place	Sweden
Sixth Place	Japan

THE NINETEENTH OLYMPIC WINTER GAMES

SALT LAKE CITY, UNITED STATES, February 9–24, 2002 (Men);
February 11–21, 2002 (Women)

FINAL PLACINGS: MEN

GOLD MEDAL	Canada
SILVER MEDAL	United States
BRONZE MEDAL	Russia
Fourth Place	Belarus
Fifth Place	Sweden
Sixth Place	Finland
Seventh Place	Czech Republic
Eighth Place	Germany
Ninth Place	Latvia
Tenth Place	Ukraine
Eleventh Place	Switzerland
Twelfth Place	Austria
Thirteenth Place	Slovakia
Fourteenth Place	France

FINAL PLACINGS: WOMEN

GOLD MEDAL	Canada
SILVER MEDAL	United States
BRONZE MEDAL	Sweden
Fourth Place	Finland
Fifth Place	Russia
Sixth Place	Germany
Seventh Place	China
Eighth Place	Kazakhstan

THE TWENTIETH OLYMPIC WINTER GAMES

TURIN, ITALY, February 10–26, 2006 (Men);
February 11–20, 2006 (Women)

FINAL PLACINGS: MEN

GOLD MEDAL   Sweden
SILVER MEDAL   Finland
BRONZE MEDAL   Czech Republic
Fourth Place   Russia
Fifth Place   Slovakia
Sixth Place   Switzerland
Seventh Place   Canada
Eighth Place   United States
Ninth Place   Kazakhstan
Tenth Place   Germany
Eleventh Place Italy
Twelfth Place   Latvia

FINAL PLACINGS: WOMEN

GOLD MEDAL   Canada
SILVER MEDAL   Sweden
BRONZE MEDAL   United States
Fourth Place   Finland
Fifth Place   Germany
Sixth Place   Russia
Seventh Place   Switzerland
Eighth Place   Italy

THE TWENTY-FIRST OLYMPIC WINTER GAMES

VANCOUVER, CANADA, February 16–18, 2010 (Men);
February 17–25, 2010 (Women)

FINAL PLACINGS: MEN

GOLD MEDAL   Canada
SILVER MEDAL   United States
BRONZE MEDAL   Finland
Fourth Place   Slovakia
Fifth Place   Sweden
Sixth Place   Russia

Seventh Place	Czech Republic
Eighth Place	Switzerland
Ninth Place	Belarus
Tenth Place	Norway
Eleventh Place	Germany
Twelfth Place	Latvia

FINAL PLACINGS: WOMEN

GOLD MEDAL	Canada
SILVER MEDAL	United States
BRONZE MEDAL	Finland
Fourth Place	Sweden
Fifth Place	Switzerland
Sixth Place	Russia
Seventh Place	China
Eighth Place	Slovakia

TRIPLE GOLD CLUB

These 24 players and one coach form the unique group that has won the IIHF World Championship, the Olympic ice hockey tournament and the Stanley Cup. To be credited with each of these honours, the player or coach must have participated in at least one game of the event.

Players are entered chronologically by the date when they achieved the final championship of the triple. If two or more players completed their triple on the same date, priority is given to the player who was the first to win his first of the three titles. If two or more players have identical accomplishments, priority is given to the player who completes the triple at the younger age.

Legend: OG=Olympic Games; SC=Stanley Cup; WS=World (Senior) Championship

1. Tomas Jonsson b. Falun, Sweden, April 12, 1960
SC 1982, 1983 (New York Islanders)
WS 1991 (Sweden)
OG 1994 (Sweden)
TGC member as of February 27, 1994 (Olympic final win vs. Canada)

2. Mats Naslund b. Timra, Sweden, October 31, 1959
SC 1986 (Montreal Canadiens)
WS 1991 (Sweden)
OG 1994 (Sweden)
TGC member as of February 27, 1994 (Olympic final win vs. Canada)

3. Hakan Loob b. Roma, Sweden, July 3, 1960
WS 1987, 1991 (Sweden)
SC 1989 (Calgary Flames)
OG 1994 (Sweden)
TGC member as of February 27, 1994 (Olympic final win vs. Canada)

4. Valeri Kamensky b. Voskresensk, Soviet Union (Russia),
April 18, 1966
WS 1986, 1989, 1990 (Soviet Union)
OG 1988 (Soviet Union)
SC 1996 (Colorado Avalanche)
TGC member as of June 10, 1996 (Stanley Cup win vs. Florida)

5. Alexei Gusarov b. Leningrad (St. Petersburg), Soviet Union
(Russia), July 8, 1964
WS 1986, 1989, 1990 (Soviet Union)
OG 1988 (Soviet Union)
SC 1996 (Colorado Avalanche)
TGC member as of June 10, 1996 (Stanley Cup win vs. Florida)

6. Peter Forsberg b. Ornskoldsvik, Sweden, July 20, 1973
WS 1992, 1998 (Sweden)
OG 1994, 2006 (Sweden)
SC 1996, 2001 (Colorado Avalanche)
TGC member as of June 10, 1996 (Stanley Cup win vs. Florida)

7. Vyacheslav Fetisov b. Moscow, Soviet Union (Russia),
April 20, 1958
WS 1978, 1981, 1982, 1983, 1986, 1989, 1990 (Soviet Union)
OG 1984, 1988 (Soviet Union)
SC 1997, 1998 (Detroit Red Wings)
TGC member as of June 7, 1997 (Stanley Cup win vs. Philadelphia)

8. Igor Larionov (b. Voskresensk, Soviet Union (Russia),
December 3, 1960)
WS 1982, 1983, 1986, 1989 (Soviet Union)
OG 1984, 1988 (Soviet Union)
SC 1997, 1998, 2002 (Detroit Red Wings)
TGC member as of June 7, 1997 (Stanley Cup win vs. Philadelphia)

9. Alexander Mogilny b. Khabarovsk, Soviet Union (Russia),
February 18, 1969
OG 1988 (Soviet Union)
WS 1989 (Soviet Union)
SC 2000 (New Jersey Devils)
TGC member as of June 10, 2000 (Stanley Cup win vs. Dallas)

10. Vladimir Malakhov b. Ekaterinburg, Soviet Union (Russia),
August 30, 1968
WS 1990 (Soviet Union)
OG 1992 (Russia)
SC 2000 (New Jersey Devils)
TGC member as of June 10, 2000 (Stanley Cup win vs. Dallas)

11. Rob Blake b. Simcoe, Ontario, Canada, December 10, 1969
WS 1994, 1997 (Canada)
SC 2001 (Colorado Avalanche)
OG 2002 (Canada)
TGC member as of February 24, 2002 (Olympic final win vs.
United States)

12. Joe Sakic b. Burnaby, British Columbia, Canada, July 7, 1969
WS 1994 (Canada)
SC 1996, 2001 (Colorado Avalanche)
OG 2002 (Canada)
TGC member as of February 24, 2002 (Olympic final win vs.
United States)

13. Brendan Shanahan b. Mimico, Ontario, Canada,
January 23, 1969
WS 1994 (Canada)
SC 1997, 1998, 2002 (Detroit Red Wings)
OG 2002 (Canada)
TGC member as of February 24, 2002 (Olympic final win vs.
United States)

14. Scott Niedermayer b. Edmonton, Alberta, Canada,
August 31, 1973
SC 1995, 2000, 2003 (New Jersey Devils), 2007 (Anaheim Ducks)
OG 2002, 2010 (Canada)
WS 2004 (Canada)
TGC member as of May 9, 2004 (World Championship final win
vs. Sweden)

15. Jaromir Jagr b. Kladno, Czechoslovakia (Czech Republic),
February 15, 1972
SC 1991, 1992 (Pittsburgh Penguins)
OG 1998 (Czech Republic)
WS 2005 (Czech Republic)
TGC member as of May 15, 2005 (World Championship final win
vs. Canada)

16. Jiri Slegr b. Jihlava, Czechoslovakia (Czech Republic),
May 30, 1971
OG 1998 (Czech Republic)
SC 2002 (Detroit Red Wings)
WS 2005 (Czech Republic)
TGC member as of May 15, 2005 (World Championship final win
vs. Canada)

17. Nicklas Lidstrom b. Vasteras, Sweden, April 28, 1970
WS 1991 (Sweden)
SC 1997, 1998, 2002 (Detroit Red Wings)
OG 2006 (Sweden)
TGC member as of February 26, 2006 (Olympic final win vs.
Finland)

18. Fredrik Modin   b. Sundsvall, Sweden, October 8, 1974
WS 1998 (Sweden)
SC 2004 (Tampa Bay Lightning)
OG 2006 (Sweden)
TGC member as of February 26, 2006 (Olympic final win vs. Finland)

19. Chris Pronger   b. Dryden, Ontario, Canada, October 10, 1974
WS 1997 (Canada)
OG 2002, 2010 (Canada)
SC 2007 (Anaheim Ducks)
TGC member as of June 6, 2007 (Stanley Cup win vs. Ottawa)

20. Niklas Kronwall   b. Stockholm, Sweden, January 12, 1981
OG 2006 (Sweden)
WS 2006 (Sweden)
SC 2008 (Detroit Red Wings)
TGC member as of June 4, 2008 (Stanley Cup win vs. Pittsburgh)

21. Henrik Zetterberg   b. Njurunda, Sweden, October 9, 1980
OG 2006 (Sweden)
WS 2006 (Sweden)
SC 2008 (Detroit Red Wings)
TGC member as of June 4, 2008 (Stanley Cup win vs. Pittsburgh)

22. Mikael Samuelsson   b. Mariefred, Sweden, December 23, 1976
OG 2006 (Sweden)
WS 2006 (Sweden)
SC 2008 (Detroit Red Wings)
TGC member as of June 4, 2008 (Stanley Cup win vs. Pittsburgh)

23. Eric Staal b. Thunder Bay, Ontario, Canada, October 29, 1984
SC 2006 (Carolina Hurricanes)
WS 2007 (Canada)
OG 2010 (Canada)
TGC member as of February 28, 2010 (Olympic final win vs. United States)

24. Jonathan Toews b. Winnipeg, Manitoba, Canada, April 29, 1988
WS 2007 (Canada)
OG 2010 (Canada)
SC 2010 (Chicago Blackhawks)
TGC member as of June 9, 2010 (Stanley Cup win vs. Philadelphia)

Triple Gold Club Coach

1. Mike Babcock (b. Saskatoon, Saskatchewan, Canada, April 29, 1963)
WS 2004 (Canada)
SC 2008 (Detroit Red Wings)
OG 2010 (Canada)
TGC member as of February 28, 2010, Olympic final win vs. United States

ANAHEIM DUCKS

(name changed from Mighty Ducks of Anaheim on June 22, 2006)
First Game Played: October 8, 1993
Detroit Red Wings 7 at Mighty Ducks of Anaheim 2
Nickname Provenance: Owners, Disney, named team after a popular kids' movie, *The Mighty Ducks* (1992)
Mascot: Wild Thing
Arena History: Arrowhead Pond, 1993–2006; Honda Centre 2006–present (capacity 17,174)
Retired Numbers: none
Hall of Famers: Players (1): Jari Kurri
Website: www.anaheimducks.com
Minor League Affiliate(s): Syracuse Crunch (AHL), Elmira Jackals (ECHL—shared with Ottawa)
Stanley Cups: (1) 2006–07
Hosted All-Star Game: none
1st Overall Draft Choices: none

ATLANTA THRASHERS

First Game Played: October 2, 1999
New Jersey Devils 4 at Atlanta Thrashers 1
Nickname Provenance: The brown thrasher is the state bird of Georgia
Mascot: Thrash (b. September 4, 1999)
Arena History: Philips Arena, 1999–present (capacity 18,545)
Retired Numbers: Dan Snyder (43, unofficial)
Hall of Famers: none
Website: www. atlantathrashers.com
Minor League Affiliate(s): Chicago Wolves (AHL), Gwinnett Gladiators (ECHL—shared with Columbus)

Stanley Cups: none
Hosted All-Star Game: (1) 2008
1st Overall Draft Choices: 1999 (Patrik Stefan), 2001 (Ilya Kovalchuk)

BOSTON BRUINS

First Game Played: December 1, 1924
Montreal Maroons 1 at Boston Bruins 2
Nickname Provenance: Named by owner Art Ross for the brown bear
Mascot: Blades (b. October 9, 2000)
Arena History: Boston Arena, 1924–28; Boston Garden, 1928–95; FleetCenter, 1995–2003; TD Banknorth Garden (same building as the FleetCenter), 2005–2009; TD Garden 2009–present (capacity 17,565)
Retired Numbers: Eddie Shore (2), Lionel Hitchman (3), Bobby Orr (4), Dit Clapper (5), Phil Esposito (7), Cam Neely (8), Johnny Bucyk (9), Milt Schmidt (15), Terry O'Reilly (24), Ray Bourque (77)
Hall of Famers: Players (47): Marty Barry, Bobby Bauer, Leo Boivin, Ray Bourque, Frank Brimsek, Johnny Bucyk, Billy Burch, Gerry Cheevers, Dit Clapper, Sprague Cleghorn, Paul Coffey, Roy Conacher, Bun Cook, Bill Cowley, Cy Denneny, Woody Dumart, Phil Esposito, Fern Flaman, Frank Fredrickson, Harvey Jackson, Tom Johnson, Duke Keats, Guy Lapointe, Brian Leetch, Harry Lumley, Mickey MacKay, Sylvio Mantha, Joe Mullen, Cam Neely, Harry Oliver, Bobby Orr, Bernie Parent, Brad Park, Jacques Plante, Babe Pratt, Bill Quackenbush, Jean Ratelle, Art Ross (inducted as Player, associated with Boston as Builder), Terry Sawchuk, Milt Schmidt, Eddie Shore, Babe Siebert, Hooley Smith, Allan Stanley, Nels Stewart, Tiny Thompson, Cooney Weiland; Builders (6): Charles Adams, Weston Adams, Walter Brown, Bud Poile (played with Boston, inducted as Builder), Glen Sather (played with Boston, inducted as Builder), Harry Sinden
Website: www.bostonbruins.com
Minor League Affiliate(s): Providence Bruins (AHL), Reading Royals (ECHL—shared with Toronto)

Stanley Cups: (5) 1928–29, 1938–39, 1940–41, 1969–70, 1971–72
Hosted All-Star Game: (2) 1971, 1996
1st Overall Draft Choices: 1982 (Gord Kluzak),
1997 (Joe Thornton)

BUFFALO SABRES

First Game Played: October 10, 1970
Buffalo Sabres 2 at Pittsburgh Penguins 1
Nickname Provenance: a contest determined the name Sabres
Mascot: Sabre-Tooth
Arena History: Memorial Auditorium ("The Aud"), 1970–96;
Marine Midland Bank Arena, 1996–2000; HSBC Arena (same building as the Marine Midland Bank Arena), 2000–present
(capacity 18,690)
Retired Numbers: Tim Horton (2), Rick Martin (7), Gilbert Perreault
(11), Rene Robert (14), Pat LaFontaine (16), Danny Gare (18)
Hall of Famers: Players (8): Dick Duff, Tim Horton, Gilbert
Perreault, Dale Hawerchuk, Clark Gillies, Grant Fuhr, Pat
LaFontaine, Marcel Pronovost (inducted as Player, associated with
Buffalo as Builder); Builders (4): Scotty Bowman, Punch Imlach,
Seymour Knox III, Roger Neilson
Website: www.sabres.com
Minor League Affiliate(s): Portland Pirates (AHL)
Stanley Cups: none
Hosted All-Star Game: 1978
1st Overall Draft Choices: 1970 (Gilbert Perreault),
1987 (Pierre Turgeon)

CALGARY FLAMES

First Game Played:
As Atlanta Flames: October 7, 1972
Atlanta Flames 3 at New York Islanders 2
As Calgary Flames: October 9, 1980
Quebec Nordiques 5 at Calgary Flames 5

Nickname Provenance: Flames was chosen by contest, representative of Atlanta during the Civil War, when much of it was burned to the ground

Mascot: Harvey the Hound

Arena History: The Omni (Atlanta), 1972–80; Stampede Corral, 1980–83; Olympic Saddledome, 1983–95; Canadian Airlines Saddledome, 1995–2001; Pengrowth Saddledome (same building as previous two Saddledomes), 2001–present (capacity 19,289)

Retired Numbers: Lanny McDonald (9), Mike Vernon (30)

Hall of Famers: Players (5): Lanny McDonald, Joe Mullen, Grant Fuhr, Brett Hull, Al MacInnis; Builders (3): Cliff Fletcher, Harley Hotchkiss, Daryl "Doc" Seaman

Website: www.calgaryflames.com

Minor League Affiliate(s): Abbotsford Heat (AHL), Utah Grizzlies (ECHL)

Stanley Cups: (1) 1988–89

Hosted All-Star Game: 1985

1st Overall Draft Choices: none

CAROLINA HURRICANES

First Game Played:

As Hartford Whalers: October 11, 1979

Hartford Whalers 1 at Minnesota North Stars 4

As Carolina Hurricanes: October 1, 1997

Carolina Hurricanes 2 at Tampa Bay Lightning 4

Nickname Provenance: Whalers adopted because it contained the letters of the WHA and it was emblematic of the region

Mascot: Stormy

Arena History: Springfield Civic Center (Hartford), 1979–80; Hartford Civic Center (Hartford), 1980–97; Greensboro Coliseum, 1997–99; Raleigh Entertainment & Sports Arena, 1999–2003; RBC Center (same building as the Raleigh Entertainment & Sports Arena), 2003–present (capacity 18,730)

Retired Numbers: Glen Wesley (2), Ron Francis (10)

Hall of Famers: Players (5): Paul Coffey (Hartford/Carolina), Gordie Howe (Hartford), Bobby Hull (Hartford), Dave Keon (Hartford), Ron Francis (Hartford/Carolina)
Website: www.carolinahcanes.com
Minor League Affiliate(s): Charlotte Checkers (AHL), Florida Everblades (ECHL—shared with Tampa Bay)
Stanley Cups: 2005–06
Hosted All-Star Game: 1986 (as Hartford Whalers)
1st Overall Draft Choices: none

CHICAGO BLACKHAWKS

First Game Played: November 17, 1926
Toronto St. Pats 1 at Chicago Blackhawks 4
Nickname Provenance: (spelling changed from "Black Hawks" to "Blackhawks" in 1986)
Mascot: Tommy the Hawk
Arena History: Chicago Coliseum, 1926–29, 1932; Chicago Stadium, 1929–94; United Center, 1995–present (opening of United Center delayed by disruption of 1994–95 NHL season, capacity 20,500)
Retired Numbers: Glenn Hall (1), Keith Magnuson (3), Pierre Pilote (3), Bobby Hull (9), Denis Savard (18), Stan Mikita (21), Tony Esposito (35)
Hall of Famers: Players (39): Sid Abel, Doug Bentley, Max Bentley, Georges Boucher, Frank Brimsek, Billy Burch, Paul Coffey, Lionel Conacher, Roy Conacher, Art Coulter, Babe Dye, Phil Esposito, Tony Esposito, Bill Gadsby, Charlie Gardiner, Herb Gardiner, Michel Goulet, Glenn Hall, George Hay, Bobby Hull, Duke Keats, Hugh Lehman, Ted Lindsay, Harry Lumley, Mickey MacKay, Stan Mikita, Howie Morenz, Bill Mosienko, Bert Olmstead, Bobby Orr, Pierre Pilote, Denis Savard, Earl Seibert, Clint Smith, Allan Stanley, Barney Stanley, Jack Stewart, Carl Voss (played for Chicago, inducted as Builder), Harry Watson; Builders (12): Al Arbour, Emile Francis (played for Chicago, inducted as Builder), Dick Irvin (played for Chicago, inducted as Builder), Tommy Ivan, John Mariucci (also

played for Chicago), Major Frederic McLaughlin, James Norris, James Norris, Jr., Rudy Pilous, Bud Poile (played for Chicago, inducted as Builder), Arthur Wirtz, William Wirtz

Website: www.chicagoblackhawks.com

Minor League Affiliate(s): Rockford IceHogs (AHL), Toledo Walleye (ECHL—shared with Detroit)

Stanley Cups: (4) 1933–34, 1937–38, 1960–61, 2009–10

Hosted All-Star Game: (4) 1948, 1961, 1974, 1991

1st Overall Draft Choices: Pat Kane

COLORADO AVALANCHE

First Game Played:

As Quebec Nordiques: October 10, 1979

Atlanta Flames 5 at Quebec Nordiques 3

As Colorado Avalanche: October 6, 1995

Detroit Red Wings 2 at Colorado Avalanche 3

Nickname Provenance: Team owners polled fans. Out of eight names offered, Avalanche was the most popular.

Mascot: Howler

Arena History: McNichols Sports Arena, 1995–99; Pepsi Center, 1999–present (capacity 18,007)

Retired Numbers: J-C Tremblay (3), Marc Tardif (8), Michel Goulet (16), Joe Sakic (19), Peter Stastny (26), Patrick Roy (33), Ray Bourque (77)

Hall of Famers: Players (6): Ray Bourque, Patrick Roy, Michel Goulet (Quebec), Jari Kurri, Guy Lafleur (Quebec), Peter Stastny (Quebec)

Website: www.coloradoavalanche.com

Minor League Affiliate(s): Lake Erie Monsters (AHL)

Stanley Cups: (2) 1995–96, 2000–01

Hosted All-Star Game: 2001

1st Overall Draft Choices: 1989 (Mats Sundin—Quebec Nordiques), 1990 (Owen Nolan—Quebec), 1991 (Eric Lindros—Quebec)

COLUMBUS BLUE JACKETS

First Game Played: October 7, 2000
Chicago Blackhawks 5 at Columbus Blue Jackets 3
Nickname Provenance: Reflects patriotism and history of the Civil War
Mascot: Stinger
Arena History: Nationwide Arena, 2000–present (capacity 18,136)
Retired Numbers: none
Hall of Famers: none
Website: www. bluejackets.com
Minor League Affiliate(s): Springfield Falcons (AHL), Gwinnett Gladiators (ECHL—shared with Atlanta)
Stanley Cups: none
Hosted All-Star Game: none
1st Overall Draft Choices: 2002 (Rick Nash)

DALLAS STARS

First Game Played:
As Minnesota North Stars: October 11, 1967
Minnesota North Stars 2 at St. Louis Blues 2
As Dallas Stars: October 5, 1993
Detroit Red Wings 4 at Dallas Stars 6
Nickname Provenance: Shortening of North Stars, consistent with Texas as the Lone Star state
Mascot: none
Arena History: Metropolitan Sports Center (also known as the Met Center), 1967–93; Reunion Arena, 1993–2001; American Airlines Center, 2001–present (capacity 18,532)
Retired Numbers: Neal Broten (7), Bill Goldsworthy (8), Bill Masterton (19)
Hall of Famers: Players (7): Mike Gartner (Minnesota), Harry Howell (Minnesota), Brett Hull, Larry Murphy (Minnesota), Gump Worsley (Minnesota), Leo Boivin (Minnesota), Dino Ciccarelli (Minnesota); Builders (3): Herb Brooks (coached Minnesota), Glen Sather (played for University of Minnesota), John Mariucci

Website: www.dallasstars.com
Minor League Affiliate(s): Allen Americans (CHL), Idaho
Steelheads (ECHL), Texas Stars (AHL)
Stanley Cups: 1998–99
Hosted All-Star Game: 1972 (as North Stars); 2007
1st Overall Draft Choices: 1978 (Bobby Smith—Minnesota North
Stars), 1983 (Brian Lawton—Minnesota), 1988 (Mike Modano—
Minnesota)

DETROIT RED WINGS

First Game Played:
As Detroit Cougars: November 18, 1926
Boston Bruins 2 at Detroit Cougars 0
As Detroit Falcons: November 13, 1930
New York Rangers 0 at Detroit Falcons 1
As Detroit Red Wings: November 10, 1932
Chicago Blackhawks 1 at Detroit Red Wings 3
Nickname Provenance: Owner James Norris, a Montreal native,
used the Winged Wheel from his hometown team and combined it
with Detroit's place in America as a car-making centre
Mascot: Al the Octopus
Arena History: Windsor Arena (Border Cities Arena), 1926–27;
Olympia, 1929–79; Joe Louis Arena, 1979–present (capacity 20,066)
Retired Numbers: Terry Sawchuk (1), Ted Lindsay (7), Gordie Howe
(9), Alex Delvecchio (10), Sid Abel (12), Steve Yzerman (19)
Hall of Famers: Players (52): Sid Abel, Jack Adams (inducted as
Player, associated with Detroit as builder), Marty Barry, Andy
Bathgate, Johnny Bucyk, Dino Ciccarelli, Paul Coffey, Charlie
Conacher, Roy Conacher, Alec Connell, Alex Delvecchio, Marcel
Dionne, Bernie Federko, Slava Fetisov, Frank Foyston, Frank
Fredrickson, Bill Gadsby, Ed Giacomin, Ebbie Goodfellow, Glenn
Hall, Doug Harvey, George Hay, Harry Holmes, Gordie Howe, Syd
Howe, Brett Hull, Duke Keats, Red Kelly, Brian Kilrea (played for

Detroit, inducted as Builder), Igor Larionov, Herbie Lewis, Ted Lindsay, Harry Lumley, Frank Mahovlich, Larry Murphy, Reg Noble, Brad Park, Bud Poile (played for Detroit, inducted as Builder), Marcel Pronovost, Bill Quackenbush, Luc Robitaille, Borje Salming, Terry Sawchuk, Earl Seibert, Darryl Sittler, Jack Stewart, Tiny Thompson, Norm Ullman, Jack Walker, Harry Watson, Cooney Weiland, Steve Yzerman; Builders (9): Al Arbour (played for Detroit, inducted as Builder), Leo Boivin (played for Detroit, inducted as Builder), Scotty Bowman, Jimmy Devellano, Tommy Ivan, Bruce Norris, James Norris, James Norris, Jr., Carl Voss (played for Detroit, inducted as Builder)
Website: www.detroitredwings.com
Minor League Affiliate(s): Grand Rapids Griffins (AHL), Toledo Walleye (ECHL—shared with Chicago)
Stanley Cups: (11) 1935–36, 1936–37, 1942–43, 1949–50, 1951–52, 1953–54, 1954–55, 1996–97, 1997–98, 2002–02, 2007–08
Hosted All-Star Game: (5) 1950, 1952, 1954, 1955, 1980
1st Overall Draft Choices: 1977 (Dale McCourt), 1986 (Joe Murphy)

EDMONTON OILERS

First Game Played: October 10, 1979
Edmonton Oilers 2 at Chicago Black Hawks 4
Nickname Provenance: From Alberta Oilers and later Edmonton Oilers of WHA, to refer to Alberta's place as an oil capital in Canada
Mascot: none
Arena History: Northlands Coliseum, 1979–99; Skyreach Centre, 1999–2003; Rexall Place, 2005–present (all three are the same building, capacity 16,839)
Retired Numbers: Al Hamilton (3), Paul Coffey (7), Glenn Anderson (9) Mark Messier (11), Jari Kurri (17), Grant Fuhr (31), Wayne Gretzky (99—leaguewide recognition)
Hall of Famers: Players (6): Glenn Anderson, Paul Coffey, Grant Fuhr, Wayne Gretzky, Jari Kurri, Mark Messier; Builders (1): Glen Sather

Website: www.edmontonoilers.com
Minor League Affiliate(s): Oklahoma City Barons (AHL), Stockton Thunder (ECHL—shared with San Jose)
Stanley Cups: (5) 1983–84, 1984–85, 1986–87, 1987–88, 1989–90
Hosted All-Star Game: 1989
1st Overall Draft Choices: 2010 (Taylor Hall)

FLORIDA PANTHERS

First Game Played: October 6, 1993
Florida Panthers 4 at Chicago Blackhawks 4
Nickname Provenance: Named for the animal, which is common in Florida
Mascot: Stanley C. Panther
Arena History: Miami Arena, 1993–99; National Car Rental Center, 1999–2002; Office Depot Center, 2002–03; BankAtlantic Center, 2005–present (previous three are the same building, capacity 19,250)
Retired Numbers: none
Hall of Famers: Players (2): Dino Ciccarelli, Igor Larionov
Website: www.floridapanthers.com
Minor League Affiliate(s): Rochester Americans (AHL), Florida Everblades (ECHL—shared with Carolina)
Stanley Cups: none
Hosted All-Star Game: 2003
1st Overall Draft Choices: 1994 (Ed Jovanovski)

LOS ANGELES KINGS

First Game Played: October 14, 1967
Philadelphia Flyers 2 at Los Angeles Kings 4
Nickname Provenance: Named by owner Jack Kent Cooke to give the team a royal (i.e., important) sound to it
Mascot: Bailey
Arena History: Long Beach Arena, October 1967; Los Angeles

Sports Arena, November–December 1967; The Forum, 1967–88; Great Western Forum, 1988–99 (same building as The Forum); Staples Center, 1999–present (capacity 18,118)

Retired Numbers: Marcel Dionne (16), Dave Taylor (18), Luc Robitaille (20), Rogie Vachon (30), Wayne Gretzky (99—leaguewide recognition)

Hall of Famers: Players (14): Paul Coffey, Marcel Dionne, Dick Duff, Grant Fuhr, Wayne Gretzky, Harry Howell, Jari Kurri, Larry Murphy, Bob Pulford, Larry Robinson, Luc Robitaille, Terry Sawchuk, Steve Shutt, Billy Smith; Builders (1): Brian Kilrea (played for Los Angeles, inducted as Builder)

Website: www.lakings.com

Minor League Affiliate(s): Manchester Monarchs (AHL), Ontario Reign (ECHL)

Stanley Cups: none

Hosted All-Star Game: (2) 1981, 2002

1st Overall Draft Choices: none

MINNESOTA WILD

First Game Played: October 6, 2000
Minnesota Wild 1 at Mighty Ducks of Anaheim 3

Nickname Provenance: Selected by fan contest

Mascot: Nordy

Arena History: Xcel Energy Center, 2000–present (capacity 18,064)

Retired Numbers: none

Hall of Famers: none

Website: www.wild.com

Minor League Affiliate(s): Houston Aeros (AHL), Bakersfield Condors (ECHL)

Stanley Cups: none

Hosted All-Star Game: (1) 2004

1st Overall Draft Choices: none

MONTREAL CANADIENS

First Game Played:

In NHA: January 19, 1910
Montreal Canadiens 4 at Renfrew Millionaires 9
In NHL: December 19, 1917
Ottawa Senators 4 at Montreal Canadiens 7

Nickname Provenance: As a Canadian team based in Quebec, simply called Canadians in French (they are also known as "the Habs," short for "*les habitants*," a name given to the early settlers of the province)

Mascot: Youppi

Arena History: Westmount Arena, 1909–1918; Jubilee Arena, 1918–20; Mount Royal Arena, 1920–24; Montreal Forum, 1924–96 (refurbished in 1968); Molson Centre, 1996–2002; Bell Centre, 2002–present (same building as Molson Centre, capacity 21,273)

Retired Numbers: Jacques Plante (1), Doug Harvey (2), Emile "Butch" Bouchard (3), Jean Beliveau (4), Bernie Geoffrion (5), Howie Morenz (7), Maurice Richard (9), Guy Lafleur (10), Yvan Cournoyer (12), Dickie Moore (12), Henri Richard (16), Elmer Lach (16), Serge Savard (18), Larry Robinson (19), Bob Gainey (23), Ken Dryden (29), Patrick Roy (33)

Hall of Famers: Players (50): Marty Barry, Harry Cameron, Gord Drillon, Dick Duff, Tony Esposito, Rod Langway, Roy Worters, Dick Irvin (inducted as Player, associated with Montreal as Builder), Howie Morenz, Georges Vezina, Aurel Joliat, Newsy Lalonde, Joe Malone, Sprague Cleghorn, Herb Gardiner, Sylvio Mantha, Joe Hall, George Hainsworth, Maurice Richard, Jack Laviolette, Didier Pitre, Bill Durnan, Babe Siebert, Toe Blake, Emile Bouchard, Elmer Lach, Ken Reardon, Tom Johnson, Jean Beliveau, Bernie Geoffrion, Doug Harvey, Dickie Moore, Jacques Plante, Henri Richard, Patrick Roy, Gump Worsley, Frank Mahovlich, Yvan Cournoyer, Ken Dryden, Jacques Lemaire, Bert Olmstead, Serge Savard, Jacques Laperriere, Guy Lafleur, Buddy O'Connor, Bob Gainey, Guy Lapointe, Steve Shutt, Larry Robinson, Denis Savard; Builders (12):

Cliff Fletcher, William Northey, Hon. Donat Raymond, Frank Selke, Ambrose O'Brien, Leo Dandurand, Tommy Gorman, Hon. Hartland de Montarville Molson, Joseph Cattarinich, Sam Pollock, Scotty Bowman, Glen Sather (played with Montreal, inducted as Builder)

Website: www.canadiens.com
Minor League Affiliate(s): Hamilton Bulldogs (AHL)
Stanley Cups: (23) 1923–24, 1929–30, 1930–31, 1943–44, 1945–46, 1952–53, 1955–56, 1956–57, 1957–58, 1958–59, 1959–60, 1964–65, 1065–66, 1967–68, 1968–69, 1970–71, 1972–73, 1975–76, 1976–77, 1977–78, 1978–79, 1985–86, 1992–93
Hosted All-Star Game: (12) 1953, 1956, 1957, 1958, 1959, 1960, 1965, 1967, 1969, 1975, 1993, 2009
1st Overall Draft Choices: 1969 (Rejean Houle), 1971 (Guy Lafleur), 1980 (Doug Wickenheiser)

NASHVILLE PREDATORS

First Game Played: October 10, 1998
Florida Panthers 1 at Nashville Predators 0
Nickname Provenance: selected by fans
Mascot: Gnash
Arena History: Nashville Arena, 1998–99, 2007; Gaylord Entertainment Center, 1999–2007; Sommet Centre, 2007–2010; Bridgestone Arena, 2010–present (all refer to the same building, capacity 17,113)
Retired Numbers: none
Hall of Famers: none
Website: www.nashvillepredators.com
Minor League Affiliate(s): Milwaukee Admirals (AHL)
Stanley Cups: none
Hosted All-Star Game: none
1st Overall Draft Choices: none

NEW JERSEY DEVILS

First Game Played:
As Kansas City Scouts: October 9, 1974
Kansas City Scouts 2 at Toronto Maple Leafs 6
As Colorado Rockies: October 5, 1976
Toronto Maple Leafs 2 at Colorado Rockies 4
As New Jersey Devils: October 5, 1982
Pittsburgh Penguins 3 at New Jersey Devils 3
Nickname Provenance: Selected by fans in reference to legend of a demonic baby produced by one Mrs. Leeds in 1735, her 13th child
Mascot: The Devil
Arena History: Kemper Arena (Kansas City), 1974–76; McNichols Sports Arena (Colorado), 1976–82; Brendan Byrne Arena, 1982–83; Byrne Meadowlands Arena, 1983–92 (same building as Brendan Byrne Arena); Meadowlands Arena (same building as Byrne Meadowlands Arena), 1992–96; Continental Airlines Arena (same building as Meadowlands Arena), 1996–2007; Prudential Center, 2007–present (capacity 17,625)
Retired Numbers: Ken Daneyko (3), Scott Stevens (4)
Hall of Famers: Players (5): Slava Fetisov, Igor Larionov, Lanny McDonald (Colorado Rockies), Peter Stastny, Scott Stevens; Builders (2): Herb Brooks, Lou Lamoriello
Website: www.newjerseydevils.com
Minor League Affiliate(s): Albany Devils (AHL), Trenton Devils (ECHL)
Stanley Cups: (3) 1994–95, 1999–2000, 2002–03
Hosted All-Star Game: 1984
1st Overall Draft Choices: 1979 (Rob Ramage—Colorado Rockies)

NEW YORK ISLANDERS

First Game Played: October 7, 1972
Atlanta Flames 3 at New York Islanders 2
Nickname Provenance: Named, simply, because the team is located on Long Island, New York

Mascot: none
Arena History: Nassau Veterans' Memorial Coliseum, 1972–present (capacity 16,234)
Retired Numbers: Denis Potvin (5), Clark Gillies (9), Bryan Trottier (19), Mike Bossy (22), Bob Nystrom (23), Billy Smith (31)
Hall of Famers: Players (6): Mike Bossy, Pat LaFontaine, Denis Potvin, Billy Smith, Bryan Trottier, Clark Gillies; Builders (2): Al Arbour, Bill Torrey
Website: www.newyorkislanders.com
Minor League Affiliate(s): Bridgeport Sound Tigers (AHL), Kalamazoo Wings (ECHL), Odessa Jackalopes (CHL)
Stanley Cups: (4) 1979–80, 1980–81, 1981–82, 1982–83
Hosted All-Star Game: 1983
1st Overall Draft Choices: 1972 (Billy Harris), 1973 (Denis Potvin), 2000 (Rick DiPietro), 2009 (John Tavares)

NEW YORK RANGERS

First Game Played: November 16, 1926
Montreal Maroons 0 at New York Rangers 1
Nickname Provenance: Emerged when sportswriters in New York called the new franchise Tex's Rangers, in reference to Tex Rickard, the president of Madison Square Garden and the man who assembled the executive for the team in 1926
Mascot: none
Arena History: Madison Square Garden, 1926–68; Madison Square Garden, 1968–present (newly built, capacity 18,200)
Retired Numbers: Ed Giacomin (1), Brian Leetch (2), Harry Howell (3), Rod Gilbert (7), Andy Bathgate (9), Adam Graves (9) Mark Messier (11), Mike Richter (35)
Hall of Famers: Players (47): Glenn Anderson, Dick Duff, Howie Morenz, Lester Patrick, Bill Cook, Frank Boucher, Ching Johnson, Babe Siebert, Earl Seibert, Doug Bentley, Max Bentley, Babe Pratt, Neil Colville, Bryan Hextall, Bill Gadsby, Terry Sawchuk, Bernie Geoffrion, Doug Harvey, Charlie Rayner, Art Coulter, Johnny

Bower, Tim Horton, Andy Bathgate, Jacques Plante, Harry Howell, Lynn Patrick, Pat LaFontaine, Harry Lumley, Gump Worsley, Allan Stanley, Rod Gilbert, Phil Esposito, Jean Ratelle, Ed Giacomin, Guy Lafleur, Buddy O'Connor, Brad Park, Clint Smith, Marcel Dionne, Edgar Laprade, Bun Cook, Wayne Gretzky, Mike Gartner, Jari Kurri, Mark Messier, Brian Leetch, Luc Robitaille; Builders (9): Herb Brooks, Bud Poile (played with Rangers, inducted as Builder), Emile Francis (also played for Rangers), William Jennings, John Kilpatrick, Roger Neilson, Craig Patrick, Glen Sather (played with Rangers, inducted as Builder), Carl Voss (played with Rangers, inducted as Builder)
Website: www.newyorkrangers.com
Minor League Affiliate(s): Hartford Wolf Pack (AHL), Greenville Road Warriors (ECHL—shared with Philadelphia)
Stanley Cups: (4) 1927–28, 1932–33, 1939–40, 1993–94
Hosted All-Star Game: (2) 1973, 1994
1st Overall Draft Choices: none

OTTAWA SENATORS

First Game Played: October 8, 1992
Montreal Canadiens 3 at Ottawa Senators 5
Nickname Provenance: From original team of same name from 1917–34
Mascot: Spartacat
Arena History: Civic Centre, 1992–96; Palladium, 1996; Corel Centre, 1996–2006; Scotiabank Place, 2006–present (same building as Palladium and Corel Centre, capacity 19,153)
Retired Numbers: Frank Finnigan (8)
Hall of Famers: none
Website: www.ottawasenators.com
Minor League Affiliate(s): Binghamton Senators (AHL), Elmira Jackals (ECHL—shared with Anaheim)
Stanley Cups: none
Hosted All-Star Game: none

1st Overall Draft Choices: 1993 (Alexandre Daigle), 1995 (Bryan Berard), 1996 (Chris Phillips)

PHILADELPHIA FLYERS

First Game Played: October 11, 1967
Philadelphia Flyers 1 at Oakland Seals 5
Nickname Provenance: Named by a nine-year-old in a fan contest
Mascot: none
Arena History: The Spectrum, 1967–96; CoreStates Center, 1996–98; First Union Center, 1998–2003 (same building as CoreStates Center); Wachovia Center, 2003–2010 (same building as First Union Center); Wells Fargo Center, 2010–present (same building as Wachovia Center, capacity 19,537)
Retired Numbers: Bernie Parent (1), Barry Ashbee (4), Bill Barber (7), Bobby Clarke (16)
Hall of Famers: Players (7): Paul Coffey, Bernie Parent, Bobby Clarke, Bill Barber, Dale Hawerchuk, Darryl Sittler, Allan Stanley; Builders (2): Ed Snider, Keith Allen
Website: www.philadelphiaflyers.com
Minor League Affiliate(s): Adirondack Phantoms (AHL), Greenville Road Warriors (ECHL—shared with NY Rangers)
Stanley Cups: (2) 1973–74, 1974–75
Hosted All-Star Game: (2) 1976, 1992
1st Overall Draft Choices: 1975 (Mel Bridgman)

PHOENIX COYOTES

First Game Played:
As Winnipeg Jets: October 10, 1979
Winnipeg Jets 2 at Pittsburgh Penguins 4
As Phoenix Coyotes: October 5, 1996
Phoenix Coyotes 0 at Hartford Whalers 1
Nickname Provenance: Logo depicts a Kachina coyote, indigenous to the region
Mascot: Howler
Arena History: Winnipeg Arena (Winnipeg), 1979–96; America West

Arena, 1996–98; Cellular One Ice Den (same building as America West Arena), 1998–99; America West Arena, 1999–2000; Alltel Ice Den, 2000–03 (same building as America West Arena); Glendale Arena, 2003–2008; Jobing.com Arena (same building as Glendale Arena, capacity 17,799)

Retired Numbers: Bobby Hull (9—Winnipeg), Dale Hawerchuk (10—Winnipeg), Thomas Steen (25), Teppo Humminen (27)

Hall of Famers: Players (5): Mike Gartner, Brett Hull, Bobby Hull (Winnipeg), Dale Hawerchuk (Winnipeg), Serge Savard (Winnipeg)

Website: www.phoenixcoyotes.com

Minor League Affiliate(s): San Antonio Rampage (AHL), Las Vegas Wranglers (ECHL)

Stanley Cups: none

Hosted All-Star Game: none

1st Overall Draft Choices: 1981 (Dale Hawerchuk—Winnipeg Jets)

PITTSBURGH PENGUINS

First Game Played: October 11, 1967
Montreal Canadiens 2 at Pittsburgh Penguins 1

Nickname Provenance: After the Pittsburgh arena opened in 1961, it was dubbed "The Igloo" for its shape. As a result, when Pittsburgh was awarded an NHL team in 1967, owners opted for a nickname compatible with "Igloo" and decided on "Penguins."

Mascot: Iceburgh

Arena History: Civic Arena ("The Igloo"), 1967–2000; Mellon Arena, 2000–2010 (same building as Civic Arena); Consol Energy Center, 2010–present (capacity 18,087)

Retired Numbers: Michel Briere (21), Mario Lemieux (66)

Hall of Famers: Players (11): Leo Boivin, Paul Coffey, Tim Horton, Red Kelly (inducted as Player, associated with Pittsburgh as Builder), Andy Bathgate, Mario Lemieux, Larry Murphy, Bryan Trottier, Joe Mullen, Ron Francis, Luc Robitaille; Builders (4): Scotty Bowman, Bob Johnson, Craig Patrick, Glen Sather (played

for Pittsburgh, inducted as Builder)
Website: www.pittsburghpenguins.com
Minor League Affiliate(s): Wilkes-Barre/Scranton Penguins (AHL), Wheeling Nailers (ECHL)
Stanley Cups: (3) 1990–91, 1991–92, 2008–09
Hosted All-Star Game: 1990
1st Overall Draft Choices: 1984 (Mario Lemieux), 2003 (Marc-Andre Fleury), 2005 (Sidney Crosby)

ST. LOUIS BLUES

First Game Played: October 11, 1967
Minnesota North Stars 2 at St. Louis Blues 2
Nickname Provenance: Named to remember the city's place in the history of music
Mascot: Louie
Arena History: St. Louis Arena, 1967–94; Kiel Center, 1994–2000; Savvis Center, 2000–2008, Scottrade Center, 2008–present (same building as Kiel Center and Savvis Center, capacity 19,022)
Retired Numbers: Al MacInnis (2), Bob Gassoff (3), Barclay Plager (8), Brian Sutter (11), Brett Hull (16), Bernie Federko (24)
Hall of Famers: Players (15): Glenn Anderson, Grant Fuhr, Bernie Federko, Dale Hawerchuk, Joe Mullen, Wayne Gretzky, Peter Stastny, Guy Lapointe, Jacques Plante, Glenn Hall, Dickie Moore, Doug Harvey, Al MacInnis, Scott Stevens, Brett Hull; Builders (7): Roger Neilson, Al Arbour, Scotty Bowman, Emile Francis, Craig Patrick (played for St. Louis, inducted as Builder), Lynn Patrick, Glen Sather (played for St. Louis, inducted as Builder)
Website: www.stlouisblues.com
Minor League Affiliate(s): Peoria Rivermen (AHL), Alaska Aces (ECHL)
Stanley Cups: none
Hosted All-Star Game: (2) 1970, 1988
1st Overall Draft Choices: none

SAN JOSE SHARKS

First Game Played: October 4, 1991
San Jose Sharks 3 at Vancouver Canucks 4
Nickname Provenance: named by team owners after a fan contest
Mascot: S.J. Sharkie (b. January 1992)
Arena History: Cow Palace, 1991–93; San Jose Arena, 1993–2001; Compaq Center, 2001–03; HP Pavilion, 2003–present (same building as Compaq Center and San Jose Arena, capacity 17,496)
Retired Numbers: none
Hall of Famers: (1) Igor Larionov
Website: www.sjsharks.com
Minor League Affiliate(s): Worcester Sharks (AHL), Stockton Thunder (ECHL—shared with Edmonton)
Stanley Cups: none
Hosted All-Star Game: 1997
1st Overall Draft Choices: none

TAMPA BAY LIGHTNING

First Game Played: October 7, 1992
Chicago Blackhawks 3 at Tampa Bay Lightning 7
Nickname Provenance: Tampa Bay is, statistically, the lightning capital of the world.
Mascot: Thunder Bug
Arena History: Expo Hall, 1992–93; ThunderDome, 1993–96 (five home games played at Orlando Arena); Ice Palace, 1998–2003; *St. Petersburg Times* Forum, 2003–present (same building as Ice Palace, capacity 19,758)
Retired Numbers: none
Hall of Famers: Players (2): Dino Ciccarelli, Denis Savard
Website: www.tampabaylightning.com
Minor League Affiliate(s): Norfolk Admirals (AHL), Florida Everblades (ECHL—shared with Carolina), Colorado Eagles (CHL)

Stanley Cups: 2003–04
Hosted All-Star Game: 1999
1st Overall Draft Choices: 1992 (Roman Hamrlik), 1998 (Vincent Lecavalier), 2008 (Steve Stamkos)

TORONTO MAPLE LEAFS

First Game Played:
As Toronto Arenas: December 19, 1917
Toronto Arenas 9 at Montreal Wanderers 10
As Toronto St. Pats: December 23, 1919
Toronto St. Pats 0 at Ottawa Senators 3
As Toronto Maple Leafs: February 17, 1927
New York Americans 1 at Toronto Maple Leafs 4
Nickname Provenance: Named by owner Conn Smythe after a World War I regiment
Mascot: Carlton the Bear
Arena History: Arena Gardens (Mutual Street Arena), 1917–31; Maple Leaf Gardens, 1931–99; Air Canada Centre, 1999–present (capacity 18,819)
Retired Numbers: Bill Barilko (5), Ace Bailey (6)
Honoured Numbers: Turk Broda (1), Johnny Bower (1), Red Kelly (4), King Clancy (7), Tim Horton (7), Charlie Conacher (9), Ted Kennedy (9), Syl Apps (10), George Armstrong (10), Wendel Clark (17), Borje Salming (21), Frank Mahovlich (27), Darryl Sittler (27), Doug Gilmour (93)
Hall of Famers: Players (59): Jack Adams, Glenn Anderson, Syl Apps, Al Arbour, George Armstrong, Ace Bailey, Andy Bathgate, Max Bentley, Leo Boivin, Johnny Bower, Turk Broda, Harry Cameron, Gerry Cheevers, King Clancy, Sprague Cleghorn, Charlie Conacher, Rusty Crawford, Hap Day, Gord Drillon, Dick Duff, Babe Dye, Fern Flaman, Grant Fuhr, Mike Gartner, Eddie Gerard, George Hainsworth, Harry Holmes, Red Horner, Tim Horton, Syd Howe, Harvey Jackson, Red Kelly, Ted Kennedy, Dave Keon, Brian Leetch,

Harry Lumley, Frank Mahovlich, Lanny McDonald, Dickie Moore, Larry Murphy, Frank Nighbor, Reg Noble, Bert Olmstead, Bernie Parent, Pierre Pilote, Jacques Plante, Babe Pratt, Joe Primeau, Marcel Pronovost, Bob Pulford, Borje Salming, Terry Sawchuk, Sweeney Schriner, Darryl Sittler, Allan Stanley, Norm Ullman, Carl Voss, Harry Watson, Ron Francis; Builders (12): Harold Ballard, J.P. Bickell, Cliff Fletcher, Foster Hewitt, William Hewitt, Punch Imlach, Dick Irvin (played for Toronto, inducted as Builder), Frank Mathers (played for Toronto, inducted as Builder), Rudy Pilous, Bud Poile (played for Toronto, inducted as Builder), Frank Selke, Conn Smythe
Website: www.torontomapleleafs.com
Minor League Affiliate(s): Toronto Marlies (AHL), Reading Royals (ECHL—shared with Boston)
Stanley Cups: (13) 1917–18, 1921–22, 1931–32, 1941–42, 1944–45, 1946–47, 1947–48, 1948–49, 1950–51, 1961–62, 1962–63, 1963–64, 1966–67
Hosted All-Star Game: (8) 1947, 1949, 1951, 1962, 1963, 1964, 1968, 2000
1st Overall Draft Choices: 1985 (Wendel Clark)

VANCOUVER CANUCKS

First Game Played: October 9, 1970
Los Angeles Kings 3 at Vancouver Canucks 1
Nickname Provenance: Continuation of WHL franchise nickname
Mascot: Fin the Whale
Arena History: Pacific Coliseum, 1970–95; General Motors (GM) Place, 1995–2010; Rogers Arena, 2010–present (same building as GM Place, capacity 18,810)
Retired Numbers: Wayne Maki (11, unofficial, later worn by Mark Messier but not before or since), Stan Smyl (12), Trevor Linden (16)
Hall of Famers: (3) Igor Larionov, Cam Neely, Mark Messier
Website: www.canucks.com
Minor League Affiliate(s): Manitoba Moose (AHL), Victoria Salmon Kings (ECHL)

Stanley Cups: none
Hosted All-Star Game: (2) 1977, 1998
1st Overall Draft Choices: none

WASHINGTON CAPITALS

First Game Played: October 9, 1974
Washington Capitals 3 at New York Rangers 6
Nickname Provenance: So called because the team plays in the capital city of the USA
Mascot: Slapshot
Arena History: Capital Centre, 1974–93; US Air Arena, 1993–97 (same building as Capital Centre); US Airways Arena, 1997 (same building as US Air Arena); MCI Center, 1997–2006; Verizon Center, 2006–present (same building as MCI Center—capacity 18,277)
Retired Numbers: Rod Langway (5), Yvon Labre (7), Mike Gartner (11), Dale Hunter (32)
Hall of Famers: Players (5): Dino Ciccarelli, Mike Gartner, Rod Langway, Larry Murphy, Scott Stevens; Builders (1): Craig Patrick (played for Washington, inducted as Builder)
Website: www.washingtoncaps.com
Minor League Affiliate(s): Hershey Bears (AHL), South Carolina Stingrays (ECHL)
Stanley Cups: none
Hosted All-Star Game: 1982
1st Overall Draft Choices: 1974 (Greg Joly), 1976 (Rick Green), (2005) Alexander Ovechkin

FINAL STANDINGS, REGULAR SEASON, 2009–10

EASTERN CONFERENCE

Northeast Division	GP	W	L	OT	GF	GA	Pts
Buffalo	82	45	27	10	235	207	100
Ottawa	82	44	32	6	225	238	94
Boston	82	39	30	13	206	200	91
Montreal	82	39	33	10	217	223	88
Toronto	82	30	38	14	214	267	74

Southeast Division							
Washington	82	54	15	13	318	233	121
Atlanta	82	35	34	13	234	256	83
Carolina	82	35	37	10	230	256	80
Tampa Bay	82	34	36	12	217	260	80
Florida	82	32	37	13	208	244	77

Atlantic Division							
New Jersey	82	48	27	7	222	191	103
Pittsburgh	82	47	28	7	257	237	101
Philadelphia	82	41	35	6	236	225	88
NY Rangers	82	38	33	11	222	218	87
NY Islanders	82	34	37	11	222	264	79

WESTERN CONFERENCE

Central Division							
Chicago	82	52	22	8	271	209	112
Detroit	82	44	24	14	229	216	102
Nashville	82	47	29	6	225	225	100
St. Louis	82	40	32	10	225	223	90
Columbus	82	32	35	15	216	259	79

Northwest Division

Vancouver	82	49	28	5	272	222	103
Colorado	82	43	30	9	244	233	95
Calgary	82	40	32	10	204	210	90
Minnesota	82	38	36	8	219	246	84
Edmonton	82	27	47	8	214	284	62

Pacific Division

San Jose	82	51	20	11	264	215	113
Phoenix	82	50	25	7	225	202	107
Los Angeles	82	46	27	9	241	219	101
Anaheim	82	39	32	11	238	251	89
Dallas	82	37	31	14	237	254	88

SCORING LEADERS & GOALIE LEADERS, 2009–10

(Nationality and NHL affiliation in parentheses)

Points

Henrik Sedin (SWE-VAN)	112
Sidney Crosby (CAN-PIT)	109
Alexander Ovechkin (RUS-WAS)	109
Nicklas Backstrom (SWE-WAS)	101
Steve Stamkos (CAN-TB)	95
Martin St. Louis (CAN-TB)	94
Brad Richards (CAN-DAL)	91
Joe Thornton (CAN-STL)	89
Patrick Kane (USA-CHI)	88
Marian Gaborik (SVK-NYR)	86

Goals

Sidney Crosby (CAN-PIT)	51
Steve Stamkos (CAN-TB)	51
Alexander Ovechkin (RUS-WAS)	50
Patrick Marleau (CAN-SJ)	44
Marian Gaborik (SVK-NYR)	42
Ilya Kovalchuk (RUS-ATL/NJ)	41
Alexander Semin (RUS-WAS)	40
Dany Heatley (CAN-SJ)	39
Zach Parise (USA-NJ)	38
Alexandre Burrows (CAN-VAN)	35
Bobby Ryan (USA-ANA)	35

Assists

Henrik Sedin (SWE-VAN)	83
Joe Thornton (CAN-SJ)	69
Nicklas Backstrom (RUS-WAS)	68

Brad Richards (CAN-DAL)	67
Martin St. Louis (CAN-TB)	65
Alexander Ovechkin (RUS-WAS)	59
Paul Stastny (USA-COL)	59
Sidney Crosby (CAN-PIT)	58
Patrick Kane (USA-CHI)	58
Mike Green (CAN-WAS)	57

Penalty Minutes

Zenon Konopka (CAN-TB)	265
Colton Orr (CAN-TOR)	239
Steve Downie (CAN-TB)	208
Daniel Carcillo (CAN-PHI)	207
Matt Carkner (CAN-OTT)	190
Cam Janssen (USA-STL)	190
Chris Neil (CAN-OTT)	175
Brandon Crombeen (USA-STL)	168
Brandon Prust (CAN-CAL/NYR)	163
Ian Laperriere (CAN-PHI)	162

Wins, Goalie

Martin Brodeur (CAN-NJ)	45
Evgeni Nabokov (RUS-SJ)	44
Ilya Bryzgalov (RUS-PHO)	42
Ryan Miller (USA-BUF)	41
Roberto Luongo (CAN-VAN)	40
Jonathan Quick (USA-LA)	39
Craig Anderson (USA-COL)	38
Jimmy Howard (USA-DET)	37
Marc-Andre Fleury (CAN-PIT)	37
Miikka Kiprusoff (FIN-CAL)	35
Henrik Lundqvist (SWE-NYR)	35

Losses, Goalie

Miikka Kiprusoff (FIN-CAL)	28
Tomas Vokoun (CZE-FLO)	28
Jess Deslauriers (CAN-EDM)	28
Henrik Lundqvist (SWE-NYR)	27
Steve Mason (CAN-CBJ)	26
Martin Brodeur (CAN-NJ)	25
Craig Anderson (USA-COL)	25
Jonathan Quick (USA-LA)	24
Jonas Hiller (SUI-ANA)	23
Niklas Backstrom (FIN-MIN)	23
Cam Ward (CAN-CAR)	23

Minutes Played

Martin Brodeur (CAN-NJ)	4,499:01
Jonathan Quick (USA-LA)	4,258:27
Craig Anderson (USA-COL)	4,235:21
Miikka Kiprusoff (FIN-CAL)	4,235:19
Henrik Lundqvist (SWE-NYR)	4,203:49
Evgeni Nabokov (RUS-SJ)	4,194:07
Ilya Bryzgalov (RUS-PHO)	4,084:27
Ryan Miller (USA-BUF)	4,047:10
Roberto Luongo (CAN-VAN)	3,899:24
Marc-Andre Fleury (CAN-PIT)	3,798:17

Shutouts

Martin Brodeur (CAN-NJ)	9
Ilya Bryzgalov (RUS-PHO)	8
Craig Anderson (USA-COL)	7
Pekka Rinne (FIN-NAS)	7
Antti Niemi (FIN-CHI)	7
Tomas Vokoun (CZE-FLO)	7
Ryan Miller (USA-BUF)	5

Brian Elliott (CAN-OTT)	5
Jaroslav Halak (SVK-MON)	5
Tuukka Rask (FIN-BOS)	5
Steve Mason (CAN-CBJ)	5
Tim Thomas (USA-BOS)	5

Goals-Against Average

Tuukka Rask (FIN-BOS)	1.97
Ryan Miller (USA-BUF)	2.22
Martin Brodeur (CAN-NJ)	2.24
Antti Niemi (FIN-CHI)	2.25
Jimmy Howard (USA-DET)	2.26
Ilya Bryzgalov (RUS-PHO)	2.29
Miikka Kiprusoff (FIN-CAL)	2.31
Henrik Lundqvist (SWE-NYR)	2.38
Jaroslav Halak (SVK-MON)	2.40
Evgeni Nabokov (RUS-SJ)	2.43

PLAYERS WHO PLAYED IN 2008–09, BUT NOT IN 2009–10

PLAYER	2008–09 STATUS
Armstrong, Riley	played for Abbotsford & Grand Rapids (AHL)
Arnason, Tyler	played in AHL & KHL
Axelsson, P.J.	played for Frolunda (SWE)
Babchuk, Anton	played for Avangard Omsk (KHL)
Backman, Christian	played for Frolunda (SWE)
Bass, Cody	played for Binghamton (AHL)
Bayda, Ryan	played for Wilkes Barre/Scranton (AHL)
Bell, Brendan	played for Peoria & Syracuse (AHL)
Bentivoglio, Sean	played for Bridgeport (AHL)
Bishop, Ben	played for Peoria (AHL)
Bonk, Radek	played in CZE & KHL
Boucher, Philippe	retired
Boulerice, Jesse	played for Wilkes-Barre/Scranton (AHL)
Brisebois, Patrice	retired
Brookbank, Wade	played for Wilkes-Barre/Scranton (AHL)
Cavanagh, Tom	played for Manchester (AHL)
Chucko, Kris	played for Abbotsford (AHL)
Collins, Sean	played for Hershey (AHL)
Colliton, Jeremy	played for Rogle (SWE)
Crabb, Joey	played for Chicago (AHL)
Cullimore, Jassen	played for Rockford (AHL)
Dandenault, Mathieu	played for Hartford (AHL)
Denis, Marc	retired
Devereaux, Boyd	played for Lugano (SUI)
de Vries, Greg	retired
Downey, Aaron	retired
Fedorov, Sergei	played for Magnitogorsk (KHL)

Fernandez, Manny	retired
Fraser, Jamie	played for Houston (AHL)
Fritsch, Jamie	played in ECHL & AHL
Fritsche, Dan	played for Syracuse (AHL)
Fritz, Mitch	played for Norfolk (AHL)
Frogren, Jonas	played for Toronto (AHL)
Gauthier, Denis	retired
Gerber, Martin	played for Mytischi (KHL)
Gillies, Colton	played for Houston (AHL)
Gragnani, Marc-Andre	played for Portland (AHL)
Gratton, Chris	retired
Gratton, Josh	played in KHL & AHL
Greentree, Kyle	played for Rockford (AHL)
Hall, Adam	played for Norfolk (AHL)
Hamilton, Jeff	played for Lugano (SUI)
Havelid, Niclas	played for Linkoping (SWE)
Hedican, Bret	retired
Helenius, Riku	played in AHL & SWE
Helmer, Bryan	played for Hershey (AHL)
Henry, Alex	played for Hamilton (AHL)
Heward, Jamie	retired
Hinote, Dan	played for MoDo (SWE)
Holik, Bobby	retired
Hollweg, Ryan	played for San Antonio (AHL)
Holt, Chris	played for Binghamton (AHL)
Hudler, Jiri	played for Moscow Dynamo (KHL)
Hutchinson, Andrew	played for Texas (AHL)
Iggulden, Mike	played for Riga Dynamo (KHL)
James, Connor	played for Augsburg (GER)
Jancevski, Dan	played for Texas (AHL)
Joseph, Curtis	retired
Kaberle, Frantisek	played for Kladno (CZE)
Kalinin, Dmitri	played for Ufa Salavat Yulayev (KHL)

Karsums, Martins	played in AHL & KHL
Kaspar, Lukas	played in AHL & FIN
Kinrade, Geoff	played for Binghamton (AHL)
Klee, Ken	retired
Kolanos, Krys	played for Adirondack (AHL)
Kolzig, Olaf	retired
Kozlov, Viktor	played for Ufa Salavat Yulayev (KHL)
Krahn, Brent	played for Texas (AHL)
Krog, Jason	played for Chicago (AHL)
Kukkonen, Lasse	played for Avangard Omsk (KHL)
LaCosta, Daniel	played for Syracuse (AHL)
LaCouture, Dan	played for Providence (AHL)
Lavallee-Smotherman, Jordan	played for Syracuse (AHL)
Ledin, Per	played for HV 71 Jonkoping (SWE)
Lehman, Scott	played for Chicago (AHL)
Lemieux, Claude	retired
Lewis, Grant	played for Chicago & Hershey (AHL)
Lindstrom, Joakim	played for Nizhny Novgorod (KHL)
Lundqvist, Joel	played for Frolunda (SWE)
MacDonald, Craig	played for DEG Metro (GER)
Macias, Ray	played for Lake Erie (AHL)
MacKenzie, Aaron	played in ECHL & CZE
Malik, Marek	played in CZE & SUI
Mannino, Peter	played for Chicago (AHL)
McCarty, Darren	retired
McCormick, Cody	played for Portland (AHL)
McIver, Nathan	played for Manitoba (AHL)
McKenna, Mike	played for Lowell (AHL)
McLean, Brett	played for Bern (SUI)
McLean, Kurtis	played for Lukko Rauma (FIN)
Melichar, Josef	played for Ceske Budejovice (CZE)
Mink, Graham	played for Rochester (AHL)
Mojzis, Tomas	played for MoDo (SWE)

Montoya, Al	played for San Antonio (AHL)
Motzko, Joe	played for Ingoldstadt (GER)
Murray, Garth	played for Abbotsford (AHL)
Naslund, Markus	played for MoDo (SWE)
Negrin, John	played for Abbotsford (AHL)
Nikulin, Alexander	played for CSKA Moscow (KHL)
Niskala, Janne	played for Frolunda (SWE)
Norrena, Fredrik	played for Linkoping (SWE)
Novotny, Jiri	played for Mytischi (KHL)
Numminen, Teppo	retired
Nycholat, Lawrence	played for Manitoba (AHL)
Nylander, Michael	played in AHL & FIN
Ondrus, Ben	played for Toronto (AHL)
Oreskovic, Phil	played for Toronto (AHL)
Ouellet, Michel	played for Fribourg (SUI)
Paddock, Cam	played for Peoria (AHL)
Peca, Michael	retired
Pelech, Matt	played for Abbotsford (AHL)
Pelletier, Pascal	played for Syracuse & Peoria (AHL)
Peltonen, Ville	played for Minsk (KHL)
Perrin, Eric	played for Avangard Omsk (KHL)
Pesonen, Janne	played for Ak Bars Kazan (KHL)
Petiot, Richard	played for Rockford (AHL)
Petruzalek, Jakub	played for Lukko Rauma (FIN)
Pihlstrom, Antti	played in SWE & FIN
Plihal, Tomas	played for TPS Turku (FIN)
Pock, Thomas	played for Rapperswil (SUI)
Pogge, Justin	played in ECHL & AHL
Porter, Chris	played for Peoria (AHL)
Quick, Kevin	played for Norfolk (AHL)
Raduns, Nate	played for Pontebba (ITA)
Ramo, Karri	played for Avangard Omsk (KHL)
Regier, Steve	played for Salzburg (AUT)
Reitz, Eric	played for Novosibirsk (KHL)

Richardson, Luke	retired
Rissmiller, Pat	played for Hartford & Grand Rapids (AHL)
Roberts, Gary	retired
Roenick, Jeremy	retired
Roy, Andre	retired
Ryan, Michael	played for Albany (AHL)
Sabourin, Dany	played for Providence (AHL)
Sakic, Joe	retired
Salcido, Brian	played for Manitoba (AHL)
Sanford, Curtis	played for Hamilton (AHL)
Sauer, Mike	played for Hartford (AHL)
Schwarz, Marek	played for Mlada Boleslav (CZE)
Semenov, Alexei	played for Dynamo Moscow (KHL)
Shanahan, Brendan	retired
Sillinger, Mike	retired
Skinner, Brett	played for Lake Erie (AHL)
Sloane, David	played in ECHL & AHL
Smith, Jason	retired
Smith, Trevor	played for Bridgeport (AHL)
Smith, Zach	did not play
Sprukts, Janis	played for Dynamo Riga (KHL)
Stafford, Garrett	played for Texas (AHL)
Stephan, Tobias	played for Geneve Servette (SUI)
Sterling, Brett	played for Chicago (AHL)
Stewart, Anthony	played for Chicago (AHL)
Stuart, Colin	played for Abbotsford (AHL)
Sundin, Mats	retired
Tallackson, Barry	played for Peoria (AHL)
Tellqvist, Mikael	played in KHL & FIN
Thomas, Bill	played in AHL & SUI
Tikhonov, Viktor	played in AHL & KHL
Tjarnqvist, Daniel	played for Yaroslavl (KHL)
Tordjman, Josh	played for San Antonio (AHL)

Turris, Kyle	played for San Antonio (AHL)
Vaananen, Ossi	played for Dynamo Minsk (KHL)
Van der Gulik, David	played for Abbotsford (AHL)
Van Ryn, Mike	did not play—injured
Vernace, Mike	played for Chicago & Hamilton (AHL)
Vrana, Petr	played for Vitkovice (CZE)
Wagner, Steve	played for Peoria & Wilkes-Barre/Scranton (AHL)
Ward, Jason	played for Adirondack (AHL)
Weber, Mike	played for Portland (AHL)
Weekes, Kevin	retired
Welch, Noah	played for Chicago (AHL)
Weller, Craig	played for Chicago (AHL)
Westgarth, Kevin	played for Manchester (AHL)
Williams, Jeremy	played for Grand Rapids (AHL)
Wilson, Landon	played for Texas (AHL)
Wishart, Ty	played for Norfolk (AHL)
York, Mike	played for Rochester (AHL)
Zednik, Richard	played for Yaroslavl (KHL)
Zeiler, John	played for Manchester (AHL)
Zherdev, Nikolai	played for Mytischi (KHL)
Zigomanis, Mike	played for Toronto (AHL)
Zubov, Ilja	played for Ufa & CSKA Moscow (KHL)
Zubov, Sergei	played for St. Petersburg (KHL)

2010 PLAYOFF RESULTS

Eastern Conference Quarterfinals

Montreal (8) vs. Washington (1)

April 15	Montreal 3 at Washington 2 (Plekanec 13:19 OT)
April 17	Montreal 5 at Washington 6 (Backstrom 0:31 OT)
April 19	Washington 5 at Montreal 1
April 21	Washington 6 at Montreal 3
April 23	Montreal 2 at Washington 1
April 26	Washington 1 at Montreal 4
April 28	Montreal 2 at Washington 1

Montreal wins best-of-seven 4–3

Philadelphia (7) vs. New Jersey (2)

April 14	Philadelphia 2 at New Jersey 1
April 16	Philadelphia 3 at New Jersey 5
April 18	New Jersey 2 at Philadelphia 3 (Carcillo 3:35 OT)
April 20	New Jersey 1 at Philadelphia 4
April 22	Philadelphia 3 at New Jersey 0

Philadelphia wins best-of-seven 4–1

Boston (6) vs. Buffalo (3)

April 15	Boston 1 at Buffalo 2
April 17	Boston 5 at Buffalo 3
April 19	Buffalo 1 at Boston 2
April 21	Buffalo 2 at Boston 3 (Satan 27:41 OT)
April 23	Boston 1 at Buffalo 4
April 26	Buffalo 3 at Boston 4

Boston wins best-of-seven 4–2

Ottawa (5) vs. Pittsburgh (4)

April 14	Ottawa 5 at Pittsburgh 4
April 16	Ottawa 1 at Pittsburgh 2

April 18   Pittsburgh 4 at Ottawa 2
April 20   Pittsburgh 7 at Ottawa 4
April 22   Ottawa 4 at Pittsburgh 3 (Carkner 47:06 OT)
April 24   Pittsburgh 4 at Ottawa 3 (Dupuis 9:56 OT)
Pittsburgh wins best-of-seven 4–2

Western Conference Quarterfinals

Colorado (8) vs. San Jose (1)
April 14   Colorado 2 at San Jose 1
April 16   Colorado 5 at San Jose 6 (Setoguchi 5:22 OT)
April 18   San Jose 0 at Colorado 1 (R. O'Reilly 0:51) [Anderson]
April 20   San Jose 2 at Colorado 1 (Pavelski 10:24 OT)
April 22   Colorado 0 at San Jose 5 [Nabokov]
April 24   San Jose 5 at Colorado 2
San Jose wins best-of-seven 4–2

Nashville (7) vs. Chicago (2)
April 16   Nashville 4 at Chicago 1
April 18   Nashville 0 at Chicago 2 [Niemi]
April 20   Chicago 1 at Nashville 4
April 22   Chicago 3 at Nashville 0 [Niemi]
April 24   Nashville 4 at Chicago 5 (Hossa 4:07 OT)
April 26   Chicago 5 at Nashville 3
Chicago wins best-of-seven 4–2

Los Angeles (6) vs. Vancouver (3)
April 15   Los Angeles 2 at Vancouver 3 (Samuelsson 8:52 OT)
April 17   Los Angeles 3 at Vancouver 2 (Kopitar 7:28 OT)
April 19   Vancouver 3 at Los Angeles 5
April 21   Vancouver 6 at Los Angeles 4
April 23   Los Angeles 2 at Vancouver 7
April 25   Vancouver 4 at Los Angeles 2
Vancouver wins best-of-seven 4–2

Detroit (5) vs. Phoenix (4)

April 14	Detroit 2 at Phoenix 3
April 16	Detroit 7 at Phoenix 4
April 18	Phoenix 4 at Detroit 2
April 20	Phoenix 0 at Detroit 3 [Howard]
April 23	Detroit 4 at Phoenix 2
April 25	Phoenix 5 at Detroit 2
April 27	Detroit 6 at Phoenix 1

Detroit wins best-of-seven 4–3

Eastern Conference Semifinals

Montreal (8) vs. Pittsburgh (4)

April 30	Montreal 3 at Pittsburgh 6
May 2	Montreal 3 at Pittsburgh 1
May 4	Pittsburgh 2 at Montreal 0 [Marc-Andre Fleury]
May 6	Pittsburgh 2 at Montreal 3
May 8	Montreal 1 at Pittsburgh 2
May 10	Pittsburgh 3 at Montreal 4
May 12	Montreal 5 at Pittsburgh 2

Montreal wins best-of-seven 4–3

Philadelphia (7) vs. Boston (6)

May 1	Philadelphia 4 at Boston 5 (Savard 13:52 OT)
May 3	Philadelphia 2 at Boston 3
May 5	Boston 4 at Philadelphia 1
May 7	Boston 4 at Philadelphia 5 (Gagne 14:40 OT)
May 10	Philadelphia 4 at Boston 0 [Boucher/Leighton]
May 12	Boston 1 at Philadelphia 2
May 12	Philadelphia 4 at Boston 3

Philadelphia wins best-of-seven 4–3

Western Conference Semifinals

Detroit (5) vs. San Jose (1)

April 29	Detroit 3 at San Jose 4
May 2	Detroit 3 at San Jose 4
May 4	San Jose 4 at Detroit 3 (Marleau 7:07 OT)
May 6	San Jose 1 at Detroit 7
May 8	Detroit 1 at San Jose 2

San Jose wins best-of-seven 4–1

Vancouver (3) vs. Chicago (2)

May 1	Vancouver 5 at Chicago 1
May 3	Vancouver 2 at Chicago 4
May 5	Chicago 5 at Vancouver 2
May 7	Chicago 7 at Vancouver 4
May 9	Vancouver 3 at Chicago 5
May 11	Chicago 5 at Vancouver 1

Chicago wins best-of-seven 4–2

Eastern Conference Finals

Montreal (8) vs. Philadelphia (7)

May 16	Montreal 0 at Philadelphia 6 [Leighton]
May 18	Montreal 0 at Philadelphia 3 [Leighton]
May 20	Philadelphia 1 at Montreal 5
May 22	Philadelphia 3 at Montreal 0 [Leighton]
May 24	Montreal 2 at Philadelphia 4

Philadelphia wins best-of-seven 4–1

Western Conference Finals

Chicago (2) vs. San Jose (1)

May 16	Chicago 2 at San Jose 1
May 18	Chicago 4 at San Jose 2
May 21	San Jose 2 at Chicago 3 (Byfuglien 12:24 OT)
May 23	San Jose 2 at Chicago 4

Chicago wins best-of-seven 4–0

Stanley Cup Finals

May 29	Philadelphia 5 at Chicago 6
May 31	Philadelphia 1 at Chicago 2
June 2	Chicago 3 at Philadelphia 4 (Giroux 5:59 OT)
June 4	Chicago 3 at Philadelphia 5
June 6	Philadelphia 4 at Chicago 7
June 9	Chicago 4 at Philadelphia 3 (Kane 4:06 OT)

Chicago wins Stanley Cup 4–2

PLAYER STATISTICS BY TEAM, 2010 PLAYOFFS

Boston Bruins

	GP	G	A	P	Pim
Dennis Wideman	13	1	11	12	4
Patrice Bergeron	13	4	7	11	2
Mark Recchi	13	6	4	10	6
Miroslav Satan	13	5	5	10	16
Milan Lucic	13	5	4	9	19
David Krejci	9	4	4	8	2
Zdeno Chara	13	2	5	7	29
Johnny Boychuk	13	2	4	6	6
Blake Wheeler	13	1	5	6	6
Matt Hunwick	13	0	6	6	2
Michael Ryder	13	4	1	5	2
Marc Savard	7	1	2	3	12
Vladimir Sobotka	13	0	2	2	15
Daniel Paille	13	0	2	2	2
Steve Begin	13	1	0	1	10
Andrew Ference	13	0	1	1	18
Tuukka Rask	13	0	1	1	0
Adam McQuaid	9	0	0	0	6
Mark Stuart	4	0	0	0	6
Shawn Thornton	12	0	0	0	4
Marco Sturm	7	0	0	0	4
Trent Whitfield	4	0	0	0	0

In Goal	GP	W-L	Mins	GA	SO	GAA
Tuukka Rask	13	7–6	829:03	36	0	2.61

Buffalo Sabres

	GP	G	A	P	Pim
Jason Pominville	6	2	2	4	2
Tyler Ennis	6	1	3	4	0
Thomas Vanek	3	2	1	3	2
Tim Kennedy	6	1	2	3	4
Mike Grier	6	2	0	2	2
Patrick Kaleta	6	1	1	2	22
Adam Mair	6	1	1	2	4
Nathan Gerbe	2	1	1	2	0
Cody McCormick	3	0	2	2	14
Raffi Torres	4	0	2	2	12
Derek Roy	6	0	2	2	4
Henrik Tallinder	6	0	2	2	2
Craig Rivet	6	1	0	1	11
Steve Montador	6	1	0	1	4
Tyler Myers	6	1	0	1	4
Matt Ellis	3	1	0	1	0
Paul Gaustad	6	0	1	1	8
Toni Lydman	6	0	1	1	6
Tim Connolly	6	0	1	1	2
Andrej Sekera	6	0	0	0	7
Ryan Miller	6	0	0	0	2
Drew Stafford	3	0	0	0	0

In Goal	GP	W-L	Mins	GA	SO	GAA
Ryan Miller	6	2–4	383:30	15	0	2.34

Chicago Blackhawks

	GP	G	A	P	Pim
Jonathan Toews	22	7	22	29	4
Patrick Kane	22	10	18	28	6
Patrick Sharp	22	11	11	22	16
Duncan Keith	22	2	15	17	10
Dustin Byfuglien	22	11	5	16	20
Dave Bolland	22	8	8	16	30
Marian Hossa	22	3	12	15	25
Kris Versteeg	22	6	8	14	14
Brent Seabrook	22	4	7	11	14
Troy Brouwer	19	4	4	8	8
Niklas Hjalmarsson	22	1	7	8	6
Tomas Kopecky	17	4	2	6	8
Andrew Ladd	19	3	3	6	12
Brent Sopel	22	1	5	6	8
Brian Campbell	19	1	4	5	2
Ben Eager	18	1	2	3	20
John Madden	22	1	1	2	2
Bryan Bickell	4	0	1	1	2
Antti Niemi	22	0	0	0	2
Adam Burish	15	0	0	0	2
Jordan Hendry	15	0	0	0	2
Nick Boynton	3	0	0	0	2
Colin Fraser	3	0	0	0	0
Cristobal Huet	1	0	0	0	0

In Goal	GP	W-L	Mins	GA	SO	GAA
Antti Niemi	22	16–6	1,321:51	58	2	2.63
Cristobal Huet	1	0–0	19:56	0	0	0.00

Colorado Avalanche

	GP	G	A	P	Pim
Paul Stastny	6	1	4	5	4
Brandon Yip	6	2	2	4	6
Chris Stewart	6	3	0	3	4
Matt Duchene	6	0	3	3	0
John-Michael Liles	6	1	1	2	4
Kyle Kumiskey	6	1	1	2	2
T.J. Galiardi	6	0	2	2	6
Ryan O'Reilly	6	1	0	1	2
Marek Svatos	3	1	0	1	2
Milan Hejduk	3	1	0	1	0
Adam Foote	6	0	1	1	10
Ryan Wilson	4	0	1	1	0
Craig Anderson	6	0	1	1	0
Kyle Quincey	6	0	0	0	8
Cody McLeod	6	0	0	0	5
Scott Hannan	6	0	0	0	4
Darcy Tucker	6	0	0	0	2
Stephane Yelle	6	0	0	0	2
Ryan Stoa	1	0	0	0	2
Matt Hendricks	6	0	0	0	0
Kevin Porter	4	0	0	0	0
Peter Budaj	1	0	0	0	0
Brett Clark	1	0	0	0	0
Chris Durno	1	0	0	0	0
Ruslan Salei	1	0	0	0	0

In Goal	GP	W-L	Mins	GA	SO	GAA
Craig Anderson	6	2–4	366:19	16	1	2.62
Peter Budaj	1	0–0	8:56	1	0	6.67

Detroit Red Wings

	GP	G	A	P	Pim
Johan Franzen	12	6	12	18	16
Henrik Zetterberg	12	7	8	15	6
Pavel Datsyuk	12	6	7	13	8
Brian Rafalski	12	3	8	11	2
Todd Bertuzzi	12	2	9	11	12
Nicklas Lidstrom	12	4	6	10	2
Valtteri Filppula	12	4	5	9	6
Tomas Holmstrom	12	4	3	7	12
Brad Stuart	12	2	4	6	8
Niklas Kronwall	12	0	5	5	12
Dan Cleary	12	2	0	2	4
Justin Abdelkader	11	1	1	2	36
Drew Miller	12	1	1	2	4
Jonathan Ericsson	12	0	2	2	8
Darren Helm	12	1	0	1	4
Kris Draper	12	0	0	0	16
Andreas Lilja	11	0	0	0	14
Jimmy Howard	12	0	0	0	2
Patrick Eaves	8	0	0	0	2
Jason Williams	3	0	0	0	0
Brett Lebda	2	0	0	0	0
Mattias Ritola	1	0	0	0	0

In Goal	GP	W-L	Mins	GA	SO	GAA
Jimmy Howard	12	5–7	720:26	33	1	2.75

Los Angeles Kings

	GP	G	A	P	Pim
Drew Doughty	6	3	4	7	4
Jack Johnson	6	0	7	7	6
Michal Handzus	6	3	2	5	4
Anze Kopitar	6	2	3	5	2
Dustin Brown	6	1	4	5	6
Fredrik Modin	6	3	1	4	2
Alexander Frolov	6	1	3	4	0
Wayne Simmonds	6	2	1	3	9
Ryan Smyth	6	1	1	2	6
Brad Richardson	6	1	1	2	2
Jarret Stoll	6	1	0	1	4
Sean O'Donnell	6	0	1	1	4
Justin Williams	3	0	1	1	2
Matt Greene	6	0	1	1	0
Rob Scuderi	6	0	0	0	6
Rich Clune	4	0	0	0	5
Jeff Halpern	6	0	0	0	4
Randy Jones	4	0	0	0	2
Jonathan Quick	6	0	0	0	0
Scott Parse	4	0	0	0	0
Peter Harrold	2	0	0	0	0
Erik Ersberg	1	0	0	0	0
Raitis Ivanins	1	0	0	0	0

In Goal	GP	W-L	Mins	GA	SO	GAA
Jonathan Quick	6	2–4	360:27	21	0	3.50
Erik Ersberg	1	0–0	12:56	2	0	9.23

Montreal Canadiens

	GP	G	A	P	Pim
Mike Cammalleri	19	13	6	19	6
Brian Gionta	19	9	6	15	14
Scott Gomez	19	2	12	14	25
Tomas Plekanec	19	4	7	11	20
Roman Hamrlik	19	0	9	9	15
Andrei Kostitsyn	19	3	5	8	12
P.K. Subban	14	1	7	8	6
Marc-Andre Bergeron	19	2	4	6	10
Dominic Moore	19	4	1	5	6
Maxim Lapierre	19	3	1	4	20
Tom Pyatt	18	2	2	4	2
Jaroslav Spacek	10	1	3	4	6
Andrei Markov	8	0	4	4	0
Travis Moen	19	2	1	3	4
Josh Gorges	19	0	2	2	14
Benoit Pouliot	18	0	2	2	6
Glen Metropolit	16	0	2	2	4
Hal Gill	18	0	1	1	20
Mathieu Darche	11	0	1	1	2
Ryan O'Byrne	13	0	0	0	10
Carey Price	1	0	0	0	4
Jaroslav Halak	18	0	0	0	0
Sergei Kostitsyn	5	0	0	0	0
Ben Maxwell	1	0	0	0	0

In Goal	GP	W-L	Mins	GA	SO	GAA
Jaroslav Halak	18	9–9	1,013:24	43	0	2.55
Carey Price	1	0–1	134:40	8	0	3.56

Nashville Predators

	GP	G	A	P	Pim
David Legwand	6	2	5	7	8
Martin Erat	6	4	1	5	4
Joel Ward	6	2	2	4	2
J-P Dumont	6	2	2	4	0
Shea Weber	6	2	1	3	4
Steve Sullivan	6	0	3	3	2
Jason Arnott	6	2	0	2	0
Kevin Klein	6	0	2	2	4
Dan Hamhuis	6	0	2	2	2
Denis Grebeshkov	2	0	2	2	0
Jerred Smithson	6	1	0	1	6
Patric Hornqvist	2	0	1	1	4
Marcel Goc	6	0	1	1	2
Jordan Tootoo	6	0	1	1	2
Cody Franson	4	0	1	1	2
Colin Wilson	6	0	1	1	0
Francis Bouillon	6	0	0	0	6
Pekka Rinne	6	0	0	0	0
Nick Spaling	6	0	0	0	0
Ryan Suter	6	0	0	0	0
Dustin Boyd	4	0	0	0	0

In Goal	GP	W-L	Mins	GA	SO	GAA
Pekka Rinne	6	2–4	357:59	16	0	2.68

New Jersey Devils

	GP	G	A	P	Pim
Ilya Kovalchuk	5	2	4	6	6
Zach Parise	5	1	3	4	0
Patrik Elias	5	0	4	4	2
Brian Rolston	5	2	1	3	0
Andy Greene	5	1	1	2	6
Travis Zajac	5	1	1	2	2
Colin White	5	1	0	1	8
Dainius Zubrus	5	1	0	1	8
Jamie Langenbrunner	5	0	1	1	4
Mike Mottau	5	0	1	1	0
David Clarkson	5	0	0	0	22
P-L Letourneau-Leblond	5	0	0	0	10
Rob Niedermayer	5	0	0	0	6
Bryce Salvador	5	0	0	0	6
Dean McAmmond	5	0	0	0	4
Rod Pelley	3	0	0	0	2
Matthew Corrente	2	0	0	0	2
Martin Brodeur	5	0	0	0	0
Paul Martin	5	0	0	0	0
Martin Skoula	4	0	0	0	0
Mark Fraser	1	0	0	0	0

In Goal	GP	W-L	Mins	GA	SO	GAA
Martin Brodeur	5	1–4	298:44	15	0	3.01

Ottawa Senators

	GP	G	A	P	Pim
Matt Cullen	6	3	5	8	0
Daniel Alfredsson	6	2	6	8	2
Jason Spezza	6	1	6	7	4
Erik Karlsson	6	1	5	6	4
Chris Kelly	6	1	5	6	2
Mike Fisher	6	2	3	5	6
Chris Neil	6	3	1	4	20
Peter Regin	6	3	1	4	6
Jarkko Ruutu	6	2	1	3	34
Chris Campoli	6	0	2	2	4
Anton Volchenkov	6	0	2	2	4
Matt Carkner	6	1	0	1	12
Nick Foligno	6	0	1	1	2
Andy Sutton	6	0	0	0	8
Zack Smith	6	0	0	0	5
Chris Phillips	6	0	0	0	4
Jesse Winchester	6	0	0	0	0
Brian Elliott	4	0	0	0	0
Pascal Leclaire	3	0	0	0	0
Shean Donovan	2	0	0	0	0
Ryan Shannon	2	0	0	0	0
Jonathan Cheechoo	1	0	0	0	0
Milan Michalek	1	0	0	0	0

In Goal	GP	W-L	Mins	GA	SO	GAA
Pascal Leclaire	3	1–2	210:43	10	0	2.84
Brian Elliott	4	1–2	202:53	14	0	4.14

Philadelphia Flyers

	GP	G	A	P	Pim
Danny Briere	23	12	18	30	18
Mike Richards	23	7	16	23	18
Claude Giroux	23	10	11	21	4
Ville Leino	19	7	14	21	6
Chris Pronger	23	4	14	18	36
Scott Hartnell	23	8	9	17	25
Matt Carle	23	1	12	13	8
Simon Gagne	19	9	3	12	0
Kimmo Timonen	23	1	10	11	20
Jeff Carter	12	5	2	7	2
Arron Asham	23	4	3	7	10
James van Riemsdyk	21	3	3	6	4
Daniel Carcillo	17	2	4	6	34
Braydon Coburn	23	1	3	4	22
Lukas Krajicek	22	0	3	3	8
Blair Betts	23	1	1	2	4
Ryan Parent	17	1	0	1	2
Darroll Powe	23	0	1	1	6
Ian Laperriere	13	0	1	1	6
Oskars Bartulis	7	0	0	0	4
Michael Leighton	14	0	0	0	2
Brian Boucher	12	0	0	0	2
David Laliberte	1	0	0	0	2
Andreas Nodl	10	0	0	0	0
Jared Ross	3	0	0	0	0
Johan Backlund	1	0	0	0	0

In Goal	GP	W-L	Mins	GA	SO	GAA
Michael Leighton	14	8–3	757:13	31	3	2.46
Brian Boucher	12	6–6	655:37	27	1	2.47
Johan Backlund	1	0–0	1:24	0	0	0.00

Phoenix Coyotes

	GP	G	A	P	Pim
Matt Lombardi	7	1	5	6	2
Wojtek Wolski	7	4	1	5	0
Keith Yandle	7	2	3	5	4
Radim Vrbata	7	2	2	4	4
Derek Morris	7	1	3	4	11
Petr Prucha	7	1	2	3	4
Martin Hanzal	7	0	3	3	10
Vernon Fiddler	6	1	1	2	14
Shane Doan	3	1	1	2	4
Taylor Pyatt	7	1	1	2	2
Adrian Aucoin	7	0	2	2	10
Zbynek Michalek	7	0	2	2	2
Lee Stempniak	7	0	2	2	0
Sami Lepisto	7	1	0	1	6
Ed Jovanovski	7	1	0	1	4
Lauri Korpikoski	7	1	0	1	2
Mathieu Schneider	3	1	0	1	0
Robert Lang	4	0	1	1	0
Petter Nokelainen	5	0	0	0	2
Ilya Bryzgalov	7	0	0	0	0
Daniel Winnik	7	0	0	0	0

In Goal	GP	W-L	Mins	GA	SO	GAA
Ilya Bryzgalov	7	3–4	419:14	24	0	3.44

Pittsburgh Penguins

	GP	G	A	P	Pim
Sidney Crosby	13	6	13	19	6
Sergei Gonchar	13	2	10	12	4
Evgeni Malkin	13	5	6	11	6
Chris Kunitz	13	4	7	11	8
Bill Guerin	11	4	5	9	2
Alex Goligoski	13	2	7	9	2
Pascal Dupuis	13	2	6	8	4
Kris Letang	13	5	2	7	6
Matt Cooke	13	4	2	6	22
Maxime Talbot	13	2	4	6	11
Jordan Staal	11	3	2	5	6
Alexei Ponikarovsky	11	1	4	5	4
Craig Adams	13	2	1	3	15
Mark Eaton	13	0	3	3	4
Brooks Orpik	13	0	2	2	12
Mark Letestu	4	0	1	1	0
Mike Rupp	11	0	0	0	8
Ruslan Fedotenko	6	0	0	0	4
Marc-Andre Fleury	13	0	0	0	2
Tyler Kennedy	10	0	0	0	2
Jordan Leopold	8	0	0	0	2
Jay McKee	5	0	0	0	2
Chris Conner	1	0	0	0	0
Brent Johnson	1	0	0	0	0

In Goal	GP	W-L	Mins	GA	SO	GAA
Brent Johnson	1	0–0	31:29	1	0	1.94
Marc-Andre Fleury	13	7–6	798:12	37	1	2.78

San Jose Sharks

	GP	G	A	P	Pim
Joe Pavelski	15	9	8	17	6
Dan Boyle	15	2	12	14	8
Patrick Marleau	14	8	5	13	8
Dany Heatley	14	2	11	13	16
Joe Thornton	15	3	9	12	18
Ryane Clowe	15	2	8	10	28
Devon Setoguchi	15	5	4	9	6
Douglas Murray	15	1	6	7	8
Jason Demers	15	1	4	5	8
Logan Couture	15	4	0	4	4
Marc-Edouard Vlasic	15	0	3	3	4
Scott Nichol	15	1	1	2	17
Rob Blake	15	1	1	2	10
Torrey Mitchell	15	0	2	2	2
Dwight Helminen	7	1	0	1	4
Manny Malhotra	15	1	0	1	0
Jed Ortmeyer	4	0	1	1	0
Jamie McGinn	15	0	0	0	8
Kent Huskins	15	0	0	0	6
Niclas Wallin	6	0	0	0	2
Evgeni Nabokov	15	0	0	0	0
Thomas Greiss	1	0	0	0	0

In Goal	GP	W-L	Mins	GA	SO	GAA
Evgeni Nabokov	15	8–7	889:51	38	1	2.56
Thomas Greiss	1	0–0	40:00	2	0	3.00

Vancouver Canucks

	GP	G	A	P	Pim
Mikael Samuelsson	12	8	7	15	16
Daniel Sedin	12	5	9	14	12
Henrik Sedin	12	3	11	14	6
Ryan Kesler	12	1	9	10	4
Kevin Bieksa	12	3	5	8	14
Christian Ehrhoff	12	3	4	7	8
Kyle Wellwood	12	2	5	7	0
Alexandre Burrows	12	3	3	6	22
Alexander Edler	12	2	4	6	10
Pavol Demitra	11	2	4	6	4
Sami Salo	12	1	5	6	2
Steve Bernier	12	4	1	5	0
Mason Raymond	12	3	1	4	6
Shane O'Brien	12	1	2	3	25
Jannik Hansen	12	1	2	3	4
Michael Grabner	9	1	0	1	0
Andrew Alberts	10	0	1	1	27
Rick Rypien	7	0	1	1	7
Ryan Johnson	4	0	0	0	2
Roberto Luongo	12	0	0	0	0
Tanner Glass	4	0	0	0	0
Nolan Baumgartner	1	0	0	0	0
Matt Pettinger	1	0	0	0	0
Andrew Raycroft	1	0	0	0	0
Aaron Rome	1	0	0	0	0

In Goal	GP	W-L	Mins	GA	SO	GAA
Andrew Raycroft	1	0–0	24:38	1	0	2.40
Roberto Luongo	12	6–6	706:52	38	0	3.22

Washington Capitals

	GP	G	A	P	Pim
Alexander Ovechkin	7	5	5	10	0
Nicklas Backstrom	7	5	4	9	4
Mike Knuble	7	2	4	6	6
Eric Fehr	7	3	1	4	4
John Carlson	7	1	3	4	0
Tom Poti	6	0	4	4	5
Brooks Laich	7	2	1	3	4
Matt Bradley	7	1	2	3	2
Jason Chimera	7	1	2	3	2
Mike Green	7	0	3	3	12
Joe Corvo	7	1	1	2	4
Boyd Gordon	6	1	1	2	0
Alexander Semin	7	0	2	2	4
Tomas Fleischmann	6	0	1	1	6
Eric Belanger	7	0	1	1	4
Jeff Schultz	7	0	1	1	4
Brendan Morrison	5	0	1	1	2
Shaone Morrisonn	5	0	0	0	2
Semyon Varlamov	6	0	0	0	0
David Steckel	3	0	0	0	0
Tyler Sloan	2	0	0	0	0
Jose Theodore	2	0	0	0	0
Karl Alzner	1	0	0	0	0
Scott Walker	1	0	0	0	0

In Goal	GP	W-L	Mins	GA	SO	GAA
Semyon Varlamov	6	3–3	348:30	14	0	2.41
Jose Theodore	2	0–1	81:08	5	0	3.70

ALL REGULAR-SEASON SCORES, 2009–10

October 1

Washington 4 at Boston 1 (Ovechkin (WAS) two goals, one assist)
Montreal 4 at Toronto 3 (Gorges 4:47 OT)
San Jose 2 at Colorado 5 (Avs retired Joe Sakic's # 19)
Vancouver 3 at Calgary 5 (eight different scorers)

October 2

Florida 4 at Chicago 3 (SO) (played in Helsinki)
Detroit 3 at St. Louis 4 (no scoring in 3rd) (played in Stockholm)
Philadelphia 2 at Carolina 0 [Emery]
NY Rangers 2 at Pittsburgh 3 (Penguins raise Cup banner in home
    opener)

October 3

Chicago 4 at Florida 0 [Niemi] (played in Helsinki)
St. Louis 5 at Detroit 3 (Red Wings led 2–0 early in 1st) (played in
    Stockholm)
Vancouver 0 at Colorado 3 (C. Anderson)
Carolina 2 at Boston 7 (Bruins led 5–0 midway through game)
Montreal 2 at Buffalo 1 (Gionta 2:42 OT)
Philadelphia 5 at New Jersey 2 (Flyers led 3–0 after 2nd)
Pittsburgh 4 at NY Islanders 3 (Tavares (NYI) scored in 1st NHL
    game) (SO)
Ottawa 2 at NY Rangers 5 (no scoring after 1st)
Toronto 4 at Washington 6 (Leafs scored only three goals of 3rd)
Tampa Bay 3 at Atlanta 6 (Kovalchuk (ATL), Peverley (ATL),
    St. Louis (TB) two goals each)
Minnesota 1 at Columbus 2 (no scoring in first half of game)
Nashville 3 at Dallas 2 (SO)
San Jose 4 at Anaheim 1 (Ducks scored only goal of 3rd)
Calgary 4 at Edmonton 3 (Moss scored game winner at 19:11 of 3rd
    off giveaway by goalie Khabibulin)

Phoenix 6 at Los Angeles 3 (Coyotes scored two goals in each period)

October 5

NY Rangers 3 at New Jersey 2 (Devils had early 1–0 lead)
Columbus 5 at Vancouver 3 (Jackets scored three goals in 2nd)

October 6

Ottawa 2 at Toronto 1 (Senators scored goals in 37 seconds in 2nd)
Washington 5 at Philadelphia 6 (Briere 3:52 OT)
Tampa Bay 1 at Carolina 2 (SO)
Montreal 3 at Calgary 4 (Flames scored only goal of 3rd)
Anaheim 3 at Minnesota 4 (Brunette 3:08 OT)
Dallas 4 at Edmonton 5 (SO)
San Jose 4 at Los Angeles 6 (Kings led 4–0 midway through game)

October 7

Phoenix 3 at Pittsburgh 0 [Bryzgalov]
Montreal 1 at Vancouver 7 (Canucks led 3–1 early in 2nd)

October 8

Anaheim 6 at Boston 1 (Bruins led 1–0 after 1st)
Phoenix 1 at Buffalo 2 (all goals in 3rd)
NY Islanders 2 at Ottawa 3 (Fisher 0:32 OT)
Pittsburgh 5 at Philadelphia 4 (Briere & Carter (PHI) two goals each)
NY Rangers 4 at Washington 3 (game tied 2–2 early in 3rd)
New Jersey 4 at Tampa Bay 3 (SO)
Chicago 2 at Detroit 3 (Red Wings all goals in 2nd)
Atlanta 4 at St. Louis 2 (Kovalchuk (ATL) two goals)
Colorado 2 at Nashville 3 (Avs led 2–1 early in 3rd)
Calgary 4 at Edmonton 3 (SO)
Minnesota 3 at Los Angeles 6 (Kings led 3–0 early in 2nd)
Columbus 3 at San Jose 6 (Heatley (SJ) hat trick)

October 9

Florida 2 at Carolina 7 (nine different scorers)
Dallas 5 at Calgary 2 (Stars led 2–0 early in 2nd)

October 10

NY Islanders 3 at Boston 4 (SO)
Pittsburgh 5 at Toronto 2 (Crosby (PIT) two goals)
Atlanta 2 at Ottawa 4 (game tied 2–2 after 1st)
Anaheim 3 at Philadelphia 2 (SO)
New Jersey 3 at Florida 2 (Clarkson (NJ) at 16:25 breaks 2–2 tie)
Washington 2 at Detroit 3 (Holmstrom (DET) at 13:07 breaks 2–2 tie)
Carolina 2 at Tampa Bay 5 (Lightning score only three goals of 3rd)
Los Angeles 2 at St. Louis 1 (Kings led 2–0 after 2nd)
Buffalo 1 at Nashville 0 (Grier 16:35 3rd) [Miller]
Colorado 3 at Chicago 4 (SO)
Columbus 2 at Phoenix 0 [Garon]
Montreal 2 at Edmonton 3 (Oilers led 3–0 late in 2nd)
Minnesota 2 at San Jose 4 (Wild led 2–0 midway through 2nd)

October 11

Anaheim 0 at NY Rangers 3 [Valiquette]
Dallas 3 at Vancouver 3 (SO)

October 12

Colorado 4 at Boston 3 (game tied 2–2 midway through 2nd)
Los Angeles 2 at NY Islanders 1 (Kings led 2–0 early in 3rd)
Toronto 2 at NY Rangers 7 (Rangers scored only four goals of 3rd)
New Jersey 3 at Washington 2 (SO)
Pittsburgh 4 at Ottawa 1 (Kennedy two goals in 2nd)
Florida 2 at Tampa Bay 3 (Lightning only two goals of 3rd)
Edmonton 6 at Nashville 1 (Oilers led 6–0 late in 2nd)
Calgary 5 at Chicago 6 (Flames led 5–0 late in 1st—Seabrook
    0:26 OT)
Phoenix 1 at San Jose 0 [Bryzgalov]

October 13

Detroit 2 at Buffalo 6 (Vanek (BUF) two goals in 2nd)
Calgary 1 at Columbus 2 (no scoring in 3rd)
Colorado 4 at Toronto 1 (no scoring in 3rd)

October 14

Los Angeles 2 at NY Rangers 4 (game tied 1–1 early in 1st)
Edmonton 3 at Chicago 4 (Grebeshkov broke 3–3 tie at 19:12 of 3rd)
Nashville 0 at Dallas 6 [Turco]
Minnesota 2 at Anaheim 3 (Ducks led 3–0 late in 2nd)

October 15

San Jose 1 at Washington 4 (Ovechkin two goals)
Colorado 3 at Montreal 2 (R. O'Reilly at 13:42 of 3rd broke 2–2 tie)
Tampa Bay 1 at Ottawa 7 (M. Michalek hat trick)
Los Angeles 2 at Detroit 5 (Kings led 1–0 after 1st)
Chicago 3 at Nashville 1 (game tied 1–1 early in 2nd)
St. Louis 2 at Phoenix 3 (Jovanovski 3:37 OT)

October 16

Atlanta 4 at New Jersey 2 (Thrashers scored three goals in 3rd)
NY Islanders 3 at Buffalo 6 (nine different scorers)
Philadelphia 2 at Florida 4 (Panthers scored only two goals of 3rd)
Boston 3 at Dallas 0 [Thomas]
Vancouver 3 at Calgary 5 (Flames led 5–0 after 2nd)
Minnesota 2 at Edmonton 5 (Penner & Brule (EDM) two goals each)

October 17

Atlanta 4 at Buffalo 2 (Kovalchuk (ATL) two goals)
NY Rangers 4 at Toronto 1 (Leafs led 1–0 early in 1st)
Ottawa 3 at Montreal 1 (Sens scored in every period)
Carolina 0 at New Jersey 2 (Brodeur)
San Jose 4 at NY Islanders 1 (Islanders led 1–0 after 1st)
Nashville 2 at Washington 3 (SO)

Colorado 4 at Detroit 3 (SO)
Los Angeles 1 at Columbus 4 (Kings led 1–0 late in 1st)
Tampa Bay 1 at Pittsburgh 4 (Penguins led 2–0 after 1st)
Dallas 4 at Chicago 3 (Stars scored three goals in 2nd)
Boston 1 at Phoenix 4 (no scoring in 3rd)
Minnesota 1 at Vancouver 2 (Canucks scored only goal of 3rd)
St. Louis 5 at Anaheim 0 [Conklin]

October 19

San Jose 7 at NY Rangers 3 (Setoguchi (SJ) two goals in 2nd)
Los Angeles 4 at Dallas 1 (Stars led 1–0 early in 2nd)
Vancouver 1 at Edmonton 2 (Canucks led 1–0 after 1st)

October 20

St. Louis 1 at Pittsburgh 5 (Penguins led 4–0 midway through 2nd)
Atlanta 1 at Montreal 2 (SO)
Columbus 3 at Calgary 6 (nine different scorers)

October 21

Nashville 2 at Boston 3 (Bruins scored only goal of 3rd)
Carolina 3 at NY Islanders 4 (SO)
Buffalo 5 at Florida 2 (Sabres led 5–1 after 1st)
Colorado 2 at Minnesota 3 (SO)
Vancouver 3 at Chicago 2 (Canucks trailed 2–1 after 2nd)
Dallas 4 at Anaheim 2 (Stars led 3–0 midway through 2nd)

October 22

NY Islanders 1 at Montreal 5 (Habs led 3–0 after 2nd)
New Jersey 4 at NY Rangers 2 (Devils scored only two goals of 3rd)
Boston 3 at Philadelphia 4 (SO)
Washington 5 at Atlanta 4 (Caps led 5–2 after 2nd)
Nashville 6 at Ottawa 5 (Weber 2:11 OT)
San Jose 2 at Tampa Bay 5 (Stamkos (TB) two goals)

Columbus 4 at Edmonton 6 (Oilers scored only three goals of 3rd)
Detroit 2 at Phoenix 3 (Aucoin 1:57 OT)
Dallas 4 at Los Angeles 5 (Handzus 0:55 OT)

October 23

Florida 2 at Pittsburgh 3 (SO)
Minnesota 1 at St. Louis 3 (Blues scored in every period)
Carolina 4 at Colorado 5 (P. Stastny (COL) two goals)

October 24

Toronto 1 at Vancouver 3 (Canucks led 2–0 after 1st)
NY Rangers 4 at Montreal 5 (Cammalleri 2:42 OT to complete
    hat trick)
Boston 4 at Ottawa 3 (SO)
Washington 3 at NY Islanders 2 (Laich 1:00 OT)
Florida 1 at Philadelphia 5 (game tied 1–1 late in 1st)
San Jose 4 at Atlanta 3 (Sharks led 3–0 early in 3rd)
New Jersey 4 at Pittsburgh 1 (Devils led 3–0 early in 3rd)
Buffalo 3 at Tampa Bay 2 (SO)
Dallas 4 at St. Louis 1 (Blues scored late in 3rd)
Carolina 2 at Minnesota 3 (Clutterbuck 1:55 OT)
Nashville 0 at Chicago 2 [Huet]
Los Angeles 5 at Phoenix 3 (D. Brown (LA) & Doan (PHO) two
    goals each)
Detroit 1 at Colorado 3 (Avs scored only two goals of 3rd)
Columbus 6 at Anaheim 4 (Ducks led 1–0 early in 2nd)
Edmonton 2 at Calgary 5 (Flames scored three goals in 2nd)

October 25

San Jose 4 at Philadelphia 1 (game tied 1–1 midway through 1st)
Columbus 2 at Los Angeles 6 (Kings scored two goals in each
    period)
Edmonton 0 at Vancouver 2 [Luongo]

October 26

Phoenix 2 at NY Rangers 5 (Gaborik (NYR) two goals)
NY Islanders 2 at Montreal 3 (Hamrlik 1:32 OT)
Minnesota 1 at Chicago 3 (Hawks led 2–0 after 1st & 2nd)
Toronto 6 at Anaheim 3 (game tied 1–1 late in 3rd)

October 27

Philadelphia 2 at Washington 4 (Caps scored only two goals of 3rd)
Colorado 3 at Edmonton 0 [C. Anderson]
Detroit 5 at Vancouver 4 (Wings scored four goals in 3rd)

October 28

Buffalo 4 at New Jersey 1 (Sabres led 2–0 after 1st)
NY Rangers 1 at NY Islanders 3 (Islanders scored in each period)
St. Louis 5 at Carolina 2 (Blues led 3–0 late in 1st)
Phoenix 4 at Columbus 1 (Blue Jackets led 1–0 midway
    through 2nd)
Montreal 1 at Pittsburgh 6 (Crosby hat trick)
Ottawa 4 at Florida 3 (Sens scored three goals in 2nd)
Nashville 4 at Minnesota 3 (Wild scored all goals in 2nd)
Toronto 3 at Dallas 4 (Neal 2:57 OT)
Colorado 3 at Calgary 2 (game tied 2–2 after 1st & 2nd)
Los Angeles 1 at San Jose 2 (SO)

October 29

New Jersey 2 at Boston 1 (Devils scored only goal of 3rd)
Washington 4 at Atlanta 3 (Caps led 3–0 after 2nd)
Ottawa 2 at Tampa Bay 5 (Stamkos (TB) two goals)
Phoenix 2 at St. Louis 0 [Bryzgalov]
Chicago 0 at Nashville 2 [Rinne]
Detroit 5 at Edmonton 6 (SO)
Vancouver 2 at Los Angeles 1 (SO)

October 30

NY Islanders 4 at Washington 3 (Streit 0:53 OT)

Pittsburgh 4 at Columbus 3 (SO)

Toronto 2 at Buffalo 3 (Connolly 1:04 OT)

NY Rangers 2 at Minnesota 2 (game tied 1–1 early in 2nd)

Montreal 2 at Chicago 3 (Hawks scored only goal of 3rd)

Florida 6 at Dallas 5 (SO)

Vancouver 2 at Anaheim 7 (Perry & Ryan (ANA) two goals each)

Colorado 1 at San Jose 3 (no scoring for first 39 minutes)

October 31

Edmonton 0 at Boston 2 [Rask]

Carolina 1 at Philadelphia 6 (Coburn two goals in 1:30 in 3rd)

Atlanta 3 at Ottawa 1 (Thrashers score in every period)

New Jersey 2 at Tampa Bay 1 (SO)

Toronto 4 at Montreal 5 (SO)

Buffalo 0 at NY Islanders 5 [Biron]

Minnesota 2 at Pittsburgh 1 (all goals in 1st)

Florida 4 at St. Louis 0 [Vokoun]

Dallas 2 at Nashville 4 (Predators only three goals of 3rd)

Anaheim 2 at Phoenix 3 (SO)

Detroit 3 at Calgary 1 (no scoring in 1st)

November 1

Boston 0 at NY Rangers 1 (Gaborik 15:51 2nd) [Lundqvist]

San Jose 5 at Carolina 1 (Hurricanes led 1–0 early in 2nd)

Columbus 5 at Washington 4 (Umberger 1:45 OT)

Colorado 0 at Vancouver 3 [Raycroft]

November 2

Edmonton 1 at NY Islanders 3 (game tied 1–1 after 1st)

Tampa Bay 2 at Philadelphia 6 (Richards & Carter (PHI) two goals each)

Los Angeles 5 at Phoenix 3 (Kings scored only three goals of 3rd)

November 3

Boston 0 at Detroit 2 [Osgood]
Tampa Bay 2 at Toronto 1 (Malone 2:21 OT)
Atlanta 5 at Montreal 4 (game tied 3–3 early in 3rd)
NY Rangers 1 at Vancouver 4 (Samuelsson two goals)
Pittsburgh 4 at Anaheim 3 (game tied 2–2 after 2nd)

November 4

NY Islanders 0 at Buffalo 3 (Miller)
Washington 2 at New Jersey 3 (Bergfors (NJ) two goals in 3rd)
San Jose 3 at Columbus 2 (SO)
Carolina 0 at Florida 3 [Vokoun]
Calgary 3 at Dallas 2 (Iginla 1:25 OT)
Phoenix 1 at Colorado 4 (Avs led 1–0 after 1st & 2nd)

November 5

Montreal 2 at Boston 1 (SO)
Columbus 4 at Atlanta 3 (Torres (CBJ) two goals)
Tampa Bay 2 at Ottawa 3 (Spezza 4:17 OT)
San Jose 1 at Detroit 2 (SO)
Calgary 2 at St. Louis 1 (Phaneuf 2:50 OT)
Vancouver 5 at Minnesota 2 (Canucks scored three goals in 2nd)
Chicago 1 at Phoenix 3 (no scoring in 3rd)
NY Rangers 4 at Edmonton 2 (Rangers led 2–0 midway through 2nd)
Nashville 0 at Anaheim 4 [Hiller]
Pittsburgh 2 at Los Angeles 5 (Kings scored only four goals of 3rd)

November 6

NY Islanders 1 at New Jersey 2 (no scoring in 3rd)
Toronto 3 at Carolina 2 (Leafs scored only goal of 3rd)
Philadelphia 5 at Buffalo 2 (Carcillo (PHI) two goals)
Washington 4 at Florida 1 (Caps led 3–0 midway through 3rd)
Vancouver 1 at Dallas 2 (no scoring in 1st)
Chicago 3 at Colorado 4 (SO)

November 7

Nashville 3 at Los Angeles 1 (Predators led 2–0 early in 3rd)

Buffalo 2 at Boston 4 (Bruins led 3–0 early in 2nd)

Detroit 1 at Toronto 5 (Leafs led 3–0 early in 3rd)

Tampa Bay 3 at Montreal 1 (no scoring in 3rd)

New Jersey 3 at Ottawa 2 (Devils scored only two goals of 3rd)

Atlanta 3 at NY Islanders 6 (nine different scorers)

St. Louis 1 at Philadelphia 2 (SO)

Florida 4 at Washington 7 (Knuble & Fleischmann (WAS) two goals each)

Carolina 2 at Columbus 3 (Blue Jackets scored all goals in 3rd)

Dallas 2 at Minnesota 3 (game tied 2–2 late in 2nd)

Phoenix 3 at Anaheim 4 (Coyotes scored all goals in 3rd)

NY Rangers 1 at Calgary 3 (Flames scored in each period)

Pittsburgh 0 at San Jose 5 [Nabokov]

November 8

St. Louis 2 at Atlanta 3 (SO)

Edmonton 5 at Colorado 3 (game tied 1–1 midway through 1st)

November 9

Los Angeles 1 at Chicago 4 (Hawks scored only three goals of 3rd)

November 10

Pittsburgh 0 at Boston 3 [Thomas]

Minnesota 5 at Toronto 2 (Wild scored three goals in 2nd)

Calgary 1 at Montreal 0 (Iginla 14:55 1st) [Kiprusoff]

Edmonton 3 at Ottawa 4 (SO)

Vancouver 1 at St. Louis 6 (Blues led 4–0 after 1st)

Nashville 3 at San Jose 4 (Boyle broke 3–3 tie at 19:00 of 3rd)

November 11

Edmonton 1 at Buffalo 3 (Sabres scored in every period)

Anaheim 1 at New Jersey 3 (no scoring in 3rd)

NY Islanders 4 at Washington 5 (SO)
Los Angeles 5 at Carolina 2 (T. Ruutu both CAR goals)
Detroit 9 at Columbus 1 (Red Wings led 4–0 after 1st)
Colorado 2 at Chicago 3 (SO)

November 12

Florida 1 at Boston 0 [Vokoun]
Atlanta 5 at NY Rangers 3 (game tied 1–1 after 1st)
Ottawa 1 at Philadelphia 5 (Briere two goals)
New Jersey 4 at Pittsburgh 1 (Penguins led 1–0 midway through 2nd)
Minnesota 3 at Tampa Bay 4 (SO)
Vancouver 1 at Detroit 3 (Red Wings scored only two goals of 3rd)
Nashville 3 at St. Louis 1 (Blues led 1–0 midway through 2nd)
Montreal 4 at Phoenix 2 (game tied 1–1 early in 3rd)
Dallas 3 at San Jose 2 (SO)

November 13

Minnesota 1 at Washington 3 (Caps scored only two goals of 3rd)
NY Islanders 4 at Carolina 3 (Okposo 4:45 OT)
Anaheim 2 at Columbus 3
Calgary 1 at Buffalo 2 (SO)
Los Angeles 0 at Atlanta 7 (Kovalchuk & Afinogenov two goals each)
Toronto 2 at Chicago 3 (Hawks led 3–0 early in 3rd)

November 14

Calgary 5 at Toronto 2 (Flames led 2–0 at 1:37 of 1st)
NY Rangers 2 at Ottawa 1 (SO)
Washington 2 at New Jersey 5 (Caps led 1–0 early in 1st)
Buffalo 3 at Philadelphia 2 (Sabres led 2–0 after 2nd)
NY Islanders 4 at Florida 5 (SO)
Anaheim 4 at Detroit 7 (Red Wings outscored Ducks 5–3 in 3rd)
Boston 5 at Pittsburgh 6 (Dupuis 1:24 OT)
Los Angeles 2 at Tampa Bay 1 (SO)
Dallas 2 at Phoenix 3 (no scoring in 1st)

San Jose 3 at St. Louis 1 (Blues led 1–0 after 1st)
Montreal 0 at Nashville 2 [Rinne]
Vancouver 8 at Colorado 2 (H. Sedin hat trick)

November 15

Minnesota 4 at Carolina 5 (SO)
Edmonton 2 at Atlanta 3 (Thrashers scored only goal of 3rd)
San Jose 3 at Chicago 4 (Seabrook 0:41 OT)

November 16

NY Islanders 4 at Boston 1 (Moulson two goals)
New Jersey 2 at Philadelphia 3 (Flyers scored in each period)
Edmonton 2 at Columbus 3 (SO)
Anaheim 2 at Pittsburgh 5 (Penguins led 3–1 after 2nd)
Los Angeles 4 at Florida 3 (SO)
Tampa Bay 4 at Phoenix 1 (Coyotes only goal late in 1st)

November 17

Washington 4 at NY Rangers 2 (Rangers led 1–0 early in 1st)
Carolina 2 at Montreal 3 (SO)
Toronto 2 at Ottawa 3 (no scoring in 3rd)
San Jose 3 at Nashville 4 (Predators scored two goals in 1st & 2nd)
Colorado 3 at Calgary 2 (game tied 1–1 midway through 2nd)

November 18

Florida 6 at Buffalo 2 (Panthers scored four goals in 3rd)
Dallas 3 at Detroit 1 (Stars scored in each period)
Phoenix 3 at Minnesota 2 (game tied 1–1 early in 3rd)
Colorado 4 at Edmonton 6 (Hejduk (COL) two goals)
Philadelphia 3 at Los Angeles 2 (Kings led 1–0 after 1st)

November 19

Toronto 5 at Carolina 6 (SO)
Boston 4 at Atlanta 3 (SO)

Pittsburgh 2 at Ottawa 6 (Phillips (OTT) two goals in 3rd)
Phoenix 2 at St. Louis 3 (E. Johnson 0:17 OT)
New Jersey 2 at Nashville 3 (SO)
Columbus 4 at Dallas 1 (Blue Jackets led 4–0 midway through 2nd)
Chicago 7 at Calgary 1 (Hawks scored five goals in 2nd)
Tampa Bay 3 at Anaheim 4 (S. Niedermayer 0:52 OT)

November 20

Montreal 3 at Washington 2 (Caps led 1–0 after 1st)
Boston 2 at Buffalo 1 (Bergeron 0:47 OT)
Florida 2 at Detroit 1 (McCabe 0:40 OT)
NY Islanders 2 at Minnesota 3 (Wild scored only two goals of 3rd)
Colorado 2 at Vancouver 5 (Canucks scored only four goals of 3rd)
Philadelphia 3 at San Jose 6 (Heatley (SJ) hat trick)

November 21

Calgary 5 at Los Angeles 2 (Iginla hat trick)
Washington 1 at Toronto 2 (SO)
Detroit 3 at Montreal 2 (SO)
Buffalo 3 at Ottawa 5 (Senators outscored Sabres 3–2 in 3rd)
Florida 3 at NY Rangers 2 (Rangers led 1–0 early in 2nd)
Tampa Bay 1 at Carolina 3 (Lightning led 1–0 after 1st)
Pittsburgh 3 at Atlanta 2 (Thrashers scored only two goals of 3rd)
Philadelphia 1 at Phoenix 3 (game tied 1–1 midway through 2nd)
NY Islanders 1 at St. Louis 4 (Islanders led 1–0 early in 1st)
Columbus 3 at Nashville 4 (SO)
New Jersey 3 at Dallas 5 (Rolston (NJ) & Robidas (DAL) two goals each)
San Jose 3 at Anaheim 2 (Sharks scored only goal of 3rd)
Chicago 5 at Edmonton 2 (game tied 1–1 early in 1st)

November 22

Tampa Bay 4 at Atlanta 3 (Stamkos 2:56 OT)
Chicago 1 at Vancouver 0 (Bickell 1:12 3rd) [Niemi]

November 23

Detroit 1 at Nashville 3 (Predators scored in each period)

NY Islanders 4 at Toronto 3 (Bailey 4:17 OT)

Columbus 4 at NY Rangers 7 (Rangers scored all goals in first 33 minutes)

Washington 3 at Ottawa 4 (Fisher 1:14 OT)

Pittsburgh 3 at Florida 2 (Crosby 3:07 OT)

Boston 4 at St. Louis 2 (game tied 1–1 midway through 1st)

Carolina 0 at Dallas 2 [Turco]

Philadelphia 4 at Colorado 5 (game tied 2–2 early in 2nd)

Phoenix 0 at Edmonton 4 [Drouin-Deslauriers]

Calgary 2 at Anaheim 3 (SO)

November 24

Columbus 3 at Montreal 5 (Vermette (CBJ) & Bergeron (MON) two goals each)

November 25

Ottawa 1 at New Jersey 3 (game tied 1–1 after 1st)

Philadelphia 2 at NY Islanders 1 (Islanders led 1–0 after 1st)

Buffalo 0 at Washington 2 [Varlamov]

Toronto 4 at Tampa Bay 3 (no scoring in 3rd)

Montreal 1 at Pittsburgh 3 (Penguins led 3–0 after 2nd)

NY Rangers 2 at Florida 1 (SO)

Atlanta 2 at Detroit 0 [Pavelec]

Boston 2 at Minnesota 1 (SO)

St. Louis 4 at Dallas 3 (SO)

Nashville 4 at Colorado 3 (Legwand 3:07 OT)

Phoenix 1 at Calgary 2 (Dawes broke 1–1 tie at 14:16 of 3rd)

Los Angeles 3 at Edmonton 1 (Oilers led 1–0 after 1st)

Carolina 2 at Anaheim 3 (Hurricanes led 1–0 late in 2nd)

Chicago 7 at San Jose 2 (nine different scorers)

November 26

Columbus 1 at Ottawa 2 (game tied 1–1 after 1st & 2nd)

Los Angeles 1 at Vancouver 4 (Canucks scored only three goals of 3rd)

November 27

New Jersey 2 at Boston 1 (SO)

Buffalo 4 at Philadelphia 2 (Flyers scored both goals in final minute of 1st)

Colorado 3 at Minnesota 5 (Kobasew (MIN) hat trick)

Pittsburgh 2 at NY Islanders 3 (Islanders scored only two goals of 3rd)

Chicago 0 at Anaheim 3 [Giguere]

Atlanta 6 at Carolina 4 (Thrashers scored only five goals of 3rd)

NY Rangers 1 at Tampa Bay 5 (Rangers scored final goal of game late in 3rd)

Toronto 6 at Florida 4 (game tied 3–3 after 2nd)

Calgary 3 at Detroit 0 [Kiprusoff]

St. Louis 3 at Nashville 1 (Blues led 1–0 after 2nd)

San Jose 5 at Edmonton 3

Dallas 2 at Phoenix 5 (Korpikoski (PHO) two goals)

November 28

NY Islanders 1 at New Jersey 6 (Islanders led 1–0 after 1st)

Ottawa 3 at Boston 4 (SO)

Carolina 1 at Buffalo 5 (Hurricanes led 1–0 after 1st & 2nd)

Washington 4 at Montreal 3 (SO)

Philadelphia 0 at Atlanta 1 (Peverley 11:07 2nd) [Hedberg]

Calgary 4 at Columbus 3

NY Rangers 3 at Pittsburgh 8 (Crosby (PIT) hat trick)

Detroit 4 at St. Louis 3 (SO)

Florida 1 at Nashville 4 (Predators scored only three goals of 3rd)

Tampa Bay 3 at Dallas 4 (Wandell 2:12 OT)

Minnesota 3 at Colorado 2 (SO)
Edmonton 3 at Vancouver 7 (Vancouver led 5–1 after 1st)
Chicago 1 at Los Angeles 2 (SO)

November 29

Phoenix 3 at Anaheim 2 (Doan 1:18 OT)
San Jose 4 at Vancouver 2 (game tied 1–1 after 1st)

November 30

Buffalo 3 at Toronto 0 [Miller]
Pittsburgh 5 at NY Rangers 2 (Crosby, Rupp (PIT) & Gaborik
   (NYR) two goals each)
Washington 3 at Carolina 2 (Carolina led 1–0 early in 1st)
Florida 3 at Atlanta 4 (Afinogenov broke 3–3 tie at 19:54 of 3rd)
St. Louis 2 at Columbus 5 (Umberger hat trick)
Colorado 3 at Tampa Bay 0 [Anderson]
Dallas 1 at Detroit 4 (game tied 1–1 after 1st)
Calgary 5 at Nashville 0 [Kiprusoff]

December 1

Toronto 3 at Montreal 0 [MacDonald/Gustavsson]
Columbus 3 at Chicago 4 (SO)
Los Angeles 4 at Anaheim 3 (Richardson broke 3–3 tie at
   17:40 of 3rd)
Ottawa 2 at San Jose 5 (M. Michalek (OTT) & Marleau (SJ) two
   goals each)

December 2

Tampa Bay 1 at Boston 4 (Bruins led 4–0 after 2nd)
Vancouver 5 at New Jersey 2 (Canucks led 3–2 after 1st & 2nd)
Colorado 5 at Florida 6 (SO)
Nashville 4 at Minnesota 5 (Ebbett 1:26 OT)

December 3

Montreal 2 at Buffalo 6 (eight different scorers)

Vancouver 3 at Philadelphia 0 [Luongo]

Florida 2 at Washington 6 (Caps scored two goals in each period)

NY Islanders 4 at Atlanta 1 (Moulson hat trick)

Toronto 6 at Columbus 3 (Kessel & Blake (TOR) two goals each)

Colorado 1 at Pittsburgh 4 (game tied 1–1 after 1st & 2nd)

Edmonton 4 at Detroit 1 (O'Sullivan two goals)

Anaheim 1 at Dallas 3 (Ducks led 1–0 after 1st & 2nd)

Calgary 1 at Phoenix 2 (Flames led 1–0 after 1st)

Ottawa 3 at Los Angeles 6 (Fisher (OTT) & Williams (LA) two goals each)

St. Louis 3 at San Jose 2 (SO)

December 4

Tampa Bay 2 at New Jersey 3 (Devils scored all goals in 3rd)

Anaheim 4 at Minnesota 5 (SO)

Boston 1 at Montreal 5 (Habs scored four goals in 2nd)

Nashville 4 at Chicago 1 (Hawks led 1–0 midway through 1st)

December 5

Vancouver 3 at Carolina 5 (Cole (CAR) hat trick)

Edmonton 3 at Dallas 2 (SO)

St. Louis 5 at Los Angeles 4 (SO)

Toronto 2 at Boston 7 (Savard hat trick)

NY Rangers 2 at Buffalo 1 (Sabres scored in final minute)

Detroit 3 at New Jersey 4 (SO)

Washington 8 at Philadelphia 2 (Fleischmann & Green (WAS) two goals each)

Atlanta 2 at Florida 1 (SO)

Colorado 3 at Columbus 2 (Avs led 2–0 after 2nd)

Chicago 2 at Pittsburgh 1 (Versteeg 2:38 OT)

NY Islanders 0 at Tampa Bay 4 [M. Smith]

Minnesota 5 at Nashville 3 (Predators led 1–0 late in 1st)

Calgary 2 at San Jose 1 (Flames scored only goal of 3rd)

Ottawa 2 at Phoenix 3 (Sens scored only two goals of 3rd)

December 6

Detroit 3 at NY Rangers 1 (game tied 1–1 after 2nd)

Ottawa 4 at Anaheim 3 (SO)

December 7

New Jersey 3 at Buffalo 0 [Brodeur]

Atlanta 2 at Toronto 5 (Leafs scored all goals in 2nd)

Philadelphia 1 at Montreal 3 (Flyers led 1–0 after 1st)

Carolina 3 at Pittsburgh 2 (no scoring in 3rd)

Washington 3 at Tampa Bay 0 [Varlamov]

Edmonton 3 at Florida 2 (SO)

Colorado 4 at St. Louis 0 [Budaj]

Minnesota 0 at Phoenix 2 [Bryzgalov]

Calgary 1 at Los Angeles 2 (game tied 1–1 after 1st)

December 8

NY Islanders 2 at Philadelphia 6 (Tavares (NYI) & Richards & Carter (PHI) two goals each)

Montreal 4 at Ottawa 1 (game tied 1–1 early in 2nd)

Vancouver 2 at Nashville 4 (Erat (NAS) two goals)

Dallas 3 at Anaheim 4 (S. Koivu 4:13 OT)

December 9

Washington 0 at Buffalo 3 [Miller]

NY Islanders 2 at Toronto 3 (Tavares (NYI) two goals in 3rd)

Carolina 2 at New Jersey 4 (Devils led 3–0 early in 3rd)

Florida 0 at Columbus 3 [S. Mason]

Edmonton 3 at Tampa Bay 2 (no scoring in 3rd)

St. Louis 1 at Detroit 0 (Boyes 1:56 1st) [Conklin]

NY Rangers 1 at Chicago 2 (Byfuglien 3:43 OT)

Minnesota 1 at Colorado 0 (Miettinen 5:57 1st) [N. Backstrom]
Atlanta 1 at Calgary 3 (no scoring in 1st)
Los Angeles 5 at San Jose 4 (D. Brown 1:16 OT)

December 10

Toronto 2 at Boston 5 (Recchi (BOS) two goals)
Ottawa 2 at Philadelphia 0 (Elliott)
Pittsburgh 3 at Montreal 2 (Penguins scored only goal of 3rd)
Columbus 3 at Nashville 4 (SO)
Atlanta 2 at Vancouver 4 (D. Sedin hat trick)
Phoenix 2 at Los Angeles 3 (SO)

December 11

Florida 4 at New Jersey 2 (Frolik (FLO) two goals)
Carolina 3 at Washington 4 (Green 1:16 OT)
Chicago 1 at Buffalo 2 (no scoring in 1st)
Anaheim 2 at Detroit 3 (Bertuzzi 1:07 OT)
Edmonton 5 at St. Louis 3 (Oilers scored only four goals of 3rd)
Tampa Bay 1 at Colorado 2 (SO)
Minnesota 2 at Calgary 1 (Havlat 3:15 OT)
Dallas 3 at San Jose 2 (SO)

December 12

Washington 3 at Toronto 6 (Leafs scored three goals in 2nd & 3rd)
Carolina 2 at Ottawa 4 (Sens scored only two goals of 3rd)
Philadelphia 1 at New Jersey 4 (Devils led 3–0 after 1st)
Boston 2 at NY Islanders 3 (Nielsen 0:24 OT)
Buffalo 3 at NY Rangers 2 (no scoring last half of game)
Montreal 3 at Atlanta 4 (Kovalchuk 1:18 OT)
Anaheim 3 at Columbus 1 (Ducks scored in each period)
Florida 2 at Pittsburgh 3 (Malkin 0:37 OT)
San Jose 1 at Phoenix 2 (Coyotes led 2–0 early in 2nd)
Detroit 3 at Nashville 2 (Bertuzzi 0:24 OT)

Minnesota 3 at Vancouver 4 (Canucks led 3–2 after 1st)
Dallas 2 at Los Angeles 3 (SO)

December 13

Tampa Bay 0 at Chicago 4 [Niemi]
Calgary 2 at Colorado 3 (Avs led 2–0 midway through 2nd)

December 14

Philadelphia 3 at Boston 1 (Flyers scored only three goals of 3rd)
Ottawa 2 at Toronto 3 (Leafs led 1–0 midway through game)
Florida 7 at NY Islanders 1 (Horton hat trick)
Atlanta 3 at NY Rangers 2 (SO)
Nashville 5 at Columbus 3 (Sullivan (NAS) hat trick)
Buffalo 4 at Montreal 3 (teams scored two goals each in 3rd)
Phoenix 2 at Detroit 3 (no scoring in 3rd)
Los Angeles 1 at Vancouver 3 (Canucks led 2–0 late in 1st)

December 15

Philadelphia 1 at Pittsburgh 6 (J. Staal two goals)
Calgary 3 at St. Louis 4 (Blues scored only goal of 3rd)
Tampa Bay 4 at Nashville 7 (Predators scored five goals in 2nd)
Columbus 1 at Minnesota 2 (game tied 1–1- after 2nd)
Washington 6 at Colorado 1 (Fleischmann two goals)
Los Angeles 3 at Edmonton 2 (Kings led 2–0 early in 2nd)

December 16

Montreal 1 at New Jersey 2 (Habs led 1–0 after 1st)
NY Islanders 2 at NY Rangers 1 (Rangers' only goal came in the final minute)
Dallas 3 at Carolina 5 (T. Ruutu (CAR) hat trick)
Phoenix 6 at Toronto 3 (Coyotes won 2nd period 4–2)
Buffalo 0 at Ottawa 2 [Elliott]
Atlanta 3 at Florida 4 (Frolik broke 3–3 tie at 18:39 of 3rd)

St. Louis 0 at Chicago 3 [Huet]
Anaheim 3 at Vancouver 2 (S. Koivu broke 2–2 tie at 15:47 of 3rd)

December 17

Minnesota 3 at Montreal 1 (game tied 1–1 early in 1st)
NY Rangers 5 at NY Islanders 2 (Callahan (NYR) two goals)
Pittsburgh 3 at Philadelphia 2 (SO)
Dallas 5 at Atlanta 6 (Peverley 1:16 OT)
Phoenix 2 at Columbus 1 (SO)
Tampa Bay 0 at Detroit 3 [Howard]
Los Angeles 1 at Calgary 2 (Flames led 1–0 after 1st & 2nd)
Nashville 6 at Edmonton 3 (Oilers led 2–0 early in 1st)
Anaheim 1 at San Jose 4 (Thornton two goals)

December 18

Ottawa 2 at New Jersey 4 (game tied 2–2 midway through 2nd)
Toronto 2 at Buffalo 5 (Sabres scored only four goals of 2nd)
Carolina 3 at Florida 6 (nine different scorers)
Tampa Bay 6 at St. Louis 3 (Stamkos & Halpern (TB) two
    goals each)
Boston 4 at Chicago 5 (SO)
Washington 2 at Vancouver 3 (Canucks only goal of 3rd)

December 19

NY Rangers 2 at Philadelphia 1 (no scoring final 35 minutes)
Detroit 3 at Dallas 4 (game tied 3–3 after 2nd)
Phoenix 2 at Anaheim 4 (game tied 1–1 midway through 2nd)
Nashville 5 at Calgary 3 (game tied 2–2 early in 2nd)
Pittsburgh 2 at Buffalo 1 (SO)
Boston 0 at Toronto 2 (Gustavsson)
Minnesota 1 at Ottawa 4 (Sens led 4–0 early in 3rd)
Montreal 3 at NY Islanders 0 [Halak]
Florida 2 at Carolina 3 (Hurricanes led 3–0 after 2nd)

New Jersey 5 at Atlanta 4 (McAmmond (NJ) two goals)
Columbus 2 at Colorado 5 (Avs led 4–0 after 1st)
Washington 4 at Edmonton 2 (Caps scored only four goals of 3rd)

December 20

Detroit 0 at Chicago 3 [Huet]
St. Louis 3 at Vancouver 1 (game tied 1–1 after 1st)

December 21

Buffalo 3 at Toronto 2 (D. Roy 3:35 OT)
Tampa Bay 4 at NY Islanders 2 (Islanders led 2–1 late in 2nd)
NY Rangers 3 at Carolina 1 (Hurricanes led 1–0 early in 2nd)
Montreal 4 at Atlanta 3 (M. Bergeron 2:23 OT)
Boston 2 at Ottawa 0 [Thomas]
Florida 4 at Philadelphia 1 (Horton two goals)
New Jersey 4 at Pittsburgh 0 [Brodeur]
Colorado 4 at Minnesota 3 (Wild scored only two goals of 3rd)
San Jose 4 at Dallas 2 (Marleau (SJ) two goals)
St. Louis 7 at Edmonton 2 (game tied 1–1 midway through 1st)
Columbus 2 at Phoenix 5 (Upshall (PHO) two goals)

December 22

San Jose 3 at Chicago 2 (Sharks led 2–0 after 2nd)
Anaheim 4 at Colorado 2 (Avs led 2–0 early in 3rd)
Nashville 1 at Vancouver 4 (Predators scored final goal)

December 23

Edmonton 1 at Minnesota 3 (Wild scored in each period)
Atlanta 4 at Boston 6 (ten different scorers)
Toronto 1 at NY Islanders 3 (Islanders led 2–0 after 2nd)
Florida 1 at NY Rangers 4 (Prospal two goals)
Ottawa 2 at Pittsburgh 8 (game tied 1–1 after 1st)
Buffalo 2 at Washington 5 (N. Backstrom (WAS) two goals)

Montreal 5 at Carolina 1 (Habs led 4–1 after 1st)
Philadelphia 5 at Tampa Bay 2 (game tied 2–2 after 2nd)
Chicago 3 at Detroit 0 [Niemi]
Columbus 1 at Dallas 3 (Neal two goals)
Anaheim 0 at Phoenix 4 [Bryzgalov]
St. Louis 2 at Calgary 1 (SO)

December 26

Montreal 3 at Toronto 2 (A. Kostitsyn 0:34 OT)
NY Islanders 3 at NY Rangers 2 (Okposo 4:13 OT)
New Jersey 1 at Washington 4 (Caps led 2–1 after 1st)
Philadelphia 4 at Carolina 3 (SO)
Columbus 1 at Detroit 2 (Blue Jackets led 1–0 after 1st)
Ottawa 3 at Buffalo 2 (SO)
Atlanta 3 at Tampa Bay 4 (game tied 2–2 after 2nd)
Los Angeles 2 at Phoenix 3 (Kings led 1–0 early in 1st)
Chicago 4 at Nashville 1 (game tied 1–1 early in 2nd)
St. Louis 3 at Minnesota 4 (game tied 1–1 after 2nd)
Dallas 1 at Colorado 4 (Stewart two goals)
Edmonton 1 at Vancouver 4 (no scoring in 1st)
Anaheim 2 at San Jose 5 (Marleau (SJ) two goals in 1st)

December 27

Philadelphia 2 at NY Islanders 1 (game tied 1–1 early in 2nd)
Boston 2 at Florida 1 (Panthers led 1–0 late in 2nd)
Buffalo 5 at St. Louis 3 (Sabres scored only three goals of 3rd)
Nashville 4 at Chicago 5 (Hawks scored four goals in 3rd)
Toronto 4 at Pittsburgh 3 (White broke 3–3 tie at 18:38 of 3rd)
Vancouver 5 at Calgary 1 (Flames led 1–0 early in 1st)

December 28

Atlanta 2 at New Jersey 3 (Devils led 2–1 after 1st & 2nd)
Carolina 6 at Washington 3 (E. Staal (CAR) two goals)

Detroit 0 at Columbus 1 (Modin 3:12 OT) [S. Mason]
Montreal 2 at Ottawa 4 (Habs led 2–0 midway through 1st)
Boston 1 at Tampa Bay 2 (Lightning led 1–0 after 1st & 2–0 after 2nd)
Calgary 4 at Edmonton 1 (R. Bourque hat trick)
Minnesota 4 at Los Angeles 3 (E. Belanger broke 3–3 tie at
    17:35 of 3rd)
Phoenix 2 at San Jose 3 (SO)

December 29

Pittsburgh 3 at Buffalo 4 (Penguins led 3–0 midway through 2nd)
Columbus 1 at NY Islanders 2 (SO)
Nashville 4 at St. Louis 3 (Predators led 4–1 early in 3rd)
Chicago 4 at Dallas 5 (Hawks led 3–2 after 1st)
Vancouver 2 at Phoenix 3 (SO)
Minnesota 2 at Anaheim 4 (game tied 1–1 late in 1st)

December 30

Atlanta 0 at Boston 4 [Rask]
Pittsburgh 0 at New Jersey 2 [Brodeur]
Philadelphia 6 at NY Rangers 0 [Leighton]
Montreal 2 at Tampa Bay 1 (Plekanec 3:32 OT)
Colorado 4 at Ottawa 3 (Shannon (OTT) two goals)
Los Angeles 1 at Calgary 2 (game tied 1–1 early in 2nd)
Toronto 1 at Edmonton 3 (O'Sullivan two PP goals)
Washington 2 at San Jose 5 (Sharks led 3–0 after 2nd)

December 31

Montreal 5 at Florida 4 (nine different scorers)
San Jose 3 at Phoenix 2 (SO)
NY Islanders 2 at Ottawa 3 (SO)
Colorado 2 at Detroit 4 (game tied 2–2 midway through 3rd)
Nashville 2 at Columbus 1 (Legwand 0:28 OT)
Vancouver 4 at St. Louis 3 (Ehrhoff 2:24 OT)
Los Angeles 5 at Minnesota 2 (Kings led 4–0 early in 2nd)
Anaheim 3 at Dallas 5 (Eriksson (DAL) hat trick)

NY Rangers 2 at Carolina 1 (game tied 1–1 after 1st & 2nd)
New Jersey 1 at Chicago 5 (Devils scored final goal late in 3rd)
Edmonton 1 at Calgary 2 (Oilers scored with 1:29 remaining)

January 1

Philadelphia 1 at Boston 2 (Sturm 1:57 OT)
Atlanta 3 at Buffalo 4 (D. Roy 4:02 OT)

January 2

Carolina 2 at NY Rangers 1 (Whitney 3:45 OT)
Vancouver 3 at Dallas 1 (game tied 1–1 early in 3rd)
Pittsburgh 1 at Tampa Bay 3 (game tied 1–1 after 1st)
Washington 1 at Los Angeles 2 (Kings scored only goal of 3rd)
Toronto 1 at Calgary 3 (Leafs led 1–0 after 1st)
Atlanta 5 at NY Islanders 6 (SO)
Colorado 3 at Columbus 2 (Blue Jackets led 2–1 after 2nd)
Detroit 4 at Phoenix 1 (game tied 1–1 early in 2nd)
New Jersey 5 at Minnesota 3 (Langenbrunner (NJ) hat trick)
Chicago 6 at St. Louis 3 (Hawks scored two goals in each period)
Anaheim 1 at Nashville 3 (Ducks led 1–0 after 1st)
Edmonton 1 at San Jose 4 (Sharks led 3–0 early in 2nd)

January 3

Philadelphia 4 at Ottawa 7 (Kovalev (OTT) four goals)
Buffalo 1 at Montreal 0 (Connolly 6:56 2nd) [Miller]
Pittsburgh 2 at Florida 6 (Penguins led 2–0)
Anaheim 2 at Chicago 5 (Hawks scored last two goals of game)

January 4

Boston 2 at NY Rangers 3 (Higgins broke 2–2 tie at 18:31 of 3rd)
Los Angeles 6 at San Jose 2 (Kings led 5–0 after 2nd)

January 5

Montreal 2 at Washington 4 (Semin (WAS) two goals)
Florida 2 at Toronto 3 (Panthers led 2–1 after 1st)

Dallas 0 at New Jersey 4 [Brodeur]
Boston 4 at Ottawa 1 (Bruins led 4–0 after 1st)
Atlanta 2 at Pittsburgh 5 (Slater (ATL) & J. Staal (PIT) two goals each)
Calgary 3 at Nashville 1 (Flames had empty-netter)
Minnesota 1 at Chicago 4 (Wild led 1–0 late in 1st)
Phoenix 5 at Edmonton 4 (Doan 1:37 OT)
Detroit 1 at Anaheim 4 (Ducks led 2–0 after 1st & 2nd)
Columbus 3 at Vancouver 7 (Burrows (VAN) hat trick)

January 6

Toronto 2 at Philadelphia 6 (Flyers led 3–0 after 2nd)
Tampa Bay 3 at Buffalo 5 (no scoring in 3rd)
Dallas 2 at NY Rangers 5 (seven different scorers)
Calgary 1 at Minnesota 4 (Flames led 1–0 early in 1st)
NY Islanders 3 at Colorado 2 (Okposo broke 2–2 tie at 16:43 of 3rd)
St. Louis 1 at San Jose 2 (Heatley 4:06 OT)

January 7

NY Rangers 1 at Atlanta 2 (SO)
Ottawa 2 at Washington 5 (Backstrom (WAS) two goals)
Chicago 5 at Boston 2 (Bruins led 2–0 early in 1st)
Philadelphia 7 at Pittsburgh 4 (Flyers led 5–2 early in 2nd)
Florida 0 at Montreal 2 [Halak]
Carolina 2 at Nashville 4 (game tied 1–1 late in 1st)
Columbus 4 at Edmonton 2 (game tied 1–1 late in 2nd)
St. Louis 2 at Anaheim 4 (game tied 1–1 after 2nd)
Phoenix 0 at Vancouver 4 [Luongo]
Detroit 2 at Los Angeles 1 (Helm broke 1–1 tie at 19:42 of 3rd)

January 8

Tampa Bay 4 at New Jersey 2 (Stamkos (TB) two goals)
Colorado 1 at Carolina 2 (Avs scored in final minute)
Toronto 2 at Buffalo 3 (Leafs scored only two goals of 3rd)

NY Islanders 3 at Dallas 4 (Stars scored three goals in 2nd)
Columbus 3 at Calgary 2 (Blue Jackets scored in every period)

January 9

NY Rangers 3 at Boston 1 (Bruins scored last goal late in 3rd)
New Jersey 2 at Montreal 1 (Parise 2:38 OT)
Pittsburgh 4 at Toronto 1 (Gonchar two goals)
Florida 3 at Ottawa 0 [Vokoun]
Tampa Bay 1 at Philadelphia 4 (Flyers scored three goals in 3rd)
Washington 8 at Atlanta 1 (Knuble & Semin (WAS) two goals each)
Colorado 4 at Buffalo 3 (SO)
NY Islanders 5 at Phoenix 4 (SO)
Chicago 5 at Minnesota 6 (SO)
Anaheim 3 at Nashville 2 (Predators scored only two goals of 3rd)
Calgary 3 at Vancouver 2 (SO)
Detroit 4 at San Jose 1 (Red Wings scored three goals in 2nd)
St. Louis 4 at Los Angeles 3 (game tied 1–1 early in 2nd)

January 10

Ottawa 1 at Carolina 4 (Senators led 1–0 early in 2nd)
Anaheim 3 at Chicago 1 (Ducks had empty net goal)
Dallas 0 at Columbus 2 [Garon]

January 11

Pittsburgh 3 at Minnesota 4 (Crosby (PIT) two goals)
Colorado 3 at Calgary 2 (SO)
Nashville 3 at Vancouver 2 (Predators only goal of 3rd)
San Jose 2 at Los Angeles 1 (no scoring in 3rd)

January 12

New Jersey 1 at NY Rangers 0 [Brodeur]
Ottawa 1 at Atlanta 6 (game tied 1–1 midway through 1st)
Carolina 4 at Toronto 2 (Hurricanes scored only two goals of 3rd)

Detroit 0 at NY Islanders 6 [Roloson]
Dallas 3 at Philadelphia 6 (Flyers scored four goals in 2nd)
Washington 4 at Tampa Bay 7 (Green (WAS) in 3rd & Stamkos
    (TB) in 2nd, two power-play goals each)
Columbus 1 at St. Louis 4 (Blues led 3–0 after 1st)
Nashville 5 at Edmonton 3 (Predators led 4–0 early in 2nd)
San Jose 3 at Phoenix 1 (Marleau two goals in 1st)

January 13

Vancouver 2 at Minnesota 5 (Wild scored only three goals of 3rd)
Washington 5 at Florida 4 (SO)
Pittsburgh 3 at Calgary 1 (Penguins scored in each period)
Boston 3 at Anaheim 4 (Ducks scored only two goals of 3rd)

January 14

Philadelphia 0 at Toronto 4 [Toskala]
Buffalo 2 at Atlanta 1 (D. Roy 2:27 OT)
Ottawa 2 at NY Rangers 0 [Mike Brodeur]
Carolina 1 at Detroit 3 (Red Wings scored in each period)
Florida 3 at Tampa Bay 2 (Lightning led 2–1 after 1st & 2nd)
Dallas 3 at Montreal 5 (game tied 3–3 after 2nd)
Minnesota 0 at St. Louis 1 (Oshie 0:26 3rd) [C. Mason]
Columbus 0 at Chicago 3 [Huet]
New Jersey 3 at Phoenix 4 (game tied 2–2 after 2nd)
Pittsburgh 3 at Edmonton 2 (Penguins scored only three
    goals of 3rd)
Boston 2 at San Jose 1 (SO)
Anaheim 0 at Los Angeles 4 [Quick]

January 15

Toronto 1 at Washington 6 (Capitals scored two goals in
    each period)
Nashville 1 at Calgary 0 (Hornqvist 13:38 of 3rd) [Ellis]

January 16

Detroit 2 at Dallas 3 (SO)
Chicago 6 at Columbus 5 (Hawks scored three goals in 1st & 3rd)
New Jersey 1 at Colorado 3 (Avs led 2–0 after 1st & 2nd)
Boston 3 at Los Angeles 4 (SO)
Edmonton 2 at San Jose 4 (game tied 1–1 late in 1st)
Buffalo 2 at NY Islanders 3 (SO)
Ottawa 4 at Montreal 2 (Habs led 2–1 early in 2nd)
Tampa Bay 2 at Florida 5 (Stillman & Olesz (FLO) two goals each)
Minnesota 4 at Phoenix 6 (Latendresse (MIN) hat trick)
NY Rangers 1 at St. Louis 4 (game tied 1–1 after 2nd)
Atlanta 5 at Carolina 3 (Thrashers empty-net goal)
Pittsburgh 2 at Vancouver 6 (eight different scorers)

January 17

Philadelphia 3 at Washington 5 (Flyers led 2–1 early in 1st)
Chicago 4 at Detroit 3 (SO)
Montreal 2 at NY Rangers 6 (Habs led 2–0 after 1st)
Calgary 4 at Anaheim 5 (Ducks scored only two goals of 3rd)

January 18

Ottawa 5 at Boston 1 (Alfredsson hat trick)
New Jersey 0 at NY Islanders 4 [DiPietro]
Buffalo 7 at Phoenix 2 (Sabres led 3–0 early in 2nd)
Tampa Bay 3 at Carolina 2 (Lightning scored in each period)
St. Louis 2 at Columbus 4 (Torres (CBJ) two goals)
Atlanta 0 at Florida 1 (Campbell 7:18 of 2nd) [Vokoun]
Toronto 4 at Nashville 3 (Leafs led 3–0 late in 2nd)
Minnesota 3 at Dallas 4 (Stars led 4–0 middle of 2nd)
Edmonton 0 at Colorado 6 [Anderson]
Calgary 1 at San Jose 9 (Sharks scored three goals in each period)

January 19

Toronto 3 at Atlanta 4 (Leads led 2–0 after 1st)
Tampa Bay 2 at NY Rangers 8 (ten different scorers)
Detroit 2 at Washington 3 (no scoring in 1st)
Columbus 3 at Philadelphia 5 (game tied 2–2 midway through 2nd)
NY Islanders 4 at Pittsburgh 6 (Malkin (PIT) hat trick)
Chicago 1 at Ottawa 4 (Senators led 2–0 after 1st)
Buffalo 4 at Anaheim 5 (nine different scorers)
San Jose 5 at Los Angeles 1 (Marlowe & Clowe two goals each)

January 20

Florida 0 at New Jersey 2 [Brodeur]
St. Louis 4 at Montreal 3 (McDonald 3:19 OT)
Vancouver 3 at Edmonton 2 (D. Sedin 1:39 OT)

January 21

NY Rangers 0 at Philadelphia 2 [Emery]
Toronto 2 at Tampa Bay 3 (St. Louis 4:50 OT)
Carolina 5 at Atlanta 2 (E. Staal hat trick)
Florida 1 at NY Islanders 2 (SO)
St. Louis 2 at Ottawa 3 (Senators led 2–0 midway through 2nd)
Columbus 3 at Boston 2 (Blue Jackets scored only two goals of 3rd)
Washington 6 at Pittsburgh 3 (game tied 3–3 after 2nd)
Detroit 4 at Minnesota 3 (SO)
Nashville 2 at Phoenix 4 (Upshall hat trick)
Chicago 3 at Calgary 1 (Hawks scored only two goals of 3rd)
Dallas 3 at Vancouver 4 (both teams scored in all periods)
Buffalo 3 at Los Angeles 4 (SO)
Anaheim 1 at San Jose 3 (Sharks got empty-net goal)

January 22

Montreal 3 at New Jersey 1 (Devils led 1–0 early in 1st)
Nashville 1 at Colorado 2 (Avs led 2–0 early in 2nd)
Dallas 4 at Edmonton 3 (Neal broke 3–3 tie at 19:37 of 3rd)

January 23

Ottawa 2 at Boston 1 (game tied 1–1 midway through 2nd)
Carolina 2 at Philadelphia 4 (Carter (PHI) two goals)
New Jersey 4 at NY Islanders 2 (Devils scored only two goals of 2nd)
NY Rangers 0 at Montreal 6 [Halak]
Toronto 0 at Florida 2 [Vokoun]
Los Angeles 3 at Detroit 2 (Red Wings left 2–1 after 2nd)
Phoenix 2 at Washington 4 (game tied 1–1 after 1st)
Atlanta 1 at Tampa Bay 2 (SO)
Anaheim 4 at St. Louis 3 (SO)
Columbus 2 at Minnesota 4 (M. Koivu (MIN) two goals)
Chicago 1 at Vancouver 5 (Canucks led 3–0 after 1st & 2nd)
Buffalo 2 at San Jose 5 (Sabres led 1–0 after 1st)

January 24

Pittsburgh 2 at Philadelphia 1 (game tied 1–1 after 1st & 2nd)
Boston 1 at Carolina 5 (Hurricanes led 5–0 early in 3rd)
Dallas 0 at Colorado 4 [Anderson]

January 25

Pittsburgh 4 at NY Rangers 2 (game tied 1–1 after 2nd)
St. Louis 2 at Calgary 0 [Conklin]
Buffalo 2 at Vancouver 3 (game tied 1–1 midway through 2nd)

January 26

Washington 7 at NY Islanders 2 (Caps led 4–1 after 1st)
Nashville 2 at Columbus 3 (no scoring in 1st)
Anaheim 1 at Atlanta 2 (Thrashers had only goal of 3rd)
Los Angeles 5 at Toronto 3 (both teams scored in all periods)
New Jersey 0 at Ottawa 3 [Elliott]
Montreal 1 at Florida 2 (Habs led 1–0 after 2nd)
Phoenix 5 at Detroit 4 (Doan 3:50 OT)
Chicago 4 at Edmonton 2 (Hawks scored three goals in 2nd)

January 27

New Jersey 1 at Buffalo 2 (SO)
Carolina 5 at NY Rangers 1 (Samsonov two goals)
Anaheim 1 at Washington 5 (game tied 1–1 after 2nd)
Montreal 0 at Tampa Bay 3 [Niittymaki]
Detroit 2 at Minnesota 5 (Wild led 3–2 after 1st & 2nd)
Calgary 3 at Dallas 4 (SO)
St. Louis 2 at Vancouver 3 (game tied 1–1 after 1st & 2nd)

January 28

NY Islanders 1 at Carolina 4 (Hurricanes empty-net goal)
Ottawa 4 at Pittsburgh 1 (Senators led 1–0 early in 1st)
Atlanta 4 at Philadelphia 3 (Thrashers scored only three goals of 3rd)
Los Angeles 4 at Columbus 1 (Kopitar two goals)
Calgary 2 at Phoenix 3 (SO)
Minnesota 1 at Colorado 0 (Havlat 15:11 of 3rd) [Harding]
St. Louis 2 at Edmonton 1 (game tied 1–1 after 2nd)
Chicago 4 at San Jose 3 (Brouwer 1:37 OT)

January 29

Toronto 4 at New Jersey 5 (Zajac 4:14 OT)
Florida 1 at Washington 4 (game tied 1–1 early in 2nd)
Boston 1 at Buffalo 2 (no scoring in 3rd)
Nashville 2 at Detroit 4 (game tied 1–1 after 1st)
Anaheim 2 at Tampa Bay 1 (SO)
Colorado 2 at Dallas 3 (Stars scored only goal of 3rd)

January 30

Montreal 2 at Ottawa 3 (Fisher 3:33 OT)
NY Islanders 1 at Philadelphia 2 (no goals in final 25 minutes)
Chicago 2 at Carolina 4 (game tied 1–1 early 2nd)
Vancouver 5 at Toronto 3 (Leafs led 3–0 after 1st)
Los Angeles 3 at Boston 2 (SO)
NY Rangers 2 at Phoenix 3 (Coyotes led 3–0 after 1st & 2nd)

Atlanta 3 at Nashville 4 (Predators only goal of 3rd)
Columbus 3 at St. Louis 2 (Russell 1:32 OT)
Edmonton 1 at Calgary 6 (Boyd & Iginla two goals each)
Minnesota 2 at San Jose 5 (game tied 1–1 midway through 1st)

January 31

Tampa Bay 2 at Washington 3 (Ovechkin broke 2–2 tie at 13:34 of 3rd)
Detroit 1 at Pittsburgh 2 (SO)
NY Islanders 0 at Florida 2 [Vokoun]
Los Angeles 3 at New Jersey 4 (Devils led 2–0 midway through 2nd)
Phoenix 4 at Dallas 2 (Coyotes led 2–0 early in 2nd)
NY Rangers 3 at Colorado 1 (Avs scored final goal in 3rd)

February 1

Buffalo 4 at Pittsburgh 5 (Crosby (PIT) hat trick)
Anaheim 3 at Florida 0 [Hiller]
Philadelphia 3 at Calgary 0 [Emery]
Carolina 2 at Edmonton 4 (no scoring in 3rd)

February 2

Washington 4 at Boston 1 (Caps scored only three goals of 3rd)
New Jersey 0 at Toronto 3 [Giguere]
Tampa Bay 2 at Atlanta 1 (no scoring in final 37 minutes)
Vancouver 2 at Montreal 3 (game tied 1–1 midway through 1st)
Phoenix 1 at Nashville 0 (SO) [Bryzgalov/Rinne]
Minnesota 2 at Dallas 4 (Stars led 2–0 late in 2nd)
Columbus 1 at Colorado 5 (Blue Jackets led 1–0 early in 1st)
NY Rangers 1 at Los Angeles 2 (Rangers goal late in 3rd)
Detroit 4 at San Jose 2 (game tied 2–2 after 1st & 2nd)

February 3

Ottawa 4 at Buffalo 2 (game tied 2–2 early in 3rd)
St. Louis 3 at Chicago 2 (Blues scored only three goals in 2nd)
Carolina 1 at Calgary 4 (game tied 1–1 midway through 2nd)

Philadelphia 0 at Edmonton 1 (Potulny 19:43 of 3rd) [Drouin-Deslauriers]

Detroit 1 at Anaheim 3 (Ducks led 3–0 midway through 2nd)

February 4

Montreal 3 at Boston 2 (SO)

Washington 6 at NY Rangers 5 (Caps scored only two goals of 3rd)

Dallas 1 at Columbus 2 (Blue Jackets led 1–0 after 1st & 2nd)

Vancouver 1 at Ottawa 3 (Senators led 2–0 after 1st & 2nd)

NY Islanders 2 at Tampa Bay 5 (Stamkos (TB) two goals)

San Jose 4 at St. Louis 2 (Sharks scored in each period)

Colorado 3 at Nashville 5 (Predators scored four goals in 2nd)

Edmonton 2 at Minnesota 4 (game tied 1–1 after 2nd)

Anaheim 4 at Los Angeles 6 (both teams scored three goals in 3rd)

February 5

Toronto 3 at New Jersey 4 (Devils scored only three goals of 3rd)

Atlanta 2 at Washington 5 (game tied 1–1 early in 2nd)

Carolina 4 at Buffalo 3 (game tied 1–1 after 1st & 2nd)

Calgary 2 at Florida 1 (no scoring in 3rd)

Phoenix 2 at Chicago 1 (SO)

February 6

Vancouver 3 at Boston 2 (SO)

Pittsburgh 3 at Montreal 5 (game tied 1–1 after 1st)

Detroit 3 at Los Angeles 4 (Kings scored only goal of 3rd)

Phoenix 0 at Dallas 4 [Turco]

Ottawa 0 at Toronto 5 [Giguere]

Carolina 3 at NY Islanders 1 (game tied 1–1 midway through 2nd)

New Jersey 1 at NY Rangers 3 (Rangers scored only three goals of 2nd)

Florida 2 at Atlanta 4 (Panthers led 2–0 after 1st)

Calgary 1 at Tampa Bay 2 (Meszaros 1:58 OT)

Buffalo 0 at Columbus 4 [S. Mason]

Chicago 2 at St. Louis 1 (Hawks led 2–0 after 1st & 2nd)

San Jose 4 at Nashville 3 (Heatley (SJ) & Dumont (NAS) two goals each)

Philadelphia 1 at Minnesota 2 (no scoring in 3rd)

Edmonton 0 at Colorado 3 [Anderson]

February 7

Boston 3 at Montreal 0 [Rask]

Pittsburgh 4 at Washington 5 (Knuble 2:49 OT)

February 8

San Jose 3 at Toronto 2 (Sharks only goal of 3rd)

New Jersey 2 at Philadelphia 3 (game tied 2–2 after 2nd)

St. Louis 2 at Colorado 5 (game tied 2–2 after 1st)

Edmonton 1 at Phoenix 6 (Lombardi two goals)

Los Angeles 2 at Anaheim 4 (no scoring in 3rd)

February 9

Boston 3 at Buffalo 2 (SO)

Nashville 3 at NY Islanders 4 (SO)

Florida 1 at Carolina 4 (game tied 1–1 midway through 2nd)

Calgary 2 at Ottawa 3 (no scoring in 3rd)

Vancouver 1 at Tampa Bay 3 (game tied 1–1 after 2nd)

Detroit 3 at St. Louis 4 (SO)

Dallas 3 at Chicago 4 (SO)

February 10

Philadelphia 3 at New Jersey 2 (Gagne 3:27 OT)

Nashville 2 at NY Rangers 1 (no scoring in 3rd)

San Jose 0 at Columbus 3 [S. Mason]

Phoenix 3 at Minnesota 2 (Wild led 1–0 early in 1st)

Washington 5 at Montreal 6 (Plekanec 4:52 OT)

NY Islanders 1 at Pittsburgh 3 (no scoring in first half of game)

Atlanta 3 at Colorado 4 (Cumiskey 0:09 OT)

Edmonton 2 at Anaheim 3 (Ducks scored only goal of 3rd)

February 11

Washington 5 at Ottawa 6 (Semin (WAS) hat trick)
Buffalo 3 at Carolina 4 (Samsonov 1:47 OT)
Boston 5 at Tampa Bay 4 (Bruins led 5–0 early in 2nd)
Vancouver 3 at Florida 0 [Luongo]
San Jose 3 at Detroit 2 (SO)
Dallas 3 at Calgary 1 (Flames led 1–0 midway through 2nd)
Edmonton 3 at Los Angeles 2 (SO)

February 12

Nashville 2 at New Jersey 5 (Devils scored only three goals of 3rd)
Montreal 2 at Philadelphia 3 (Flyers led 3–0 after 2nd)
Vancouver 4 at Columbus 3 (Blue Jackets led 3–0 midway
     through 2nd)
NY Rangers 3 at Pittsburgh 2 (O. Jokinen 1:02 OT)
Toronto 0 at St. Louis 4 [C. Mason]
Atlanta 3 at Minnesota 2 (game tied 2–2 after 1st & 2nd)
Phoenix 1 at Colorado 2 (Avs scored only goal of 3rd)

February 13

Tampa Bay 4 at NY Islanders 5 (Park (NYI) two goals)
San Jose 1 at Buffalo 3 (Sabres scored all goals in 2nd)
Philadelphia 6 at Montreal 2 (Briere hat trick)
New Jersey 2 at Carolina 5 (Hurricanes led 4–0 early in 3rd)
Boston 3 at Florida 2 (SO)
Ottawa 1 at Detroit 4 (Red Wings led 2–0 after 1st)
Dallas 3 at Phoenix 0 [Turco]
Washington 3 at St. Louis 4 (SO)
Atlanta 4 at Chicago 5 (SO)
Anaheim 1 at Calgary 3 (game tied 1–1 after 1st)
Colorado 0 at Los Angeles 3 [Quick]

February 14

Tampa Bay 2 at NY Rangers 5 (Lightning led 2–0 after 1st)
Nashville 4 at Pittsburgh 3 (SO)
Vancouver 2 at Minnesota 6 (eight different scorers)
Ottawa 4 at NY Islanders 3 (Senators scored only three goals of 3rd)
Chicago 5 at Columbus 4 (SO)
Anaheim 7 at Edmonton 3 (Ducks scored four goals in 3rd)

OLYMPICS BREAK

March 1

Detroit 3 at Colorado 2 (Red Wings scored only goal of 3rd)

March 2

Montreal 4 at Boston 1 (Bruins led 1–0 after 1st & 2nd)
Carolina 5 at Toronto 1 (Leafs scored game's final goal)
Chicago 3 at NY Islanders 5 (Islanders scored four goals in 2nd)
Florida 2 at Atlanta 4 (game tied 2–2 after 1st)
Vancouver 4 at Columbus 3 (Ehrhoff 1:33 OT)
NY Rangers 4 at Ottawa 1 (Senators led 1–0 after 1st)
Buffalo 2 at Pittsburgh 3 (Penguins scored in each period)
Philadelphia 7 at Tampa Bay 2 (Flyers scored only five goals of 3rd)
Edmonton 3 at Nashville 4 (both teams scored in all periods)
Los Angeles 5 at Dallas 1 (Kings led 4–0 after 2nd)
St. Louis 5 at Phoenix 2 (Coyotes led 1–0 early in 1st)
New Jersey 4 at San Jose 3 (Devils led 4–0 early in 3rd)

March 3

Washington 3 at Buffalo 1 (game tied 1–1 after 2nd)
Philadelphia 4 at Florida 7 (Panthers outscored Flyers 4–3 in 2nd)
Vancouver 6 at Detroit 3 (game tied 2–2 early in 2nd)
Edmonton 2 at Chicago 5 (Hawks scored only three goals of 3rd)
Colorado 4 at Anaheim 3 (Ducks led 2–0 early in 2nd)
Minnesota 4 at Calgary 0 [N. Backstrom]

March 4

Toronto 2 at Boston 3 (SO)

Pittsburgh 5 at NY Rangers 4 (Malkin 3:42 OT)

Tampa Bay 4 at Washington 5 (Lecavalier (TB), Walker &
Knuble (WAS) two goals each)

Ottawa 1 at Carolina 4 (Hurricanes led 3–0 after 2nd)

NY Islanders 3 at Atlanta 6 (nine different scorers)

Los Angeles 2 at Nashville 4 (game tied 1–1 after 1st)

St. Louis 6 at Dallas 1 (game tied 1–1 late in 1st)

Colorado 1 at Phoenix 3 (Coyotes scored only two goals of 3rd)

Montreal 2 at San Jose 3 (Sharks scored only two goals of 3rd)

March 5

Philadelphia 2 at Buffalo 3 (Connolly 2:31 OT)

Nashville 2 at Detroit 5 (Helm (DET) two goals)

Vancouver 3 at Chicago 6 (Hawks led 5–1 after 1st)

New Jersey 3 at Calgary 5 (Devils led 1–0 after 1st)

Minnesota 1 at Edmonton 2 (SO)

March 6

Dallas 3 at Pittsburgh 6 (Crosby (PIT) two goals)

Boston 3 at NY Islanders 2 (game tied 1–1 early in 2nd)

Toronto 2 at Ottawa 1 (SO)

NY Rangers 0 at Washington 2 [Theodore]

Carolina 1 at Florida 4 (Panthers led 2–0 after 1st & 2nd)

Atlanta 2 at Tampa Bay 6 (Stamkos (TB) two goals)

Anaheim 0 at Phoenix 4 [Bryzgalov]

St. Louis 3 at Colorado 7 (Stewart (COL) hat trick)

Montreal 4 at Los Angeles 2 (game tied 1–1 after 1st)

Columbus 1 at San Jose 2 (Sharks scored only two goals of 3rd)

March 7

Vancouver 4 at Nashville 2 (Predators led 2–1 after 2nd)

Calgary 5 at Minnesota 2 (Iginla hat trick)

Boston 1 at Pittsburgh 2 (game tied 1–1 after 2nd)
Carolina 4 at Atlanta 0 [Legace]
Detroit 5 at Chicago 4 (Red Wings scored all goals in 2nd)
Buffalo 2 at NY Rangers 1 (Kaleta 2:22 OT)
Toronto 1 at Philadelphia 3 (game tied 1–1 midway through 2nd)
Montreal 4 at Anaheim 3 (SO)
New Jersey 0 at Edmonton 2 [Drouin-Deslauriers]

March 8

Dallas 4 at Washington 3 (SO)
Columbus 0 at Los Angeles 6 [Quick]

March 9

Boston 3 at Toronto 4 (Kulemin 4:10 OT)
NY Islanders 2 at Philadelphia 3 (Flyers scored only two goals of 3rd)
Nashville 2 at Atlanta 1 (no scoring in final 39 minutes)
Tampa Bay 3 at Montreal 5 (Darche (MON) two goals)
Calgary 4 at Detroit 2 (Flames scored only three goals of 3rd)
Florida 3 at Minnesota 2 (SO)
Vancouver 6 at Colorado 4 (Samuelsson (VAN) hat trick)
Ottawa 4 at Edmonton 1 (game tied 1–1 after 2nd)
Columbus 5 at Anaheim 2 (both teams scored twice in 3rd)

March 10

Dallas 3 at Buffalo 5 (game tied 3–3 after 1st)
NY Rangers 3 at New Jersey 6 (nine different scorers)
Carolina 3 at Washington 4 (Fleischmann 3:20 OT)
Los Angeles 2 at Chicago 3 (Sharp 2:08 OT)
Vancouver 3 at Phoenix 4 (SO)

March 11

Tampa Bay 3 at Toronto 4 (Kessel 3:33 OT)
St. Louis 2 at NY Islanders 1 (SO)

Boston 5 at Philadelphia 1 (game tied 1–1 early in 2nd)
Pittsburgh 3 at Carolina 4 (Pothier 0:23 OT)
Atlanta 1 at Columbus 2 (Thrashers scored only goal of 3rd)
Edmonton 4 at Montreal 5 (SO)
Minnesota 1 at Detroit 5 (Red Wings led 3–0 late in 1st)
Florida 0 at Colorado 3 [Anderson]
Ottawa 0 at Calgary 2 [Kiprusoff]
Nashville 5 at San Jose 8 (Sharks scored six goals in 3rd)

March 12

Pittsburgh 1 at New Jersey 3 (game tied 1–1 after 1st & 2nd)
Tampa Bay 3 at Washington 2 (game tied 1–1 after 1st)
Minnesota 3 at Buffalo 2 (Sabres scored only two goals of 3rd)
NY Rangers 5 at Atlanta 2 (Rangers led 3–0 after 1st)
Los Angeles 2 at Dallas 1 (SO)
Nashville 1 at Anaheim 0 (Weber 17:54 of 1st) [Rinne]

March 13

Chicago 2 at Philadelphia 3 (all goals in 3rd)
Edmonton 4 at Toronto 6 (Kessel (TOR) two goals)
Boston 2 at Montreal 3 (Habs led 2–0 after 1st)
New Jersey 2 at NY Islanders 4 (game tied 1–1 after 1st)
Phoenix 4 at Carolina 0 [Bryzgalov]
Buffalo 2 at Detroit 3 (Rafalski 0:31 OT)
St. Louis 5 at Columbus 1 (Blues led 4–0 early in 3rd)
Ottawa 1 at Vancouver 5 (Samuelsson two goals)
Florida 3 at San Jose 2 (B. Allen 2:46 OT)

March 14

Nashville 3 at Los Angeles 2 (game tied 1–1 after 1st & 2nd)
Colorado 5 at Dallas 3 (P. Stastny (COL) two goals)
Philadelphia 1 at NY Rangers 3 (Flyers led 1–0 after 1st)
Toronto 1 at NY Islanders 4 (Leafs led 1–0 early in 1st)
Phoenix 3 at Atlanta 2 (SO)

Pittsburgh 2 at Tampa Bay 1 (Penguins scored only two goals of 3rd)
St. Louis 2 at Minnesota 4 (Wild led 4–0 late in 2nd)
Washington 4 at Chicago 3 (N. Backstrom 3:10 OT)
San Jose 2 at Anaheim 4 (Ducks led 3–0 after 1st & 2nd)
Calgary 1 at Vancouver 3 (Canucks led 3–0 after 1st & 2nd)

March 15

Boston 2 at New Jersey 3 (Devils led 3–0 after 1st)
Edmonton 3 at Columbus 5 (eight different scorers)
Detroit 2 at Calgary 1 (Flames led 1–0 late in 2nd)

March 16

Montreal 3 at NY Rangers 1 (game tied 1–1 after 2nd)
Boston 5 at Carolina 2 (Cole both Hurricanes goals)
Buffalo 3 at Atlanta 4 (Thrashers led 3–1 after 1st)
Toronto 4 at Ottawa 1 (Leafs led 3–0 late in 2nd)
Phoenix 2 at Tampa Bay 1 (no scoring in 3rd)
Washington 7 at Florida 3 (Laich (WAS) two goals)
Colorado 5 at St. Louis 3 (game tied 2–2 early in 2nd)
Philadelphia 3 at Nashville 4 (SO)
Edmonton 2 at Minnesota 4 (game tied 1–1 midway through 2nd)
San Jose 2 at Dallas 8 (Stars led 4–0 midway through 2nd)
NY Islanders 5 at Vancouver 2 (Tavares (NYI) two goals)

March 17

Pittsburgh 2 at New Jersey 5 (Penguins led 1–0 early in 1st)
Calgary 3 at Colorado 2 (Flames led 3–0 midway through 2nd)
Chicago 2 at Anaheim 4 (Ducks with empty-net goal)

March 18

Pittsburgh 3 at Boston 0 [Fleury]
St. Louis 4 at NY Rangers 3 (Rangers led 2–1 after 1st)
Washington 3 at Carolina 4 (Whitney 4:02 OT)
Ottawa 3 at Atlanta 6 (Thrashers scored only three goals of 3rd)

New Jersey 1 at Toronto 2 (SO)
Buffalo 6 at Tampa Bay 2 (Sabres led 4–0 after 2nd)
Phoenix 4 at Florida 3 (SO)
Minnesota 0 at Nashville 5 [Rinne]
Philadelphia 3 at Dallas 2 (Stars led 1–0 in 1st)
San Jose 2 at Vancouver 3 (Canucks led 2–0 after 1st)
Chicago 3 at Los Angeles 0 [Niemi]

March 19

Minnesota 2 at Columbus 4 (Wild led 2–1 after 2nd)
San Jose 3 at Calgary 4 (Sharks scored only two goals of 3rd)
Detroit 2 at Edmonton 3 (SO)
NY Islanders 4 at Anaheim 5 (S. Koivu 0:14 OT)

March 20

Carolina 3 at Pittsburgh 2 (McBain 4:59 OT)
Ottawa 4 at Dallas 5 (Spezza (OTT) hat trick)
Montreal 2 at Toronto 3 (SO)
St. Louis 1 at New Jersey 0 (Steen 19:47 of 1st) [Conklin]
Philadelphia 2 at Atlanta 5 (Armstrong (ATL) two goals)
Buffalo 3 at Florida 1 (Sabres scored in each period)
Washington 3 at Tampa Bay 1 (game tied 1–1 in 1st)
Columbus 0 at Nashville 1 (Franson 1:54 OT) [Rinne]
Chicago 4 at Phoenix 5 (SO)
Detroit 4 at Vancouver 3 (Zetterberg 4:59 OT)
NY Islanders 0 at Los Angeles 1 (Richardson 13:35 of 1st) [Quick]

March 21

Calgary 3 at Minnesota 4 (Kobasew (MIN) two goals)
NY Rangers 1 at Boston 2 (no scoring in 1st)
Buffalo 5 at Carolina 3 (Sabres scored four goals in 2nd)
Tampa Bay 2 at Florida 5 (Lightning led 1–0 midway through 1st)
Nashville 3 at St. Louis 2 (Boyd broke 2–2 tie at 17:14 of 3rd)
Phoenix 3 at Dallas 2 (SO)

Atlanta 3 at Philadelphia 1 (Thrashers led 2–0 after 1st & 2nd)
Colorado 2 at Anaheim 5 (Ducks led 4–0 after 2nd)
San Jose 1 at Edmonton 5 (Sharks scored last goal of game
   late in 3rd)

March 22

Pittsburgh 1 at Detroit 3 (Zetterberg two goals)
Ottawa 2 at Montreal 0 [Elliott]
Colorado 3 at Los Angeles 4 (Doughty 3:40 OT)

March 23

Florida 4 at Toronto 1 (Panthers led 1–0 after 1st & 2nd)
Columbus 3 at New Jersey 6 (Parise & Zajac (NJ) two goals each)
Boston 4 at Atlanta 0 [Rask]
Philadelphia 0 at Ottawa 2 [Elliott]
Carolina 2 at Tampa Bay 3 (St. Louis 0:29 OT)
Dallas 3 at Nashville 1 (game tied 1–1 after 2nd)
San Jose 4 at Minnesota 1 (Sharks scored only two goals of 3rd)
Phoenix 0 at Chicago 2 [Niemi]
Anaheim 1 at Calgary 3 (game tied 1–1 late in 2nd)
Vancouver 2 at Edmonton 3 (no scoring in 3rd)

March 24

NY Islanders 0 at NY Rangers 5 [Lundqvist]
Pittsburgh 3 at Washington 4 (SO)
Montreal 2 at Buffalo 3 (SO)
St. Louis 2 at Detroit 4 (Blues led 1–0 after 1st)
Los Angeles 3 at Colorado 4 (SO)
Anaheim 1 at Vancouver 4 (Canucks led 3–0 after 1st)

March 25

Tampa Bay 5 at Boston 3 (Stamkos (TB) two goals)
NY Rangers 4 at New Jersey 3 (SO)
Calgary 2 at NY Islanders 3 (Flames led 2–1 after 2nd)

Minnesota 4 at Philadelphia 3 (Brodziak 2:33 OT)
Washington 2 at Carolina 3 (SO)
Toronto 2 at Atlanta 1 (Grabovski 0:39 OT)
Chicago 3 at Columbus 8 (Blue Jackets led 2–1 early in 2nd)
Florida 1 at Montreal 4 (Habs led 2–0 after 1st & 2nd)
Los Angeles 1 at St. Louis 3 (Blues scored in every period)
Phoenix 3 at Nashville 4 (SO)
Dallas 0 at San Jose 3 [Nabokov]

March 26

Ottawa 4 at Buffalo 2 (Senators led 2–0 early in 2nd)
Minnesota 2 at Detroit 6 (Franzen (DET) two goals)
Anaheim 3 at Edmonton 2 (Perry (ANA) two goals)

March 28

Calgary 0 at Boston 5 [Thomas]
Philadelphia 1 at Pittsburgh 4 (Flyers led 1–0 late in 1st)
Tampa Bay 1 at Buffalo 7 (Roy hat trick)
NY Rangers 2 at Toronto 3 (Kulemin 0:39 OT)
New Jersey 4 at Montreal 2 (Devils scored only goal of 3rd)
Florida 2 at Ottawa 3 (no scoring in 1st)
Atlanta 4 at Carolina 0 [Hedberg]
NY Islanders 4 at Columbus 3 (Bailey 2:58 OT)
Detroit 1 at Nashville 0 [Howard]
Colorado 2 at Phoenix 6 (Coyotes scored only three goals of 3rd)
Vancouver 2 at San Jose 4 (Canucks led 1–0 early in 2nd)
Dallas 4 at Los Angeles 1 (Richards two goals)

March 28

Calgary 5 at Washington 3 (Flames led 4–0 after 1st)
Toronto 4 at Pittsburgh 5 (SO)
Edmonton 1 at St. Louis 2 (Blues scored only goal of 3rd)
New Jersey 1 at Philadelphia 5 (Flyers led 4–0 after 2nd)

Columbus 4 at Chicago 2 (Voracek (CBJ) two goals)
Colorado 3 at San Jose 4 (Mueller (COL) & Setoguchi (SJ) two goals each)

March 29

Carolina 4 at Atlanta 1 (Thrashers led 1–0 after 1st)
Buffalo 3 at Boston 2 (game tied 1–1 midway through 1st)
Nashville 3 at Florida 2 (Bouillon 1:00 OT)
Los Angeles 2 at Minnesota 3 (no scoring in 1st)
Dallas 1 at Anaheim 3 (all goals in 2nd)

March 30

Atlanta 3 at Toronto 2 (Stalberg both goals for Leafs)
Boston 1 at New Jersey 0 (Bergeron 4:41 OT) [Rask]
NY Rangers 4 at NY Islanders 3 (Rangers scored only three goals of 2nd)
Ottawa 5 at Washington 4 (Kovalev 4:41 OT)
Tampa Bay 2 at Columbus 3 (Lightning led 2–1 after 2nd)
Edmonton 4 at Detroit 5 (Red Wings led 4–0 late in 2nd)
Chicago 2 at St. Louis 4 (game tied 1–1 late in 1st)
Los Angeles 2 at Nashville 0 [Bernier]
Phoenix 1 at Vancouver 4 (Canucks led 3–1 after 1st)

March 31

Florida 2 at Buffalo 6 (Sabres scored two goals in each period)
Carolina 2 at Montreal 1 (Habs led 1–0 after 1st)
Tampa Bay 2 at Pittsburgh 0 [M. Smith]
Chicago 4 at Minnesota 0 [Niemi]
San Jose 1 at Dallas 5 (game tied 1–1 early in 1st)
Anaheim 5 at Colorado 2 (Ducks led 2–0 midway trough 2nd)
Phoenix 1 at Calgary 2 (no scoring in first 34 minutes)

April 1

Philadelphia 4 at NY Islanders 6 (Islanders led 4–0 early in 2nd)
Buffalo 2 at Toronto 4 (Leafs scored only two goals of 3rd)
Atlanta 1 at Washington 2 (Capitals scored only goal of 3rd)
Florida 1 at Boston 0 (Ballard 7:15 of 1st) [Clemmensen]
Carolina 3 at Ottawa 4 (SO)
Columbus 2 at Detroit 3 (Red Wings scored in every period)
St. Louis 2 at Nashville 3 (game tied 2–2 after 2nd)
Vancouver 3 at Los Angeles 8 (Brown (LA) hat trick)

April 2

Montreal 1 at Philadelphia 0 (Plekanec 9:25 of 1st) [Halak]
Chicago 2 at New Jersey 1 (SO)
NY Rangers 5 at Tampa Bay 0 [Lundqvist]
San Jose 3 at Minnesota 2 (Couture (SJ) scored only goal of 3rd
    at 16:09)
Edmonton 3 at Dallas 6 (Stars scored three goals in 1st & 3rd;
    Oilers scored three in 2nd)
Calgary 2 at Colorado 1 (no scoring in 1st)
Vancouver 5 at Anaheim 4 (SO)

April 3

Atlanta 3 at Pittsburgh 4 (Leopold 2:50 OT)
Ottawa 1 at NY Islanders 4 (Islanders scored only three goals of 2nd)
Nashville 4 at Detroit 3 (Suter 0:16 OT)
New Jersey 4 at Carolina 0 [Brodeur]
NY Rangers 4 at Florida 1 (Panthers led 1–0 after 2nd)
Boston 2 at Toronto 1 (Satan 3:25 OT)
Buffalo 0 at Montreal 3 [Halak]
Washington 3 at Columbus 2 (Capitals led 3–0 midway through 1st)
Dallas 1 at St. Louis 2 (game tied 1–1 after 2nd)
Edmonton 2 at Phoenix 3 (SO)
Anaheim 2 at Los Angeles 1 (SO)

April 4

Calgary 1 at Chicago 4 (Hawks scored in every period)
Detroit 3 at Philadelphia 4 (Flyers led 2–0 early in 1st)
San Jose 4 at Colorado 5 (Liles 2:59 OT)
Minnesota 3 at Vancouver 4 (Salo 2:15 OT)

April 5

Boston 2 at Washington 3 (Laich 0:44 OT)
Columbus 1 at St. Louis 2 (E. Johnson 3:59 OT)
Minnesota 1 at Edmonton 4 (Moreau two goals)

April 6

New Jersey 3 at Atlanta 0 [Brodeur]
NY Rangers 2 at Buffalo 5 (game tied 2–2 after 1st)
Philadelphia 2 at Toronto 0 [Boucher]
Montreal 3 at NY Islanders 4 (SO)
Washington 6 at Pittsburgh 3 (Ovechkin (WAS) & Leopold (PIT)
    two goals each)
Ottawa 5 at Florida 2 (Senators led 1–0 after 1st)
Carolina 8 at Tampa Bay 5 (Lightning led 1–0 early in 1st)
Chicago 5 at Dallas 2 (Fraser (CHI) two goals)
San Jose 2 at Calgary 1 (Sharks led 2–0 after 2nd)
Colorado 4 at Vancouver 3 (SO)
Los Angeles 5 at Anaheim 4 (SO)

April 7

Toronto 1 at NY Rangers 5 (Rangers led 3–0 after 1st & 2nd)
Columbus 3 at Detroit 4 (Blue Jackets led 2–1 after 1st & 2nd)
St. Louis 5 at Chicago 6 (Hawks led 6–2 after 2nd)
Colorado 4 at Edmonton 5 (Whitney 3:50 OT)
Nashville 2 at Phoenix 5 (Coyotes scored three goals in 3rd)

April 8

Buffalo 1 at Boston 3 (Sabres led 1–0 after 1st)
Montreal 2 at Carolina 5 (E. Staal hat trick)
New Jersey 2 at Florida 3 (game tied 1–1 after 2nd)
NY Islanders 3 at Pittsburgh 7 (Penguins led 4–2 after 1st)
Ottawa 3 at Tampa Bay 4 (SO)
Anaheim 2 at Dallas 3 (SO)
Minnesota 2 at Calgary 1 (SO)
Vancouver 2 at San Jose 4 (Sharks led 4–0 after 2nd)
Phoenix 3 at Los Angeles 2 (SO)

April 9

Philadelphia 3 at NY Rangers 4 (no scoring in 3rd)
Atlanta 2 at Washington 5 (Ovechkin & Backstrom (WAS) two goals each)
Detroit 1 at Columbus 0 (SO) [Howard]
Anaheim 3 at St. Louis 6 (Blues scored only three goals of 3rd)
Chicago 5 at Colorado 2 (Fraser (CHI) two goals)

April 10

Carolina 2 at Boston 4 (Bruins get empty-net goal)
Edmonton 4 at Los Angeles 3 (SO)
NY Islanders 1 at New Jersey 7 (Devils led 5–0 after 2nd)
Pittsburgh 0 at Atlanta 1 (Little 9:26 of 2nd) [Hedberg]
Buffalo 5 at Ottawa 2 (Vanek four goals)
Toronto 4 at Montreal 3 (Phaneuf 2:06 OT)
Florida 3 at Tampa Bay 4 (SO)
St. Louis 1 at Nashville 2 (SO)
Dallas 4 at Minnesota 3 (SO)
Calgary 3 at Vancouver 7 (D. Sedin (VAN) hat trick)
Phoenix 2 at San Jose 3 (SO)

April 11

Los Angeles 2 at Colorado 1 (D. Brown 1:31 OT)
Detroit 3 at Chicago 2 (B. Stuart 3:11 OT)
NY Rangers 1 at Philadelphia 2 (SO)
Boston 4 at Washington 3 (SO)
Pittsburgh 6 at NY Islanders 5 (Leopold 4:25 OT)
Buffalo 1 at New Jersey 2 (Devils scored only goal of 3rd)
Tampa Bay 3 at Florida 1 (Lightning led 2–1 after 1st & 2nd)
Edmonton 2 at Anaheim 7 (Carter (ANA) two goals)

SHOOTOUT LEADERS, 2009–10

SKATERS

Shots

Radim Vrbata (PHO)	18
Lauri Korpikoski (PHO)	17
Jack Johnson (LA)	17
Anze Kopitar (LA)	16
Brad Richards (DAL)	16
Patrick Kane (CHI)	15
Wojtek Wolski (COL/PHO)	15
Jonathan Toews (CHI)	14
Pavel Datsyuk (DET)	14
Corey Perry (ANA)	13
Patrice Bergeron (BOS)	13
Steve Reinprecht (FLO)	13
Blake Wheeler (BOS)	13

Goals

Sidney Crosby (PIT)	8	(10 shots)
Jonathan Toews (CHI)	8	(14 shots)
Anze Kopitar (LA)	8	(16 shots)
Radim Vrbata (PHO)	8	(18 shots)
Brad Boyes (STL)	7	(12 shots)
Pavel Datsyuk (DET)	7	(14 shots)
Lauri Korpikoski (PHO)	7	(17 shots)
Adrian Aucoin (PHO)	6	(9 shots)
Frans Nielsen (NYI)	6	(11 shots)
Jack Johnson (LA)	6	(17 shots)

Shooting Percentage (minimum 5 shots)

Sidney Crosby (PIT)	80.00%	(8/10)
Adrian Aucoin (PHO)	66.67%	(6/9)
Vyacheslav Kozlov (ATL)	66.67%	(4/6)

Michal Handzus (LA)	62.50%	(5/8)
Robert Lang (PHO)	62.50%	(5/8)
T.J. Oshie (STL)	62.50%	(5/8)
Brian Gionta (MON)	60.00%	(3/5)
Claude Giroux (PHI)	60.00%	(3/5)
Gilbert Brule (EDM)	60.00%	(3/5)
Jeff Tambellini (NYI)	60.00%	(3/5)
Ryan Kesler (VAN)	60.00%	(3/5)
Ryan Potulny (EDM)	60.00%	(3/5)

Worst Shooting Percentage (minimum 5 shots)

James Neal (DAL)	0.00%	(0/10)
Sam Gagner (EDM)	0.00%	(0/7)
Wojtek Wolski (COL/PHO)	6.67%	(1/15)
Mike Ribeiro (DAL)	8.33%	(1/12)
Vincent Lecavalier (TB)	12.50%	(1/8)
Mike Modano (DAL)	14.29%	(1/7)
Tim Connelly (BUF)	14.29%	(1/7)
Blake Wheeler (BOS)	15.38%	(2/13)
Dany Heatley (SJ)	16.67%	(1/6)
Dustin Penner (EDM)	16.67%	(1/6)
Guillaume Latendresse (MON/MIN)	16.67%	(1/6)
Mike Richards (PHI)	16.67%	(1/6)
Ryan Smyth (LA)	16.67%	(1/6)
Tomas Plekanec (MON)	16.67%	(1/6)

GOALIES

Wins

Ilya Bryzgalov (PHO)	8	(13 SO)
Jonathan Quick (LA)	8	(14 SO)
Craig Anderson (COL)	7	(11 SO)
Jason LaBarbera (PHO)	6	(7 SO)
Antti Niemi (CHI)	6	(8 SO)

Marc-Andre Fleury (PIT)   6 (8 SO)
Pekka Rinne (NAS)   6 (9 SO)
Martin Brodeur (NJ)   6 (10 SO)
Evgeni Nabokov (SJ)   6 (12 SO)

Save Percentage (minimum 15 shots faced)

Alex Auld (DAL)   86.7% (13/15)
Antti Niemi (CHI)   81.3% (26/32)
Antero Niittymaki (TB)   78.3% (18/23)
Jaroslav Halak (MON)   76.2% (16/21)
Johan Hedberg (ATL)   76.2% (16/21)
Pekka Rinne (NAS)   75.6% (34/45)
Manny Legace (CAR)   75.0% (12/16)
Evgeni Nabokov (SJ)   74.0% (37/50)
Marc-Andre Fleury (PIT)   73.9% (17/23)
Semyon Varlamov (WAS)   72.7% (24/33)
Tim Thomas (BOS)   72.7% (24/33)

TEAM RECORDS

Most Shootouts

Team	SO	W	L
Phoenix	20	14	6
Boston	19	10	9
Los Angeles	18	10	8
Dallas	17	7	10
Florida	16	6	10
Chicago	15	9	6
Detroit	15	6	9
Edmonton	14	8	6
NY Islanders	14	8	6
San Jose	13	7	6
Anaheim	13	5	8

Fewest Shootouts

Team	SO	W	L
Philadelphia	7	4	3
NY Rangers	7	3	4
Toronto	8	4	4
Vancouver	8	4	4
Carolina	9	4	5
Pittsburgh	10	8	2
Ottawa	10	5	5
Atlanta	10	4	6
Buffalo	10	4	6
Calgary	10	3	7

NATIONALITY OF ALL PLAYERS, 2009–10

SUMMARY

(figures in parentheses show leaguewide representation as a percentage)

TOTAL	962
CANADA	519 (54.0%)
Alberta	91
British Columbia	53
Manitoba	31
New Brunswick	1
Newfoundland	5
Nova Scotia	10
Ontario	201
Prince Edward Island	4
Quebec	71
Saskatchewan	52
UNITED STATES	208 (21.6%)
SWEDEN	52 (5.4%)
CZECH REPUBLIC	49 (5.1%)
FINLAND	38 (4.0%)
RUSSIA	32 (3.3%)
SLOVAKIA	17 (1.8%)
GERMANY	10 (1.0%)
DENMARK	6 (0.6%)
LATVIA	5 (0.5%)
AUSTRIA	3 (0.3%)
BELARUS	3 (0.3%)
KAZAKHSTAN	3 (0.3%)
SWITZERLAND	3 (0.5%)
UKRAINE	2 (0.2%)

BAHAMAS	1 (0.1%)
BRAZIL	1 (0.1%)
BRUNEI	1 (0.1%)
FRANCE	1 (0.1%)
ITALY	1 (0.1%)
JAPAN	1 (0.1%)
LITHUANIA	1 (0.1%)
NORWAY	1 (0.1%)
POLAND	1 (0.1%)
SLOVENIA	1 (0.1%)
SOUTH KOREA	1 (0.1%)
UNITED KINGDOM	1 (0.1%)

[NOTE: Owen Nolan was born in Belfast, which is not in Ireland (i.e., Eire), but Northern Ireland, which is part of the U.K.]

NATIONALITY BREAKDOWN

CANADA	**520**	
Alberta	**91**	
Airdrie	1	Zach Boychuk
Banff	1	Ryan Smyth
Beaverlodge	1	Matt Walker
Bonnyville	1	Jon Kalinski
Calgary	17	Cody Almond, Nolan Baumgartner, Jay Beagle, Mike Brodeur, Braydon Coburn, Patrick Eaves, T.J. Galiardi, Mike Green, Chad Johnson, Nick Johnson, Robert Nilsson, Chris Phillips, Jeff Schultz, Tyler Sloan, Brent Sopel, Ryan Stone, Jeff Tambellini
Caroline	2	Kris Russell, Jim Vandermeer
Castor	1	Darcy Tucker

Cochrane	1	Mason Raymond
Cold Lake	1	Alexander Auld
Coleman	1	Rick Rypien
Drumheller	1	Andrew Bodnarchuk
Edmonton	31	Shawn Belle, Blair Betts, Jay Bouwmeester, Johnny Boychuk, Gilbert Brule, Jason Chimera, Erik Christensen, Mike Comrie, Derek Engelland, Tyler Ennis, Andrew Ference, Vernon Fiddler, Mark Fistric, Jarome Iginla, Dustin Kohn, Daymond Langkow, Bryan Little, Jamie Lundmark, Joffrey Lupul, Derek Morris, Scott Nichol, Scott Niedermayer, Matt Pettinger, Dion Phaneuf, Fernando Pisani, Steve Reinprecht, David Schlemko, Nathan Smith, Jason Strudwick, Brian Sutherby, Darryl Sydor
Elk Point	2	Mark Letestu, Sheldon Souray
Forestburg	1	Evan Oberg
Fort McMurray	1	Scottie Upshall
Fort Saskatchewan	2	Mike Commodore, Ray Whitney
Grand Cache	1	Dean McAmmond
Halkirk	1	Shane Doan
Hinton	1	Dave Scatchard
Lac La Biche	1	Rene Bourque
Leduc	1	Matt Climie
Lethbridge	2	Spencer Machacek, Kris Versteeg
Lloydminster	1	Clarke MacArthur
Mannville	1	Kyle Calder
Medicine Hat	1	Brooks Laich
Olds	1	Jay Rosehill
Peace River	1	Chris Osgood

Red Deer	2	Trent Hunter, Chris Mason
Redwater	1	Todd Fedoruk
Rimbey	1	Jason Jaffray
Rocky Mountain House	2	Brad Stuart, Nick Tarnasky
St. Paul	1	Kyle Brodziak
Sherwood Park	1	Cam Ward
Stony Plain	1	Steve Goertzen
Strathmore	1	Keaton Ellerby
Taber	1	Devin Setoguchi
Vermilion	1	Jeff Woywitka
Viking	1	Brett Sutter
Westlock	1	Kyle Chipchura

British Columbia	**53**	
Abbotsford	2	Ryan Craig, Kyle Cumiskey
Burnaby	3	Karl Alzner, Jason LaBarbera, Greg Zanon
Cassiar	1	Rob Niedermayer
Comox	1	Brett McLean
Cranbrook	1	Brad Lukowich
Hope	1	Jeff Hoggan
Invermere	1	Wade Dubielewicz
Kamloops	1	Mark Recchi
Kelowna	1	Josh Gorges
Kitimat	1	Rod Pelley
Maple Ridge	1	Andrew Ladd
Murrayville	1	Dean Arsene
North Vancouver	1	Ben Maxwell
Osoyoos	1	Chuck Kobasew
Pitt Meadows	1	Brendan Morrison
Port McNeill	2	Willie Mitchell, Clayton Stoner
Quesnel	2	Brett Festerling, Aaron Gagnon
Richmond	4	Scott Hannan, Raymond Sawada, Brent Seabrook, Brandon Segal

Salmon Arm	2	Cody Franson, Scott Jackson
Sicamous	2	Colin Fraser, Shea Weber
Smithers	1	Dan Hamhuis
Trail	2	Shawn Horcoff, Barret Jackman
Vancouver	13	Troy Brouwer, Tyler Eckford, Zach Hamill, Evander Kane, Paul Kariya, Milan Lucic, Steve Montador, Shaone Morrisonn, Carey Price, Mike Santorelli, MacGregor Sharp, Aaron Voros, Brandon Yip
Vernon	4	Eric Brewer, Andrew Ebbett, Eric Godard, Jerred Smithson
Victoria	2	Jamie Benn, Ryan O'Byrne
White Rock	1	Jason Garrison
Manitoba	**31**	
Binscarth	1	Cody McLeod
Brandon	4	Alex Plante, Bryce Salvador, Brock Trotter, Ryan White
Churchill	1	Jordin Tootoo
Neepawa	2	Triston Grant, Shane Hnidy
Nesbitt	1	Aaron Rome
Portage La Prairie	2	Arron Asham, Troy Bodie
Selkirk	1	Andrew Murray
Snowflake	1	Justin Falk
Steinbach	1	Jeff Penner
Thompson	2	Chris Minard, Jody Shelley
Winkler	2	Eric Fehr, Dustin Penner
Winnipeg	13	Cam Barker, Dustin Boyd, Riley Cote, Nigel Dawes, Darren Helm, Duncan Keith, Frazer McLaren, Derek Meech, Colton Orr, Alexander Steen, Jonathan Toews, Ian White, Travis Zajac

Ontario	**201**	
Ajax	1	Brent Burns
Alfred	1	Benoit Pouliot
Almonte	1	Kent Huskins
Barrie	1	John Madden
Beaconsfield	1	Ben Walter
Belleville	4	Matt Cooke, Andrew Raycroft, Brad Richardson, Derek Smith
Blyth	1	Justin Peters
Bowmanville	1	Bryan Bickell
Bramalea	1	Mike Weaver
Brampton	2	Rick Nash, Kris Newbury
Brantford	1	Paul Szczechura
Brights Grove	1	Brad Staubitz
Cambridge	3	Tim Brent, Trevor Gillies, Scott Walker
Carp	1	Kurtis Foster
Chatham	1	Ryan Jones
Clinton	1	Ryan O'Reilly
Cobourg	1	Justin Williams
Collingwood	1	Jason Arnott
Dryden	1	Chris Pronger
Elliot Lake	1	Zack Stortini
Fergus	1	Jamie McGinn
Gloucester	1	Grant Clitsome
Grimsby	1	Kevin Bieksa
Guelph	5	Krys Barch, Logan Couture, David Jones, Kirk Maltby, Rich Peverley
Haliburton	1	Matt Duchene
Hamilton	4	Ray Emery, Adam Mair, Brian McGratton, Steve Staios
Hearst	1	Claude Giroux
Huntsville	1	Ethan Moreau
Kanata	2	Cory Murphy, Todd White

Kenora	1	Mike Richards
King City	2	Daniel Carcillo, Alex Pietrangelo
Kingston	6	Bryan Allen, John Erskine, Jay McClement, Jay McKee, Mike Smith, Andy Sutton
Kitchener	4	Kevin Klein, Kyle Quincey, Gregory Stewart, Dennis Wideman
London	12	Gregory Campbell, Jeff Carter, Drew Doughty, Sam Gagner, Nazem Kadri, Mark Mancari, Curtis McElhinney, Brandon Prust, Bryan Rodney, Joe Thornton, Jason Williams, Brian Willsie
Long Sault	1	Jesse Winchester
Markdale	1	Chris Neil
Markham	1	Steve Stamkos
Millgrove	1	Danny Syvret
Mississauga	8	Brad Boyes, Matt Corrente, Tom Kostopoulos, Manny Malhotra, Shawn Matthias, Jason Spezza, Matt Stajan, John Tavares
Moose Factory	1	Jonathan Cheechoo
Newmarket	2	Steve Downie, Brian Elliott
Niagara-on-the-Lake	1	Zenon Konopka
Nobleton	1	Nick Boynton
North Bay	1	Craig Rivet
Oakville	2	Steve Mason, Kyle Wilson
Oshawa	5	Josh Bailey, Michael Haley, Jay Harrison, James Neal, Shawn Thornton
Ottawa	12	Derek Armstrong, Adrian Aucoin, Dan Boyle, Rod Brind'Amour, Ben Eager, Mark Fraser, Marc Methot, Sean O'Donnell, Derek Roy, Marc Savard, Martin St. Pierre, Stephane Yelle
Palmerston	1	Nick Spaling

Peterborough	3	Mike Fisher, Corey Perry, Cory Stillman
Petrolia	1	Michael Leighton
Pickering	1	Sean Avery
Port Hope	1	Shane O'Brien
Richmond Hill	3	Mike Cammalleri, Derek Joslin, Theo Peckham
Sarnia	1	Dustin Jeffrey
Sault Ste. Marie	4	Matt D'Agostini, Tyler Kennedy, Chris Thorburn, Marty Turco
Simcoe	2	Rob Blake, Dwayne Roloson
St. Catharines	4	Rob Davison, Bryan McCabe, Andrew Peters, John Scott
St. Isidore	1	Francis Wathier
Stittsville	1	Matt Bradley
Stoney Creek	1	Mark Popovic
Stouffville	1	Michael del Zotto
Strathroy	2	Brian Campbell, Andy McDonald
Sudbury	3	Todd Bertuzzi, Andrew Brunette, Derek MacKenzie
Thornhill	1	Dominic Moore
Thunder Bay	8	Taylor Chorney, Ryan Johnson, Taylor Pyatt, Tom Pyatt, Patrick Sharp, Eric Staal, Jordan Staal, Marc Staal
Timmins	2	Shean Donovan, Steve Sullivan
Toronto	37	Mike Blunden, Dave Bolland, Chris Campoli, Luca Caputi, David Clarkson, Rich Clune, Andrew Cogliano, Carlo Colaiacovo, Trevor Daley, Kris Draper, Mike Duco, Chris Durno, Adam Foote, Mark Giordano, Matt Halischuk, Darren Haydar, Brayden Irwin, Chris Kelly, Mike Knuble, Manny Legace, Corey Locke, Brad May, Jamal Mayers, Kenndal McArdle, Glen Metropolit,

		Matt Moulson, Cal O'Reilly, Wayne Primeau, Liam Reddox, Wayne Simmonds, Chris Stewart, P.K. Subban, Raffi Torres, Stephen Valiquette, Joel Ward, Stephen Weiss, Daniel Winnick
Waterloo	1	John Mitchell
Welland	6	Paul Bissonnette, Cal Clutterbuck, Matt Ellis, Daniel Girardi, Nathan Horton, Daniel Paille
Winchester	1	Matt Carkner
Whitby	2	Victor Oreskevich, Paul Ranger
Windsor	7	Matt Beleskey, Ed Jovanovski, Matt Martin, Wes O'Neill, Aaron Ward, Kyle Wellwood, Ryan Wilson
Woodbridge	1	Steve Eminger
Quebec	**71**	
Alma	1	Guillaume Desbiens
Amos	1	Guillaume Lefebvre
L'Ancienne-Lorette	1	Patrice Bergeron
Beauceville	1	Stephane Veilleux
Chandler	1	Mathieu Garon
Dorval	1	Jason Demers
Drummondville	1	Mathieu Perreault
Gatineau	3	Daniel Briere, Mathieu Carle, Alexandre Picard (b. Jul '85)
Greenfield Park	1	Jerome Samson
Hull	2	Derick Brassard, P-A Parenteau
Île-Bizard	1	Vincent Lecavalier
Lac-St-Charles	1	Martin Biron
Lafontaine	1	Yann Danis
Laval	4	Pascal Dupuis, Philippe Dupuis, Martin St. Louis, Jose Theodore
Lemoyne	1	Maxime Talbot

Lévis	1	Pierre-Luc Letourneau-Leblond
Longueuil	2	Maxime Fortunas, Bruno Gervais
Montreal	18	Alexandre Bolduc, Martin Brodeur, Corey Crawford, Mathieu Darche, J-P Dumont, J-S Giguere, Ben Guite, Ian Laperriere, Georges Laraque, Kris Letang, Charles Linglet, Matt Lombardi, Roberto Luongo, Torrey Mitchell, Maxim Noreau, Joel Perrault, Mike Ribeiro, Marc-Edouard Vlasic
Pointe-Claire	1	Alex Burrows
Quebec City	6	Steve Bernier, David Desharnais, Alexandre Giroux, Marc-Antoine Pouliot, Paul Stastny, Yan Stastny
Repentigny	2	Pascal Leclaire, Jason Pominville
Rouyn-Noranda	1	Marc-Andre Cliché
St-Agapit	1	Antoine Vermette
St-Bonaventure	1	Patrick Lalime
Ste-Cathérine	1	Guillaume Latendresse
Ste-Foy	1	Simon Gagne
St-Georges	1	Mathieu Roy
St-Jean-sur-Richelieu	2	Jeff Drouin-Deslauriers, David Laliberte
Ste-Justine	1	Alex Tanguay
St-Léonard	1	Maxim Lapierre
St-Louis-de-France	1	Marc-Andre Bergeron
Les Saules	1	Alexandre Picard (b. Oct '85)
Sherbrooke	4	Eric Belanger, Pierre-Marc Bouchard, David Perron, Stephane Robidas
Sorel	2	Francois Beauchemin, Marc-Andre Fleury
Terrebonne	1	J-F Jacques
Trois-Rivières	1	Steve Begin

New Brunswick   1
Quispamsis   1   Randy Jones

Newfoundland   5
Bonavista   1   Adam Pardy
Carbonear   1   Daniel Cleary
St. John's   3   Ryane Clowe, Teddy Purcell, Michael
                                Ryder

Nova Scotia   10
Halifax   5   Eric Boulton, Sidney Crosby, Andrew
                                Gordon, Brad Marchand, James
                                Sheppard
Judique   1   Andrew MacDonald
New Glasgow   2   Jon Sim, Colin White
Pictou   1   Joey MacDonald
Port Hawkesbury   1   Aaron Johnson
Prince Edward Island   4
Charlottetown   2   Mark Flood, Adam McQuaid
Murray Harbour   1   Brad Richards
Summerside   1   Steve Ott

Saskatchewan   52
Alameda   1   Trent Whitfield
Aneroid   1   Patrick Marleau
Brock   1   Steve MacIntyre
Carlyle   1   Brenden Morrow
Central Butte   1   Blair Jones
Craik   1   Garnet Exelby
Humboldt   2   Dustin Tokarski, Brendan Witt
Kamsack   1   Darcy Hordichuk
Kindersley   2   Derek Dorsett, Curtis Glencross
Lanigan   1   Sheldon Brookbank
Leroy   1   Nathan Paetsch

Lloydminster	2	Colby Armstrong, Wade Redden
Meadow Lake	2	Blake Comeau, Dwayne King
Melfort	1	Tyson Strachan
Melville	2	Shaun Heshka, Jarret Stoll
Nipawin	1	Dane Byers
Nokomis	1	Jordan Henry
Prince Albert	1	Ryan Parent
Regina	10	Tyler Bozak, Brett Carson, Devan Dubnyk, Ryan Getzlaf, Tanner Glass, Josh Harding, Scott Hartnell, Chris Kunitz, Brendan Mikkelson, Nathan Oystrick
Rosetown	1	Quintin Laing
Saskatoon	12	Wade Belak, Byron Bitz, Derek Boogaard, Jared Cowen, Dan Ellis, Ryan Keller, Warren Peters, Darroll Powe, Cory Sarich, Brayden Schenn, Luke Schenn, James Wright
Stewart Valley	1	Travis Moen
Strasbourg	1	Nick Schultz
Swift Current	1	Boyd Kane
Unity	1	Boyd Gordon
Wapella	1	Brett Clark
Yorkton	1	Matt Zaba

USA **209**

Alabama	1	Jared Ross
Alaska	6	Matt Carle, Ty Conklin, Brandon Dubinsky, Scott Gomez, Nate Thompson, Tim Wallace
California	2	Brooks Orpik, Casey Wellman
Colorado	2	Brandon Crombeen, David Hale
Connecticut	10	Nick Bonino, Chris Clark, Chris Drury, Ron Hainsey, Colin McDonald, Max

		Pacioretty, Jonathan Quick, Ryan Shannon, Jamie Sifers, Colin Wilson
Delaware	1	Mark Eaton
Illinois	9	Craig Anderson, Jarred Boll, Mike Brown, Chris Chelios, Joe Corvo, Robbie Earl, Brett Lebda, Tim Stapleton, Andy Wozniewski
Indiana	3	Donald Brashear, Jack Johnson, John-Michael Liles
Iowa	1	Scott Clemmensen
Maine	1	Greg Moore
Maryland	2	Jeremy Duchesne, Jeff Halpern
Massachusetts	22	Keith Aucoin, Chris Bourque, Brian Boyle, Bobby Butler, Joe Callahan, John Carlson, Rick DiPietro, Benn Ferriero, Hal Gill, Bill Guerin, Josh Hennessy, Doug Janik, Greg Mauldin, John McCarthy, Mike Mottau, Jay Pandolfo, Brian Pothier, Tom Poti, Cory Schneider, Keith Tkachuk, Ryan Whitney, Keith Yandle
Michigan	33	Justin Abdelkader, David Booth, Drayson Bowman, Chris Conner, Patrick Davis, Corey Elkins, Jeff Finger, Nathan Gerbe, Tim Gleason, Andy Greene, Matt Greene, Mike Grier, Dwight Helminen, T.J. Hensick, Andy Hilbert, Matt Hunwick, Brent Johnson, Ryan Kesler, Chad LaRose, David Legwand, Alec Martinez, Ryan Miller, Mike Modano, David Moss, Scott Parse, Kevin Porter, Corey Potter, Brian Rafalski, Brian Rolston, Jim Slater, Tim Thomas, Doug Weight, James

		Wisniewski
Minnesota	40	Andrew Alberts, David Backes, Keith Ballard, Jason Blake, Brandon Bochenski, Casey Borer, Dustin Byfuglien, Ryan Carter, Tim Conboy, Matt Cullen, John Curry, Trevor Frischmon, Tom Gilbert, Alex Goligoski, Matt Hendricks, Erik Johnson, Jamie Langenbrunner, Brian Lee, Jordan Leopold, Mike Lundin, Paul Martin, Jamie McBain, Peter Mueller, Matt Niskanen, Kyle Okposo, Zach Parise, Mark Parrish, Derek Peltier, Toby Petersen, Tom Preissing, Nate Prosser, Kurt Sauer, Dan Sexton, Matt Smaby, Ryan Stoa, Mark Stuart, Jeff Taffe, Blake Wheeler, Clay Wilson, J.T. Wyman
Missouri	2	Chris Butler, Cam Janssen
Nebraska	1	Jed Ortmeyer
New Hampshire	2	Ben Lovejoy, Freddy Meyer
New Jersey	5	Paul Mara, Drew Miller, Bobby Ryan, Bobby Sanguinetti, James van Riemsdyk
New York	32	Zach Bogosian, Francis Bouillon, Dustin Brown, Ryan Callahan, Erik Cole, Tim Connolly, Craig Conroy, Nick Foligno, Matt Gilroy, Brian Gionta, Chris Higgins, Jimmy Howard, Patrick Kaleta, Patrick Kane, Tim Kennedy, Mike Komisarek, Drew Larman, Matt Lashoff, Jay Leach, Todd Marchant, Eric Nystrom, Nick Palmieri, Marty Reasoner, Mathieu Schneider, Rob

Schremp, Rob Scuderi, Tim Sestito, Tom Sestito, Lee Stempniak, Brandon Sutter, Ryan Vesce, Steven Zalewski

North Carolina	1	Patrick O'Sullivan
North Dakota	4	Paul Gaustad, Danny Irmen, Tim Jackman, Ryan Potulny
Ohio	2	Peter Harrold, Mike Rupp
Oregon	1	Jack Hillen
Pennsylvania	9	Nate Guenin, Christian Hanson, Chad Kolarik, Ryan Malone, Justin Mercier, George Parros, Dylan Reese, Eric Tangradi, R.J. Umberger
Rhode Island	1	Brian Boucher
Texas	1	Tyler Myers
Utah	1	Trevor Lewis
Washington	2	Pat Dwyer, T.J. Oshie
Wisconsin	11	Adam Burish, Jake Dowell, Davis Drewiske, Phil Kessel, Joe Pavelski, Joel Rechlicz, Jack Skille, Drew Stafford, David Steckel, Ryan Suter, Brad Winchester
SWEDEN	52	Daniel Alfredsson, Johan Backlund, Mikael Backlund, Nicklas Backstrom, Niklas Bergfors, Patrik Berglund, Fabian Brunnstrom, Alexander Edler, Jhonas Enroth, Tobias Enstrom, Jonathan Ericsson, Anders Eriksson, Loui Eriksson, Erik Ersberg, Johan Franzen, Nicklas Grossman, Carl Gunnarsson, Jonas Gustavsson, Johan Hedberg, Viktor Hedman, Niklas Hjalmarsson, Tomas Holmstrom, Patrik Hornqvist, Kristian Huselius, Kim Johnsson, Jonas

Junland, Eric Karlsson, Niklas Kronwall, Staffan Kronwall, Nicklas Lidstrom, Andreas Lilja, Henrik Lundqvist, Fredrik Modin, Oscar Moller, Johan Motin, Doug Murray, John Oduya, Mattias Ohlund, Samuel Pahlsson, Mattias Ritola, Mikael Samuelsson, Daniel Sedin, Henrik Sedin, Fredrik Sjostrom, Viktor Stalberg, Anton Stralman, Henrik Tallinder, Andreas Thuresson, Niclas Wallin, Rickard Wallin, Tom Wandell, Henrik Zetterberg

CZECH REPUBLIC	49	Radek Dvorak, Patrik Elias, Martin Erat, Tomas Fleischmann, Michael Frolik, Roman Hamrlik, Martin Hanzal, Martin Havlat, Jan Hejda, Milan Hejduk, Ales Hemsky, Tomas Kaberle, Petr Kalus, Tomas Kana, Jakub Kindl, Rostislav Klesla, David Koci, Ales Kotalik, Lukas Krajicek, David Krejci, Kamil Kreps, Filip Kuba, Pavel Kubina, Robert Lang, Radek Martinek, Milan Michalek, Zbynek Michalek, Vladimir Mihalek, Michal Neuvirth, Rostislav Olesz, Ondrej Pavelec, Tomas Plekanec, Roman Polak, Vaclav Prospal, Petr Prucha, Michal Repik, Michal Rozsival, Alexander Salak, Martin Skoula, Ladislav Smid, Radek Smolenak, Vladimir Sobotka, Jaroslav Spacek, Petr Sykora, Jiri Tlusty, Tomas Vokoun, Jakub Voracek, Radim Vrbata, Marek Zidlicky

FINLAND	38	Niklas Backstrom, Sean Bergenheim, Valtteri Filppula, Niklas Hagman, Ilkka Heikkinen, Jesse Joensuu, Jussi Jokinen, Olli Jokinen, Miikka Kiprusoff, Ville Koistinen, Mikko Koivu, Saku Koivu, Lauri Korpikoski, Teemu Laakso, Jere Lehtinen, Kari Lehtonen, Mikko Lehtonen, Ville Leino, Sami Lepisto, Perttu Lindgren, Toni Lydman, Antti Miettinen, Antti Niemi, Antero Niittymaki, Petteri Nokelainen, Oskar Osala, Ilkka Pikkarainen, Joni Pitkanen, Mika Pyorala, Tuukka Rask, Pekka Rinne, Jarkko Ruutu, Tuomo Ruutu, Anssi Salmela, Sami Salo, Teemu Selanne, Kimmo Timonen, Vesa Toskala
RUSSIA	32	Maxim Afinogenov, Artem Anisimov, Evgeni Artyukin, Ilya Bryzgalov, Evgeni Dadonov, Pavel Datsyuk, Nikita Filatov, Alexander Frolov, Sergei Gonchar, Denis Grebeshkov, Nikolai Khabibulin, Anton Klementyev, Ilya Kovalchuk, Alexei Kovalev, Vyacheslav Kozlov, Nikolai Kulemin, Dmitri Kulikov, Enver Lisin, Andrei Loktionov, Evgeni Malkin, Andrei Markov, Maxim Mayorov, Alexander Ovechkin, Alexander Pechurski, Sergei Samsonov, Alexander Semin, Sergei Shirokov, Fedor Tyutin, Simeon Varlamov, Ivan Vishnevskiy, Anton Volchenkov, Vladimir Zharkov

SLOVAKIA	17	Mario Bliznak, Peter Budaj, Zdeno Chara, Pavol Demitra, Marian Gaborik, Jaroslav Halak, Michal Handzus, Marian Hossa, Milan Jurcina, Tomas Kopecky, Andrei Meszaros, Peter Olvecky, Miroslav Satan, Andrej Sekera, Marek Svatos, Boris Valabik, Lubomir Visnovsky
GERMANY	10	Christian Ehrhoff, Marcel Goc, Mikhail Grabovski, Thomas Greiss, Dany Heatley, Jochen Hecht, Christoph Schubert, Dennis Seidenberg, Marco Sturm, Alexander Sulzer
DENMARK	6	Mikkel Boedker, Lars Eller, Jannik Hansen, Philip Larsen, Frans Nielsen, Peter Regin
LATVIA	5	Oskars Bartulis, Kaspars Daugavins, Raitis Ivanins, Arturs Kulda, Karlis Skrastins
AUSTRIA	3	Michael Grabner, Andreas Nodl, Thomas Vanek
BELARUS	3	Andrei Kostitsyn, Sergei Kostitsyn, Ruslan Salei
KAZAKHSTAN	3	Nik Antropov, Antonin Khudobin, Evgeny Nabokov
SWITZERLAND	3	Jonas Hiller, Mark Streit, Yannick Weber

UKRAINE	2	Ruslan Fedotenko, Alexei Ponikarovsky
BAHAMAS	1	Andre Deveaux
BRAZIL	1	Robyn Regehr
BRUNEI	1	Craig Adams
FRANCE	1	Cristobal Huet
ITALY	1	Luca Sbisa
JAPAN	1	Ryan O'Marra
LITHUANIA	1	Dainius Zubrus
NORWAY	1	Ole-Kristian Tollefsen
POLAND	1	Wojtek Wolski
SLOVENIA	1	Anze Kopitar
SOUTH KOREA	1	Richard Park
UNITED KINGDOM	1	Owen Nolan

FIRST GAMES PLAYED, 2009–10

Player (NAT)	Team (date)	G Mins	A W-L	P	Pim GA
Cody Almond (CAN)	MIN (Feb. 12)	0	0	0	0
Dean Arsene (CAN)	EDM (Nov. 16)	0	0	0	0
Johan Backlund (SWE)	PHI (Mar. 27)	40:00	L	2	
Oskars Bartulis (LAT)	PHI (Nov. 12)	0	0	0	0
Jamie Benn (CAN)	DAL (Oct. 3)	0	0	0	2
Mario Bliznak (SVK)	VAN (Oct. 30)	0	0	0	0
Andrew Bodnarchuk (CAN)	BOS (Apr. 3)	0	0	0	0
Nick Bonino (USA)	ANA (Mar. 26)	0	0	0	2
Drayson Bowman (USA)	CAR (Jan. 16)	0	0	0	0
Tyler Bozak (CAN)	TOR (Oct. 13)	0	1	1	0
Mike Brodeur (CAN)	OTT (Dec. 19)	60:00	W	1	
Bobby Butler (USA)	OTT (Apr. 1)	0	0	0	0
Mathieu Carle (CAN)	MON (Nov. 3)	0	0	0	2
John Carlson (USA)	WAS (Nov. 20)	0	0	0	0
Marc-Andre Cliché (CAN)	LA (Mar. 2)	0	0	0	0
Grant Clitsome (CAN)	CBJ (Mar. 2)	0	2	2	2
Rich Clune (CAN)	LA (Feb. 11)	0	0	0	0
Matt Corrente (CAN)	NJ (Nov. 21)	0	0	0	0
Logan Couture (CAN)	SJ (Oct. 25)	0	0	0	2
Jared Cowen (CAN)	OTT (Apr. 8)	0	0	0	2
Evgeni Dadonov (RUS)	FLO (Apr. 6)	0	0	0	0
Kaspars Daugavins (LAT)	OTT (Jan. 14)	0	0	0	0
Michael Del Zotto (CAN)	NYR (Oct. 2)	0	0	0	0
Jason Demers (CAN)	SJ (Oct. 1)	0	0	0	0
Guillaume Desbiens (CAN)	VAN (Oct. 11)	0	0	0	2
David Desharnais (CAN)	MTL (Nov. 25)	0	0	0	0
Devan Dubnyk (CAN)	EDM (Nov. 28)	51:35	ND	3	
Mike Duco (CAN)	FLO (Dec. 2)	0	0	0	2
Matt Duchene (CAN)	COL (Oct. 1)	0	1	1	0

Jeremy Duchesne (USA)	PHI (Apr. 1)	16:44	ND	1	
Tyler Eckford (CAN)	NJ (Nov. 19)	0	0	0	2
Corey Elkins (USA)	LA (Dec. 15)	0	0	0	0
Lars Eller (DEN)	STL (Nov. 5)	1	0	1	0
Keaton Ellerby (CAN)	FLO (Jan. 14)	0	0	0	0
Deryk Engelland (CAN)	PIT (Nov. 10)	0	0	0	0
Tyler Ennis (CAN)	BUF (Nov. 14)	1	0	1	0
Jhonas Enroth (SWE)	BUF (Nov. 7)	58:18	L	4	
Justin Falk (CAN)	MIN (Mar. 19)	0	0	0	0
Benn Ferriero (USA)	SJ (Oct. 1)	0	0	0	0
Mark Flood (CAN)	NYI (Mar. 25)	0	0	0	0
Maxime Fortunas (CAN)	DAL (Dec. 19)	0	0	0	0
Cody Franson (CAN)	NAS (Oct. 17)	0	0	0	0
Trevor Frischmon (USA)	CBJ (Mar. 28)	0	0	0	4
Aaron Gagnon (CAN)	DAL (Oct. 16)	0	0	0	0
Matt Gilroy (USA)	NYR (Oct. 2)	0	0	0	0
Michael Grabner (AUT)	VAN (Oct. 16)	0	1	1	0
Carl Gunnarsson (SWE)	TOR (Nov. 14)	0	0	0	0
Jonas Gustavsson (SWE)	TOR (Oct. 3)	38:13	L	3	
Michael Haley (CAN)	NYI (Apr. 10)	0	0	0	5
Zach Hamill (CAN)	BOS (Apr. 11)	0	1	1	0
Victor Hedman (SWE)	TB (Oct. 3)	0	1	1	0
Ilkka Heikkinen (FIN)	NYR (Dec. 5)	0	0	0	0
Shaun Heshka (CAN)	PHO (Nov. 7)	0	0	0	2
Danny Irmen (USA)	MIN (Nov. 18)	0	0	0	0
Brayden Irwin (CAN)	TOR (Apr. 1)	0	0	0	2
Scott Jackson (CAN)	TB (Apr. 11)	0	0	0	0
Chad Johnson (CAN)	NYR (Dec. 30)	40:00	ND	3	
Nick Johnson (CAN)	PIT (Jan. 21)	1	0	1	0
Nazem Kadri (CAN)	TOR (Feb. 8)	0	0	0	0
Tomas Kana (CZE)	CBJ (Mar. 30)	0	0	0	0
Evander Kane (CAN)	ATL (Oct. 3)	0	1	1	0
Erik Karlsson (SWE)	OTT (Oct. 3)	0	1	1	0
Ryan Keller (CAN)	OTT (Nov. 25)	0	0	0	0

Anton Khudobin (KAZ)	MIN (Feb. 4)	9:33	W	0	
Jakub Kindl (CZE)	DET (Dec. 3)	0	0	0	0
Anton Klementyev (RUS)	NYI (Mar. 27)	0	0	0	0
Dustin Kohn (CAN)	NYI (Jan. 21)	0	1	1	0
Chad Kolarik (USA)	CBJ (Apr. 5)	0	0	0	0
Arturs Kulda (LAT)	ATL (Feb. 12)	0	0	0	0
Dmitri Kulikov (RUS)	FLO (Oct. 2)	0	0	0	0
Teemu Laakso (FIN)	NAS (Oct. 3)	0	0	0	0
David Laliberte (CAN)	PHI (Oct. 31)	1	1	2	0
Philip Larsen (DEN)	DAL (Apr. 8)	0	0	0	0
Mark Letestu (CAN)	PIT (Nov. 14)	0	0	0	0
Charles Linglet (CAN)	EDM (Apr. 2)	0	0	0	0
Perttu Lindgren (FIN)	DAL (Oct. 19)	0	0	0	0
Andrei Loktionov (RUS)	LA (Nov. 25)	0	0	0	0
Spencer Machacek (CAN)	ATL (Mar.16)	0	0	0	0
Brad Marchand (CAN)	BOS (Oct. 21)	0	1	1	0
Matthew Martin (CAN)	NYI (Feb. 9)	0	2	2	2
Alec Martinez (USA)	LA (Oct. 3)	0	0	0	0
Jamie McBain (USA)	CAR (Mar. 16)	0	1	1	0
John McCarthy (USA)	SJ (Jan. 9)	0	0	0	0
Colin McDonald (USA)	EDM (Nov. 27)	0	0	0	0
Frazer McLaren (CAN)	SJ (Oct. 3)	0	1	1	0
Adam McQuaid (CAN)	BOS (Dec. 19)	0	0	0	0
Justin Mercier (USA)	COL (Dec. 9)	0	0	0	0
Johan Motin (SWE)	EDM (Mar. 3)	0	0	0	0
Tyler Myers (USA)	BUF (Oct. 3)	0	0	0	0
Maxim Noreau (CAN)	MIN (Apr. 8)	0	0	0	0
Evan Oberg (CAN)	VAN (Jan. 9)	0	0	0	0
Ryan O'Marra (JPN)	EDM (Nov. 10)	0	0	0	0
Ryan O'Reilly (CAN)	COL (Oct. 1)	0	1	1	0
Victor Oreskovich (CAN)	FLO (Oct. 31)	0	0	0	0
Nick Palmieri (USA)	NJ (Jan. 20)	0	1	1	0
Scott Parse (USA)	LA (Oct. 24)	0	1	1	0
Alexander Pechurski (RUS)	PIT (Jan. 16)	35:31	ND	1	

Jeff Penner (CAN)	BOS (Mar. 9)	0	0	0	0
Mathieu Perreault (CAN)	WAS (Nov. 4)	0	2	2	0
Justin Peters (CAN)	CAR (Feb. 6)	59:54	W	1	
Ilkka Pikkarainen (FIN)	NJ (Oct. 5)	0	0	0	2
Alex Plante (CAN)	EDM (Feb. 1)	0	1	1	0
Nate Prosser (USA)	MIN (Apr. 5)	0	1	1	4
Tom Pyatt (CAN)	MTL (Nov. 5)	0	0	0	0
Mika Pyorala (FIN)	PHI (Oct. 2)	0	0	0	0
Dylan Reese (USA)	NYI (Mar. 4)	0	0	0	0
Jay Rosehill (CAN)	TOR (Oct. 1)	0	0	0	5
Alexander Salak (CZE)	FLO (Oct. 9)	18:28	ND	2	
Jerome Samson (CAN)	CAR (Jan. 7)	0	1	1	2
Bobby Sanguinetti (USA)	NYR (Nov. 27)	0	0	0	0
Brayden Schenn (CAN)	LA (Nov. 26)	0	0	0	0
Dan Sexton (USA)	ANA (Dec. 4)	0	0	0	0
MacGregor Sharp (CAN)	ANA (Nov. 19)	0	0	0	0
Sergei Shirokov (RUS)	VAN (Oct. 1)	0	0	0	0
Derek Smith (CAN)	OTT (Feb. 13)	0	0	0	0
Nick Spaling (CAN)	NAS (Dec. 15)	0	1	1	0
Viktor Stalberg (SWE)	TOR (Oct. 1)	0	1	1	0
Ryan Stoa (USA)	COL (Dec. 13)	0	0	0	0
Clayton Stoner (CAN)	MIN (Dec. 17)	0	0	0	0
P.K. Subban (CAN)	MON (Feb. 12)	0	1	1	2
Eric Tangradi (USA)	PIT (Apr. 11)	0	0	0	0
John Tavares (CAN)	NYI (Oct. 3)	1	1	2	0
Andreas Thuresson (SWE)	NAS (Oct. 31)	0	0	0	0
Dustin Tokarski (CAN)	TB (Jan. 16)	20:00	ND	0	
Brock Trotter (CAN)	MON (Feb. 6)	0	0	0	0
James van Riemsdyk (USA)	PHI (Oct. 2)	0	1	1	0
Francis Wathier (CAN)	DAL (Oct. 21)	0	0	0	5
Casey Wellman (USA)	MIN (Mar. 19)	0	1	1	0
Ryan White (CAN)	MON (Nov. 5)	0	1	1	0
Colin Wilson (USA)	NAS (Oct. 12)	0	0	0	0
Kyle Wilson (CAN)	WAS (Dec. 5)	0	2	2	0

Ryan Wilson (CAN)	COL (Oct. 15)	0	0	0	0
James Wright (CAN)	TB (Oct. 3)	0	0	0	0
J.T. Wyman (USA)	MON (Nov. 24)	0	0	0	0
Brandon Yip (CAN)	COL (Dec. 19)	0	0	0	2
Matt Zaba (CAN)	NYR (Jan. 23)	33:43	ND	2	
Steven Zalewski (USA)	SJ (Oct. 12)	0	0	0	0
Vladimir Zharkov (RUS)	NJ (Nov. 28)	0	0	0	0

BY NATION

Canada	75
United States	30
Sweden	9
Russia	7
Finland	5
Czech Republic	3
Latvia	3
Denmark	2
Austria	1
Japan	1
Kazakhstan	1
Slovakia	1
TOTAL	**138**

BY NHL TEAM

Anaheim	3
Atlanta	6
Boston	5
Buffalo	3
Calgary	0
Carolina	4
Columbus	4
Chicago	0

Colorado	7
Dallas	6
Detroit	1
Edmonton	7
Florida	6
Los Angeles	7
Minnesota	8
Montreal	7
Nashville	4
New Jersey	5
NY Islander	7
NY Rangers	6
Ottawa	7
Pittsburgh	5
Philadelphia	6
Phoenix	1
San Jose	6
St. Louis	1
Tampa Bay	4
Toronto	7
Vancouver	5
Washington	3

PLAYER REGISTER, REGULAR SEASON, 2009–10

Skater YEAR	GP	G	A	P	Pim	
Goalie YEAR	GP	W-L-OTL-T	Mins	GA	SO	GAA

Abdelkader, Justin b. Muskegon, Michigan, February 25, 1987

2009–10 DET	50	3	3	6	35	
NHL Totals	54	3	3	6	37	

Adams, Craig b. Seria, Brunei, April 26, 1977

2009–10 PIT	82	0	10	10	72	
NHL Totals	589	37	63	100	455	

Afinogenov, Maxim b. Moscow, Soviet Union (Russia), September 4, 1979

2009–10 ATL	82	24	37	61	46	
NHL Totals	651	158	237	395	486	

Alberts, Andrew b. Minneapolis, Minnesota, June 30, 1981

2009–10 CAR/VAN	76	3	9	12	87	
NHL Totals	339	5	39	44	379	

• traded by Carolina to Vancouver on March 3, 2010, for a 3rd-round draft choice in 2010

Alfredsson, Daniel b. Gothenburg, Sweden, December 11, 1972

2009–10 OTT	70	20	51	71	22	
NHL Totals	1,002	375	617	992	431	

Allen, Bryan b. Kingston, Ontario, August 21, 1980

2009–10 FLO	74	4	9	13	99	
NHL Totals	447	24	63	87	566	

Almond, Cody b. Calgary, Alberta, July 24, 1989

2009–10 MIN	7	1	0	1	9
NHL Totals	7	1	0	1	9

Alzner, Karl b. Burnaby, British Columbia, September 24, 1988

2009–10 WAS	21	0	5	5	8
NHL Totals	51	1	9	10	10

Anderson, Craig b. Park Ridge, Illinois, May 21, 1981

2009–10 COL	71	38–25–0–7	4,235	186	7	2.64
NHL Totals	180	74–68–2–10	10,052	464	14	2.77

Anisimov, Artem b. Yaroslavl, Soviet Union (Russia), May 24, 1988

2009–10 NYR	82	12	16	28	32
NHL Totals	83	12	16	28	32

Antropov, Nik b. Vost, Soviet Union (Kazakhstan), February 18, 1980

2009–10 ATL	76	24	43	67	44
NHL Totals	603	156	215	371	527

Armstrong, Colby b. Lloydminster, Saskatchewan, November 23, 1982

2009–10 ATL	79	15	14	29	61
NHL Totals	360	78	100	178	317

Armstrong, Derek b. Ottawa, Ontario, April 23, 1973

2009–10 STL	6	0	0	0	2
NHL Totals	477	72	149	221	355

Arnott, Jason b. Collingwood, Ontario, October 11, 1974

2009–10 NAS	63	19	27	46	26
NHL Totals	1,099	383	490	873	1,176

Arsene, Dean b. Murrayville, British Columbia, July 20, 1980

2009–10 EDM	13	0	0	0	41
NHL Totals	13	0	0	0	41

Artyukin, Evgeni b. Moscow, Soviet Union (Russia), April 4, 1983

2009–10 ANA/ATL	54	9	7	16	72
NHL Totals	199	19	30	49	313

• traded by Anaheim to Atlanta on March 1, 2010, for Nathan Oystrick and a conditional draft choice in 2011

Asham, Arron b. Portage La Prairie, Manitoba, April 13, 1978

2009–10 PHI	72	10	14	24	126
NHL Totals	648	82	97	179	818

Aucoin, Adrian b. Ottawa, Ontario, July 3, 1973

2009–10 PHO	82	8	20	28	56
NHL Totals	933	116	248	364	683

Aucoin, Keith b. Waltham, Massachusetts, November 6, 1978

2009–10 WAS	9	1	4	5	0
NHL Totals	74	8	18	26	18

Auld, Alexander b. Cold Lake, Alberta, January 7, 1981

2009–10 DAL/NYR	24	9–7–3	1299	64	0	2.96
NHL Totals	207	83–82–2–26	11,592	537	6	2.78

• claimed off waivers by the Rangers from Dallas on February 27, 2010

Avery, Sean b. Pickering, Ontario, April 10, 1980

2009–10 NYR	69	11	20	31	160
NHL Totals	489	84	136	220	1,338

Backes, David b. Blaine, Minnesota, May 1, 1984

2009–10 STL	79	17	31	48	106
NHL Totals	282	71	85	156	407

Backlund, Johan b. Skelleftea, Sweden, July 24, 1981

2009–10 PHI	1	0–1–0–0	40	2	0	3.00
NHL Totals	1	0–1–0–0	40	2	0	3.00

Backlund, Mikael b. Vasteras, Sweden, March 17, 1989

2009–10 CAL	23	1	9	10	6
NHL Totals	24	1	9	10	6

Backstrom, Nicklas b. Gavle, Sweden, November 23, 1987

2009–10 WAS	82	33	68	101	50
NHL Totals	246	69	189	258	120

Backstrom, Niklas b. Helsinki, Finland, February 13, 1978

2009–10 MIN	60	26–23–0–8	3,489	158	2	2.72
NHL Totals	230	119–68–0–30	13,213	521	19	2.37

Bailey, Josh b. Oshawa, Ontario, October 2, 1989

2009–10 NYI	73	16	19	35	18
NHL Totals	141	23	37	60	34

Ballard, Keith b. Baudette, Minnesota, November 26, 1982

2009–10 FLO	82	8	20	28	88
NHL Totals	397	33	116	149	403

Barch, Krys b. Guelph, Ontario, March 26, 1980

2009–10 DAL	63	0	6	6	130
NHL Totals	209	8	15	23	475

Barker, Cam b. Winnipeg, Manitoba, April 4, 1986

2009–10 CHI/MIN	70	5	16	21	68
NHL Totals	219	18	69	87	229

• traded by Chicago to Minnesota on February 12, 2010, for Kim Johnsson and Nick Leddy

Bartulis, Oskars b. Ogre, Soviet Union (Latvia), January 21, 1987

2009–10 PHI	53	1	8	9	28
NHL Totals	53	1	8	9	28

Baumgartner, Nolan b. Calgary, Alberta, March 23, 1976

2009–10 VAN	12	1	1	2	2
NHL Totals	143	7	40	47	69

Beagle, Jay b. Calgary, Alberta, October 16, 1985

2009–10 WAS	7	1	1	2	2
NHL Totals	10	1	1	2	4

Beauchemin, Francois b. Sorel, Quebec, June 4, 1980

2009–10 TOR	82	5	21	26	32
NHL Totals	328	26	90	116	205

Begin, Steve b. Trois-Rivières, Quebec, June 14, 1978

2009–10 BOS	77	5	9	14	53
NHL Totals	486	52	48	100	535

Belak, Wade b. Saskatoon, Saskatchewan, July 3, 1976

2009–10 NAS	39	0	2	2	58
NHL Totals	534	8	25	33	1,245

Belanger, Eric b. Sherbrooke, Quebec, December 16, 1977

2009–10 MIN/WAS	77	15	26	41	32
NHL Totals	634	121	178	299	283

• traded by Minnesota to Washington on March 3, 2010, for a 2nd-round draft choice in 2010

Beleskey, Matt b. Windsor, Ontario, June 7, 1988

2009–10 ANA	60	11	7	18	35
NHL Totals	62	11	7	18	35

Belle, Shawn b. Edmonton, Alberta, January 3, 1985

| 2009–10 MON | 2 | 0 | 0 | 0 | 0 |
| NHL Totals | 11 | 0 | 1 | 1 | 0 |

Benn, Jamie b. Victoria, British Columbia, July 18, 1989

| 2009–10 DAL | 82 | 22 | 19 | 41 | 45 |
| NHL Totals | 82 | 22 | 19 | 41 | 45 |

Bergenheim, Sean b. Helsinki, Finland, February 8, 1984

| 2009–10 NYI | 63 | 10 | 13 | 23 | 45 |
| NHL Totals | 246 | 40 | 40 | 80 | 195 |

Bergeron, Marc-Andre b. St-Louis-de-France, Quebec, October 13, 1980

| 2009–10 MON | 60 | 13 | 21 | 34 | 16 |
| NHL Totals | 399 | 75 | 119 | 194 | 177 |

Bergeron, Patrice b. L'Ancienne-Lorette, Quebec, July 24, 1985

| 2009–10 BOS | 73 | 19 | 33 | 52 | 28 |
| NHL Totals | 376 | 99 | 181 | 280 | 116 |

Bergfors, Niklas b. Sodertalje, Sweden, March 7, 1987

| 2009–10 NJ/ATL | 81 | 21 | 23 | 44 | 10 |
| NHL Totals | 90 | 22 | 23 | 45 | 10 |

• traded by New Jersey to Atlanta on February 4, 2010, with Johnny Oduya, Patrice Cormier and a 1st- and 2nd-round draft choice in 2010 for Ilya Kovalchuk, Anssi Salmela and a 2nd-round draft choice in 2010

Berglund, Patrik b. Vasteras, Sweden, June 2, 1988

| 2009–10 STL | 71 | 13 | 13 | 26 | 16 |
| NHL Totals | 147 | 34 | 39 | 72 | 32 |

Bernier, Jonathan b. Laval, Quebec, August 7, 1988

| 2009–10 LA | 3 | 3–0–0–0 | 185 | 4 | 1 | 1.30 |
| NHL Totals | 7 | 4–3–0–0 | 423 | 20 | 1 | 2.83 |

Bernier, Steve b. Quebec City, Quebec, March 31, 1985

2009–10 VAN	59	11	11	22	21
NHL Totals	317	71	73	144	176

Bertuzzi, Todd b. Sudbury, Ontario, February 2, 1975

2009–10 DET	82	18	26	44	80
NHL Totals	941	273	395	668	1,301

Betts, Blair b. Edmonton, Alberta, February 16, 1980

2009–10 PHI	63	8	10	18	14
NHL Totals	402	36	30	66	110

Bickell, Bryan b. Bowmanville, Ontario, March 9, 1986

2009–10 CHI	16	3	1	4	5
NHL Totals	23	5	1	6	7

Bieksa, Kevin b. Grimsby, Ontario, June 16, 1981

2009–10 VAN	55	3	19	22	85
NHL Totals	281	28	97	125	483

Biron, Martin b. Lac-St-Charles, Quebec, August 15, 1977

2009–10 NYI	29	9–14–0–4	1,634	89	1	3.27
NHL Totals	462	208–176–25–24	26,058	1,142	26	2.63

Bissonnette, Paul b. Welland, Ontario, March 11, 1985

2009–10 PHO	41	3	2	5	117
NHL Totals	56	3	3	6	139

Bitz, Byron b. Saskatoon, Saskatchewan, July 21, 1984

2009–10 BOS/FLO	52	5	6	11	33
NHL Totals	87	9	9	18	51

• traded by Boston to Florida on March 3, 2010, with Craig Weller and a 2nd-round draft choice in 2010 for Dennis Seidenberg and Matt Bartkowski

Blake, Jason b. Moorhead, Minnesota, September 2, 1973

2009–10 TOR/ANA	82	16	25	41	36
NHL Totals	750	190	252	442	408

• traded by Toronto to Anaheim on January 31, 2010, with Vesa Toskala for J-S Giguere

Blake, Rob b. Simcoe, Ontario, December 10, 1969

2009–10 SJ	70	7	23	30	60
NHL Totals	1,270	240	537	777	1,679

Bliznak, Mario b. Trencin, Czechoslovakia (Czech Republic), March 6, 1987

2009–10 VAN	2	0	0	0	0
NHL Totals	2	0	0	0	0

Blunden, Mike b. Toronto, Ontario, December 15, 1986

2009–10 CBJ	40	2	2	4	59
NHL Totals	50	2	2	4	69

Bochenski, Brandon b. Blaine, Minnesota, April 4, 1982

2009–10 TB	28	4	9	13	2
NHL Totals	156	28	40	68	54

Bodie, Troy b. Portage La Prairie, Manitoba, January 25, 1985

2009–10 ANA	44	5	2	7	80
NHL Totals	48	5	2	7	80

Bodnarchuk, Andrew b. Drumheller, Alberta, July 11, 1988

2009–10 BOS	5	0	0	0	2
NHL Totals	5	0	0	0	2

Boedker, Mikkel b. Brondby, Denmark, December 16, 1989

2009–10 PHO	14	1	2	3	0
NHL Totals	92	12	19	31	18

Bogosian, Zach b. Massena, New York, July 15, 1990

2009–10 ATL	81	10	13	23	61
NHL Totals	128	19	23	42	108

Bolduc, Alexandre b. Montreal, Quebec, June 26, 1985

2009–10 VAN	15	0	0	0	13
NHL Totals	22	0	1	1	17

Boll, Jarred b. Crystal Lake, Illinois, May 13, 1986

2009–10 CBJ	68	4	3	7	149
NHL Totals	218	13	18	31	555

Bolland, Dave b. Toronto, Ontario, June 5, 1986

2009–10 CHI	39	6	10	16	28
NHL Totals	160	29	51	80	108

Bonino, Nick b. Hartford, Connecticut, April 20, 1988

2009–10 ANA	9	1	1	2	6
NHL Totals	9	1	1	2	6

Boogaard, Derek b. Saskatoon, Saskatchewan, June 23, 1982

2009–10 MIN	57	0	4	4	105
NHL Totals	255	2	12	14	544

Booth, David b. Detroit, Michigan, November 24, 1984

2009–10 FLO	28	8	8	16	23
NHL Totals	221	64	62	126	99

Borer, Casey b. Minneapolis, Minnesota, July 28, 1985

2009–10 CAR	2	0	0	0	0
NHL Totals	16	1	2	3	9

Bouchard, Pierre-Marc b. Sherbrooke, Quebec, April 27, 1984

2009–10 MIN	1	0	0	0	2
NHL Totals	426	77	190	267	138

Boucher, Brian b. Woonsocket, Rhode Island, January 2, 1977

| 2009–10 PHI | 33 | 9–18–0–3 | 1,742 | 80 | 1 | 2.76 |
| NHL Totals | 280 | 101–121–30–10 | 15,644 | 709 | 17 | 2.72 |

Bouillon, Francis b. New York, New York, October 17, 1975

| 2009–10 NAS | 81 | 3 | 8 | 11 | 50 |
| NHL Totals | 566 | 24 | 89 | 113 | 421 |

Boulton, Eric b. Halifax, Nova Scotia, August 17, 1976

| 2009–10 ATL | 62 | 2 | 6 | 8 | 113 |
| NHL Totals | 480 | 21 | 42 | 63 | 1,063 |

Bourque, Chris b. Boston, Massachusetts, January 29, 1986

| 2009–10 PIT/WAS | 21 | 0 | 3 | 3 | 10 |
| NHL Totals | 33 | 1 | 3 | 4 | 12 |

• claimed off waivers by Washington from Pittsburgh on December 5, 2009

Bourque, Rene b. Lac La Biche, Alberta, December 10, 1981

| 2009–10 CAL | 73 | 27 | 31 | 58 | 88 |
| NHL Totals | 314 | 81 | 92 | 173 | 294 |

Bouwmeester, Jay b. Edmonton, Alberta, September 27, 1983

| 2009–10 CAL | 82 | 3 | 26 | 29 | 48 |
| NHL Totals | 553 | 56 | 176 | 232 | 377 |

Bowman, Drayson b. Grand Rapids, Michigan, March 8, 1989

| 2009–10 CAR | 9 | 2 | 0 | 2 | 4 |
| NHL Totals | 9 | 2 | 0 | 2 | 4 |

Boychuk, Johnny b. Edmonton, Alberta, January 19, 1984

| 2009–10 BOS | 51 | 5 | 10 | 15 | 43 |
| NHL Totals | 56 | 5 | 10 | 15 | 43 |

Boychuk, Zach b. Airdrie, Alberta, October 4, 1989

2009–10 CAR	31	3	6	9	2
NHL Totals	33	3	6	9	2

Boyd, Dustin b. Winnipeg, Manitoba, July 16, 1986

2009–10 CAL/NAS	78	11	13	24	19
NHL Totals	210	31	31	62	39

• traded by Calgary to Nashville on March 3, 2010, for a 4th-round draft choice in 2010

Boyes, Brad b. Mississauga, Ontario, April 17, 1982

2009–10 STL	82	14	28	42	26
NHL Totals	410	133	161	294	133

Boyle, Brian b. Dorchester, Massachusetts, December 18, 1984

2009–10 NYR	71	4	2	6	47
NHL Totals	107	12	4	16	93

Boyle, Dan b. Ottawa, Ontario, July 12, 1976

2009–10 SJ	76	15	43	58	70
NHL Totals	676	107	300	407	460

Boynton, Nick b. Nobleton, Ontario, January 14, 1979

2009–10 ANA/CHI	49	1	7	8	71
NHL Totals	554	33	103	136	822

• traded by Anaheim to Chicago on March 2, 2010 for future considerations

Bozak, Tyler b. Regina, Saskatchewan, March 19, 1986

2009–10 TOR	37	8	19	27	6
NHL Totals	37	8	19	27	6

Bradley, Matt b. Stittsville, Ontario, June 13, 1978

2009–10 WAS	77	10	14	24	47
NHL Totals	569	52	78	130	463

Brashear, Donald b. Bedford, Indiana, January 7, 1972

2009–10 NYR	36	0	1	1	73
NHL Totals	1,025	85	120	205	2,634

Brassard, Derick b. Hull, Quebec, September 22, 1987

2009–10 CBJ	79	9	27	36	48
NHL Totals	127	20	43	63	71

Brent, Tim b. Cambridge, Ontario, March 10, 1984

2009–10 TOR	1	0	0	0	0
NHL Totals	19	1	0	1	8

Brewer, Eric b. Vernon, British Columbia, April 17, 1979

2009–10 STL	59	8	7	15	46
NHL Totals	682	56	138	194	537

Briere, Daniel b. Gatineau, Quebec, October 6, 1977

2009–10 PHI	75	26	27	53	71
NHL Totals	666	230	296	526	530

Brind'Amour, Rod b. Ottawa, Ontario, August 9, 1970

2009–10 CAR	80	9	10	19	36
NHL Totals	1,484	452	732	1,184	1,100

Brodeur, Martin b. Montreal, Quebec, May 6, 1972

2009–10 NJ	77	45–25–0–6	4,499	168	9	2.24
NHL Totals	1,076	602–324–105–29	63,520	2,340	110	2.21

Brodeur, Mike b. Calgary, Alberta, March 30, 1983

2009–10 OTT	3	3–0–0–0	180	3	1	1.00
NHL Totals	3	3–0–0–0	180	3	1	1.00

Brodziak, Kyle b. St. Paul, Alberta, May 25, 1984

2009–10 MIN	82	9	23	32	22
NHL Totals	257	35	56	91	82

Brookbank, Sheldon b. Lanigan, Saskatchewan, October 3, 1980

2009–10 ANA	66	0	9	9	114
NHL Totals	157	1	21	22	265

Brouwer, Troy b. Vancouver, British Columbia, August 17, 1985

2009–10 CHI	78	22	18	40	66
NHL Totals	159	32	35	67	123

Brown, Dustin b. Ithaca, New York, November 4, 1984

2009–10 LA	82	24	32	56	41
NHL Totals	431	113	135	248	310

Brown, Mike b. Northbrook, Illinois, June 24, 1985

2009–10 ANA	75	6	1	7	106
NHL Totals	142	9	3	12	306

Brule, Gilbert b. Edmonton, Alberta, January 1, 1987

2009–10 EDM	65	17	20	37	38
NHL Totals	222	31	41	72	102

Brunette, Andrew b. Sudbury, Ontario, August 24, 1973

2009–10 MIN	82	25	36	61	12
NHL Totals	950	238	422	660	294

Brunnstrom, Fabian b. Jonstorp, Sweden, February 6, 1985

2009–10 DAL	44	2	9	11	10
NHL Totals	99	19	21	40	18

Bryzgalov, Ilya b. Togliatti, Soviet Union (Russia), June 22, 1980

2009–10 PHO	69	42–20–0–6	4,084	156	8	2.29
NHL Totals	258	120–96–0–25	7,225	621	16	2.55

Budaj, Peter b. Banska Bystrica, Czechoslovakia (Slovakia), September 18, 1982

2009–10 COL	15	5–5–0–2	728	32	1	2.64
NHL Totals	197	86–70–0–23	10,872	497	8	2.74

Burish, Adam b. Madison, Wisconsin, January 6, 1983

2009–10 CHI	13	1	3	4	14
NHL Totals	169	11	10	21	323

Burns, Brent b. Ajax, Ontario, March 9, 1985

2009–10 MIN	47	3	17	20	32
NHL Totals	373	38	99	137	227

Burrows, Alex b. Pointe-Claire, Quebec, April 11, 1981

2009–10 VAN	82	35	32	67	121
NHL Totals	370	85	85	170	604

Butler, Bobby b. Marlborough, Massachusetts, April 26, 1987

2009–10 OTT	2	0	0	0	0
NHL Totals	2	0	0	0	0

Butler, Chris b. St. Louis, Missouri, October 27, 1986

2009–10 BUF	59	1	20	21	22
NHL Totals	106	3	24	27	40

Byers, Dane b. Nipawin, Saskatchewan, February 21, 1986

2009–10 NYR	5	1	0	1	31
NHL Totals	6	1	0	1	31

Byfuglien, Dustin b. Minneapolis, Minnesota, March 27, 1985

2009–10 CHI	82	17	17	34	94
NHL Totals	260	55	54	109	268

Calder, Kyle b. Mannville, Alberta, January 5, 1979

2009–10 ANA	14	0	2	2	8
NHL Totals	590	114	180	294	309

Callahan, Joe b. Brockton, Massachusetts, December 20, 1982

2009–10 SJ	1	0	1	1	0
NHL Totals	19	0	3	3	4

Callahan, Ryan b. Rochester, New York, March 21, 1985

2009–10 NYR	77	19	18	37	48
NHL Totals	224	53	43	96	133

Cammalleri, Mike b. Richmond Hill, Ontario, June 8, 1982

2009–10 MON	65	26	24	50	16
NHL Totals	429	158	179	337	230

Campbell, Brian b. Strathroy, Ontario, May 23, 1979

2009–10 CHI	68	7	31	38	18
NHL Totals	561	49	236	285	161

Campbell, Gregory b. London, Ontario, December 17, 1983

2009–10 FLO	60	2	15	17	53
NHL Totals	363	29	56	85	312

Campoli, Chris b. North York (Toronto), Ontario, July 9, 1984

2009–10 OTT	67	4	14	18	16
NHL Totals	320	29	85	114	156

Caputi, Luca b. Toronto, Ontario, October 1, 1988

2009–10 PIT/TOR	23	2	6	8	12
NHL Totals	28	3	6	9	16

• traded by Pittsburgh to Toronto on March 2, 2010, with Martin Skoula for Alexei Ponikarovsky

Carcillo, Daniel b. King City, Ontario, January 28, 1985

2009–10 PHI	76	12	10	22	207
NHL Totals	225	32	35	67	859

Carkner, Matt b. Winchester, Ontario, November 3, 1980

2009–10 OTT	81	2	9	11	190
NHL Totals	83	2	10	12	192

Carle, Mathieu b. Gatineau, Quebec, September 30, 1987

2009–10 MON	3	0	0	0	4
NHL Totals	3	0	0	0	4

Carle, Matt b. Anchorage, Alaska, September 25, 1984

2009–10 PHI	80	6	29	35	16
NHL Totals	307	27	97	124	108

Carlson, John b. Natick, Massachusetts, January 10, 1990

2009–10 WAS	22	1	5	6	8
NHL Totals	22	1	5	6	8

Carson, Brett b. Regina, Saskatchewan, November 29, 1985

2009–10 CAR	54	2	10	12	12
NHL Totals	59	2	10	12	16

Carter, Jeff b. London, Ontario, January 1, 1985

2009–10 PHI	74	33	28	61	38
NHL Totals	381	145	132	277	249

Carter, Ryan b. White Bear Lake, Minnesota, August 3, 1983

2009–10 ANA	38	4	5	9	31
NHL Totals	120	11	15	26	119

Chara, Zdeno b. Trencin, Czechoslovakia (Slovakia), March 18, 1977

2009–10 BOS	80	7	37	44	87
NHL Totals	847	111	252	363	1,297

Cheechoo, Jonathan b. Moose Factory, Ontario, July 15, 1980

2009–10 OTT	61	5	9	14	20
NHL Totals	501	170	135	305	324

Chelios, Chris b. Chicago, Illinois, January 25, 1962

2009–10 ATL	7	0	0	0	0
NHL Totals	1,651	185	763	948	2,891

Chimera, Jason b. Edmonton, Alberta, May 2, 1979

2009–10 CBJ/WAS	78	15	19	34	98
NHL Totals	500	88	101	189	516

• traded by Columbus to Washington on December 28, 2009, for Chris Clark and Milan Jurcina

Chipchura, Kyle b. Westlock, Alberta, February 19, 1986

2009–10 MON/ANA	74	6	6	12	72
NHL Totals	123	10	16	26	87

• traded by Montreal to Anaheim on December 2, 2009, for a 4th-round draft choice in 2011

Chorney, Taylor b. Thunder Bay, Ontario, April 27, 1987

2009–10 EDM	42	0	3	3	12
NHL Totals	44	0	3	3	12

Christensen, Erik b. Edmonton, Alberta, December 17, 1983

2009–10 ANA/NYR	58	8	18	26	26
NHL Totals	275	50	74	124	136

• claimed off waivers by the Rangers from Anaheim on December 2, 2009

Clark, Brett b. Wapella, Saskatchewan, December 23, 1976

2009–10 COL	64	3	17	20	28
NHL Totals	517	34	105	139	259

Clark, Chris b. South Windsor, Connecticut, March 8, 1976

2009–10 WAS/CBJ	74	7	13	20	48
NHL Totals	554	98	101	199	662

• traded by Washington to Columbus on December 28, 2009, with Milan Jurcina for Jason Chimera

Clarkson, David b. Toronto, Ontario, March 31, 1984

2009–10 NJ	46	11	13	24	85
NHL Totals	216	40	42	82	438

Cleary, Daniel b. Carbonear, Newfoundland, December 18, 1978

2009–10 DET	64	15	19	34	29
NHL Totals	678	113	170	283	365

Clemmensen, Scott b. Des Moines, Iowa, July 23, 1977

2009–10 FLO	23	9–8–0–2	1,215	59	1	2.91
NHL Totals	91	42–28–0–7	4,916	219	5	2.67

Cliché, Marc-Andre b. Rouyn-Noranda, Quebec, March 23, 1987

2009–10 LA	1	0	0	0	0
NHL Totals	1	0	0	0	0

Climie, Matt b. Leduc, Alberta, February 11, 1983

2009–10 DAL	1	0–1–0–0	60	5	0	5.00
NHL Totals	4	2–2–0–0	245	14	0	2.43

Clitsome, Grant b. Gloucester, Ontario, April 14, 1985

2009–10 CBJ	11	1	2	3	6
NHL Totals	11	1	2	3	6

Clowe, Ryane b. St. John's, Newfoundland, September 30, 1982

2009–10 SJ	82	19	38	57	131
NHL Totals	244	60	93	153	291

Clune, Rich　b. Toronto, Ontario, April 25, 1987

2009–10 LA	14	0	2	2	26
NHL Totals	14	0	2	2	26

Clutterbuck, Cal　b. Welland, Ontario, November 18, 1987

2009–10 MIN	74	13	8	21	52
NHL Totals	154	24	15	39	128

Coburn, Braydon　b. Calgary, Alberta, February 27, 1985

2009–10 PHI	81	5	14	19	54
NHL Totals	297	24	71	95	275

Cogliano, Andrew　b. Toronto, Ontario, June 14, 1987

2009–10 EDM	82	10	18	28	31
NHL Totals	246	46	65	111	73

Colaiacovo, Carlo　b. Toronto, Ontario, January 27, 1983

2009–10 STL	67	7	25	32	60
NHL Totals	241	22	72	94	146

Cole, Erik　b. Oswego, New York, November 6, 1978

2009–10 CAR	40	11	5	16	29
NHL Totals	538	158	180	338	508

Comeau, Blake　b. Meadow Lake, Saskatchewan, February 18, 1986

2009–10 NYI	61	17	18	35	40
NHL Totals	168	32	43	75	94

Commodore, Mike　b. Fort Saskatchewan, Alberta, November 7, 1979

2009–10 CBJ	57	2	9	11	62
NHL Totals	434	21	77	98	601

Comrie, Mike b. Edmonton, Alberta, September 11, 1980

2009–10 EDM	43	13	8	21	30
NHL Totals	568	167	192	359	425

Conboy, Tim b. Farmington, Minnesota, March 22, 1981

2009–10 CAR	12	0	0	0	24
NHL Totals	59	0	6	6	121

Conklin, Ty b. Anchorage, Alaska, March 30, 1976

2009–10 STL	26	10–10–0–2	1,451	60	4	2.48
NHL Totals	175	83–53–4–12	9,437	403	14	2.56

Conner, Chris b. Westland, Michigan, December 23, 1983

2009–10 PIT	8	2	1	3	0
NHL Totals	79	9	15	24	20

Connolly, Tim b. Syracuse, New York, May 7, 1981

2009–10 BUF	73	17	48	65	28
NHL Totals	559	105	248	353	240

Conroy, Craig b. Potsdam, New York, September 4, 1971

2009–10 CAL	63	3	12	15	25
NHL Totals	991	180	360	540	595

Cooke, Matt b. Belleville, Ontario, September 7, 1978

2009–10 PIT	79	15	15	30	106
NHL Totals	738	114	157	271	859

Corrente, Matt b. Mississauga, Ontario, March 17, 1988

2009–10 NJ	12	0	0	0	24
NHL Totals	12	0	0	0	24

Corvo, Joe b. Oak Park, Illinois, June 20, 1977

| 2009–10 CAR/WAS | 52 | 6 | 12 | 18 | 12 |
| NHL Totals | 486 | 68 | 150 | 218 | 186 |

• traded by Carolina to Washington on March 3, 2010, for Brian Pothier, Oskar Osala and a 2nd-round draft choice in 2011

Cote, Riley b. Winnipeg, Manitoba, March 16, 1982

| 2009–10 PHI | 15 | 0 | 0 | 0 | 24 |
| NHL Totals | 156 | 1 | 6 | 7 | 411 |

Couture, Logan b. Guelph, Ontario, March 28, 1989

| 2009–10 SJ | 25 | 5 | 4 | 9 | 6 |
| NHL Totals | 25 | 5 | 4 | 9 | 6 |

Cowen, Jared b. Saskatoon, Saskatchewan, January 25, 1991

| 2009–10 OTT | 1 | 0 | 0 | 0 | 2 |
| NHL Totals | 1 | 0 | 0 | 0 | 2 |

Craig, Ryan b. Abbotsford, British Columbia, January 6, 1982

| 2009–10 TB | 3 | 0 | 0 | 0 | 5 |
| NHL Totals | 184 | 32 | 31 | 63 | 126 |

Crawford, Corey b. Montreal, Quebec, December 31, 1984

| 2009–10 CHI | 1 | 0-1-0-0 | 59 | 3 | 0 | 3.05 |
| NHL Totals | 8 | 1-3-0-1 | 370 | 16 | 1 | 2.60 |

Crombeen, Brandon b. Denver, Colorado, July 10, 1985

| 2009–10 STL | 79 | 7 | 8 | 15 | 168 |
| NHL Totals | 168 | 19 | 20 | 39 | 355 |

Crosby, Sidney b. Halifax, Nova Scotia, August 7, 1987

| 2009–10 PIT | 81 | 51 | 58 | 109 | 71 |
| NHL Totals | 371 | 183 | 323 | 506 | 356 |

Cullen, Matt b. Virginia, Minnesota, November 2, 1976

2009–10 CAR/OTT	81	16	32	48	34
NHL Totals	880	169	292	461	392

• traded by Carolina to Ottawa on February 12, 2010, for Alexandre Picard and a 2nd-round draft choice in 2010

Cumiskey, Kyle b. Abbotsford, British Columbia, December 2, 1986

2009–10 COL	61	7	13	20	20
NHL Totals	114	8	19	27	38

Curry, John b. Shorewood, Minnesota, February 27, 1984

2009–10 PIT	1	0–1–0–0	24	5	0	12.50
NHL Totals	4	2–2–0–0	174	11	0	3.79

Dadonov, Evgeni b. Chelyabinsk, Soviet Union (Russia), March 12, 1989

2009–10 FLO	4	0	0	0	0
NHL Totals	4	0	0	0	0

D'Agostini, Matt b. Sault Ste. Marie, Ontario, October 23, 1986

2009–10 MON/STL	47	2	2	4	28
NHL Totals	101	14	11	25	46

• traded by Montreal to St. Louis on March 3, 2010, for Aaron Palushaj

Daley, Trevor b. Toronto, Ontario, October 9, 1983

2009–10 DAL	77	6	16	22	25
NHL Totals	416	26	77	103	347

Danis, Yann b. Lafontaine, Quebec, June 21, 1981

2009–10 NJ	12	3–2–0–1	467	16	0	2.06
NHL Totals	49	16–21–0–4	2,540	114	3	2.69

Darche, Mathieu b. Montreal, Quebec, November 26, 1976

2009–10 MON	29	5	5	10	4
NHL Totals	130	13	21	34	30

Datsyuk, Pavel b. Sverdlovsk, Soviet Union (Russia), July 20, 1978

2009–10 DET	80	27	43	70	18
NHL Totals	606	198	394	592	157

Daugavins, Kaspars b. Riga, Soviet Union (Latvia), May 18, 1988

2009–10 OTT	1	0	0	0	0
NHL Totals	1	0	0	0	0

Davis, Patrick b. Sterling, Michigan, December 28, 1986

2009–10 NJ	8	1	0	1	0
NHL Totals	9	1	0	1	0

Davison, Rob b. St. Catharines, Ontario, May 1, 1980

2009–10 NJ	1	0	0	0	0
NHL Totals	219	3	15	18	321

Dawes, Nigel b. Winnipeg, Manitoba, February 9, 1985

2009–10 CAL	66	14	18	32	18
NHL Totals	199	39	44	83	43

Del Zotto, Michael b. Stouffville, Ontario, June 24, 1990

2009–10 NYR	80	9	28	37	32
NHL Totals	80	9	28	37	32

Demers, Jason b. Dorval, Quebec, June 9, 1988

2009–10 SJ	51	4	17	21	21
NHL Totals	51	4	17	21	21

Demitra, Pavol b. Dubnica, Czechoslovakia (Slovakia), November 29, 1974

| 2009–10 VAN | 28 | 3 | 13 | 16 | 0 |
| NHL Totals | 847 | 304 | 464 | 768 | 284 |

Desbiens, Guillaume b. Alma, Quebec, April 20, 1985

| 2009–10 VAN | 1 | 0 | 0 | 0 | 2 |
| NHL Totals | 1 | 0 | 0 | 0 | 2 |

Desharnais, David b. Quebec City, Quebec, September 14, 1986

| 2009–10 MON | 6 | 0 | 1 | 1 | 0 |
| NHL Totals | 6 | 0 | 1 | 1 | 0 |

Deveaux, Andre b. Freeport, Bahamas, February 23, 1984

| 2009–10 TOR | 1 | 0 | 0 | 0 | 0 |
| NHL Totals | 22 | 0 | 1 | 1 | 75 |

DiPietro, Rick b. Winthrop, Massachusetts, September 19, 1981

| 2009–10 NYI | 8 | 2–5–0–0 | 462 | 20 | 1 | 2.60 |
| NHL Totals | 281 | 119–117–8–21 | 16,136 | 749 | 15 | 2.79 |

Doan, Shane b. Halkirk, Alberta, October 10, 1976

| 2009–10 PHO | 82 | 18 | 37 | 55 | 41 |
| NHL Totals | 1,047 | 276 | 402 | 678 | 956 |

Donovan, Shean b. Timmins, Ontario, January 22, 1975

| 2009–10 OTT | 30 | 2 | 3 | 5 | 40 |
| NHL Totals | 951 | 112 | 129 | 241 | 705 |

Dorsett, Derek b. Kindersley, Saskatchewan, December 20, 1986

| 2009–10 CBJ | 51 | 4 | 10 | 14 | 105 |
| NHL Totals | 103 | 8 | 11 | 19 | 255 |

Doughty, Drew b. London, Ontario, December 8, 1989

2009–10 LA	82	16	43	59	54
NHL Totals	163	22	64	86	110

Dowell, Jake b. Eau Claire, Wisconsin, March 4, 1985

2009–10 CHI	3	1	1	2	5
NHL Totals	23	3	2	5	17

Downie, Steve b. Newmarket, Ontario, April 3, 1987

2009–10 TB	79	22	24	46	208
NHL Totals	140	31	33	64	346

Draper, Kris b. Toronto, Ontario, May 24, 1971

2009–10 DET	81	7	15	22	28
NHL Totals	1,110	155	198	353	778

Drewiske, Davis b. Hudson, Wisconsin, November 22, 1984

2009–10 LA	42	1	7	8	14
NHL Totals	59	1	10	11	32

Drouin-Deslauriers, Jeff b. St-Jean-sur-Richelieu, Quebec, May 15, 1984

2009–10 EDM	48	16–28–0–4	2,798	152	3	3.26
NHL Totals	58	20–31–0–4	3,337	182	3	3.27

Drury, Chris b. Trumbull, Connecticut, August 20, 1976

2009–10 NYR	77	14	18	32	31
NHL Totals	868	254	356	610	460

Dubielewicz, Wade b. Invermere, British Columbia, January 30, 1978

2009–10 MIN	3	1–1–0–0	101	5	0	2.97
NHL Totals	43	18–16–1–1	2,195	97	0	2.65

Dubinsky, Brandon b. Anchorage, Alaska, April 29, 1986

2009–10 NYR	69	20	24	44	54
NHL Totals	239	47	78	125	247

Dubnyk, Devan b. Regina, Saskatchewan, May 4, 1986

2009–10 EDM	19	4–10–2	1,075	64	0	3.57
NHL Totals	19	4–10–2	1,075	64	0	3.57

Duchene, Matt b. Haliburton, Ontario, January 16, 1991

2009–10 COL	81	24	31	55	16
NHL Totals	81	24	31	55	16

Duchesne, Jeremy b. Silver Spring, Maryland, October 17, 1986

2009–10 PHI	1	0–0–0	17	1	0	3.53
NHL Totals	1	0–0–0	17	1	0	3.53

Duco, Mike b. Toronto, Ontario, July 8, 1987

2009–10 FLO	10	0	0	0	50
NHL Totals	10	0	0	0	50

Dumont, J-P b. Montreal, Quebec, April 1, 1978

2009–10 NAS	74	17	28	45	20
NHL Totals	752	204	300	504	348

Dupuis, Pascal b. Laval, Quebec, April 7, 1979

2009–10 PIT	81	18	20	38	16
NHL Totals	587	113	127	240	244

Dupuis, Philippe b. Laval, Quebec, April 24, 1985

2009–10 COL	4	0	1	1	2
NHL Totals	12	0	1	1	6

Durno, Chris b. Scarborough (Toronto), Ontario, October 31, 1980

2009–10 COL	41	4	4	8	47
NHL Totals	43	4	4	8	47

Dvorak, Radek b. Tabor, Czechoslovakia (Czech Republic), March 9, 1977

2009–10 FLO	76	14	18	32	20
NHL Totals	1,052	208	326	534	370

Dwyer, Pat b. Spokane, Washington, June 22, 1983

2009–10 CAR	58	7	5	12	6
NHL Totals	71	8	5	13	6

Eager, Ben b. Ottawa, Ontario, January 22, 1984

2009–10 CHI	60	7	9	16	120
NHL Totals	255	27	25	52	621

Earl, Robbie b. Chicago, Illinois, June 2, 1985

2009–10 MIN	32	6	0	6	6
NHL Totals	41	6	1	7	6

Eaton, Mark b. Wilmington, Delaware, May 6, 1977

2009–10 PIT	79	3	13	16	26
NHL Totals	531	23	55	78	220

Eaves, Patrick b. Calgary, Alberta, May 1, 1984

2009–10 DET	65	12	10	22	26
NHL Totals	307	57	55	112	125

Ebbett, Andrew b. Vernon, British Columbia, January 2, 1983

2009–10 ANA/ CHI/MIN	61	9	6	15	8
NHL Totals	112	17	30	47	34

• claimed off waivers by Chicago from Anaheim on October 17, 2009
• claimed off waivers by Minnesota from Chicago on November 21, 2009

Eckford, Tyler b. Vancouver, British Columbia, September 8, 1985

2009–10 NJ	3	0	1	1	4
NHL Totals	3	0	1	1	4

Edler, Alexander b. Stockholm, Sweden, April 21, 1986

2009–10 VAN	76	5	37	42	40
NHL Totals	253	24	78	102	142

Ehrhoff, Christian b. Moers, West Germany (Germany), July 6, 1982

2009–10 VAN	80	14	30	44	42
NHL Totals	421	39	137	176	286

Elias, Patrik b. Trebic, Czechoslovakia (Czech Republic), April 13, 1976

2009–10 NJ	58	19	29	48	40
NHL Totals	880	314	440	754	443

Elkins, Corey b. West Bloomfield, Michigan, February 23, 1985

2009–10 LA	3	1	0	1	0
NHL Totals	3	1	0	1	0

Eller, Lars b. Herlev, Denmark, May 8, 1989

2009–10 STL	7	2	0	2	4
NHL Totals	7	2	0	2	4

Ellerby, Keaton b. Strathmore, Alberta, November 5, 1988

2009–10 FLO	22	0	0	0	2
NHL Totals	22	0	0	0	2

Elliott, Brian b. Newmarket, Ontario, April 9, 1985

2009–10 OTT	59	25–18–0–4	3,038	130	5	2.57
NHL Totals	87	46–26–0–7	4,765	208	6	2.62

Ellis, Dan b. Saskatoon, Saskatchewan, June 19, 1980

2009–10 NAS	31	15–13–1–1	1,715	77	1	2.69
NHL Totals	111	50–42–0–8	5,968	263	10	2.64

Ellis, Matt b. Welland, Ontario, August 31, 1981

2009–10 BUF	72	3	10	13	12
NHL Totals	187	13	20	33	56

Emery, Ray b. Hamilton, Ontario, September 28, 1982

2009–10 PHI	29	16–11–0–1	1,684	74	3	2.64
NHL Totals	163	87–51–0–15	9,103	409	11	2.70

Eminger, Steve b. Woodbridge, Ontario, October 31, 1983

2009–10 ANA	63	4	12	16	30
NHL Totals	346	15	70	85	301

Engelland, Derek b. Edmonton, Alberta, April 3, 1982

2009–10 PIT	9	0	2	2	17
NHL Totals	9	0	2	2	17

Ennis, Tyler b. Edmonton, Alberta, October 6, 1989

2009–10 BUF	10	3	6	9	6
NHL Totals	10	3	6	9	6

Enroth, Jhonas b. Stockholm, Sweden, June 25, 1988

2009–10 BUF	1	0–1–0–0	58	4	0	4.12
NHL Totals	1	0–1–0–0	58	4	0	4.12

Enstrom, Tobias b. Nordingra, Sweden, November 5, 1984

2009–10 ATL	82	6	44	50	30
NHL Totals	246	16	104	120	124

Erat, Martin b. Trebic, Czechoslovakia (Czech Republic), August 28, 1981

2009–10 NAS	74	21	28	49	50
NHL Totals	552	123	229	352	348

Ericsson, Jonathan b. Karlskrona, Sweden, March 2, 1984

2009–10 DET	62	4	9	13	44
NHL Totals	89	6	12	18	63

Eriksson, Anders b. Bollnas, Sweden, January 9, 1975

2009–10 PHO/NYR	20	0	5	5	2
NHL Totals	572	22	154	176	242

• traded by Phoenix to the Rangers on March 3, 2010, for Miika Wiikman and a 7th-round draft choice in 2011

Eriksson, Loui b. Gothenburg, Sweden, July 17, 1985

2009–10 DAL	82	29	42	71	26
NHL Totals	292	85	99	184	86

Ersberg, Erik b. Sala, Sweden, March 8, 1982

2009–10 LA	11	4–3–0–2	551	22	0	2.40
NHL Totals	53	18–19–0–10	2,827	120	2	2.55

Erskine, John b. Kingston, Ontario, June 26, 1980

2009–10 WAS	50	1	5	6	66
NHL Totals	323	7	24	31	630

Exelby, Garnet b. Craik, Saskatchewan, August 16, 1981

2009–10 TOR	51	1	3	4	73
NHL Totals	408	7	43	50	584

Falk, Justin b. Snowflake, Manitoba, October 11, 1988

2009–10 MIN	3	0	0	0	0
NHL Totals	3	0	0	0	0

Fedoruk, Todd b. Redwater, Alberta, February 13, 1979

2009–10 TB	50	3	3	6	54
NHL Totals	545	32	65	97	1,050

Fedotenko, Ruslan   b. Kiev, Soviet Union (Ukraine),
January 18, 1979

2009–10 PIT	80	11	19	30	50
NHL Totals	677	150	158	308	419

Fehr, Eric   b. Winkler, Manitoba, September 7, 1985

2009–10 WAS	69	21	18	39	24
NHL Totals	178	36	37	73	62

Ference, Andrew   b. Edmonton, Alberta, March 17, 1979

2009–10 BOS	51	0	8	8	16
NHL Totals	570	24	117	141	504

Ferriero, Benn   b. Boston, Massachusetts, April 29, 1987

2009–10 SJ	24	2	3	5	8
NHL Totals	24	2	3	5	8

Festerling, Brett   b. Quesnel, British Columbia, March 3, 1986

2009–10 ANA	42	0	3	3	15
NHL Totals	82	0	8	8	33

Fiddler, Vernon   b. Edmonton, Alberta, May 9, 1980

2009–10 PHO	76	8	22	30	46
NHL Totals	381	53	70	123	236

Filatov, Nikita   b. Moscow, Soviet Union (Russia), May 25, 1990

2009–10 CBJ	13	2	0	2	8
NHL Totals	21	6	0	6	8

Filppula, Valtteri   b. Vantaa, Finland, March 20, 1984

2009–10 DET	55	11	24	35	24
NHL Totals	290	52	77	129	116

Finger, Jeff b. Houghton, Michigan, December 18, 1979

2009–10 TOR	39	2	8	10	20
NHL Totals	199	17	40	57	114

Fisher, Mike b. Peterborough, Ontario, June 5, 1980

2009–10 OTT	79	25	28	53	59
NHL Totals	620	153	171	324	521

Fistric, Mark b. Edmonton, Alberta, June 1, 1986

2009–10 DAL	67	1	9	10	69
NHL Totals	140	1	15	16	135

Fleischmann, Tomas b. Koprivnice, Czechoslovakia (Czech Republic), May 16, 1984

2009–10 WAS	69	23	28	51	28
NHL Totals	260	56	72	128	74

Fleury, Marc-Andre b. Sorel, Quebec, November 28, 1984

2009–10 PIT	67	37–21–0–6	3,798	168	1	2.65
NHL Totals	302	148–106–2–30	17,165	808	16	2.82

Flood, Mark b. Charlottetown, Prince Edward Island, September 29, 1984

2009–10 NYI	6	0	1	1	0
NHL Totals	6	0	1	1	0

Foligno, Nick b. Buffalo, New York, October 31, 1987

2009–10 OTT	61	9	17	26	53
NHL Totals	187	32	35	67	132

Foote, Adam b. Toronto, Ontario, July 10, 1971

2009–10 COL	67	0	9	9	64
NHL Totals	1,107	66	234	300	1,501

Fortunus, Maxime b. Longueil, Quebec, July 28, 1983

2009–10 DAL	8	0	0	0	4
NHL Totals	8	0	0	0	4

Foster, Kurtis b. Carp, Ontario, November 24, 1981

2009–10 TB	71	8	34	42	48
NHL Totals	257	29	90	119	203

Franson, Cody b. Salmon Arm, British Columbia, August 8, 1987

2009–10 NAS	61	6	15	21	16
NHL Totals	61	6	15	21	16

Franzen, Johan b. Landsbro, Sweden, December 23, 1979

2009–10 DET	27	10	11	21	22
NHL Totals	319	93	71	164	190

Fraser, Colin b. Sicamous, British Columbia, January 28, 1985

2009–10 CHI	70	7	12	19	44
NHL Totals	157	13	23	36	108

Fraser, Mark b. Ottawa, Ontario, September 29, 1986

2009–10 NJ	61	3	3	6	36
NHL Totals	68	3	3	6	43

Frischmon, Trevor b. Ham Lake, Minnesota, August 5, 1981

2009–10 CBJ	3	0	0	0	4
NHL Totals	3	0	0	0	4

Frolik, Michael b. Kladno, Czechoslovakia (Czech Republic), February 17, 1988

2009–10 FLO	82	21	22	43	43
NHL Totals	161	42	46	88	65

Frolov, Alexander b. Moscow, Soviet Union (Russia),
June 19, 1982

| 2009–10 LA | 81 | 19 | 32 | 51 | 26 |
| NHL Totals | 536 | 168 | 213 | 381 | 210 |

Gaborik, Marian b. Trencin, Czechoslovakia (Slovakia),
February 14, 1982

| 2009–10 NYR | 76 | 42 | 44 | 86 | 37 |
| NHL Totals | 578 | 261 | 262 | 523 | 338 |

Gagne, Simon b. Ste-Foy, Quebec, February 29, 1980

| 2009–10 PHI | 58 | 17 | 23 | 40 | 47 |
| NHL Totals | 664 | 259 | 265 | 524 | 278 |

Gagner, Sam b. London, Ontario, August 10, 1989

| 2009–10 EDM | 68 | 15 | 26 | 41 | 33 |
| NHL Totals | 223 | 44 | 87 | 131 | 107 |

Gagnon, Aaron b. Quesnel, British Columbia, April 24, 1986

| 2009–10 DAL | 2 | 0 | 0 | 0 | 0 |
| NHL Totals | 2 | 0 | 0 | 0 | 0 |

Galiardi, T.J. b. Calgary, Alberta, April 22, 1988

| 2009–10 COL | 70 | 15 | 24 | 39 | 28 |
| NHL Totals | 81 | 18 | 25 | 43 | 34 |

Garon, Mathieu b. Chandler, Quebec, January 9, 1978

| 2009–10 CBJ | 35 | 12–9–0–6 | 1,771 | 83 | 2 | 2.81 |
| NHL Totals | 239 | 106–92–3–16 | 13,009 | 615 | 16 | 2.84 |

Garrison, Jason b. White Rock, British Columbia, November 13, 1984

| 2009–10 FLO | 39 | 2 | 6 | 8 | 23 |
| NHL Totals | 40 | 2 | 6 | 8 | 23 |

Gaustad, Paul b. Fargo, North Dakota, February 3, 1982

2009–10 BUF	65	12	10	22	82
NHL Totals	342	52	81	133	414

Gerbe, Nathan b. Oxford, Michigan, July 24, 1987

2009–10 BUF	10	2	3	5	4
NHL Totals	20	2	4	6	8

Gervais, Bruno b. Longueuil, Quebec, October 3, 1984

2009–10 NYI	71	3	14	17	31
NHL Totals	278	9	53	62	134

Getzlaf, Ryan b. Regina, Saskatchewan, May 10, 1985

2009–10 ANA	66	19	50	69	79
NHL Totals	363	107	232	339	382

Giguere, Jean-Sebastien b. Montreal, Quebec, May 16, 1977

2009–10 ANA/TOR	35	10–15–7	2,023	96	3	2.85
NHL Totals	492	220–184–25–38	28,144	1,180	34	2.52

• traded by Anaheim to Toronto on January 31, 2010, for Vesa Toskala and Jason Blake

Gilbert, Tom b. Minneapolis, Minnesota, January 10, 1983

2009–10 EDM	82	5	26	31	16
NHL Totals	258	24	91	115	62

Gill, Hal b. Concord, Massachusetts, April 6, 1975

2009–10 MON	68	2	9	11	68
NHL Totals	919	33	129	162	868

Gillies, Trevor b. Cambridge, Ontario, January 30, 1979

2009–10 NYI	14	0	1	1	75
NHL Totals	15	0	1	1	96

Gilroy, Matt b. North Bellmore, New York, July 30, 1984

2009–10 NYR	69	4	11	15	23
NHL Totals	69	4	11	15	23

Gionta, Brian b. Rochester, New York, January 18, 1979

2009–10 MON	61	28	18	46	26
NHL Totals	534	180	178	358	253

Giordano, Mark b. Toronto, Ontario, March 10, 1983

2009–10 CAL	82	11	19	30	81
NHL Totals	195	20	45	65	184

Girardi, Daniel b. Welland, Ontario, April 29, 1984

2009–10 NYR	82	6	18	24	53
NHL Totals	280	20	60	80	128

Giroux, Alexandre b. Quebec City, Quebec, June 16, 1981

2009–10 WAS	9	1	2	3	4
NHL Totals	31	4	5	9	16

Giroux, Claude b. Hearst, Ontario, January 12, 1988

2009–10 PHI	82	16	31	47	23
NHL Totals	126	25	49	74	37

Glass, Tanner b. Regina, Saskatchewan, November 29, 1983

2009–10 VAN	67	4	7	11	115
NHL Totals	111	5	8	13	161

Gleason, Tim b. Southfield, Michigan, January 29, 1983

2009–10 CAR	61	5	14	19	78
NHL Totals	393	12	72	84	385

Glencross, Curtis b. Kindersley, Saskatchewan, December 28, 1982

2009–10 CAL	67	15	18	33	58
NHL Totals	212	44	55	99	155

Goc, Marcel b. Calw, West Germany (Germany), August 24, 1983

2009–10 NAS	73	12	18	30	14
NHL Totals	338	32	52	84	90

Godard, Eric b. Vernon, British Columbia, March 7, 1980

2009–10 PIT	45	1	2	3	76
NHL Totals	316	6	9	15	728

Goertzen, Steve b. Stony Plain, Alberta, May 26, 1984

2009–10 CAR	6	0	0	0	5
NHL Totals	68	2	2	4	83

Goligoski, Alex b. Grand Rapids, Minnesota, July 30, 1985

2009–10 PIT	69	8	29	37	22
NHL Totals	117	14	45	59	40

Gomez, Scott b. Anchorage, Alaska, December 23, 1979

2009–10 MON	78	12	47	59	60
NHL Totals	784	160	477	637	518

Gonchar, Sergei b. Chelyabinsk, Soviet Union (Russia),
April 13, 1974

2009–10 PIT	62	11	39	50	49
NHL Totals	991	202	482	684	842

Gordon, Andrew b. Halifax, Nova Scotia, December 13, 1985

2009–10 WAS	2	0	0	0	0
NHL Totals	3	0	0	0	0

Gordon, Boyd b. Unity, Saskatchewan, October 19, 1983

2009–10 WAS	36	4	6	10	12
NHL Totals	303	24	52	76	66

Gorges, Josh b. Kelowna, British Columbia, August 14, 1984

2009–10 MON	82	3	7	10	39
NHL Totals	328	8	44	52	165

Grabner, Michael b. Villach, Austria, October 5, 1987

2009–10 VAN	20	5	6	11	8
NHL Totals	20	5	6	11	8

Grabovski, Mikhail b. Potsdam, East Germany (Germany),
January 31, 1984

2009–10 TOR	59	10	23	35	10
NHL Totals	164	33	59	92	110

Grant, Triston b. Neepawa, Manitoba, February 2, 1984

2009–10 NAS	3	0	0	0	9
NHL Totals	11	0	1	1	19

Grebeshkov, Denis b. Yaroslavl, Soviet Union (Russia),
October 11, 1983

2009–10 EDM/NAS	51	7	14	21	32
NHL Totals	227	17	67	84	112

• traded by Edmonton to Nashville on March 1, 2010, for a 2nd-round draft
choice in 2010

Green, Mike b. Calgary, Alberta, October 12, 1985

2009–10 WAS	75	19	57	76	54
NHL Totals	317	71	149	220	238

Greene, Andy b. Trenton, Michigan, October 30, 1982

2009–10 NJ	78	6	31	37	14
NHL Totals	209	11	51	62	64

Greene, Matt b. Grand Ledge, Michigan, May 13, 1983

2009–10 LA	75	2	7	9	83
NHL Totals	308	5	31	36	399

Greiss, Thomas b. Straubing, West Germany (Germany),
January 29, 1986

2009–10 SJ	16	7–4–1	782	35	0	2.69
NHL Totals	19	7–5–0–2	911	42	0	2.77

Grier, Mike b. Detroit, Michigan, January 5, 1975

2009–10 BUF	73	10	12	22	14
NHL Totals	987	157	210	367	498

Grossman, Nicklas b. Stockholm, Sweden, January 22, 1985

2009–10 DAL	71	0	7	7	32
NHL Totals	222	2	24	26	109

Guenin, Nate b. Sewickley, Pennsylvania, December 10, 1982

2009–10 PIT	2	0	0	0	0
NHL Totals	14	0	2	2	6

Guerin, Bill b. Worcester, Massachusetts, November 9, 1970

2009–10 PIT	78	21	24	45	75
NHL Totals	1,263	429	427	856	1,660

Guite, Ben b. Montreal, Quebec, July 17, 1978

2009–10 NAS	6	0	0	0	4
NHL Totals	175	19	26	45	97

Gunnarsson, Carl b. Orebro, Sweden, November 9, 1986

2009–10 TOR	43	3	12	15	10
NHL Totals	43	3	12	15	10

Gustavsson, Jonas b. Stockholm, Sweden, October 24, 1984

2009–10 TOR	42	16–15–9	2,340	112	1	2.87
NHL Totals	42	16–15–9	2,340	112	1	2.87

Hagman, Niklas b. Espoo, Finland, December 5, 1979

2009–10 TOR/CAL	82	25	19	44	25
NHL Totals	628	127	124	251	182

• traded by Toronto to Calgary on January 31, 2010, with Ian White, Matt Stajan and Jamal Mayers for Dion Phaneuf, Fredrik Sjostrom and Keith Aulie

Hainsey, Ron b. Bolton, Connecticut, March 24, 1981

2009–10 ATL	80	5	21	26	39
NHL Totals	406	31	119	150	214

Halak, Jaroslav b. Bratislava, Czechoslovakia (Slovakia), May 13, 1985

2009–10 MON	45	26–13–0–5	2,630	105	5	2.40
NHL Totals	101	56–34–0–7	5,757	251	9	2.62

Hale, David b. Colorado Springs, Colorado, June 18, 1981

2009–10 TB	39	0	4	4	25
NHL Totals	302	3	21	24	236

Haley, Michael b. Oshawa, Ontario, March 30, 1986

2009–10 NYI	2	0	0	0	9
NHL Totals	2	0	0	0	9

Halischuk, Matt b. Toronto, Ontario, June 1, 1988

2009–10 NJ	20	1	1	2	2
NHL Totals	21	1	2	3	2

Halpern, Jeff b. Potomac, Maryland, May 3, 1976

2009–10 TB/LA	71	9	10	19	39
NHL Totals	720	131	185	316	554

• traded by Tampa Bay to Los Angeles on March 3, 2010, for Teddy Purcell and a 3rd-round draft choice in 2010

Hamhuis, Dan b. Smithers, British Columbia, December 13, 1982

2009–10 NAS	78	5	19	24	49
NHL Totals	483	32	129	161	375

Hamill, Zach b. Vancouver, British Columbia,
September 23, 1988

2009–10 BOS	1	0	1	1	0
NHL Totals	1	0	1	1	0

Hamrlik, Roman b. Zlin, Czechoslovakia (Czech Republic),
April 12, 1974

2009–10 MON	75	6	20	26	56
NHL Totals	1,232	148	442	590	1,285

Handzus, Michal b. Banska Bystrica, Czechoslovakia (Slovakia),
March 11, 1977

2009–10 LA	81	20	22	42	38
NHL Totals	762	160	245	405	428

Hannan, Scott b. Richmond, British Columbia, January 23, 1979

2009–10 COL	81	2	14	16	40
NHL Totals	752	30	144	174	450

Hansen, Jannick b. Herlev, Denmark, March 15, 1986

2009–10 VAN	47	9	6	15	18
NHL Totals	107	15	21	36	57

Hanson, Christian b. Venetia, Pennsylvania, March 10, 1986

2009–10 TOR	31	2	5	7	16
NHL Totals	36	3	6	9	18

Hanzal, Martin b. Pisek, Czechoslovakia (Czech Republic),
February 20, 1987

2009–10 PHO	81	11	22	33	104
NHL Totals	227	30	69	99	172

Harding, Josh b. Regina, Saskatchewan, June 18, 1984

2009–10 MIN	25	9–12–0–0	1,300	66	1	3.05
NHL Totals	83	28–39–0–4	4,286	190	4	2.66

Harrison, Jay b. Oshawa, Ontario, November 3, 1982

2009–10 CAR	38	1	5	6	50
NHL Totals	58	1	7	8	68

Harrold, Peter b. Kirtland Hills, Ohio, June 8, 1983

2009–10 LA	39	1	2	3	8
NHL Totals	145	7	15	22	46

Hartnell, Scott b. Regina, Saskatchewan, April 18, 1982

2009–10 PHI	81	14	30	44	155
NHL Totals	679	161	197	358	1,001

Havlat, Martin b. Mlada Bolslav, Czechoslovakia (Czech Republic), April 19, 1981

2009–10 MIN	73	18	36	54	34
NHL Totals	543	187	263	450	280

Haydar, Darren b. Toronto, Ontario, October 22, 1979

2009–10 COL	1	0	0	0	0
NHL Totals	23	1	7	8	2

Heatley, Dany b. Freiburg, West Germany (Germany), January 21, 1981

2009–10 SJ	82	39	43	82	54
NHL Totals	589	299	326	625	510

Hecht, Jochen b. Mannheim, West Germany (Germany), June 21, 1977

2009–10 BUF	79	21	21	42	35
NHL Totals	697	165	247	412	394

Hedberg, Johan b. Leksand, Sweden, May 3, 1973

2009–10 ATL	47	21–16–0–6	2,632	115	3	2.62
NHL Totals	293	123–114–14–15	16,341	799	14	2.93

Hedman, Victor b. Ornskoldsvik, Sweden, December 18, 1990

2009–10 TB	74	4	16	20	79
NHL Totals	74	4	16	20	79

Heikkinen, Ilkka b. Rauma, Finland, November 13, 1984

2009–10 NYR	7	0	0	0	0
NHL Totals	7	0	0	0	0

Hejda, Jan b. Prague, Czechoslovakia (Czech Republic),
June 18, 1978

2009–10 CBJ	62	3	10	13	36
NHL Totals	264	7	49	56	155

Hejduk, Milan b. Usti-nad-Labem, Czechoslovakia (Czech
Republic), February 14, 1976

2009–10 COL	56	23	21	44	10
NHL Totals	839	335	366	701	284

Helm, Darren b. Winnipeg, Manitoba, January 21, 1987

2009–10 DET	75	11	13	24	18
NHL Totals	98	11	14	25	24

Helminen, Dwight b. Hancock, Michigan, June 22, 1983

2009–10 SJ	4	1	0	1	0
NHL Totals	27	2	1	3	0

Hemsky, Ales b. Pardubice, Czechoslovakia (Czech Republic),
August 13, 1983

2009–10 EDM	22	7	15	22	8
NHL Totals	443	100	253	353	206

Hendricks, Matt b. Blaine, Minnesota, June 17, 1981

2009–10 COL	56	9	7	16	74
NHL Totals	60	9	7	16	87

Hendry, Jordan b. Nokomis, Saskatchewan, February 23, 1984

2009–10 CHI	43	2	6	8	10
NHL Totals	92	3	9	12	36

Hennessy, Josh b. Brockton, Massachusetts, February 7, 1985

2009–10 OTT	4	0	0	0	0
NHL Totals	20	1	0	1	4

Hensick, T.J. b. Lansing, Michigan, December 10, 1985

2009–10 COL	7	1	2	3	0
NHL Totals	90	11	24	35	16

Heshka, Shaun b. Melville, Saskatchewan, July 30, 1985

2009–10 PHO	8	0	2	2	4
NHL Totals	8	0	2	2	4

Higgins, Chris b. Smithtown, New York, June 2, 1983

2009–10 NYR/CAL	67	8	9	17	32
NHL Totals	349	92	76	168	128

• traded by the Rangers to Calgary on February 1, 2010, with Ales Kotalik for Olli Jokinen and Brandon Prust

Hilbert, Andy b. Lansing, Michigan, February 6, 1981

2009–10 MIN	4	0	0	0	2
NHL Totals	307	42	62	104	132

Hillen, Jack b. Portland, Oregon, January 24, 1986

2009–10 NYI	69	3	18	21	44
NHL Totals	111	4	24	28	64

Hiller, Jonas b. Felben Wellhausen, Switzerland, February 12, 1982

2009–10 ANA	59	30–23–0–4	3,358	152	2	2.73
NHL Totals	128	63–45–0–6	7,047	293	6	2.49

Hjalmarsson, Niklas b. Eksjo, Sweden, June 6, 1987

2009–10 CHI	77	2	15	17	20
NHL Totals	111	3	18	21	33

Hnidy, Shane b. Neepawa, Manitoba, November 8, 1975

2009–10 MIN	70	2	12	14	66
NHL Totals	547	16	55	71	631

Hoggan, Jeff b. Hope, British Columbia, February 1, 1978

2009–10 PHO	4	0	0	0	2
NHL Totals	107	2	9	11	76

Holmstrom, Tomas b. Pitea, Sweden, January 23, 1973

2009–10 DET	68	25	20	45	60
NHL Totals	879	214	255	469	667

Horcoff, Shawn b. Trail, British Columbia, September 17, 1978

2009–10 EDM	77	13	23	36	51
NHL Totals	637	133	241	374	417

Hordichuk, Darcy b. Kamsack, Saskatchewan, August 10, 1980

2009–10 VAN	56	1	1	2	142
NHL Totals	431	18	15	33	998

Hornqvist, Patric b. Sollentuna, Sweden, January 1, 1987

2009–10 NAS	80	30	21	51	40
NHL Totals	108	32	26	58	56

Horton, Nathan b. Welland, Ontario, May 29, 1985

2009–10 FLO	65	20	37	57	42
NHL Totals	422	142	153	295	382

Hossa, Marian b. Stara Lubovna, Czechoslovakia (Slovakia), January 12, 1979

2009–10 CHI	57	24	27	51	18
NHL Totals	832	363	407	770	476

Howard, Jimmy b. Syracuse, New York, March 26, 1984

2009–10 DET	63	37–15–0–10	3,740	141	3	2.26
NHL Totals	72	38–20–0–10	4,197	162	3	2.32

Huet, Cristobal b. St-Martin-d'Heres, France, September 3, 1975

2009–10 CHI	48	26–14–0–4	2,731	114	4	2.50
NHL Totals	2.72	129–90–11–21	15,261	625	24	2.46

Hunter, Trent b. Red Deer, Alberta, July 5, 1980

2009–10 NYI	61	11	17	28	18
NHL Totals	442	98	127	225	178

Hunwick, Matt b. Warren, Michigan, May 21, 1985

2009–10 BOS	76	6	8	14	32
NHL Totals	142	12	30	42	67

Huselius, Kristian b. Osterhaninge, Sweden, November 10, 1978

2009–10 CBJ	74	23	40	63	36
NHL Totals	621	176	252	428	244

Huskins, Kent b. Almonte, Ontario, May 4, 1979

2009–10 SJ	82	3	19	22	47
NHL Totals	224	9	41	50	147

Iginla, Jarome b. Edmonton, Alberta, July 1, 1977

2009–10 CAL	82	32	37	69	58
NHL Totals	1,024	441	479	920	726

Irmen, Danny b. Fargo, North Dakota, September 6, 1984

2009–10 MIN	2	0	0	0	0
NHL Totals	2	0	0	0	0

Irwin, Brayden b. Toronto, Ontario, March 24, 1987

2009–10 TOR	2	0	0	0	2
NHL Totals	2	0	0	0	2

Ivanans, Raitis b. Riga, Soviet Union (Latvia), January 1, 1979

2009–10 LA	61	0	0	0	136
NHL Totals	280	12	6	18	564

Jackman, Barret b. Trail, British Columbia, March 5, 1981

2009–10 STL	66	2	15	17	81
NHL Totals	457	19	94	113	729

Jackman, Tim b. Minot, North Dakota, November 14, 1981

2009–10 NYR	54	4	5	9	98
NHL Totals	191	11	17	28	357

Jackson, Scott b. Salmon Arm, British Columbia, February 5, 1987

2009–10 TB	1	0	0	0	0
NHL Totals	1	0	0	0	0

Jacques, Jean-Francois b. Terrebonne, Quebec, April 29, 1985

2009–10 EDM	49	4	7	11	78
NHL Totals	109	5	7	12	122

Jaffray, Jason b. Rimbey, Alberta, June 30, 1981

2009–10 CAL	3	0	0	0	0
NHL Totals	36	4	6	10	33

Janik, Doug b. Agawam, Massachusetts, March 26, 1980

2009–10 DET	13	0	2	2	18
NHL Totals	174	3	15	18	141

Janssen, Cam b. St. Louis, Missouri, April 15, 1984

2009–10 STL	43	0	0	0	190
NHL Totals	206	2	4	6	544

Jeffrey, Dustin b. Sarnia, Ontario, February 27, 1988

2009–10 PIT	1	0	0	0	0
NHL Totals	15	1	2	3	0

Joensuu, Jesse b. Pori, Finland, October 5, 1987

2009–10 NYI	11	1	0	1	4
NHL Totals	18	2	2	4	8

Johnson, Aaron b. Port Hawkesbury, Nova Scotia, April 30, 1983

2009–10 CAL/EDM	41	4	6	10	35
NHL Totals	225	14	32	46	191

• traded by Calgary to Edmonton on March 3, 2010, with a 3rd-round draft choice in either 2010 or 2011 for Steve Staios

Johnson, Brent b. Farmington, Michigan, March 12, 1977

2009–10 PIT	23	10–6–0–1	1,108	51	0	2.76
NHL Totals	270	121–100–13–13	14,870	655	13	2.64

Johnson, Chad b. Calgary, Alberta, June 10, 1986

2009–10 NYR	5	1–2–1	281	11	0	2.35
NHL Totals	5	1–2–1	281	11	0	2.35

Johnson, Erik b. Bloomington, Minnesota, March 21, 1988

2009–10 STL	79	10	29	39	79
NHL Totals	148	15	57	72	107

Johnson, Jack b. Indianapolis, Indiana, January 13, 1987

2009–10 LA	80	8	28	36	48
NHL Totals	200	17	41	58	188

Johnson, Nick b. Calgary, Alberta, December 24, 1985

2009–10 PIT	6	1	1	2	2
NHL Totals	6	1	1	2	2

Johnson, Ryan b. Thunder Bay, Ontario, June 14, 1976

2009–10 VAN	58	1	4	5	12
NHL Totals	667	37	79	116	242

Johnsson, Kim b. Malmo, Sweden, March 16, 1976

2009–10 MIN/CHI	60	7	10	17	30
NHL Totals	739	67	217	284	406

• traded by Minnesota to Chicago on February 12, 2010, with Nick Leddy for Cam Barker

Jokinen, Jussi b. Kalajoki, Finland, April 1, 1983

2009–10 CAR	81	30	35	65	36
NHL Totals	387	84	153	237	130

Jokinen, Olli b. Kuopio, Finland, December 5, 1978

2009–10 CAL/NYR	82	15	35	50	75
NHL Totals	881	252	316	568	869

• traded by Calgary to the Rangers on February 1, 2010, with Brandon Prust for Ales Kotalik and Chris Higgins

Jones, Blair b. Central Butte, Saskatchewan, September 27, 1986

2009–10 TB	14	0	0	0	10
NHL Totals	38	1	2	3	12

Jones, David b. Guelph, Ontario, August 10, 1984

2009–10 COL	23	10	6	16	2
NHL Totals	90	20	15	35	18

Jones, Randy b. Quispamsis, New Brunswick, July 23, 1981

2009–10 LA	48	5	16	21	28
NHL Totals	265	18	72	90	162

Jones, Ryan b. Chatham, Ontario, June 14, 1984

2009–10 NAS/EDM	49	8	4	12	26
NHL Totals	95	15	14	29	48

• claimed off waivers by Edmonton from Nashville on March 3, 2010

Joslin, Derek b. Richmond Hill, Ontario, March 17, 1987

2009–10 SJ	24	0	3	3	12
NHL Totals	36	0	3	3	18

Jovanovski, Ed b. Windsor, Ontario, June 26, 1976

2009–10 PHO	66	10	24	34	55
NHL Totals	969	128	339	467	1,382

Junland, Jonas b. Linkoping, Sweden, November 15, 1987

2009–10 STL	3	0	2	2	0
NHL Totals	4	0	2	2	2

Jurcina, Milan b. Liptovsky Mikulas, Czechoslovakia (Slovakia), June 7, 1983

2009–10 WAS/CBJ	44	1	6	7	24
NHL Totals	319	15	38	53	220

• traded by Washington to Columbus on March 3, 2010, for a conditional 6th-round draft choice in 2010

Kaberle, Tomas b. Rakovnik, Czechoslovakia (Czech Republic), March 2, 1978

2009–10 TOR	82	7	42	49	24
NHL Totals	820	80	402	482	230

Kadri, Nazem b. London, Ontario, October 6, 1990

2009–10 TOR	1	0	0	0	0
NHL Totals	1	0	0	0	0

Kaleta, Patrick b. Buffalo, New York, June 8, 1986

2009–10 BUF	55	10	5	15	89
NHL Totals	153	17	14	31	240

Kalinski, Jon b. Bonnyville, Alberta, May 25, 1987

2009–10 PHI	10	0	2	2	0
NHL Totals	22	1	4	5	0

Kalus, Petr b. Ostrava, Czechoslovakia (Czech Republic), June 29, 1987

2009–10 MIN	2	0	0	0	0
NHL Totals	11	4	1	5	6

Kana, Tomas b. Opava, Czechoslovakia (Czech Republic), November 29, 1987

2009–10 CBJ	6	0	2	2	2
NHL Totals	6	0	2	2	2

Kane, Boyd b. Swift Current, Saskatchewan, April 18, 1978

2009–10 WAS	3	0	0	0	2
NHL Totals	31	0	3	3	39

Kane, Evander b. Vancouver, British Columbia, August 2, 1991

2009–10 ATL	66	14	12	26	62
NHL Totals	66	14	12	26	62

Kane, Patrick b. Buffalo, New York, November 19, 1988

2009–10 CHI	82	30	58	88	20
NHL Totals	244	76	154	230	114

Kariya, Paul b. Vancouver, British Columbia, October 16, 1974

2009–10 STL	75	18	25	43	36
NHL Totals	989	402	587	989	399

Karlsson, Erik b. Landsbro, Sweden, May 31, 1990

2009–10 OTT	60	5	21	26	24
NHL Totals	60	5	21	26	24

Keith, Duncan b. Winnipeg, Manitoba, July 16, 1983

2009–10 CHI	82	14	55	69	51
NHL Totals	404	45	152	197	322

Keller, Ryan b. Saskatoon, Saskatchewan, January 6, 1984

2009–10 OTT	6	0	0	0	0
NHL Totals	6	0	0	0	0

Kelly, Chris b. Toronto, Ontario, November 11, 1980

2009–10 OTT	81	15	17	32	38
NHL Totals	406	63	90	153	222

Kennedy, Tim b. Buffalo, New York, April 30, 1986

2009–10 BUF	78	10	16	26	50
NHL Totals	79	10	16	26	50

Kennedy, Tyler b. Sault Ste. Marie, Ontario, July 15, 1986

2009–10 PIT	64	13	12	25	31
NHL Totals	186	38	41	79	96

Kesler, Ryan b. Detroit, Michigan, August 31, 1984

2009–10 VAN	82	25	50	75	104
NHL Totals	402	90	125	215	379

Kessel, Phil b. Madison, Wisconsin, October 2, 1987

2009–10 TOR	70	30	25	55	21
NHL Totals	292	96	85	181	77

Khabibulin, Nikolai b. Sverdlovsk, Soviet Union (Russia),
January 13, 1973

2009–10 EDM	18	7–9–0–2	1,089	55	0	3.03
NHL Totals	696	306–276–58–26	39,794	1,775	41	2.68

Khudobin, Anton b. Ust-Kamenogorsk, Soviet Union (Russia),
May 7, 1986

2009–10 MIN	2	2–0–0	69	1	0	0.86
NHL Totals	2	2–0–0–0	69	1	0	0.86

Kindl, Jakub b. Sumperk, Czechoslovakia (Czech Republic),
February 10, 1987

2009–10 DET	3	0	0	0	0
NHL Totals	3	0	0	0	0

King, D.J. b. Meadow Lake, Saskatchewan, June 27, 1984

2009–10 STL	12	0	0	0	33
NHL Totals	101	4	5	9	185

Kiprusoff, Miikka b. Turku, Finland, October 26, 1976

2009–10 CAL	73	35–28–0–10	4,235	163	4	2.31
NHL Totals	458	239–153–7–45	26,541	1,079	34	2.44

Klein, Kevin b. Kitchener, Ontario, December 13, 1984

2009–10 NAS	81	1	10	11	27
NHL Totals	162	6	20	26	52

Klementyev, Anton b. Togliatti, Soviet Union (Russia),
March 25, 1990

2009–10 NYI	1	0	0	0	0
NHL Totals	1	0	0	0	0

Klesla, Rostislav b. Novy Jicin, Czechoslovakia (Czech Republic),
March 21, 1982

| 2009–10 CBJ | 26 | 2 | 6 | 8 | 26 |
| NHL Totals | 470 | 38 | 85 | 123 | 482 |

Knuble, Mike b. Toronto, Ontario, July 4, 1972

| 2009–10 WAS | 69 | 29 | 24 | 53 | 59 |
| NHL Totals | 889 | 244 | 238 | 482 | 553 |

Kobasew, Chuck b. Osoyoos, British Columbia, April 17, 1982

| 2009–10 BOS/MIN | 49 | 9 | 6 | 15 | 18 |
| NHL Totals | 410 | 87 | 82 | 169 | 288 |

• traded by Boston to Minnesota on October 18, 2009, for Craig Weller,
  Alexander Fallstrom and a 2nd-round draft choice in 2011

Koci, David b. Prague, Czechoslovakia (Czech Republic),
May 12, 1981

| 2009–10 COL | 43 | 1 | 0 | 1 | 84 |
| NHL Totals | 107 | 2 | 1 | 3 | 381 |

Kohn, Dustin b. Edmonton, Alberta, February 2, 1987

| 2009–10 NYI | 22 | 0 | 4 | 4 | 4 |
| NHL Totals | 22 | 0 | 4 | 4 | 4 |

Koistinen, Ville b. Oulu, Finland, June 17, 1981

| 2009–10 FLO | 17 | 1 | 3 | 4 | 8 |
| NHL Totals | 103 | 8 | 24 | 32 | 40 |

Koivu, Mikko b. Turku, Finland, March 12, 1983

| 2009–10 MIN | 80 | 22 | 49 | 71 | 50 |
| NHL Totals | 362 | 79 | 176 | 255 | 256 |

Koivu, Saku b. Turku, Finland, November 23, 1974

| 2009–10 ANA | 71 | 19 | 33 | 52 | 36 |
| NHL Totals | 863 | 210 | 483 | 693 | 659 |

Kolarik, Chad b. Abington, Pennsylvania, January 26, 1986

2009–10 CBJ	2	0	0	0	0
NHL Totals	2	0	0	0	0

Komisarek, Mike b. Islip Terrace, New York, January 19, 1982

2009–10 TOR	34	0	4	4	40
NHL Totals	395	12	50	62	536

Konopka, Zenon b. Niagara-on-the-Lake, Ontario, January 2, 1981

2009–10 TB	74	2	3	5	265
NHL Totals	113	6	7	13	377

Kopecky, Tomas b. Ilava, Czechoslovakia (Slovakia), February 5, 1982

2009–10 CHI	74	10	11	21	28
NHL Totals	257	22	31	53	141

Kopitar, Anze b. Jesenice, Yugoslavia (Slovenia), August 24, 1987

2009–10 LA	82	34	47	81	16
NHL Totals	318	113	172	285	94

Korpikoski, Lauri b. Turku, Finland, July 28, 1986

2009–10 PHO	71	5	6	11	16
NHL Totals	139	11	14	25	30

Kostitsyn, Andrei b. Novopolosk, Soviet Union (Belarus), February 3, 1985

2009–10 MON	59	15	18	33	32
NHL Totals	245	67	74	141	119

Kostitsyn, Sergei b. Novopolsk, Soviet Union (Belarus), March 20, 1987

2009–10 MON	47	7	11	18	8
NHL Totals	155	24	44	68	123

Kostopoulos, Tom b. Mississauga, Ontario, January 24, 1979

2009–10 CAR	82	8	13	21	106
NHL Totals	458	48	78	126	574

Kotalik, Ales b. Jindrichuv Hradec, Czechoslovakia (Czech Republic), December 23, 1978

2009–10 NYR/CAL	71	11	16	27	67
NHL Totals	516	132	146	278	340

• traded by the Rangers to Calgary on February 1, 2010, with Chris Higgins for Olli Jokinen and Brandon Prust

Kovalchuk, Ilya b. Tver, Soviet Union (Russia), April 15, 1983

2009–10 ATL/NJ	76	41	44	85	53
NHL Totals	621	338	304	642	437

• traded by Atlanta to New Jersey on February 4, 2010, with Anssi Salmela and a 2nd-round draft choice in 2010 for Niclas Bergfors, Johnny Oduya, Patric Cormier and a 1st- and 2nd-round draft choice in 2010

Kovalev, Alexei b. Togliatti, Soviet Union (Russia), February 24, 1973

2009–10 OTT	77	18	31	49	54
NHL Totals	1,228	412	578	990	1,254

Kozlov, Vyacheslav b. Voskresensk, Soviet Union (Russia), May 3, 1972

2009–10 ATL	55	8	18	26	33
NHL Totals	1,182	356	497	853	704

Krajicek, Lukas b. Prostejov, Czechoslovakia (Czech Republic), March 11, 1983

2009–10 TB/PHI	50	1	2	3	35
NHL Totals	328	11	61	72	245

• released by Tampa Bay and signed by Philadelphia as a free agent on February 1, 2010

Krejci, David b. Sternberk, Czechoslovakia (Czech Republic), April 28, 1986

2009–10 BOS	79	17	35	52	26
NHL Totals	223	45	107	152	74

Kreps, Kamil b. Litomerice, Czechoslovakia (Czech Republic), November 18, 1984

2009–10 FLO	76	5	9	14	18
NHL Totals	232	18	42	60	71

Kronwall, Niklas b. Stockholm, Sweden, January 12, 1981

2009–10 DET	48	7	15	22	32
NHL Totals	308	23	121	144	224

Kronwall, Staffan b. Jarfalla, Sweden, September 10, 1982

2009–10 CAL	11	1	2	3	2
NHL Totals	66	1	3	4	23

Kuba, Filip b. Ostrava, Czechoslovakia (Czech Republic), December 29, 1976

2009–10 OTT	53	3	25	28	28
NHL Totals	655	61	214	275	295

Kubina, Pavel b. Celadna, Czechoslovakia (Czech Republic), April 15, 1977

2009–10 ATL	76	6	32	38	66
NHL Totals	822	103	245	348	987

Kulda, Arturs b. Riga, Soviet Union (Latvia), July 25, 1988

2009–10 ATL	4	0	2	2	2
NHL Totals	4	0	2	2	2

Kulemin, Nikolai b. Magnitogorsk, Soviet Union (Russia),
July 14, 1986

2009–10 TOR	78	16	20	36	16
NHL Totals	151	31	36	67	34

Kulikov, Dmitri b. Lipetsk, Soviet Union (Russia),
October 29, 1990

2009–10 FLO	68	3	13	16	32
NHL Totals	68	3	13	16	32

Kunitz, Chris b. Regina, Saskatchewan, September 26, 1979

2009–10 PIT	50	13	19	32	39
NHL Totals	385	101	141	242	354

Laakso, Teemu b. Tuusula, Finland, August 27, 1987

2009–10 NAS	7	0	0	0	2
NHL Totals	7	0	0	0	2

LaBarbera, Jason b. Burnaby, British Columbia, January 18, 1980

2009–10 PHO	17	8–5–0–1	928	33	0	2.13
NHL Totals	124	45–49–0–11	6,436	306	4	2.85

Ladd, Andrew b. Maple Ridge, British Columbia,
December 12, 1985

2009–10 CHI	82	17	21	38	67
NHL Totals	321	63	86	149	180

Laich, Brooks b. Medicine Hat, Alberta, June 23, 1983

2009–10 WAS	78	25	34	59	34
NHL Totals	393	84	105	189	157

Laing, Quintin b. Rosetown, Saskatchewan, June 8, 1979

2009–10 WAS	36	2	2	4	21
NHL Totals	79	3	8	11	31

Laliberte, David b. St. Jean-sur-Richelieu, Quebec,
March 17, 1986

2009–10 PHI	11	2	1	3	6
NHL Totals	11	2	1	3	6

Lalime, Patrick b. St-Bonaventure, Quebec, July 7, 1974

2009–10 BUF	16	4–8–0–2	854	40	0	2.81
NHL Totals	437	200–169–40–16	24,875	1,067	35	2.57

Lang, Robert b. Teplice, Czechoslovakia (Czech Republic),
December 19, 1970

2009–10 PHO	64	9	20	29	28
NHL Totals	989	261	442	703	422

Langenbrunner, Jamie b. Duluth, Minnesota, July 24, 1975

2009–10 NJ	81	19	42	61	44
NHL Totals	965	228	378	606	760

Langkow, Daymond b. Edmonton, Alberta, September 27, 1976

2009–10 CAL	72	14	23	37	30
NHL Totals	1,013	259	382	641	533

Laperriere, Ian b. Montreal, Quebec, January 19, 1974

2009–10 PHI	82	3	17	20	162
NHL Totals	1,083	121	215	336	1,956

Lapierre, Maxim b. St-Léonard, Quebec, March 29, 1985

2009–10 MON	76	7	7	14	61
NHL Totals	255	35	37	72	221

Laraque, Georges b. Montreal, Quebec, December 7, 1976

2009–10 MON	28	1	2	3	28
NHL Totals	695	53	100	153	1,126

Larman, Drew b. Buffalo, New York, May 15, 1985

2009–10 BOS	4	0	0	0	0
NHL Totals	26	2	1	3	4

LaRose, Chad b. Fraser, Michigan, March 27, 1982

2009–10 CAR	56	11	17	28	24
NHL Totals	324	48	65	113	150

Larsen, Philip b. Esbjerg, Denmark, December 7, 1989

2009–10 DAL	2	0	1	1	0
NHL Totals	2	0	1	1	0

Lashoff, Matt b. East Greenbush, New York, September 29, 1986

2009–10 TB	5	0	0	0	21
NHL Totals	63	1	14	15	53

Latendresse, Guillaume b. Ste-Cathérine, Quebec, May 24, 1987

2009–10 MON/MIN	78	27	13	40	16
NHL Totals	287	73	49	122	149

• traded by Montreal to Minnesota on November 23, 2009, for Benoit Pouliot

Leach, Jay b. Syracuse, New York, September 2, 1979

2009–10 MON/SJ	35	1	1	2	25
NHL Totals	63	1	2	3	53

• claimed off waivers by San Jose from Montreal on December 2, 2009

Lebda, Brett b. Buffalo Grove, Illinois, January 15, 1982

2009–10 DET	63	1	7	8	24
NHL Totals	326	18	50	68	201

Lecavalier, Vincent b. Île-Bizard, Quebec, April 21, 1980

2009–10 TB	82	24	46	70	63
NHL Totals	869	326	413	739	624

Leclaire, Pascal b. Repentigny, Quebec, November 7, 1982

2009–10 OTT	34	12–14–0–2	1,745	93	0	3.20
NHL Totals	159	57–69–0–14	8,643	417	10	2.89

Lee, Brian b. Moorhead, Minnesota, March 26, 1987

2009–10 OTT	23	2	1	3	12
NHL Totals	82	4	13	17	49

Lefebvre, Guillaume b. Amos, Quebec, May 7, 1981

2009–10 BOS	1	0	0	0	0
NHL Totals	39	2	4	6	13

Legace, Manny b. Toronto, Ontario, February 4, 1973

2009–10 CAR	28	10–7–0–5	1,472	69	1	2.81
NHL Totals	365	187–99–18–23	20,140	809	24	2.41

Legwand, David b. Detroit, Michigan, August 17, 1980

2009–10 NAS	82	11	27	38	24
NHL Totals	704	152	255	407	374

Lehtinen, Jere b. Espoo, Finland, June 24, 1973

2009–10 DAL	58	4	13	17	8
NHL Totals	875	243	271	514	210

Lehtonen, Kari b. Helsinki, Finland, November 16, 1983

2009–10 DAL	12	6–4–0–0	663	31	0	2.81
NHL Totals	216	100–87–0–17	12,333	590	14	2.87

Lehtonen, Mikko b. Espoo, Finland, April 1, 1987

2009–10 BOS	1	0	0	0	0
NHL Totals	2	0	0	0	0

Leighton, Michael b. Petrolia, Ontario, May 19, 1981

2009–10 CAR/PHI	34	17–9–2	1,799	85	1	2.83
NHL Totals	103	34–40–10–4	5,636	276	4	2.94

• claimed off waivers by Philadelphia form Carolina on December 15, 2009

Leino, Ville b. Savonlinna, Finland, October 6, 1983

2009–10 DET/PHI	55	6	5	11	10
NHL Totals	68	11	9	20	16

• traded by Detroit to Philadelphia on February 6, 2010, for Ole-Kristian Tollefsen and a 5th-round draft choice in 2011

Leopold, Jordan b. Golden Valley, Minnesota, August 3, 1980

2009–10 FLO/PIT	81	11	15	26	28
NHL Totals	436	40	95	135	190

• traded by Florida to Pittsburgh on March 1, 2010, for a 2nd-round draft choice in 2010

Lepisto, Sami b. Espoo, Finland, October 17, 1984

2009–10 PHO	66	1	10	11	60
NHL Totals	80	1	15	16	78

Letang, Kris b. Montreal, Quebec, April 24, 1987

2009–10 PIT	73	3	24	27	51
NHL Totals	217	21	58	79	102

Letestu, Mark b. Elk Point, Alberta, February 4, 1985

2009–10 PIT	10	1	0	1	2
NHL Totals	10	1	0	1	2

Letourneau-Leblond, Pierre-Luc b. Lévis, Quebec, June 4, 1985

2009–10 NJ	27	0	2	2	48
NHL Totals	35	0	3	3	70

Lewis, Trevor b. Salt Lake City, Utah, January 8, 1987

2009–10 LA	5	0	0	0	0
NHL Totals	11	1	2	3	0

Lidstrom, Nicklas b. Vasteras, Sweden, April 28, 1970

2009–10 DET	82	9	40	49	24
NHL Totals	1,412	237	809	1,046	466

Liles, John-Michael b. Zionsville, Indiana, November 25, 1980

2009–10 COL	59	6	25	31	30
NHL Totals	447	62	167	229	183

Lilja, Andreas b. Helsingborg, Sweden, July 13, 1975

2009–10 DET	20	1	1	2	4
NHL Totals	478	15	59	74	501

Lindgren, Perttu b. Tampere, Finland, August 26, 1987

2009–10 DAL	1	0	0	0	0
NHL Totals	1	0	0	0	0

Linglet, Charles b. Montreal, Quebec, June 22, 1982

2009–10 EDM	5	0	0	0	2
NHL Totals	5	0	0	0	2

Lisin, Enver b. Moscow, Soviet Union (Russia), April 22, 1986

2009–10 NYR	57	6	8	14	18
NHL Totals	135	24	18	42	64

Little, Bryan b. Edmonton, Alberta, November 12, 1987

2009–10 ATL	79	13	21	34	20
NHL Totals	206	50	51	101	62

Locke, Corey b. Toronto, Ontario, May 8, 1984

2009–10 NYR	3	0	0	0	0
NHL Totals	4	0	0	0	0

Loktionov, Andrei b. Voskresensk, Soviet Union (Russia),
May 30, 1990

2009–10 LA	1	0	0	0	0
NHL Totals	1	0	0	0	0

Lombardi, Matt b. Montreal, Quebec, March 18, 1982

2009–10 PHO	78	19	34	53	36
NHL Totals	444	89	147	236	275

Lovejoy, Ben b. Concord, New Hampshire, February 20, 1984

2009–10 PIT	12	0	3	3	2
NHL Totals	14	0	3	3	2

Lucic, Milan b. Vancouver, British Columbia, June 7, 1988

2009–10 BOS	50	9	11	20	44
NHL Totals	199	34	55	89	269

Lukowich, Brad b. Cranbrook, British Columbia, August 12, 1976

2009–10 VAN	13	1	1	2	4
NHL Totals	653	23	90	113	369

Lundin, Mike b. Burnsville, Minnesota, September 24, 1984

2009–10 TB	49	3	10	13	18
NHL Totals	155	3	18	21	38

Lundmark, Jamie b. Edmonton, Alberta, January 16, 1981

2009–10 CAL/TOR	36	5	7	12	20
NHL Totals	295	40	59	99	204

• claimed off waivers by Toronto from Calgary on February 13, 2010

Lundqvist, Henrik b. Are, Sweden, March 2, 1982

2009–10 NYR	73	35–27–0–10	4,204	167	4	2.38
NHL Totals	338	177–110–0–44	19,882	771	24	2.33

Luongo, Roberto b. Montreal, Quebec, April 4, 1979

2009–10 VAN	68	40–22–0–4	3,899	167	4	2.57
NHL Totals	612	270–254–33–35	34,938	1,496	51	2.57

Lupul, Joffrey b. Edmonton, Alberta, September 23, 1983

2009–10 ANA	23	10	4	14	18
NHL Totals	395	112	113	225	232

Lydman, Toni b. Lahti, Finland, September 25, 1977

2009–10 BUF	67	4	16	20	30
NHL Totals	660	33	165	198	451

MacArthur, Clarke b. Lloydminster, Alberta, April 6, 1985

2009–10 BUF/ATL	81	16	19	35	49
NHL Totals	208	44	44	88	129

• traded by Buffalo to Atlanta on March 3, 2010, for a 3rd- and 4th-round draft choice in 2010

MacDonald, Andrew b. Judique, Nova Scotia, September 7, 1986

2009–10 NYI	46	1	6	7	20
NHL Totals	49	1	6	7	22

MacDonald, Joey b. Pictou, Nova Scotia, February 7, 1980

2009–10 TOR	6	1–4–0–0	319	17	0	3.20
NHL Totals	72	18–38–0–9	4,058	223	1	3.30

Machacek, Spencer b. Lethbridge, Alberta, October 14, 1988

2009–10	2	0	0	0	0
NHL Totals	2	0	0	0	0

MacIntyre, Steve b. Brock, Saskatchewan, August 8, 1980

2009–10 EDM/FLO	22	0	1	1	24
NHL Totals	44	2	1	3	64

• claimed off waivers by Florida from Edmonton on November 10, 2009

MacKenzie, Derek b. Sudbury, Ontario, June 11, 1981

2009–10 CBJ	18	1	3	4	0
NHL Totals	64	3	5	8	30

Madden, John b. Barrie, Ontario, May 4, 1973

2009–10 CHI	79	10	13	23	12
NHL Totals	791	150	170	320	205

Mair, Adam b. Hamilton, Ontario, February 15, 1979

2009–10 BUF	69	6	8	14	73
NHL Totals	550	37	73	110	784

Malhotra, Manny b. Mississauga, Ontario, May 18, 1980

2009–10 SJ	71	14	19	33	41
NHL Totals	705	90	140	230	385

Malkin, Evgeni b. Magnitogorsk, Soviet Union (Russia), July 31, 1986

2009–10 PIT	67	28	49	77	100
NHL Totals	309	143	238	381	338

Malone, Ryan b. Pittsburgh, Pennsylvania, December 1, 1979

2009–10 TB	69	21	26	47	68
NHL Totals	438	134	127	261	467

Maltby, Kirk b. Guelph, Ontario, December 22, 1972

2009–10 DET	52	4	2	6	32
NHL Totals	1,072	128	132	260	867

Mancari, Mark b. London, Ontario, July 11, 1985

2009–10 BUF	6	1	1	2	4
NHL Totals	16	2	3	5	10

Mara, Paul b. Ridgewood, New Jersey, September 7, 1979

2009–10 MON	42	0	8	8	48
NHL Totals	681	63	184	247	688

Marchand, Brad b. Halifax, Nova Scotia, May 11, 1988

2009–10 BOS	20	0	1	1	20
NHL Totals	20	0	1	1	20

Marchant, Todd b. Buffalo, New York, August 12, 1973

2009–10 ANA	78	9	13	22	32
NHL Totals	1,116	185	305	490	748

Markov, Andrei b. Voskresensk, Soviet Union (Russia), December 20, 1978

2009–10 MON	45	6	28	34	32
NHL Totals	616	80	283	363	357

Marleau, Patrick b. Aneroid, Saskatchewan, September 15, 1979

2009–10 SJ	82	44	39	83	22
NHL Totals	953	320	373	693	325

Martin, Matt b. Windsor, Ontario, May 8, 1989

2009–10 NYI	5	0	2	2	26
NHL Totals	5	0	2	2	26

Martin, Paul b. Minneapolis, Minnesota, March 5, 1981

2009–10 NJ	22	2	9	11	2
NHL Totals	400	26	137	163	114

Martinek, Radek b. Havlickuv Brod, Czechoslovakia (Czech Republic), August 31, 1976

2009–10 NYI	16	2	1	3	12
NHL Totals	389	18	69	87	237

Martinez, Alec b. Rochester Hills, Michigan, July 26, 1987

2009–10 LA	4	0	0	0	2
NHL Totals	4	0	0	0	2

Mason, Chris b. Red Deer, Alberta, April 20, 1976

2009–10 STL	61	30–22–0–8	3,512	148	2	2.53
NHL Totals	253	115–86–1–26	13,859	587	20	2.54

Mason, Steve b. Oakville, Ontario, May 29, 1988

2009–10 CBJ	58	20–26–0–9	3,201	163	5	3.06
NHL Totals	119	53–46–0–16	6,865	303	15	2.65

Matthias, Shawn b. Mississauga, Ontario, February 19, 1988

2009–10 FLO	55	7	9	16	10
NHL Totals	75	9	11	20	14

Mauldin, Greg b. Boston, Massachusetts, June 10, 1982

2009–10 NYI	1	0	0	0	0
NHL Totals	7	0	0	0	4

Maxwell, Ben b. North Vancouver, British Columbia, March 30, 1988

2009–10 MON	13	0	0	0	6
NHL Totals	20	0	0	0	8

May, Brad b. Toronto, Ontario, November 29, 1971

2009–10 DET	40	0	1	1	66
NHL Totals	1,041	127	161	288	2,248

Mayers, Jamal b. Toronto, Ontario, October 24, 1974

2009–10 TOR/CAL	71	3	11	14	131
NHL Totals	737	81	107	188	969

• traded by Toronto to Calgary on January 31, 2010, with Ian White, Matt Stajan and Niklas Hagman for Dion Phaneuf, Fredrik Sjostrom and Keith Aulie

Mayorov, Maxim b. Andizhan, Soviet Union (Russia), March 26, 1989

2009–10 CBJ	4	0	0	0	0
NHL Totals	7	0	0	0	0

McAmmond, Dean b. Grand Cache, Alberta, June 15, 1973

2009–10 NJ	62	8	9	17	40
NHL Totals	996	186	262	448	490

McArdle, Kenndal b. Toronto, Ontario, January 4, 1987

2009–10 FLO	19	1	2	3	29
NHL Totals	22	1	2	3	31

McBain, Jamie b. Edina, Minnesota, February 25, 1988

2009–10 CAR	14	3	7	10	0
NHL Totals	14	3	7	10	0

McCabe, Bryan b. St. Catharines, Ontario, June 8, 1975

2009–10 FLO	82	8	35	43	83
NHL Totals	1,068	138	362	500	1,698

McCarthy, John b. Boston, Massachusetts, August 9, 1986

2009–10 SJ	4	0	0	0	0
NHL Totals	4	0	0	0	0

McClement, Jay b. Kingston, Ontario, March 2, 1983

2009–10 STL	82	11	18	29	22
NHL Totals	393	46	94	140	162

McDonald, Andy b. Strathroy, Ontario, August 25, 1977

2009–10 STL	79	24	33	57	18
NHL Totals	565	145	251	396	236

McDonald, Colin b. New Haven, Connecticut, September 30, 1984

2009–10 EDM	2	1	0	1	0
NHL Totals	2	1	0	1	0

McElhinney, Curtis b. London, Ontario, May 23, 1983

2009–10 CAL/ANA	20	8–5–2	1,023	51	0	2.99
NHL Totals	39	9–13–0–3	1,691	87	0	3.09

• traded by Calgary to Anaheim on March 3, 2010, for Vesa Toskala

McGinn, Jamie b. Fergus, Ontario, August 5, 1988

2009–10 SJ	59	10	3	13	38
NHL Totals	94	14	5	19	40

McGratton, Brian b. Hamilton, Ontario, September 2, 1981

2009–10 CAL	34	1	3	4	86
NHL Totals	182	3	11	14	395

McKee, Jay b. Kingston, Ontario, September 8, 1977

2009–10 PIT	62	1	9	10	54
NHL Totals	802	21	104	125	622

McLaren, Frazer b. Winnipeg, Manitoba, October 29, 1987

2009–10 SJ	23	1	5	6	54
NHL Totals	23	1	5	6	54

McLeod, Cody b. Binscarth, Manitoba, June 26, 1984

2009–10 COL	74	7	11	18	138
NHL Totals	202	26	21	47	420

McQuaid, Adam b. Charlottetown, Prince Edward Island, October 12, 1986

2009–10 BOS	19	1	0	1	21
NHL Totals	19	1	0	1	21

Meech, Derek b. Winnipeg, Manitoba, April 21, 1984

2009–10 DET	49	2	4	6	19
NHL Totals	126	4	12	16	39

Mercier, Justin b. Erie, Pennsylvania, June 25, 1987

2009–10 COL	9	1	1	2	0
NHL Totals	9	1	1	2	0

Meszaros, Andrei b. Povazska Bystrica, Czechoslovakia (Slovakia), October 13, 1985

2009–10 TB	81	6	11	17	50
NHL Totals	379	34	109	143	299

Methot, Marc b. Ottawa, Ontario, June 21, 1985

2009–10 CBJ	60	2	6	8	51
NHL Totals	155	6	23	29	126

Metropolit, Glen b. Toronto, Ontario, June 25, 1974

2009–10 MON	69	16	13	29	24
NHL Totals	407	57	102	159	148

Meyer, Freddy b. Sanbornville, New Hampshire, January 4, 1981

2009–10 NYI	64	4	11	15	40
NHL Totals	266	19	52	71	147

Michalek, Milan b. Jindrichuv Hradec, Czechoslovakia (Czech Republic), December 7, 1984

2009–10 OTT	66	22	12	34	18
NHL Totals	383	113	135	248	202

Michalek, Zbynek b. Jindrichuv Hradec, Czechoslovakia (Czech Republic), December 23, 1982

2009–10 PHO	72	3	14	17	30
NHL Totals	415	27	88	115	192

Miettinen, Antti b. Hameenlinna, Finland, July 3, 1980

2009–10 MIN	79	20	22	42	44
NHL Totals	399	73	104	177	194

Mihalik, Vladimir b. Presov, Czechoslovakia (Czech Republic), January 29, 1987

2009–10 TB	4	0	0	0	2
NHL Totals	15	0	3	3	8

Mikkelson, Brendan b. Regina, Saskatchewan, June 22, 1987

2009–10 ANA	28	0	2	2	14
NHL Totals	62	0	4	4	31

Miller, Drew b. Dover, New Jersey, February 17, 1984

2009–10 TB/DET	80	10	9	19	12
NHL Totals	133	16	18	34	35

• claimed off waivers by Detroit from Tampa Bay on November 11, 2009

Miller, Ryan b. East Lansing, Michigan, July 17, 1980

2009–10 BUF	69	41–18–0–8	4,047	150	5	2.22
NHL Totals	333	187–104–1–33	19,609	839	17	2.57

Minard, Chris b. Thompson, Manitoba, November 18, 1981

2009–10 EDM	5	0	1	1	0
NHL Totals	40	2	4	6	14

Mitchell, John b. Waterloo, Ontario, January 22, 1985

2009–10 TOR	60	6	17	23	31
NHL Totals	136	18	34	52	64

Mitchell, Torrey b. Montreal, Quebec, January 30, 1985

2009–10 SJ	56	2	9	11	27
NHL Totals	138	12	19	31	77

Mitchell, Willie b. Port McNeill, British Columbia, April 23, 1977

2009–10 VAN	48	4	8	12	48
NHL Totals	586	19	100	119	621

Modano, Mike b. Livonia, Michigan, June 7, 1970

2009–10 DAL	59	14	16	30	22
NHL Totals	1,459	557	802	1,359	922

Modin, Fredrik b. Sundsvall, Sweden, October 8, 1974

2009–10 CBJ/LA	44	5	6	11	26
NHL Totals	858	225	227	452	439

• traded by Columbus to Los Angeles on March 3, 2010, for a conditional 7th-round draft choice in 2010

Moen, Travis b. Stewart Valley, Saskatchewan, April 6, 1982

2009–10 MON	81	8	11	19	57
NHL Totals	443	37	38	75	544

Moller, Oscar b. Stockholm, Sweden, January 22, 1989

2009–10 LA	34	4	3	7	4
NHL Totals	74	11	11	22	20

Montador, Steve b. Vancouver, British Columbia, December 21, 1979

2009–10 BUF	78	5	18	23	75
NHL Totals	446	23	68	91	679

Moore, Dominic b. Thornhill, Ontario, August 3, 1980

2009–10 FLO/MON	69	10	18	28	43
NHL Totals	374	45	83	128	243

• traded by Florida to Montreal on February 11, 2010, for a 7th-round draft choice in 2011

Moore, Greg b. Lisbon, Maine, March 26, 1984

2009–10 CBJ	4	0	0	0	0
NHL Totals	10	0	0	0	0

Moreau, Ethan b. Huntsville, Ontario, September 22, 1975

2009–10 EDM	76	9	9	18	62
NHL Totals	863	145	132	277	1,066

Morris, Derek b. Edmonton, Alberta, August 24, 1978

2009–10 BOS/PHO	76	4	25	29	37
NHL Totals	869	80	289	369	831

• traded by Boston to Phoenix on March 3, 2010, for a conditional draft choice in 2011

Morrison, Brendan b. Pitt Meadows, British Columbia, August 15, 1975

2009–10 WAS	74	12	30	42	40
NHL Totals	829	187	360	547	424

Morrisonn, Shaone b. Vancouver, British Columbia, December 23, 1982

2009–10 WAS	68	1	11	12	68
NHL Totals	418	10	60	70	423

Morrow, Brenden b. Carlyle, Saskatchewan, January 16, 1979

2009–10 DAL	76	20	26	46	69
NHL Totals	667	193	242	435	1,012

Moss, David b. Dearborn, Michigan, December 28, 1981

2009–10 CAL	64	8	9	17	20
NHL Totals	227	42	43	85	64

Motin, Johan b. Karlskoga, Sweden, October 10, 1989

2009–10 EDM	1	0	0	0	0
NHL Totals	1	0	0	0	0

Mottau, Mike b. Quincy, Massachusetts, March 19, 1978

2009–10 NJ	79	2	16	18	41
NHL Totals	258	7	46	53	137

Moulson, Matt b. North York (Toronto), Ontario, November 1, 1983

2009–10 NYI	82	30	18	48	16
NHL Totals	111	36	22	58	22

Mueller, Peter b. Bloomington, Minnesota, April 14, 1988

2009–10 PHO/COL	69	13	24	37	16
NHL Totals	222	48	79	127	72

- traded by Phoenix to Colorado with Kevin Porter on March 3, 2010, for Wojtek Wolski

Murphy, Cory b. Kanata, Ontario, February 13, 1978

2009–10 NJ	12	2	1	3	2
NHL Totals	91	9	27	36	38

Murray, Andrew b. Selkirk, Manitoba, November 6, 1981

2009–10 CBJ	46	5	2	7	6
NHL Totals	152	19	9	28	28

Murray, Doug b. Bromma, Sweden, March 12, 1980

2009–10 SJ	79	4	13	17	66
NHL Totals	289	5	33	38	260

Myers, Tyler b. Houston, Texas, February 1, 190

2009–10 BUF	82	11	37	48	32
NHL Totals	82	11	37	48	32

Nabokov, Evgeni b. Ust-Kamenogorsk, Soviet Union (Kazakhstan), July 25, 1975

2009–10 SJ	71	44–16–0–10	4,194	170	3	2.43
NHL Totals	563	293–178–29–37	32,491	1,294	50	2.39

Nash, Rick b. Brampton, Ontario, June 16, 1984

2009–10 CBJ	76	33	34	67	58
NHL Totals	517	227	195	422	494

Neal, James b. Oshawa, Ontario, September 3, 1987

2009–10 DAL	78	27	28	55	64
NHL Totals	155	51	41	92	115

Neil, Chris b. Markdale, Ontario, June 18, 1979

2009–10 OTT	68	10	12	22	175
NHL Totals	579	71	85	156	1,473

Neuvirth, Michal b. Usti nad Labem, Czechoslovakia (Czech Republic), March 23, 1988

2009–10 WAS	17	9–4–0–0	872	40	0	2.75
NHL Totals	22	11–5–0–0	1,092	51	0	2.80

Newbury, Kris b. Brampton, Ontario, February 19, 1982

2009–10 DET	4	1	0	1	4
NHL Totals	48	4	3	7	64

Nichol, Scott b. Edmonton, Alberta, December 31, 1974

2009–10 SJ	79	4	15	19	72
NHL Totals	496	48	63	111	758

Niedermayer, Rob b. Cassiar, British Columbia, December 28, 1974

2009–10 NJ	71	10	12	22	45
NHL Totals	1,082	181	269	450	882

Niedermayer, Scott b. Edmonton, Alberta, August 31, 1973

2009–10 ANA	80	10	38	48	38
NHL Totals	1,263	172	568	740	784

Nielsen, Frans b. Herning, Denmark, April 24, 1984

2009–10 NYI	76	12	26	42	6
NHL Totals	166	24	52	76	24

Niemi, Antti b. Vantaa, Finland, August 29, 1983

2009–10 CHI	39	26–7–0–4	2,190	82	7	2.25
NHL Totals	42	27–8–0–5	2,332	90	7	2.32

Niittymaki, Antero b. Turku, Finland, June 18, 1980

2009–10 TB	49	21–18–0–5	2,657	127	1	2.87
NHL Totals	210	83–79–0–28	11,699	581	5	2.98

Nilsson, Robert b. Calgary, Alberta, January 10, 1985

2009–10 EDM	60	11	16	27	12
NHL Totals	252	37	81	118	90

Niskanen, Matt b. Virginia, Minnesota, December 6, 1986

2009–10 DAL	74	3	12	15	18
NHL Totals	232	16	60	76	106

Nodl, Andreas b. Vienna, Austria, February 28, 1987

2009–10 PHI	10	0	1	1	0
NHL Totals	48	1	4	5	2

Nokelainen, Petteri b. Imatra, Finland, January 16, 1986

2009–10 ANA/PHO	67	5	8	13	27
NHL Totals	189	17	17	34	66

• traded by Anaheim to Phoenix on March 3, 2010, for a 6th-round draft choice in 2010

Nolan, Owen b. Belfast, Ireland, February 12, 1972

2009–10 MIN	73	16	17	33	40
NHL Totals	1,200	422	463	885	1,793

Noreau, Maxim b. Montreal, Quebec, May 14, 1987

2009–10 MIN	1	0	0	0	0
NHL Totals	1	0	0	0	0

Nystrom, Eric b. Syosset, New York, February 14, 1983

2009–10 CAL	82	11	8	19	54
NHL Totals	204	19	20	39	191

Oberg, Evan b. Forestburg, Alberta, February 16, 1988

2009–10 VAN	2	0	0	0	0
NHL Totals	2	0	0	0	0

O'Brien, Shane b. Port Hope, Ontario, August 9, 1983

2009–10 VAN	65	2	6	8	79
NHL Totals	299	8	47	55	605

O'Byrne, Ryan b. Victoria, British Columbia, July 19, 1984

2009–10 MON	55	1	3	4	74
NHL Totals	125	2	14	16	177

O'Donnell, Sean b. Ottawa, Ontario, October 13, 1971

2009–10 LA	78	3	12	15	70
NHL Totals	1,092	30	174	204	1,699

Oduya, John b. Stockholm, Sweden, October 1, 1981

2009–10 NJ/ATL	67	3	10	13	30
NHL Totals	300	18	61	79	167

• traded by New Jersey to Atlanta on February 24, 2010, with Niklas Bergfors, Patrice Cormier and a 1st- and 2nd-round draft choice in 2010 for Ilya Kovalchuk, Anssi Salmela and a 2nd-round draft choice in 2010

Ohlund, Mattias b. Pitea, Sweden, September 9, 1976

2009–10 TB	67	0	13	13	59
NHL Totals	837	93	245	338	815

Okposo, Kyle b. St. Paul, Minnesota, April 16, 1988

2009–10 NYI	80	19	33	52	34
NHL Totals	154	39	57	96	72

Olesz, Rostislav b. Bilovec, Czechoslovakia (Czech Republic), October 10, 1985

2009–10 FLO	78	14	15	29	28
NHL Totals	305	51	64	115	104

Olvecky, Peter b. Trencin, Czechoslovakia (Slovakia), October 11, 1985

2009–10 NAS	1	0	0	0	0
NHL Totals	32	2	5	7	12

O'Marra, Ryan b. Tokyo, Japan, June 9, 1987

2009–10 EDM	3	0	1	1	0
NHL Totals	3	0	1	1	0

O'Neill, Wes b. Windsor, Ontario, March 3, 1986

2009–10 COL	2	0	0	0	2
NHL Totals	5	0	0	0	6

O'Reilly, Cal b. Toronto, Ontario, September 30, 1986

2009–10 NAS	31	2	9	11	4
NHL Totals	42	5	11	16	6

O'Reilly, Ryan b. Clinton, Ontario, February 7, 1991

2009–10 COL	81	8	18	26	18
NHL Totals	81	8	18	26	18

Oreskovich, Victor b. Whitby, Ontario, August 15, 1986

2009–10 FLO	50	2	4	6	26
NHL Totals	50	2	4	6	26

Orpik, Brooks b. San Francisco, California, September 26, 1980

2009–10 PIT	73	2	23	25	64
NHL Totals	449	8	72	80	529

Orr, Colton b. Winnipeg, Manitoba, March 3, 1982

2009–10 TOR	82	4	2	6	239
NHL Totals	327	8	9	17	788

Ortmeyer, Jed b. Omaha, Nebraska, September 3, 1978

2009–10 SJ	76	8	11	19	37
NHL Totals	306	21	30	51	145

Osala, Oskar b. Vaasa, Finland, December 26, 1987

2009–10 CAR	1	0	0	0	0
NHL Totals	3	0	0	0	0

Osgood, Chris b. Peace River, Alberta, November 26, 1972

2009–10 DET	23	7–9–0–4	1,252	63	1	3.02
NHL Totals	733	396–213–66–21	41,934	1,739	50	2.49

Oshie, T.J. b. Mt. Vernon, Washington, December 23, 1986

2009–10 STL	76	18	30	38	36
NHL Totals	133	32	55	87	66

O'Sullivan, Patrick b. Winston-Salem, North Carolina, February 1, 1985

2009–10 EDM	73	11	23	34	32
NHL Totals	280	54	95	149	110

Ott, Steve b. Summerside, Prince Edward Island, August 19, 1982

2009–10 DAL	73	22	14	36	153
NHL Totals	410	62	87	149	831

Ovechkin, Alexander b. Moscow, Soviet Union (Russia), September 17, 1985

2009–10 WAS	72	50	59	109	89
NHL Totals	396	269	260	529	305

Oystrick, Nathan b. Regina, Saskatchewan, December 17, 1982

2009–10 ANA	3	0	0	0	2
NHL Totals	56	4	8	12	52

Pacioretty, Max b. New Canaan, Connecticut, November 20, 1988

2009–10 MON	52	3	11	14	20
NHL Totals	86	6	19	25	47

Paetsch, Nathan b. Leroy, Saskatchewan, March 30, 1983

2009–10 BUF/CBJ	21	1	1	2	12
NHL Totals	167	7	35	42	114

• traded by Buffalo to Columbus on March 3, 2010, with a 2nd-round draft choice in 2010 for Raffi Torres

Pahlsson, Samuel b. Ornskoldsvik, Sweden, December 17, 1977

2009–10 CBJ	79	3	13	16	32
NHL Totals	636	57	105	162	292

Paille, Daniel b. Welland, Ontario, April 15, 1984

2009–10 BUF/BOS	76	10	10	20	12
NHL Totals	269	45	51	96	66

• traded by Buffalo to Boston on October 20, 2009, for a 3rd-round and conditional draft choice in 2010

Palmieri, Nick b. Utica, New York, July 12, 1989

2009–10 NJ	6	0	1	1	0
NHL Totals	6	0	1	1	0

Pandolfo, Jay b. Winchester, Massachusetts, December 27, 1974

| 2009–10 NJ | 52 | 4 | 5 | 9 | 6 |
| NHL Totals | 819 | 99 | 124 | 223 | 154 |

Pardy, Adam b. Bonavista, Newfoundland, March 29, 1984

| 2009–10 CAL | 57 | 2 | 7 | 9 | 48 |
| NHL Totals | 117 | 3 | 16 | 19 | 117 |

Parent, Ryan b. Prince Albert, Saskatchewan, March 17, 1987

| 2009–10 PHI | 48 | 1 | 2 | 3 | 20 |
| NHL Totals | 102 | 1 | 6 | 7 | 36 |

Parenteau, P-A b. Hull, Quebec, March 24, 1983

| 2009–10 NYR | 22 | 3 | 5 | 8 | 4 |
| NHL Totals | 27 | 3 | 6 | 9 | 6 |

Parise, Zach b. Minneapolis, Minnesota, July 28, 1984

| 2009–10 NJ | 81 | 38 | 44 | 82 | 32 |
| NHL Totals | 407 | 160 | 175 | 335 | 139 |

Park, Richard b. Seoul, South Korea, May 27, 1976

| 2009–10 NYI | 81 | 9 | 22 | 31 | 28 |
| NHL Totals | 684 | 95 | 132 | 227 | 254 |

Parrish, Mark b. Edina, Minnesota, February 2, 1977

| 2009–10 TB | 16 | 0 | 2 | 2 | 4 |
| NHL Totals | 720 | 216 | 171 | 387 | 246 |

Parros, George b. Washington, Pennsylvania, December 29, 1979

| 2009–10 ANA | 4 | 0 | 4 | 4 | 136 |
| NHL Totals | 289 | 13 | 12 | 25 | 694 |

Parse, Scott b. Portage, Michigan, September 5, 1984

| 2009–10 LA | 59 | 11 | 13 | 24 | 22 |
| NHL Totals | 59 | 11 | 13 | 24 | 22 |

Pavelec, Ondrej b. Kladno, Czechoslovakia (Czech Republic), August 31, 1987

| 2009–10 ATL | 42 | 14–18–0–7 | 2,317 | 127 | 2 | 3.29 |
| NHL Totals | 61 | 20–28–0–7 | 3,264 | 181 | 2 | 3.33 |

Pavelski, Joe b. Plover, Wisconsin, July 11, 1984

| 2009–10 SJ | 67 | 25 | 26 | 51 | 26 |
| NHL Totals | 275 | 83 | 95 | 178 | 118 |

Pechurski, Alexander b. Magnitogorsk, Soviet Union (Russia), June 4, 1990

| 2009–10 PIT | 1 | 0–0–0 | 36 | 1 | 0 | 1.69 |
| NHL Totals | 1 | 0–0–0 | 36 | 1 | 0 | 1.69 |

Peckham, Theo b. Richmond Hill, Ontario, November 10, 1987

| 2009–10 EDM | 15 | 0 | 1 | 1 | 43 |
| NHL Totals | 31 | 0 | 1 | 1 | 104 |

Pelley, Rod b. Kitimat, British Columbia, September 1, 1984

| 2009–10 NJ | 63 | 2 | 8 | 10 | 40 |
| NHL Totals | 130 | 4 | 12 | 16 | 59 |

Peltier, Derek b. Plymouth, Minnesota, March 14, 1985

| 2009–10 COL | 3 | 0 | 0 | 0 | 0 |
| NHL Totals | 14 | 0 | 0 | 0 | 2 |

Penner, Dustin b. Winkler, Manitoba, September 28, 1982

| 2009–10 EDM | 82 | 32 | 31 | 63 | 38 |
| NHL Totals | 343 | 105 | 94 | 199 | 216 |

Penner, Jeff b. Steinbach, Manitoba, April 13, 1987

| 2009–10 BOS | 2 | 0 | 0 | 0 | 0 |
| NHL Totals | 2 | 0 | 0 | 0 | 0 |

Perrault, Joel b. Montreal, Quebec, April 6, 1983

2009–10 PHO	2	1	0	1	0
NHL Totals	89	12	14	26	68

Perreault, Mathieu b. Drummondville, Quebec, January 5, 1988

2009–10 WAS	21	4	5	9	6
NHL Totals	21	4	5	9	6

Perron, David b. Sherbrooke, Quebec, May 28, 1988

2009–10 STL	82	20	27	47	60
NHL Totals	225	48	76	124	148

Perry, Corey b. Peterborough, Ontario, May 16, 1985

2009–10 ANA	82	27	49	76	111
NHL Totals	368	118	153	271	433

Peters, Andrew b. St. Catharines, Ontario, May 5, 1980

2009–10 NJ	29	0	0	0	93
NHL Totals	229	4	3	7	650

Peters, Justin b. Blyth, Ontario, August 30, 1986

2009–10 CAR	9	6–3–0	488	23	0	2.83
NHL Totals	9	6–3–0	488	23	0	2.83

Peters, Warren b. Saskatoon, Saskatchewan, July 10, 1982

2009–10 DAL	11	1	0	1	2
NHL Totals	27	2	0	2	14

Petersen, Toby b. Minneapolis, Minnesota, October 27, 1978

2009–10 DAL	78	9	6	15	6
NHL Totals	298	29	41	70	36

Pettinger, Matt b. Edmonton, Alberta, October 22, 1980

2009–10 VAN	9	1	2	3	6
NHL Totals	422	65	58	123	210

Peverley, Rich b. Guelph, Ontario, July 8, 1982

2009–10 ATL	82	22	33	55	36
NHL Totals	194	42	68	110	77

Phaneuf, Dion b. Edmonton, Alberta, April 10, 1985

2009–10 CAL/TOR	81	12	20	32	83
NHL Totals	404	77	161	238	556

• traded by Calgary to Toronto on January 31, 2010, with Fredrik Sjostrom and Keith Aulie for Matt Stajan, Ian White, Niklas Hagman and Jamal Mayers

Phillips, Chris b. Calgary, Alberta, March 9, 1978

2009–10 OTT	82	8	16	24	45
NHL Totals	863	59	169	228	623

Picard, Alexandre b. Les Saules, Quebec, October 9, 1985

2009–10 CBJ	9	0	0	0	10
NHL Totals	67	0	2	2	58

Picard, Alexandre b. Gatineau, Quebec, July 5, 1985

2009–10 OTT/CAR	54	4	11	15	26
NHL Totals	193	16	41	57	65

• traded by Ottawa to Carolina on February 12, 2010, with a 2nd-round draft choice for Matt Cullen

Pietrangelo, Alex b. King City, Ontario, January 18, 1990

2009–10 STL	9	1	1	2	6
NHL Totals	17	1	2	3	8

Pikkarainen, Ilkka b. Sonkajarvi, Finland, April 19, 1981

2009–10 NJ	31	1	3	4	10
NHL Totals	31	1	3	4	10

Pisani, Fernando b. Edmonton, Alberta, December 27, 1976

2009–10 EDM	40	4	4	8	10
NHL Totals	402	80	73	153	190

Pitkanen, Joni b. Oulu, Finland, September 19, 1983

2009–10 CAR	71	6	40	46	72
NHL Totals	411	46	175	221	396

Plante, Alex b. Brandon, Manitoba, May 9, 1989

2009–10 EDM	4	0	1	1	2
NHL Totals	4	0	1	1	2

Plekanec, Tomas b. Kladno, Czechoslovakia (Czech Republic), October 31, 1982

2009–10 MON	82	25	45	70	50
NHL Totals	393	103	151	254	214

Polak, Roman b. Ostrava, Czechoslovakia (Czech Republic), April 28, 1986

2009–10 STL	78	4	17	21	59
NHL Totals	172	5	32	37	110

Pominville, Jason b. Repentigny, Quebec, November 30, 1982

2009–10 BUF	82	24	38	62	22
NHL Totals	386	123	183	306	112

Ponikarovsky, Alexei b. Kiev, Soviet Union (Ukraine), April 9, 1980

2009–10 TOR/PIT	77	21	29	50	61
NHL Totals	493	116	150	266	335

• traded by Toronto to Pittsburgh on March 2, 2010, for Luca Caputi and Martin Skoula

Popovic, Mark b. Stoney Creek, Ontario, October 11, 1982

2009–10 ATL	37	2	2	4	10
NHL Totals	81	2	5	7	20

Porter, Kevin b. Detroit, Michigan, March 12, 1986

2009–10 PHO/COL	20	2	1	3	0
NHL Totals	54	7	6	13	4

• traded by Phoenix to Colorado on March 3, 2010, with Peter Mueller for Wojtek Wolski

Pothier, Brian b. New Bedford, Massachusetts, April 15, 1977

2009–10 WAS/CAR	61	5	10	15	21
NHL Totals	362	26	92	118	202

• traded by Washington to Carolina on March 3, 2010, with Oskar Osala and a 2nd-round draft choice in 2011 for Joe Corvo

Poti, Tom b. Worcester, Massachusetts, March 22, 1977

2009–10 WAS	70	4	20	24	42
NHL Totals	787	67	251	318	578

Potter, Corey b. Lansing, Michigan, January 5, 1984

2009–10 NYR	3	0	0	0	2
NHL Totals	8	1	1	2	2

Potulny, Ryan b. Grand Forks, North Dakota, September 5, 1984

2009–10 EDM	64	15	17	32	28
NHL Totals	116	22	27	49	54

Pouliot, Benoit b. Alfred, Ontario, September 29, 1986

2009–10 MIN/MON	53	17	11	28	43
NHL Totals	104	24	18	42	61

• traded by Minnesota to Montreal on November 23, 2009, for Guillaume Latendresse

Pouliot, Marc-Antoine b. Quebec City, Quebec, May 22, 1985

2009–10 EDM	35	7	7	14	21
NHL Totals	176	21	32	53	74

Powe, Darroll b. Saskatoon, Saskatchewan, June 22, 1985

2009–10 PHI	63	9	6	15	54
NHL Totals	123	15	11	26	89

Preissing, Tom b. Rosemount, Minnesota, December 3, 1978

2009–10 COL	4	0	1	1	0
NHL Totals	326	31	101	132	78

Price, Carey b. Vancouver, British Columbia, August 16, 1987

2009–10 MON	41	13–20–0–5	2,358	109	0	2.77
NHL Totals	134	60–48–0–18	7,807	355	4	2.73

Primeau, Wayne b. Scarborough (Toronto), Ontario, June 4, 1976

2009–10 TOR	59	3	5	8	35
NHL Totals	774	69	125	194	789

Pronger, Chris b. Dryden, Ontario, October 10, 1974

2009–10 PHI	82	10	45	55	79
NHL Totals	1,104	152	509	661	1,536

Prospal, Vaclav b. Ceske Budejovice, Czechoslovakia (Czech Republic), February 17, 1975

2009–10 NYR	75	20	38	58	32
NHL Totals	949	218	439	657	505

Prosser, Nate b. Elk River, Minnesota, May 7, 1986

2009–10 MIN	3	0	1	1	8
NHL Totals	3	0	1	1	8

Prucha, Petr b. Chrudim, Czechoslovakia (Czech Republic), September 14, 1982

2009–10 PHO	79	13	9	22	23
NHL Totals	335	78	67	145	129

Prust, Brandon b. London, Ontario, March 16, 1984

| 2009–10 CAL/NYR | 69 | 5 | 9 | 14 | 163 |
| NHL Totals | 115 | 6 | 11 | 17 | 296 |

• traded by Calgary to the Rangers on February 1, 2010, with Olli Jokinen for Ales Kotalik and Chris Higgins

Purcell, Teddy b. St. John's, Newfoundland, September 8, 1985

| 2009–10 LA/TB | 60 | 6 | 9 | 15 | 10 |
| NHL Totals | 110 | 11 | 23 | 34 | 14 |

• traded by Los Angeles to Tampa Bay on March 3, 2010, with a 3rd-round draft choice in 2010 for Jeff Halpern

Pyatt, Taylor b. Thunder Bay, Ontario, August 19, 1981

| 2009–10 PHO | 74 | 12 | 11 | 23 | 39 |
| NHL Totals | 606 | 103 | 111 | 214 | 354 |

Pyatt, Tom b. Thunder Bay, Ontario, February 14, 1987

| 2009–10 MON | 40 | 2 | 3 | 5 | 10 |
| NHL Totals | 40 | 2 | 3 | 5 | 10 |

Pyorala, Mika b. Oulu, Finland, July 13, 1981

| 2009–10 PHI | 36 | 2 | 2 | 4 | 10 |
| NHL Totals | 36 | 2 | 2 | 4 | 10 |

Quick, Jonathan b. Milford, Connecticut, January 21, 1986

| 2009–10 LA | 72 | 39–24–0–7 | 4,258 | 180 | 4 | 2.54 |
| NHL Totals | 119 | 61–44–0–9 | 6,894 | 292 | 8 | 2.54 |

Quincey, Kyle b. Kitchener, Ontario, August 12, 1985

| 2009–10 COL | 79 | 6 | 23 | 29 | 76 |
| NHL Totals | 164 | 11 | 57 | 68 | 143 |

Rafalski, Brian b. Dearborn, Michigan, September 28, 1973

| 2009–10 DET | 78 | 8 | 34 | 42 | 26 |
| NHL Totals | 770 | 75 | 392 | 467 | 260 |

Ranger, Paul b. Whitby, Ontario, September 12, 1984

2009–10 TB	8	1	1	2	6
NHL Totals	270	18	74	92	218

Rask, Tuukka b. Savonlinna, Finland, March 10, 1987

2009–10 BOS	45	22–12–0–5	2,562	84	5	1.97
NHL Totals	50	25–13–0–6	2,807	94	6	2.10

Raycroft, Andrew b. Belleville, Ontario, May 4, 1980

2009–10 VAN	21	9–5–0–1	967	39	1	2.42
NHL Totals	251	103–101–10–17	13,815	661	7	2.87

Raymond, Mason b. Cochrane, Alberta, September 17, 1985

2009–10 VAN	82	25	28	53	48
NHL Totals	203	45	52	97	74

Reasoner, Marty b. Honeoye Falls, New York, February 26, 1977

2009–10 ATL	80	4	13	17	24
NHL Totals	624	82	141	223	319

Recchi, Mark b. Kamloops, British Columbia, February 1, 1968

2009–10 BOS	81	18	25	43	34
NHL Totals	1,571	563	922	1,485	998

Rechlicz, Joel b. Brookfield, Wisconsin, June 14, 1987

2009–10 NYR	6	0	0	0	27
NHL Totals	23	0	1	1	95

Redden, Wade b. Lloydminster, Saskatchewan, June 12, 1977

2009–10 NYR	75	2	12	14	27
NHL Totals	994	106	344	450	654

Reddox, Liam b. East York (Toronto), Ontario, January 27, 1986

2009–10 EDM	9	0	2	2	4
NHL Totals	56	5	9	14	14

Reese, Dylan b. Pittsburgh, Pennsylvania, August 29, 1984

2009–10 NYI	19	2	2	4	14
NHL Totals	19	2	2	4	14

Regehr, Robyn b. Recife, Brazil, April 19, 1980

2009–10 CAL	81	2	15	17	80
NHL Totals	747	27	119	146	744

Regin, Peter b. Herning, Denmark, April 16, 1986

2009–10 OTT	75	13	16	29	20
NHL Totals	86	14	17	31	22

Reinprecht, Steve b. Edmonton, Alberta, May 7, 1976

2009–10 FLO	82	16	22	38	18
NHL Totals	634	136	236	372	180

Repik, Michal b. Vlasim, Czechoslovakia (Czech Republic), December 31, 1988

2009–10 FLO	19	3	2	5	6
NHL Totals	24	5	2	7	8

Ribeiro, Mike b. Montreal, Quebec, February 10, 1980

2009–10 DAL	66	19	34	53	38
NHL Totals	581	136	290	426	250

Richards, Brad b. Murray Harbour, Prince Edward Island, May 2, 1980

2009–10 DAL	80	24	67	91	14
NHL Totals	700	192	447	639	153

Richards, Mike b. Kenora, Ontario, February 11, 1985

2009–10 PHI	82	31	31	62	79
NHL Totals	372	110	173	283	335

Richardson, Brad b. Belleville, Ontario, February 4, 1985

2009–10 LA	81	11	16	27	37
NHL Totals	248	30	42	72	96

Rinne, Pekka b. Kempele, Finland, November 3, 1982

2009–10 NAS	58	32–16–0–5	3,246	137	7	2.53
NHL Totals	113	62–32–0–9	6,337	260	14	2.46

Ritola, Mattias b. Borlange, Sweden, March 14, 1987

2009–10 DET	5	0	0	0	0
NHL Totals	7	0	1	1	0

Rivet, Craig b. North Bay, Ontario, September 13, 1974

2009–10 BUF	78	1	14	15	100
NHL Totals	886	48	185	233	1,136

Robidas, Stephane b. Sherbrooke, Quebec, March 3, 1977

2009–10 DAL	82	10	31	41	70
NHL Totals	643	40	136	176	488

Rodney, Bryan b. London, Ontario, April 22, 1984

2009–10 CAR	22	1	10	11	8
NHL Totals	30	1	12	13	10

Roloson, Dwayne b. Simcoe, Ontario, October 12, 1969

2009–10 NYI	50	23–18–0–7	2,897	145	1	3.00
NHL Totals	512	190–216–42–32	28,999	1,286	24	2.66

Rolston, Brian b. Flint, Michigan, February 21, 1973

2009–10 NJ	80	20	17	37	22
NHL Totals	1,121	321	382	703	424

Rome, Aaron b. Nesbitt, Manitoba, September 27, 1983

2009–10 VAN	49	0	4	4	24
NHL Totals	75	1	6	7	57

Rosehill, Jay b. Olds, Alberta, July 16, 1985

2009–10 TOR	15	1	1	2	67
NHL Totals	15	1	1	2	67

Ross, Jared b. Huntsville, Alabama, September 18, 1982

2009–10 PHI	3	0	0	0	0
NHL Totals	13	0	0	0	2

Roy, Derek b. Ottawa, Ontario, May 4, 1983

2009–10 BUF	80	26	43	69	48
NHL Totals	434	134	214	348	261

Roy, Mathieu b. St. Georges, Quebec, August 10, 1983

2009–10 CBJ	31	0	10	10	17
NHL Totals	61	2	11	13	74

Rozsival, Michal b. Vlasim, Czechoslovakia (Czech Republic), September 3, 1978

2009–10 NYR	82	3	20	23	78
NHL Totals	637	57	169	226	513

Rupp, Mike b. Cleveland, Ohio, January 13, 1980

2009–10 PIT	81	13	6	19	120
NHL Totals	416	40	32	72	532

Russell, Kris b. Caroline, Alberta, May 2, 1987

2009–10 CBJ	70	7	15	22	32
NHL Totals	203	11	42	53	74

Ruutu, Jarkko b. Vantaa, Finland, August 23, 1975

2009–10 OTT	82	12	14	26	121
NHL Totals	579	55	75	130	981

Ruutu, Tuomo b. Vantaa, Finland, February 16, 1983

2009–10 CAR	54	14	21	35	50
NHL Totals	378	92	116	208	404

Ryan, Bobby b. Cherry Hill, New Jersey, March 17, 1987

2009–10 ANA	81	35	29	64	81
NHL Totals	168	71	60	131	120

Ryder, Michael b. St. John's, Newfoundland, March 31, 1980

2009–10 BOS	82	18	15	33	35
NHL Totals	470	144	149	293	217

Rypien, Rick b. Coleman, Alberta, May 16, 1984

2009–10 VAN	69	4	4	8	126
NHL Totals	110	9	6	15	195

Salak, Alexander b. Strakonice, Czechoslovakia (Czech Republic), January 5, 1987

2009–10 FLO	2	0–1–0	67	6	0	5.41
NHL Totals	2	0–1–0	67	6	0	5.41

Salei, Ruslan b. Minsk, Soviet Union (Belarus), November 2, 1974

2009–10 COL	14	1	5	6	10
NHL Totals	842	43	151	194	1,017

Salmela, Anssi b. Tampere, Finland, August 13, 1984

2009–10 ATL/NJ	38	2	6	8	22
NHL Totals	64	3	11	14	30

• traded by Atlanta to New Jersey on February 4, 2010, with Ilya Kovalchuk and a 2nd-round draft choice in 2010 for Niklas Bergfors, Johnny Oduya, Patrice Cormier and a 1st- and 2nd-round draft choice in 2010

Salo, Sami b. Turku, Finland, September 2, 1974

2009–10 VAN	68	9	19	28	18
NHL Totals	665	81	192	273	228

Salvador, Bryce b. Brandon, Manitoba, February 11, 1976

2009–10 NJ	79	4	10	14	57
NHL Totals	610	23	70	93	559

Samson, Jerome b. Greenfield Park, Quebec, September 4, 1987

2009–10 CAR	7	0	2	2	10
NHL Totals	7	0	2	2	10

Samsonov, Sergei b. Moscow, Soviet Union (Russia),
October 27, 1978

2009–10 CAR	72	14	15	29	32
NHL Totals	810	222	309	531	195

Samuelsson, Mikael b. Mariefred, Sweden, December 23, 1976

2009–10 VAN	74	30	23	53	64
NHL Totals	540	116	145	261	308

Sanguinetti, Bobby b. Trenton, New Jersey, February 29, 1988

2009–10 NYR	5	0	0	0	4
NHL Totals	5	0	0	0	4

Santorelli, Mike b. Vancouver, British Columbia, December 14, 1985

2009–10 NAS	25	2	1	3	8
NHL Totals	32	2	1	3	10

Sarich, Cory b. Saskatoon, Saskatchewan, August 16, 1978

2009–10 CAL	57	1	5	6	58
NHL Totals	749	15	107	122	894

Satan, Miroslav b. Topolcany, Czechoslovakia (Slovakia),
October 22, 1974

2009–10 BOS	38	9	5	14	12
NHL Totals	1,050	363	372	735	464

Sauer, Kurt b. St. Cloud, Minnesota, January 16, 1981

2009–10 PHO	1	0	0	0	0
NHL Totals	357	5	28	33	250

Savard, Marc b. Ottawa, Ontario, July 17, 1977

2009–10 BOS	41	10	23	33	14
NHL Totals	782	205	491	696	708

Sawada, Raymond b. Richmond, British Columbia,
February 19, 1985

2009–10 DAL	5	0	0	0	0
NHL Totals	10	1	0	1	0

Sbisa, Luca b. Ozieri, Italy, January 30, 1990

2009–10 ANA	8	0	0	0	6
NHL Totals	47	0	7	7	42

Scatchard, Dave b. Hinton, Alberta, February 20, 1976

2009–10 NAS	16	3	2	5	17
NHL Totals	651	128	140	268	1,034

Schenn, Brayden b. Saskatoon, Saskatchewan, August 22, 1991

2009–10 LA	1	0	0	0	0
NHL Totals	1	0	0	0	0

Schenn, Luke b. Saskatoon, Saskatchewan, November 2, 1989

2009–10 TOR	79	5	12	17	50
NHL Totals	149	7	24	31	121

Schlemko, David b. Edmonton, Alberta, May 7, 1987

2009–10 PHO	17	1	4	5	8
NHL Totals	20	1	5	6	8

Schneider, Cory b. Marblehead, Massachusetts, March 18, 1986

2009–10 VAN	2	0–1–0–0	79	5	0	3.80
NHL Totals	10	2–5–0–1	434	25	0	3.46

Schneider, Mathieu b. New York, New York, June 12, 1969

2009–10 VAN/PHO	25	2	7	9	16
NHL Totals	1,289	223	520	743	1,245

• traded by Vancouver to Phoenix on March 3, 2010, for Sean Zimmerman and a 6th-round draft choice in 2010

Schremp, Rob b. Syracuse, New York, July 1, 1986

2009–10 NYI	44	7	18	25	8
NHL Totals	51	7	21	28	10

Schubert, Christoph b. Munich, West Germany (Germany), February 5, 1982

2009–10 ATL	47	2	5	7	69
NHL Totals	315	25	47	72	263

Schultz, Jeff b. Calgary, Alberta, February 25, 1986

2009–10 WAS	73	3	20	23	32
NHL Totals	247	9	47	56	97

Schultz, Nick b. Strasbourg, Saskatchewan, August 25, 1982

2009–10 MIN	80	1	19	20	43
NHL Totals	607	22	86	108	254

Scott, John b. St. Catharines, Ontario, September 26, 1982

2009–10 MIN	51	1	1	2	90
NHL Totals	71	1	2	3	111

Scuderi, Rob b. Syosset, New York, December 30, 1978

2009–10 LA	73	0	11	11	21
NHL Totals	373	3	47	50	133

Seabrook, Brent b. Richmond, British Columbia, April 20, 1985

2009–10 CHI	78	4	26	30	59
NHL Totals	392	30	114	144	375

Sedin, Daniel b. Ornskoldsvik, Sweden, September 26, 1980

2009–10 VAN	63	29	56	85	28
NHL Totals	705	208	339	547	292

Sedin, Henrik b. Ornskoldsvik, Sweden, September 26, 1980

2009–10 VAN	82	29	83	112	48
NHL Totals	728	138	434	572	418

Segal, Brandon b. Richmond, British Columbia, July 12, 1983

2009–10 LA/DAL	44	6	6	12	38
NHL Totals	46	6	6	12	38

• claimed off waivers by Dallas from Los Angeles on February 11, 2010

Seidenberg, Dennis b. Schwenningen, West Germany (Germany), July 18, 1981

2009–10 FLO/BOS	79	4	28	32	39
NHL Totals	374	18	98	116	152

• traded by Florida to Boston on March 3, 2010, with Matthew Bartkowski for Craig Weller, Byron Bitz and a 2nd-round draft choice in 2010

Sekera, Andrej b. Bojnice, Czechoslovakia (Slovakia), June 8, 1986

2009–10 BUF	49	4	7	11	6
NHL Totals	157	9	29	38	46

Selanne, Teemu b. Helsinki, Finland, July 3, 1970

2009–10 ANA	54	27	21	48	16
NHL Totals	1,186	606	654	1,260	521

Semin, Alexander b. Krasnoyarsk, Soviet Union (Russia),
March 3, 1984

2009–10 WAS	73	40	44	84	66
NHL Totals	327	148	152	300	323

Sestito, Tim b. Rome, New York, August 28, 1984

2009–10 NJ	9	0	1	1	2
NHL Totals	10	0	1	1	2

Sestito, Tom b. Rome, New York, September 28, 1987

2009–10 CBJ	3	0	0	0	7
NHL Totals	4	0	0	0	24

Setoguchi, Devin b. Taber, Alberta, January 1, 1987

2009–10 SJ	70	20	16	36	19
NHL Totals	195	62	56	118	52

Sexton, Dan b. Apple Valley, Minnesota, April 29, 1987

2009–10 ANA	41	9	10	19	16
NHL Totals	41	9	10	19	16

Shannon, Ryan b. Darien, Connecticut, March 2, 1983

2009–10 OTT	66	5	11	16	20
NHL Totals	181	20	40	60	56

Sharp, MacGregor b. Vancouver, British Columbia,
October 1, 1985

2009–10 ANA	8	0	0	0	0
NHL Totals	8	0	0	0	0

Sharp, Patrick b. Thunder Bay, Ontario, December 27, 1981

2009–10 CHI	82	25	41	66	28
NHL Totals	419	126	119	245	301

Shelley, Jody b. Thompson, Manitoba, February 7, 1976

2009–10 SJ/NYR	57	2	7	9	115
NHL Totals	538	16	33	49	1,347

• traded by San Jose to the Rangers on February 12, 2010, for a 6th-round draft choice in 2011

Sheppard, James b. Halifax, Nova Scotia, April 25, 1988

2009–10 MIN	64	2	4	6	38
NHL Totals	224	11	38	49	108

Shirokov, Sergei b. Ozery, Soviet Union (Russia), March 10, 1986

2009–10 VAN	6	0	0	0	2
NHL Totals	6	0	0	0	2

Sifers, Jamie b. Stratford, Connecticut, January 18, 1983

2009–10 MIN	14	0	0	0	6
NHL Totals	37	0	2	2	24

Sim, Jon b. New Glasgow, Nova Scotia, September 29, 1977

2009–10 NYI	77	13	9	22	44
NHL Totals	435	74	61	135	292

Simmonds, Wayne b. Scarborough (Toronto), Ontario, August 26, 1988

2009–10 LA	78	16	24	40	116
NHL Totals	160	25	38	63	189

Sjostrom, Fredrik b. Fargelanda, Sweden, May 6, 1983

2009–10 CAL/TOR	65	3	8	11	12
NHL Totals	423	44	55	99	176

• traded by Calgary to Toronto on January 31, 2010, with Dion Phaneuf and Keith Aulie for Ian White, Matt Stajan, Niklas Hagman and Jamal Mayers

Skille, Jack b. Madison, Wisconsin, May 19, 1987

2009–10 CHI	6	1	1	2	0
NHL Totals	30	5	3	8	5

Skoula, Martin   b. Litomerice, Czechoslovakia (Czech Republic), October 28, 1979

2009–10 PIT/NJ	52	3	8	11	10
NHL Totals	776	44	152	196	328

- traded by Pittsburgh to Toronto on March 2, 2010, with Luca Caputi for Alexei Ponikarovsky
- traded by Toronto to New Jersey on March 3, 2010, for a 5th-round draft choice in 2010

Skrastins, Karlis   b. Riga, Soviet Union (Latvia), July 9, 1974

2009–10 DAL	79	2	11	13	24
NHL Totals	758	29	99	128	337

Slater, Jim   b. Petoskey, Michigan, December 9, 1982

2009–10 ATL	61	11	7	18	60
NHL Totals	335	42	46	88	261

Sloan, Tyler   b. Calgary, Alberta, March 15, 1981

2009–10 WAS	40	2	4	6	22
NHL Totals	66	3	8	11	36

Smaby, Matt   b. Minneapolis, Minnesota, October 14, 1984

2009–10 TB	33	0	2	2	27
NHL Totals	90	0	6	6	89

Smid, Ladislav   b. Frydlant, Czechoslovakia (Czech Republic), February 1, 1986

2009–10 EDM	51	1	8	9	39
NHL Totals	253	4	30	34	191

Smith, Derek   b. Belleville, Ontario, October 13, 1984

2009–10 OTT	2	0	0	0	0
NHL Totals	2	0	0	0	0

Smith, Mike b. Kingston, Ontario, March 22, 1982

| 2009–10 TB | 42 | 13–18–0–7 | 2,273 | 117 | 2 | 3.09 |
| NHL Totals | 140 | 54–60–0–18 | 7,903 | 354 | 10 | 2.69 |

Smith, Nathan b. Edmonton, Alberta, February 9, 1982

| 2009–10 MIN | 9 | 0 | 0 | 0 | 12 |
| NHL Totals | 26 | 0 | 0 | 0 | 14 |

Smithson, Jerred b. Vernon, British Columbia, February 4, 1979

| 2009–10 NAS | 69 | 9 | 4 | 13 | 54 |
| NHL Totals | 392 | 30 | 41 | 71 | 274 |

Smolenak, Radek b. Prague, Czechoslovakia (Czech Republic), December 3, 1986

| 2009–10 CHI | 1 | 0 | 0 | 0 | 5 |
| NHL Totals | 7 | 0 | 1 | 1 | 15 |

Smyth, Ryan b. Banff, Alberta, February 21, 1976

| 2009–10 LA | 67 | 22 | 31 | 53 | 42 |
| NHL Totals | 987 | 332 | 381 | 713 | 775 |

Sobotka, Vladimir b. Trebic, Czechoslovakia (Czech Republic), July 2, 1987

| 2009–10 BOS | 61 | 4 | 6 | 10 | 30 |
| NHL Totals | 134 | 6 | 16 | 22 | 64 |

Sopel, Brent b. Calgary, Alberta, January 7, 1977

| 2009–10 CHI | 73 | 1 | 7 | 8 | 34 |
| NHL Totals | 588 | 42 | 169 | 211 | 293 |

Souray, Sheldon b. Elk Point, Alberta, July 13, 1976

| 2009–10 EDM | 37 | 4 | 9 | 13 | 65 |
| NHL Totals | 650 | 96 | 166 | 262 | 1,020 |

Spacek, Jaroslav b. Rokycany, Czechoslovakia (Czech Republic), February 11, 1974

2009–10 MON	74	3	18	21	50
NHL Totals	775	76	248	324	565

Spaling, Nick b. Palmerston, Ontario, September 19, 1988

2009–10 NAS	28	0	3	3	0
NHL Totals	28	0	3	3	0

Spezza, Jason b. Mississauga, Ontario, June 13, 1983

2009–10 OTT	60	23	34	57	20
NHL Totals	464	171	304	475	322

Staal, Eric b. Thunder Bay, Ontario, October 29, 1984

2009–10 CAR	70	29	41	70	68
NHL Totals	479	193	235	428	357

Staal, Jordan b. Thunder Bay, Ontario, September 10, 1988

2009–10 PIT	82	21	28	49	57
NHL Totals	327	84	84	168	173

Staal, Marc b. Thunder Bay, Ontario, January 13, 1987

2009–10 NYR	82	8	19	27	44
NHL Totals	244	13	39	52	150

Stafford, Drew b. Milwaukee, Wisconsin, October 30, 1985

2009–10 BUF	71	14	20	34	35
NHL Totals	255	63	81	144	148

Staios, Steve b. Hamilton, Ontario, July 28, 1973

2009–10 EDM/CAL	58	1	9	10	75
NHL Totals	897	53	149	202	1,245

• traded by Edmonton to Calgary on March 3, 2010, for Aaron Johnson and a 3rd-round draft choice in 2010 or 2011

Stajan, Matt b. Mississauga, Ontario, December 19, 1983

2009–10 TOR/CAL	82	19	38	57	32
NHL Totals	472	90	149	239	249

• traded by Toronto to Calgary on January 31, 2010, with Ian White, Niklas Hagman and Jamal Mayers for Dion Phaneuf, Fredrik Sjostrom and Keith Aulie

Stalberg, Viktor b. Stockholm, Sweden, January 17, 1986

2009–10 TOR	40	9	5	14	30
NHL Totals	40	9	5	14	30

Stamkos, Steve b. Markham, Ontario, February 7, 1960

2009–10 TB	82	51	44	95	38
NHL Totals	161	74	67	141	77

Stapleton, Tim b. LaGrange, Illinois, July 9, 1982

2009–10 ATL	6	2	0	2	2
NHL Totals	10	3	0	3	2

Stastny, Paul b. Quebec City, Quebec, December 27, 1985

2009–10 COL	81	20	59	79	50
NHL Totals	274	83	181	264	138

Stastny, Yan b. Quebec City, Quebec, September 30, 1982

2009–10 STL	4	1	0	1	0
NHL Totals	91	6	10	16	58

Staubitz, Brad b. Brights Grove, Ontario, July 28, 1984

2009–10 SJ	47	3	3	6	110
NHL Totals	82	4	5	9	186

Steckel, David b. Milwaukee, Wisconsin, March 15, 1982

2009–10 WAS	79	5	11	16	19
NHL Totals	234	18	29	47	89

Steen, Alexander b. Winnipeg, Manitoba, March 1, 1984

| 2009–10 STL | 68 | 24 | 23 | 47 | 30 |
| NHL Totals | 382 | 80 | 117 | 197 | 160 |

Stempniak, Lee b. Buffalo, New York, February 4, 1983

| 2009–10 TOR/PHO | 80 | 28 | 20 | 48 | 26 |
| NHL Totals | 374 | 96 | 113 | 209 | 154 |

• traded by Toronto to Phoenix on March 3, 2010, for Matt Jones and a 4th- and 7th-round draft choice in 2010

Stewart, Chris b. Toronto, Ontario, October 30, 1987

| 2009–10 COL | 77 | 28 | 36 | 64 | 73 |
| NHL Totals | 130 | 39 | 44 | 83 | 127 |

Stewart, Gregory b. Kitchener, Ontario, May 21, 1986

| 2009–10 MON | 5 | 0 | 0 | 0 | 11 |
| NHL Totals | 26 | 0 | 1 | 1 | 48 |

Stillman, Cory b. Peterborough, Ontario, December 20, 1973

| 2009–10 FLO | 58 | 15 | 22 | 37 | 22 |
| NHL Totals | 960 | 266 | 422 | 688 | 465 |

St. Louis, Martin b. Laval, Quebec, June 18, 1975

| 2009–10 TB | 82 | 29 | 65 | 94 | 12 |
| NHL Totals | 772 | 267 | 412 | 679 | 238 |

Stoa, Ryan b. Bloomington, Minnesota, April 13, 1987

| 2009–10 COL | 12 | 2 | 1 | 3 | 0 |
| NHL Totals | 12 | 2 | 1 | 3 | 0 |

Stoll, Jarret b. Melville, Saskatchewan, June 25, 1982

| 2009–10 LA | 73 | 16 | 31 | 47 | 40 |
| NHL Totals | 433 | 93 | 160 | 253 | 346 |

Stone, Ryan b. Calgary, Alberta, March 20, 1985

2009–10 EDM	27	0	6	6	48
NHL Totals	35	0	7	7	55

Stoner, Clayton b. Port McNeill, British Columbia, February 19, 1985

2009–10 MIN	8	0	2	2	12
NHL Totals	8	0	2	2	12

Stortini, Zack b. Elliot Lake, Ontario, September 11, 1985

2009–10 EDM	77	4	9	13	155
NHL Totals	224	14	23	37	642

St. Pierre, Martin b. Ottawa, Ontario, August 11, 1983

2009–10 OTT	3	0	0	0	0
NHL Totals	38	3	5	8	12

Strachan, Tyson b. Melfort, Saskatchewan, October 30, 1984

2009–10 STL	8	0	2	2	4
NHL Totals	38	0	5	5	43

Stralman, Anton b. Tibro, Sweden, August 1, 1986

2009–10 CBJ	73	6	28	34	37
NHL Totals	161	10	46	56	75

Streit, Mark b. Englisberg, Switzerland, December 11, 1977

2009–10 NYI	82	11	38	49	48
NHL Totals	361	52	162	214	180

Strudwick, Jason b. Edmonton, Alberta, July 17, 1975

2009–10 EDM	72	0	6	6	50
NHL Totals	631	13	40	53	788

Stuart, Brad b. Rocky Mountain House, Alberta, November 6, 1979

2009–10 DET	82	4	16	20	22
NHL Totals	728	65	199	264	420

Stuart, Mark b. Rochester, Minnesota, April 27, 1984

2009–10 BOS	56	2	5	7	80
NHL Totals	252	12	23	35	261

Sturm, Marco b. Dingolfing, West Germany (Germany), September 8, 1978

2009–10 BOS	76	22	15	37	30
NHL Totals	855	234	232	466	398

Subban, P.K. b. Toronto, Ontario, May 13, 1989

2009–10 MON	2	0	2	2	2
NHL Totals	2	0	2	2	2

Sullivan, Steve b. Timmins, Ontario, July 6, 1974

2009–10 NAS	82	17	34	51	35
NHL Totals	846	256	404	660	515

Sulzer, Alexander b. Kaufbeuren, West Germany (Germany), May 30, 1984

2009–10 NAS	20	0	2	2	4
NHL Totals	22	0	2	2	4

Suter, Ryan b. Madison, Wisconsin, January 21, 1985

2009–10 NAS	82	4	33	37	48
NHL Totals	393	27	126	153	312

Sutherby, Brian b. Edmonton, Alberta, March 1, 1982

2009–10 DAL	46	5	4	9	66
NHL Totals	409	39	47	86	475

Sutter, Brandon b. Huntington, New York, February 14, 1989

2009–10 CAR	72	21	19	40	2
NHL Totals	122	22	24	46	18

Sutter, Brett b. Viking, Alberta, June 2, 1987

2009–10 CAL	10	0	0	0	5
NHL Totals	14	1	0	1	7

Sutton, Andy b. Kingston, Ontario, March 10, 1975

2009–10 NYI/OTT	72	5	8	13	107
NHL Totals	585	35	101	136	1,018

• traded by the Islanders to Ottawa on March 2, 2010, for a 2nd-round draft choice in 2010

Svatos, Marek b. Kosice, Czechoslovakia (Slovakia), July 17, 1982

2009–10 COL	54	7	4	11	35
NHL Totals	316	96	68	164	207

Sydor, Darryl b. Edmonton, Alberta, May 13, 1972

2009–10 STL	47	0	8	8	15
NHL Totals	1,291	98	409	507	755

Sykora, Petr b. Plzen, Czechoslovakia (Czech Republic), November 19, 1976

2009–10 MIN	14	2	1	3	8
NHL Totals	935	302	375	677	415

Syvret, Danny b. Millgrove, Ontario, June 13, 1985

2009–10 PHI	21	2	2	4	12
NHL Totals	49	2	3	5	24

Szczechura, Paul b. Brantford, Ontario, November 30, 1985

2009–10 TB	52	5	2	7	18
NHL Totals	83	9	7	16	30

Taffe, Jeff b. Hastings, Minnesota, February 19, 1981

2009–10 FLO	21	1	1	2	4
NHL Totals	174	21	23	44	40

Talbot, Maxime b. Lemoyne, Quebec, February 11, 1984

2009–10 PIT	45	2	5	7	30
NHL Totals	306	44	43	87	258

Tallinder, Henrik b. Stockholm, Sweden, January 10, 1979

2009–10 BUF	82	4	16	20	32
NHL Totals	468	20	88	108	278

Tambellini, Jeff b. Calgary, Alberta, April 13, 1984

2009–10 NYI	36	7	7	14	14
NHL Totals	180	18	28	46	70

Tangradi, Eric b. Philadelphia, Pennsylvania, February 10, 1989

2009–10 PIT	1	0	0	0	0
NHL Totals	1	0	0	0	0

Tanguay, Alex b. Ste-Justine, Quebec, November 21, 1979

2009–10 TB	80	10	27	37	32
NHL Totals	739	203	414	617	377

Tarnasky, Nick b. Rocky Mountain House, Alberta, November 25, 1984

2009–10 FLO	31	1	2	3	85
NHL Totals	245	13	17	30	297

Tavares, John b. Mississauga, Ontario, September 20, 1990

2009–10 NYI	82	24	30	54	22
NHL Totals	82	24	30	54	22

Theodore, Jose b. Laval, Quebec, September 13, 1976

2009–10 WAS	47	30-7-0-7	2,586	121	1	2.81
NHL Totals	548	245-221-30-22	30,997	1,387	29	2.68

Thomas, Tim b. Flint, Michigan, April 15, 1974

2009–10 BOS	43	17–18–0–8	2,442	104	5	2.56
NHL Totals	262	126–91–0–35	15,068	655	17	2.61

Thompson, Nate b. Anchorage, Alaska, October 5, 1984

2009–10 NYI/TB	71	2	8	10	56
NHL Totals	118	4	10	14	105

• claimed off waivers by Tampa Bay from the Islanders on January 21, 2010

Thorburn, Chris b. Sault Ste. Marie, Ontario, June 3, 1983

2009–10 ATL	76	4	9	13	89
NHL Totals	272	19	33	52	361

Thornton, Joe b. London, Ontario, July 2, 1979

2009–10 SJ	79	20	69	89	54
NHL Totals	915	285	646	931	885

Thornton, Shawn b. Oshawa, Ontario, July 23, 1977

2009–10 BOS	74	1	9	10	141
NHL Totals	290	15	25	40	496

Thuresson, Andreas b. Kristianstad, Sweden, November 18, 1987

2009–10 NAS	22	1	2	3	4
NHL Totals	22	1	2	3	4

Timonen, Kimmo b. Kuopio, Finland, March 18, 1975

2009–10 PHI	82	6	33	39	50
NHL Totals	812	96	331	427	502

Tkachuk, Keith b. Melrose, Massachusetts, March 28, 1972

2009–10 STL	67	13	19	32	56
NHL Totals	1,201	538	527	1,065	2,219

Tlusty, Jiri b. Slany, Czechoslovakia (Czech Republic), March 16, 1988

2009–10 TOR/CAR	20	1	5	6	6
NHL Totals	92	11	15	26	20

• traded by Toronto to Carolina on December 3, 2009, for Phillippe Paradis

Toews, Jonathan b. Winnipeg, Manitoba, April 29, 1988

2009–10 CHI	76	25	43	68	47
NHL Totals	222	83	108	191	142

Tokarski, Dustin b. Humboldt, Saskatchewan,
September 16, 1989

2009–10 TB	2	0–0–0	44	3	0	4.06
NHL Totals	2	0–0–0	44	3	0	4.06

Tollefsen, Ole-Kristian b. Oslo, Norway, March 29, 1984

2009–10 PHI	18	0	2	2	23
NHL Totals	163	4	8	12	296

Tootoo, Jordin b. Churchill, Manitoba, February 2, 1983

2009–10 NAS	51	6	10	16	40
NHL Totals	355	32	45	77	572

Torres, Raffi b. Toronto, Ontario, October 8, 1981

2009–10 CBJ/BUF	74	19	17	36	34
NHL Totals	432	98	84	182	312

• traded by Columbus to Buffalo on March 3, 2010, for Nathan Paetsch and
a 2nd-round draft choice in 2010

Toskala, Vesa b. Tampere, Finland, May 20, 1977

2009–10 TOR/CAL	32	9–12–3	1,604	93	1	3.48
NHL Totals	266	129–82–5–25	14,767	679	13	2.76

• traded by Toronto to Anaheim on January 31, 2010, with Jason Blake for
J-S Giguere
• traded by Anaheim to Calgary on March 3, 2010, for Curtis McElhinney

Trotter, Brock b. Brandon, Manitoba, September 18, 1987

2009–10 MON	2	0	0	0	0
NHL Totals	2	0	0	0	0

Tucker, Darcy b. Castor, Alberta, March 15, 1975

2009–10 COL	71	10	14	24	47
NHL Totals	947	215	261	476	1,410

Turco, Marty b. Sault Ste. Marie, Ontario, August 13, 1975

2009–10 DAL	53	22–20–0–11	3,088	140	4	2.72
NHL Totals	509	262–154–26–37	29,064	1,118	40	2.31

Tyutin, Fedor b. Izhevsk, Soviet Union (Russia), July 19, 1983

2009–10 CBJ	80	6	26	32	49
NHL Totals	412	30	102	132	289

Umberger, R.J. b. Pittsburgh, Pennsylvania, May 3, 1982

2009–10 CBJ	82	23	32	55	40
NHL Totals	392	98	119	217	171

Upshall, Scottie b. Fort McMurray, Alberta, October 7, 1983

2009–10 PHO	49	18	14	32	50
NHL Totals	279	64	74	138	273

Valabik, Boris b. Nitra, Czechoslovakia (Slovakia),
February 14, 1986

2009–10 ATL	23	0	2	2	36
NHL Totals	80	0	7	7	210

Valiquette, Stephen b. Etobicoke (Toronto), Ontario,
August 20, 1977

2009–10 NYR	6	2–3–0–0	305	19	1	3.74
NHL Totals	46	16–14–0–5	2,255	103	4	2.74

Vandermeer, Jim b. Caroline, Alberta, February 21, 1980

2009–10 PHO	62	4	8	12	60
NHL Totals	374	22	65	87	557

Vanek, Thomas b. Vienna, Austria, January 19, 1984

2009–10 BUF	71	28	25	53	42
NHL Totals	389	172	141	313	262

van Riemsdyk, James b. Middletown, New Jersey, May 4, 1989

2009–10 PHI	78	15	20	35	30
NHL Totals	78	15	20	35	30

Varlamov, Simeon b. Kuybyshev, Soviet Union (Russia), April 27, 1988

2009–10 WAS	26	15–4–0–6	1,527	65	2	2.55
NHL Totals	32	19–4–0–7	1,856	78	2	2.52

Veilleux, Stephane b. Beauceville, Quebec, November 16, 1981

2009–10 TB	77	3	6	9	48
NHL Totals	438	46	53	99	302

Vermette, Antoine b. St-Agapit, Quebec, July 20, 1982

2009–10 CBJ	82	27	38	65	32
NHL Totals	458	114	131	245	245

Versteeg, Kris b. Lethbridge, Alberta, May 13, 1986

2009–10 CHI	79	20	24	44	35
NHL Totals	170	44	57	101	96

Vesce, Ryan b. Lloyd Harbor, New York, April 7, 1982

2009–10 SJ	9	3	2	5	0
NHL Totals	19	3	2	5	4

Vishnevskiy, Ivan b. Barnaul, Soviet Union (Russia), February 18, 1988

2009–10 DAL	2	0	0	0	0
NHL Totals	5	0	2	2	2

Visnovsky, Lubomir b. Topolcany, Czechoslovakia (Slovakia), August 11, 1976

2009–10 EDM/ANA	73	15	30	45	20
NHL Totals	622	93	262	355	264

• traded by Edmonton to Anaheim on March 3, 2010, for Ryan Whitney and a 6th-round draft choice in 2010

Vlasic, Marc-Edouard b. Montreal, Quebec, March 30, 1987

2009–10 SJ	64	3	13	16	33
NHL Totals	309	14	78	92	117

Vokoun, Tomas b. Karlovy Vary, Czechoslovakia (Czech Republic), July 2, 1976

2009–10 FLO	63	23–28–0–11	3,695	157	7	2.55
NHL Totals	575	240–239–35–36	32,858	1,401	38	2.56

Volchenkov, Anton b. Moscow, Soviet Union (Russia), February 25, 1982

2009–10 OTT	64	4	10	14	38
NHL Totals	428	16	78	94	297

Voracek, Jakub b. Kladno, Czechoslovakia (Czech Republic), August 15, 1989

2009–10 CBJ	81	16	34	50	26
NHL Totals	161	25	63	88	70

Voros, Aaron b. Vancouver, British Columbia, July 2, 1981

2009–10 NYR	41	3	4	7	89
NHL Totals	150	18	19	37	352

Vrbata, Radim b. Mlada Boleslav, Czechoslovakia (Czech Republic), June 13, 1981

2009–10 PHO	82	24	19	43	24
NHL Totals	522	129	146	275	150

Walker, Matt b. Beaverlodge, Alberta, April 7, 1980

2009–10 TB	66	2	3	5	90
NHL Totals	306	4	26	30	444

Walker, Scott b. Cambridge, Ontario, July 19, 1973

2009–10 CAR/WAS	42	5	3	8	32
NHL Totals	829	151	246	397	1,162

• traded by Carolina to Washington on March 3, 2010, for a 7th-round draft choice in 2010

Wallace, Tim b. Anchorage, Alaska, August 6, 1984

2009–10 PIT	1	0	0	0	0
NHL Totals	17	0	2	2	7

Wallin, Niclas b. Boden, Sweden, February 20, 1975

2009–10 CAR/SJ	70	0	7	7	49
NHL Totals	540	18	53	71	414

• traded by Carolina to San Jose on February 7, 2010, with a 5th-round draft choice in 2010 for a 2nd-round draft choice in 2010

Wallin, Rickard b. Stockholm, Sweden, April 9, 1980

2009–10 TOR	60	2	7	9	20
NHL Totals	79	8	11	19	34

Walter, Ben b. Beaconsfield, Ontario, May 11, 1984

2009–10 NJ	2	0	0	0	2
NHL Totals	24	1	0	1	6

Wandell, Tom   b. Sodertalje, Sweden, January 29, 1987

2009–10 DAL	50	5	10	15	14
NHL Totals	64	6	12	18	18

Ward, Aaron   b. Windsor, Ontario, January 17, 1973

2009–10 CAR/ANA	77	1	12	13	62
NHL Totals	839	44	107	151	736

• traded by Carolina to Anaheim on March 3, 2010, for Justin Pogge and a 4th-round draft choice in 2010 or 2011

Ward, Cam   b. Sherwood Park, Alberta, February 29, 1984

2009–10 CAR	47	18–23–0–5	2,651	119	0	2.69
NHL Totals	273	138–100–0–23	15,415	717	12	2.79

Ward, Joel   b. Toronto, Ontario, December 2, 1980

2009–10 NAS	71	13	21	34	18
NHL Totals	161	30	40	70	47

Wathier, Francis   b. St. Isidore, Ontario, December 7, 1984

2009–10 DAL	5	0	0	0	5
NHL Totals	5	0	0	0	5

Weaver, Mike   b. Bramalea, Ontario, May 2, 1978

2009–10 STL	77	1	9	10	29
NHL Totals	339	4	38	42	134

Weber, Shea   b. Sicamous, British Columbia, August 14, 1985

2009–10 NAS	78	16	27	43	36
NHL Totals	320	64	102	166	267

Weber, Yannick   b. Morges, Switzerland, September 23, 1988

2009–10 MON	5	0	0	0	4
NHL Totals	8	0	1	1	6

Weight, Doug b. Warren, Michigan, January 21, 1971

2009–10 NYI	36	1	16	17	8
NHL Totals	1,220	276	748	1,024	960

Weiss, Stephen b. Toronto, Ontario, April 3, 1983

2009–10 FLO	80	28	32	60	40
NHL Totals	481	103	181	284	179

Wellman, Casey b. Brentwood, California, October 18, 1987

2009–10 MIN	12	1	3	4	0
NHL Totals	12	1	3	4	0

Wellwood, Kyle b. Windsor, Ontario, May 16, 1983

2009–10 VAN	75	14	11	25	12
NHL Totals	338	63	97	160	30

Wheeler, Blake b. Robbinsdale, Minnesota, August 31, 1986

2009–10 BOS	82	18	20	38	53
NHL Totals	163	39	44	83	99

White, Colin b. New Glasgow, Nova Scotia, December 12, 1977

2009–10 NJ	81	2	10	12	46
NHL Totals	674	20	99	119	800

White, Ian b. Winnipeg, Manitoba, June 4, 1984

2009–10 TOR/CAL	83	13	25	38	51
NHL Totals	323	32	85	117	202

• traded by Toronto to Calgary on March 31, 2010, with Matt Stajan, Niklas Hagman and Jamal Mayers for Dion Phaneuf, Fredrik Sjostrom and Keith Aulie

White, Ryan b. Brandon, Manitoba, March 17, 1988

2009–10 MON	16	0	2	2	16
NHL Totals	16	0	2	2	16

White, Todd b. Kanata, Ontario, May 21, 1975

2009–10 ATL	65	7	19	26	24
NHL Totals	635	140	239	379	226

Whitfield, Trent b. Alameda, Saskatchewan, June 17, 1977

2009–10 BOS	16	0	1	1	7
NHL Totals	193	11	18	29	104

Whitney, Ray b. Fort Saskatchewan, Alberta, May 8, 1972

2009–10 CAR	80	21	37	58	26
NHL Totals	1,072	324	545	869	395

Whitney, Ryan b. Boston, Massachusetts, February 19, 1983

2009–10 ANA/EDM	81	7	32	39	70
NHL Totals	354	41	158	199	305

• traded by Anaheim to Edmonton on March 3, 2010, with a 6th-round draft choice in 2010 for Lubomir Visnovsky

Wideman, Dennis b. Kitchener, Ontario, March 20, 1983

2009–10 BOS	76	6	24	30	34
NHL Totals	378	46	119	165	292

Williams, Jason b. London, Ontario, August 11, 1980

2009–10 DET	44	6	9	15	8
NHL Totals	420	91	129	220	147

Williams, Justin b. Cobourg, Ontario, October 4, 1981

2009–10 LA	49	10	19	29	39
NHL Totals	552	135	214	349	372

Willsie, Brian b. London, Ontario, March 16, 1978

2009–10 COL	4	0	0	0	0
NHL Totals	380	52	56	108	217

Wilson, Clay b. Sturgeon Lake, Minnesota, April 5, 1983

2009–10 FLO	2	0	0	0	0
NHL Totals	16	1	2	3	2

Wilson, Colin b. Greenwich, Connecticut, October 20, 1989

2009–10 NAS	35	8	7	15	7
NHL Totals	35	8	7	15	7

Wilson, Kyle b. Oakville, Ontario, December 15, 1984

2009–10 WAS	2	0	2	2	0
NHL Totals	2	0	2	2	0

Wilson, Ryan b. Windsor, Ontario, February 3, 1987

2009–10 COL	61	3	18	21	36
NHL Totals	61	3	18	21	36

Winchester, Brad b. Madison, Wisconsin, March 1, 1981

2009–10 STL	64	3	5	8	108
NHL Totals	247	21	21	42	350

Winchester, Jesse b. Long Sault, Ontario, October 4, 1983

2009–10 OTT	52	2	11	13	22
NHL Totals	129	5	26	31	57

Winnik, Daniel b. Toronto, Ontario, March 6, 1985

2009–10 PHO	74	4	15	19	12
NHL Totals	202	18	34	52	100

Wisniewski, James b. Canton, Michigan, February 21, 1984

2009–10 ANA	69	3	27	30	56
NHL Totals	254	17	80	97	264

Witt, Brendan b. Humboldt, Saskatchewan, February 20, 1975

2009–10 NYI	42	2	3	5	45
NHL Totals	890	25	96	121	1,424

Wolski, Wojtek b. Zabrze, Poland, February 24, 1986

2009–10 COL/PHO	80	23	42	65	27
NHL Totals	320	79	132	211	87

• traded by Colorado to Phoenix on March 3, 2010, for Peter Mueller and Kevin Porter

Woywitka, Jeff b. Vermilion, Alberta, September 1, 1983

2009–10 DAL	36	0	3	3	11
NHL Totals	188	6	32	38	117

Wozniewski, Andy b. Buffalo Grove, Illinois, May 25, 1980

2009–10 BOS	2	0	0	0	0
NHL Totals	79	2	10	12	81

Wright, James b. Saskatoon, Saskatchewan, March 24, 1990

2009–10 TB	48	2	3	5	18
NHL Totals	48	2	3	5	18

Wyman, J.T. b. Edina, Minnesota, February 27, 1986

2009–10 MON	3	0	0	0	0
NHL Totals	3	0	0	0	0

Yandle, Keith b. Boston, Massachusetts, September 9, 1986

2009–10 PHO	82	12	29	41	45
NHL Totals	201	21	64	85	104

Yelle, Stephane b. Ottawa, Ontario, May 9, 1974

2009–10 CAR/COL	70	4	4	8	32
NHL Totals	991	96	169	265	490

• traded by Carolina to Colorado on March 3, 2010, with Harrison Reed for Cedric Lalonde-McNicoll and a 6th-round draft choice in 2010

Yip, Brandon b. Vancouver, British Columbia, April 25, 1985

2009–10 COL	32	11	8	19	22
NHL Totals	32	11	8	19	22

Zaba, Matt b. Yorkton, Saskatchewan, July 14, 1983

2009–10 NYR	1	0–0–0–0	34	2	0	3.53
NHL Totals	1	0–0–0–0	34	2	0	3.53

Zajac, Travis b. Winnipeg, Manitoba, May 13, 1985

2009–10 NJ	82	25	42	67	24
NHL Totals	326	76	129	205	100

Zalewski, Steven b. Utica, New York, August 20, 1986

2009–10 SJ	3	0	0	0	0
NHL Totals	3	0	0	0	0

Zanon, Greg b. Burnaby, British Columbia, June 5, 1980

2009–10 MIN	81	2	13	15	36
NHL Totals	311	9	32	41	136

Zetterberg, Henrik b. Njurunda, Sweden, October 9, 1980

2009–10 DET	74	23	47	70	26
NHL Totals	506	206	269	475	184

Zharkov, Vladimir b. Elektrostal, Soviet Union (Russia), January 10, 1988

2009–10 NJ	40	0	10	10	8
NHL Totals	40	0	10	10	8

Zidlicky, Marek b. Most, Czechoslovakia (Czech Republic), February 3, 1977

2009–10 MIN	78	6	37	43	67
NHL Totals	461	53	207	260	442

Zubrus, Dainius b. Elektrenai, Soviet Union (Lithuania), June 16, 1978

2009–10 NJ	51	10	17	27	28
NHL Totals	904	176	289	465	584

COACHES' REGISTER, 2009–10

(OTL are listed in lost column)

	Games	W	L	T
Anderson, John b. Toronto, Ontario, March 28, 1957				
2009–10 ATL	82	35	34	13
NHL Totals	164	70	75	19

• hired June 20, 2008; fired April 14, 2010

Arniel, Scott b. Kingston, Ontario, September 17, 1962
• no NHL coaching record
• hired by Columbus, June 8, 2010

	Games	W	L	T
Babcock, Mike b. Manitouwadge, Ontario, April 29, 1963				
2009–10 DET	82	44	24	14
NHL Totals	574	326	163	85

• hired July 14, 2005

Boucher, Guy b. Notre-Dame-du-Lac, Quebec, August 3, 1971
• no NHL coaching record
• hired by Tampa Bay, June 10, 2010

	Games	W	L	T
Boudreau, Bruce b. Toronto, Ontario, January 9, 1955				
2009–10 WAS	82	54	15	13
NHL Totals	225	141	56	28

• hired November 22, 2007

	Games	W	L	T
Bylsma, Dan b. Grand Haven, Michigan, September 19, 1970				
2009–10 PIT	82	47	28	7
NHL Totals	107	65	31	11

• hired February 15, 2009

Carlyle, Randy b. Sudbury, Ontario, April 19, 1956

2009–10 ANA	82	39	32	11
NHL Totals	410	219	139	52

• hired August 1, 2005

Clouston, Cory b. Viking, Alberta, September 19, 1969

2009–10 OTT	82	44	32	6
NHL Totals	116	63	43	10

• hired February 2, 2009

Crawford, Marc b. Belleville, Ontario, February 13, 1961

2009–10 DAL	82	37	31	14
NHL Totals	1,069	507	392	170

• hired June 11, 2009

DeBoer, Peter b. Dunnville, Ontario, June 13, 1968

2009–10 FLO	82	32	37	13
NHL Totals	164	73	67	24

• hired June 13, 2008

Gordon, Scott b. Easton, Massachusetts, February 6, 1963

2009–10 NYI	82	34	37	11
NHL Totals	164	60	84	20

• hired August 12, 2008

Hitchcock, Ken b. Edmonton, Alberta, December 17, 1951

2009–10 CBJ	58	22	27	9
NHL Totals	1,041	533	350	158

• hired November 22, 2006; fired February 3, 2010

Julien, Claude b. Orleans, Ontario, April 23, 1960

2009–10 BOS	82	39	30	13
NHL Totals	484	252	164	68

• hired June 21, 2007

Laviolette, Peter b. Norwood, Massachusetts, December 7, 1964

| 2009–10 PHI | 57 | 28 | 24 | 5 |
| NHL Totals | 544 | 272 | 208 | 64 |

• hired December 4, 2009

Lemaire, Jacques b. LaSalle, Quebec, September 7, 1945

| 2009–10 NJ | 82 | 48 | 27 | 7 |
| NHL Totals | 1,213 | 588 | 441 | 184 |

• hired July 13, 2009; retired April 26, 2010

Martin, Jacques b. St. Pascal, Ontario, October 1, 1952

| 2009–10 MON | 82 | 39 | 33 | 10 |
| NHL Totals | 1,180 | 556 | 439 | 185 |

• hired June 1, 2009

Maurice, Paul b. Sault Ste. Marie, Ontario, January 30, 1967

| 2009–10 CAR | 82 | 35 | 37 | 10 |
| NHL Totals | 977 | 412 | 413 | 152 |

• hired December 3, 2008

McLellan, Todd b. Melville, Saskatchewan, October 3, 1967

| 2009–10 SJ | 82 | 51 | 20 | 11 |
| NHL Totals | 164 | 104 | 38 | 22 |

• hired June 12, 2008

Murray, Andy b. Gladstone, Manitoba, March 3, 1951

| 2009–10 STL | 40 | 17 | 17 | 6 |
| NHL Totals | 740 | 333 | 278 | 129 |

• hired December 11, 2006; fired January 2, 2010

Murray, Terry b. Shawville, Quebec, July 20, 1950

| 2009–10 LA | 82 | 46 | 27 | 9 |
| NHL Totals | 901 | 440 | 341 | 120 |

• hired July 17, 2008

Noel, Claude b. Kirkland Lake, Ontario, October 31, 1955

2009–10 CBJ	24	10	8	6
NHL Totals	24	10	8	6

• named interim coach February 4, 2010; replaced by Scott Arniel, June 8, 2010

Payne, Davis b. King City, Ontario, October 24, 1970

2009–10 ST	42	23	15	4
NHL Totals	42	23	15	4

• hired January 2, 2010

Quenneville, Joel b. Windsor, Ontario, September 15, 1958

2009–10 CHI	82	52	22	8
NHL Totals	999	535	327	137

• hired October 16, 2008

Quinn, Pat b. Hamilton, Ontario, January 29, 1943

2009–10 EDM	82	27	47	8
NHL Totals	1,400	684	528	188

• hired May 26, 2009; fired June 22, 2010

Ramsay, Craig b. March 17, 1951, Weston (Toronto), Ontario

NHL Totals	49	16	27	6

• hired by Atlanta, June 24, 2010

Richards, Todd b. Crystal, Minnesota, October 20, 1966

2009–10 MIN	82	38	36	8
NHL Totals	82	38	36	8

• hired June 16, 2009

Ruff, Lindy b. Warburg, Alberta, February 17, 1960

2009–10 BUF	82	45	27	10
NHL Totals	984	483	361	140

• hired July 21, 1997

Sacco, Joe b. Medford, Massachusetts, February 4, 1969

| 2009–10 COL | 82 | 43 | 30 | 9 |
| NHL Totals | 82 | 43 | 30 | 9 |

• hired June 4, 2009

Sutter, Brent b. Viking, Alberta, June 10, 1962

| 2009–10 CAL | 82 | 40 | 32 | 10 |
| NHL Totals | 246 | 137 | 88 | 21 |

• hired June 23, 2009

Tippett, Dave b. Moosomin, Saskatchewan, August 25, 1961

| 2009–10 PHO | 82 | 50 | 25 | 7 |
| NHL Totals | 574 | 321 | 181 | 72 |

• hired September 24, 2009

Tocchet, Rick b. Toronto, Ontario, April 9, 1964

| 2009–10 TB | 82 | 34 | 36 | 12 |
| NHL Totals | 148 | 53 | 69 | 26 |

• hired November 14, 2008; fired April 13, 2010

Tortorella, John b. Boston, Massachusetts, June 24, 1958

| 2009–10 NYR | 82 | 38 | 33 | 11 |
| NHL Totals | 642 | 289 | 265 | 88 |

• hired February 23, 2009

Trotz, Barry b. Winnipeg, Manitoba, July 15, 1962

| 2009–10 NAS | 82 | 47 | 29 | 6 |
| NHL Totals | 902 | 411 | 371 | 120 |

• hired August 6, 1997, a year before the Predators played their first NHL game

Vigneault, Alain b. Quebec City, Quebec, May 14, 1961

| 2009–10 VAN | 82 | 49 | 28 | 5 |
| NHL Totals | 594 | 291 | 232 | 71 |

• hired June 20, 2006

Wilson, Ron   b. Windsor, Ontario, May 28, 1955

2009–10 TOR	82	30	38	14
NHL Totals	1,255	582	499	174

• hired June 10, 2008

2010 NHL ENTRY DRAFT

Los Angeles, California, June 25–26, 2010

First Round
1. Edmonton—Taylor Hall (CAN)
2. Boston—Tyler Seguin (CAN)
3. Florida—Eric Gudbranson (CAN)
4. Columbus—Ryan Johansen (CAN)
5. NY Islanders—Nino Niederreiter (SUI)
6. Tampa Bay—Brett Connolly (CAN)
7. Carolina—Jeff Skinner (CAN)
8. Atlanta—Alexander Burmistrov (RUS)
9. Minnesota—Mikael Granlund (FIN)
10. NY Rangers—Dylan McIlrath (CAN)
11. Dallas—Jack Campbell (USA)
12. Anaheim—Cam Fowler (CAN)
13. Phoenix—Brandon Gormley (CAN)
14. St. Louis—Jaden Schwartz (CAN)
15. Los Angeles—Derek Forbort (USA)
16. St. Louis—Vladimir Tarasenko (RUS)
17. Colorado—Joey Hishon (CAN)
18. Nashville—Austin Watson (USA)
19. Florida—Nick Bjugstad (USA)
20. Pittsburgh—Beau Bennett (USA)
21. Detroit—Riley Sheahan (CAN)
22. Montreal—Jarred Tinordi (USA)
23. Buffalo—Mark Pysyk (CAN)
24. Chicago—Kevin Hayes (USA)
25. Florida—Quinton Howden (CAN)
26. Washington—Evgeni Kuznetsov (RUS)
27. Phoenix—Mark Visentin (CAN)
28. San Jose—Charlie Coyle (USA)

29. Anaheim—Emerson Etem (USA)
30. NY Islanders—Brock Nelson (USA)

Second Round
31. Edmonton—Tyler Pitlick (USA)
32. Boston—Jared Knight (USA)
33. Florida—John McFarland (CAN)
34. Columbus—Dalton Smith (CAN)
35. Chicago—Ludvig Rensfeldt (SWE)
36. Florida—Alexander Petrovic (CAN)
37. Carolina—Justin Falk (USA)
38. New Jersey—Jon Merrill (USA)
39. Minnesota—Brett Bulmer (CAN)
40. NY Rangers—Christian Thomas (CAN)
41. Dallas—Patrick Nemeth (SWE)
42. Anaheim—Devante Smith-Pelly (CAN)
43. Toronto—Bradley Ross (CAN)
44. St. Louis—Sebastian Wannstrom (SWE)
45. Boston—Ryan Spooner (CAN)
46. Edmonton—Martin Marincin (SVK)
47. Los Angeles—Tyler Tofoli (CAN)
48. Edmonton—Curtis Hamilton (USA)
49. Colorado—Calvin Picard (CAN)
50. Florida—Connor Brickley (USA)
51. Detroit—Calle Jarnkrok (SWE)
52. Phoenix—Philip Lane (USA)
53. Carolina—Mark Alt (USA)
54. Chicago—Justin Holl (USA)
55. Columbus—Petr Straka (CZE)
56. Minnesota—Johann Larsson (SWE)
57. Phoenix—Oscar Lindberg (SWE)
58. Chicago—Kent Simpson (CAN)
59. Minnesota—Jason Zucker (USA)
60. Chicago—Stephen Johns (USA)

Third Round

61. Edmonton—Ryan Martindale (CAN)
62. Toronto—Greg McKegg (CAN)
63. Tampa Bay—Brock Beukeboom (USA)
64. Calgary—Maxwell Reinhart (CAN)
65. NY Islanders—Kirill Kabanov (RUS)
66. Tampa Bay—Radko Gudas (CZE)
67. Carolina—Danny Biega (CAN)
68. Buffalo—Jerome Gauthier-Leduc (CAN)
69. Florida—Joe Basaraba (CAN)
70. Los Angeles—Jordan Weal (CAN)
71. Colorado—Michael Bournival (CAN)
72. Tampa Bay—Adam Janosik (SVK)
73. Calgary—Joey Leach (CAN)
74. St. Louis—Max Gardiner (USA)
75. Buffalo—Kevin Sundher (CAN)
76. Ottawa—Jakub Culek (CZE)
77. Dallas—Alexander Guptill (CAN)
78. Nashville—Taylor Aronson (USA)
79. Toronto—Sondre Olden (NOR)
80. Pittsburgh—Bryan Rust (USA)
81. Detroit—Louis-Marc Aubry (CAN)
82. NY Islanders—Jason Clark (USA)
83. Buffalo—Matt MacKenzie (CAN)
84. New Jersey—Scott Wedgewood (CAN)
85. Carolina—Austin Levi (USA)
86. Washington—Stanislav Galiev (RUS)
87. Atlanta—Julian Melchiori (CAN)
88. San Jose—Max Gaede (USA)
89. Philadelphia—Michael Chaput (CAN)
90. Chicago—Joakim Nordstrom (SWE)

Fourth Round

91. Edmonton—Jeremie Blain (CAN)
92. Florida—Sam Brittain (CAN)
93. Florida—Benjamin Gallacher (CAN)
94. Columbus—Brandon Archibald (USA)
95. Colorado—Stephen Silas (CAN)
96. Tampa Bay—Geoffrey Schemitsch (CAN)
97. Boston—Craig Cunningham (CAN)
98. Buffalo—Steven Shipley (CAN)
99. Florida—Joonas Donskoi (FIN)
100. NY Rangers—Andrew Yogan (USA)
101. Atlanta—Ivan Telegin (RUS)
102. Columbus—Mathieu Corbeil-Theriault (CAN)
103. Calgary—John Ramage (CAN)
104. St. Louis—Jani Hakanpaa (FIN)
105. Carolina—Justin Shugg (CAN)
106. Ottawa—Markus Sorensen (SWE)
107. Colorado—Sami Aittokallio (FIN)
108. Calgary—Bill Arnold (USA)
109. Dallas—Alex Theriau (CAN)
110. Pittsburgh—Tom Kuhnhackl (GER)
111. Detroit—Teemu Pulkkinen (FIN)
112. Washington—Philipp Grubauer (GER)
113. Montreal—Mark MacMillan (CAN)
114. New Jersey—Joe Faust (USA)
115. Vancouver—Patrick McNally (USA)
116. Toronto—Petter Granberg (SWE)
117. Montreal—Morgan Ellis (CAN)
118. Tampa Bay—James Mullin (USA)
119. Philadelphia—Tye McGinn (CAN)
120. Chicago—Rob Flick (CAN)

Fifth Round

121. Edmonton—Tyler Bunz (CAN)
122. Anaheim—Christopher Wagner (USA)
123. Florida—Zach Hyman (CAN)
124. Columbus—Austin Madaisky (CAN)
125. NY Islanders—Tony Dehart (USA)
126. Nashville—Patrick Cehlin (SWE)
127. San Jose—Cody Ferriero (USA)
128. Atlanta—Fredrik Pettersson-Wentzel (SWE)
129. San Jose—Freddie Hamilton (CAN)
130. NY Rangers—Jason Wilson (CAN)
131. Dallas—John Klingberg (SWE)
132. Anaheim—Tim Heed (SWE)
133. Calgary—Michael Ferland (CAN)
134. St. Louis—Cody Beach (CAN)
135. Boston—Justin Florek (USA)
136. San Jose—Isaac MacLeod (CAN)
137. Colorado—Troy Rutkowski (CAN)
138. Phoenix—Louis Domingue (CAN)
139. Colorado—Luke Walker (USA)
140. Pittsburgh—Kenneth Agostino (USA)
141. Detroit—Petr Mrazek (CZE)
142. Washington—Caleb Herbert (USA)
143. Buffalo—Gregg Sutch (CAN)
144. Toronto—Sam Carrick (CAN)
145. Vancouver—Adam Polasek (CZE)
146. Toronto—Daniel Brodin (SWE)
147. Montreal—Brendan Gallagher (CAN)
148. Los Angeles—Kevin Gravel (USA)
149. Philadelphia—Michael Parks (USA)
150. Atlanta—Yasin Cisse (CAN)

Sixth Round

151. Chicago—Mirko Hoefflin (GER)
152. Pittsburgh—Joe Rogalski (USA)
153. Florida—Corey Durocher (CAN)
154. Columbus-Dalton Prout (CAN)
155. Atlanta—Kendall McFaull (CAN)
156. Tampa Bay—Brendan O'Donnell (CAN)
157. NY Rangers—Jesper Fasth (SWE)
158. Los Angeles—Maxim Kitsyn (RUS)
159. Minnesota—Johan Gustafsson (SWE)
160. Atlanta—Tanner Lane (USA)
161. Anaheim—Andreas Dahlstrom (SWE)
162. Edmonton—Brandon Davidson (CAN)
163. San Jose—Konrad Abeltshauser (GER)
164. St. Louis—Stephen MacAulay (CAN)
165. Boston—Zane Gothberg (USA)
166. Edmonton—Drew Czerwonka (CAN)
167. Carolina—Tyler Stahl (CAN)
168. Nashville—Anthony Bitetto (USA)
169. Atlanta—Sebastian Owuya (SWE)
170. Pittsburgh—Reid McNeill (CAN)
171. Detroit—Brooks Macek (CAN)
172. Vancouver—Alex Friesen (CAN)
173. Buffalo—Cedrick Henley (CAN)
174. New Jersey—Maxime Clermont (CAN)
175. Vancouver—Jonathan Iilahti (FIN)
176. Washington—Samuel Carrier (CAN)
177. Anaheim—Kevin Lind (USA)
178. Ottawa—Mark Stone (CAN)
179. Philadelphia—Nicholas Luukko (USA)
180. Chicago—Nick Mattson (USA)

Seventh Round

181. Edmonton—Kristians Pelss (LAT)
182. Toronto—Josh Nicholls (CAN)
183. Florida—R.J. Boyd (USA)
184. Columbus—Martin Ouellette (CAN)
185. NY Islanders—Cody Rosen (CAN)
186. Tampa Bay—Teigan Zahn (CAN)
187. Carolina—Frederik Andersen (DEN)
188. San Jose—Lee Moffie (USA)
189. Minnesota—Dylan McKinlay (CAN)
190. NY Rangers—Randy McNaught (CAN)
191. Chicago—Macmillan Carruth (USA)
192. Anaheim—Brett Perlini (CAN)
193. Calgary—Patrick Holland (CAN)
194. Nashville—David Elsner (GER)
195. Boston—Maxim Chudinov (RUS)
196. Ottawa—Bryce Aneloski (USA)
197. Colorado—Luke Moffatt (USA)
198. Nashville—Joonas Rask (FIN)
199. Atlanta—Peter Stoykewych (CAN)
200. San Jose—Christopher Crane (USA)
201. Detroit—Benjamin Marshall (USA)
202. Edmonton—Kellen Jones (CAN)
203. Buffalo—Christian Isackson (USA)
204. New Jersey—Mauro Jorg (SUI)
205. Vancouver—Sawyer Hannay (CAN)
206. Philadelphia—Richard Blidstrand (SWE)
207. Montreal—John Westin (SWE)
208. Buffalo—Riley Boychuk (CAN)
209. Philadelphia—Brendan Ranford (CAN)
210. Boston—Zach Trotman (USA)

Notes:

- Nick Bjugstad (19th) is the nephew of former NHLer Scott
- Jarred Tinordi (22nd) is the son of former NHLer Mark
- Brock Nelson (30th) is the nephew of former NHLer Dave Christian
- Dalton Smith (34th) is the son of former NHLer Derrick
- Christian Thomas (40th) is the son of former NHLer Steve
- Brock Beukeboom (63rd) is the son of former NHLer Jeff
- Maxwell Reinhart (64th) is the son of former NHLer Paul
- John Ramage (103rd) is the son of former NHLer Rob
- Tom Kuhnhackl (110th) is the son of Erich, legendary German international player and IIHF Hall of Famer
- Joonas Rask (198th) is the younger brother of Boston Bruins goalie Tuukka

ALL-TIME LEADERS

MOST GAMES

1,767	Gordie Howe
1,756	Mark Messier
1,731	Ron Francis
1,651	Chris Chelios
1,639	Dave Andreychuk

MOST POINTS, REGULAR SEASON

2,857	Wayne Gretzky
1,887	Mark Messier
1,850	Gordie Howe
1,798	Ron Francis
1,771	Marcel Dionne

MOST GOALS, REGULAR SEASON

894	Wayne Gretzky
801	Gordie Howe
741	Brett Hull
731	Marcel Dionne
717	Phil Esposito

MOST ASSISTS, REGULAR SEASON

1,963	Wayne Gretzky
1,249	Ron Francis
1,193	Mark Messier
1,169	Ray Bourque
1,135	Paul Coffey

MOST PENALTY MINUTES, REGULAR SEASON

3,966	Dave "Tiger" Williams
3,565	Dale Hunter
3,515	Tie Domi

| 3,381 | Marty McSorley |
| 3,300 | Bob Probert |

MOST GAMES, GOALIE, REGULAR SEASON

1,076	Martin Brodeur
1,029	Patrick Roy
971	Terry Sawchuk
963	Ed Belfour
943	Curtis Joseph

MOST WINS, GOALIE, REGULAR SEASON

602	Martin Brodeur
551	Patrick Roy
484	Ed Belfour
454	Curtis Joseph
447	Terry Sawchuk

MOST SHUTOUTS, GOALIE, REGULAR SEASON

110	Martin Brodeur
103	Terry Sawchuk
94	George Hainsworth
84	Glenn Hall
82	Jacques Plante

YEAR-BY-YEAR STANDINGS AND STANLEY CUP FINALS RESULTS

After playoff scores, goalies who have registered a shutout will appear in square brackets (i.e., [Broda] means Turk Broda registered a shutout). All overtime goals are also recorded.

1917–18

First Half

	GP	W	L	GF	GA	PTS
Canadiens	14	10	4	81	47	20
Arenas	14	8	6	71	75	16
Ottawa	14	5	9	67	79	10
Wanderers+	6	1	5	17	35	2

Second Half

	GP	W	L	GF	GA	PTS
Arenas	8	5	3	37	34	10
Ottawa	8	4	4	35	35	8
Canadiens	8	3	5	34	37	6

+ Wanderers' rink burned down on January 2, 1918, and team withdrew from league. Arenas and Canadiens each counted a win for defaulted games with the Wanderers.

* winner of first half played winner of second half in a two-game total-goals series for a place in the Stanley Cup finals against the winner of the Pacific Coast Hockey Association and the Western Canada Hockey League. If one team won both halves, it went to the best-of-five Stanley Cup finals automatically.

* from 1917–21 games were played until a winner decided

NHL Finals
March 11   Canadiens 3 at Arenas 7
March 13   Arenas 3 at Canadiens 4
Arenas won two-game total-goals series 10–7

Stanley Cup Finals

March 20   Vancouver 3 at Toronto 5
March 23   Vancouver 6 at Toronto 4
March 26   Vancouver 3 at Toronto 6
March 28   Vancouver 8 at Toronto 1
March 30   Vancouver 1 at Toronto 2
Toronto won best-of-five finals 3–2

1918–19

First Half

	GP	W	L	GF	GA	PTS
Canadiens	10	7	3	57	50	14
Ottawa	10	5	5	39	39	10
Arenas	10	3	7	42	49	6

Second Half

	GP	W	L	GF	GA	PTS
Ottawa	8	7	1	32	14	14
Canadiens	8	3	5	31	28	6
Arenas	8	2	6	22	43	4

* Spanish influenza epidemic caused the cancellation of the Stanley Cup finals
* the 1918–19 season was supposed to be, like the ones before and after it, a
  24-game schedule. However, when Canadiens and Ottawa clinched first
  place in both halves early, Arenas manager Charlie Querrie refused to play
  the remaining games, fearing a lack of fan interest. The league almost sued
  the Arenas, but instead Canadiens and Ottawa played a best-of-seven, rather
  than a two-game total-goals series, to create extra home dates for the clubs.

NHL Finals

February 22   Ottawa 4 at Canadiens 8
February 27   Canadiens 5 at Ottawa 3
March 1   Ottawa 3 at Canadiens 6
March 3   Canadiens 3 at Ottawa 6
March 6   Ottawa 2 at Canadiens 4
Canadiens won best-of-seven series 4–1

Stanley Cup Finals

March 19 Canadiens 0 at Seattle 7 [Holmes]
March 22 Canadiens 4 at Seattle 2
March 24 Canadiens 2 at Seattle 7
March 26 Canadiens 0 at Seattle 0 (20:00 OT) [Vezina/Holmes]
March 30 Canadiens 4 at Seattle 3 (Odie Cleghorn 15:57 OT)

Finals cancelled after five games because of Spanish influenza and the death of Canadiens player Joe Hall

1919–20

First Half

	GP	W	L	GP	GA	PTS
Ottawa	12	9	3	59	23	18
Canadiens	12	8	4	62	51	16
St. Pats	12	5	7	52	62	10
Bulldogs	12	2	10	44	81	4

Second Half

	GP	W	L	GP	GA	PTS
Ottawa	12	10	2	62	41	20
St. Pats	12	7	5	67	44	14
Canadiens	12	5	7	67	62	10
Bulldogs	12	2	10	47	96	4

No NHL finals because Ottawa won both halves

Stanley Cup Finals

March 22 Seattle 2 at Ottawa 3
March 24 Seattle 0 at Ottawa 3 [Benedict]
March 27 Seattle 3 at Ottawa 1
March 30 Seattle 5 Ottawa 2*
April 1   Ottawa 6 Seattle 1*
Ottawa won best-of-five finals 3–2

* played in Toronto because of poor ice conditions in Ottawa

1920–21

First Half

	GP	W	L	GP	GA	PTS
Ottawa	10	8	2	49	23	16
St. Pats	10	5	5	39	47	10
Canadiens	10	4	6	37	51	8
Hamilton	10	3	7	34	38	6

Second Half

	GP	W	L	GP	GA	PTS
St. Pats	14	10	4	66	53	20
Canadiens	14	9	5	75	48	18
Ottawa	14	6	8	48	52	12
Hamilton	14	3	11	58	94	6

NHL Finals

March 10   St. Pats 0 at Ottawa 5 [Benedict]
March 15   Ottawa 2 at St. Pats 0 [Benedict]
Ottawa won two-game total-goals series 7–0

Stanley Cup Finals

March 21   Ottawa 1 at Vancouver 3
March 24   Ottawa 4 at Vancouver 3
March 28   Ottawa 3 at Vancouver 2
March 31   Ottawa 2 at Vancouver 3
April 4   Ottawa 2 at Vancouver 1
Ottawa won best-of-five finals 3–2

1921–22

	GP	W	L	T	GF	GA	PTS
Ottawa	24	14	8	2	106	84	30
St. Pats	24	13	10	1	98	97	27
Canadiens	24	12	11	1	88	94	25
Hamilton	24	7	17	0	88	105	14

* overtime limited to 20 minutes (not sudden-death); minor penalties reduced from three to two minutes
* top two teams advance to playoffs; winner met the Pacific Coast Hockey Association–Western Canadian Hockey League Champion for the Stanley Cup

NHL Finals
March 11   Ottawa 4 at St. Pats 5
March 13   St. Pats 0 at Ottawa 0 [Roach/Benedict]
St. Pats won two-game total-goals series 5–4

Stanley Cup Finals
March 17   Vancouver 4 at St. Pats 3
March 21   Vancouver 1 at St. Pats 2   (Dye 4:50 OT)
March 23   Vancouver 3 at St. Pats 0 [Lehman]
March 25   Vancouver 0 at St. Pats 6 [Roach]
March 28   Vancouver 1 at St. Pats 5
St. Pats won best-of-five finals 3–2

1922–23

	GP	W	L	T	GF	GA	PTS
Ottawa	24	14	9	1	77	54	29
Canadiens	24	13	9	2	73	61	28
St. Pats	24	13	10	1	82	88	27
Hamilton	24	6	18	0	81	110	12

NHL Finals
March 7   Ottawa 2 at Canadiens 0 [Benedict]
March 9   Canadiens 2 at Ottawa 1
Ottawa won two-game total-goals series 3–2

Stanley Cup Playoffs
March 16   Ottawa 1 at Vancouver 0 [Benedict]
March 19   Ottawa 1 at Vancouver 4
March 23   Ottawa 3 at Vancouver 2
March 26   Ottawa 5 at Vancouver 1
Ottawa won best-of-five semifinals 3–1

Stanley Cup Finals
March 29   Ottawa 2 Edmonton 1 (Cy Denneny 2:08 OT)*
March 31   Ottawa 1 Edmonton 0 [Benedict]*
Ottawa won best-of-three finals 2–0

* games played at Vancouver

1923–24

	GP	W	L	T	GF	GA	PTS
Ottawa	24	16	8	0	74	54	32
Canadiens	24	13	11	0	59	48	26
St. Pats	24	10	14	0	59	85	20
Hamilton	24	9	15	0	63	68	18

NHL Finals
March 8   Ottawa 0 at Canadiens 1 [Vezina]
March 11   Canadiens 4 at Ottawa 2
Canadiens won two-game total-goals series 5–2

Stanley Cup Playoffs
March 18   Vancouver 2 at Canadiens 3
March 20   Vancouver 1 at Canadiens 2
Canadiens won best-of-three semifinals 2–0

Stanley Cup Finals
March 22   Calgary 1 at Canadiens 6
March 25   Canadiens 3 Calgary 0 [Vezina]*
Canadiens won best-of-three finals 2–0

* played at Ottawa

1924–25

	GP	W	L	T	GF	GA	PTS
Hamilton	30	19	10	1	90	60	39
St. Pats	30	19	11	0	90	84	38
Canadiens	30	17	11	2	93	56	36
Ottawa	30	17	12	1	83	66	35
Maroons	30	9	19	2	45	65	20
Boston	30	6	24	0	49	119	12

* the top two teams (Hamilton and Toronto) were supposed to compete for the NHL championship and the right to advance to the Stanley Cup Finals against the WCHL winners. However, the Tigers' players demanded more money for these extra games and the NHL simply disqualified the team. Thus, the St. Pats played the Canadiens.

NHL Finals
March 13   Canadiens 2 at St. Pats 0
March 19   St. Pats 2 at Canadiens 3
Canadiens won two-game total-goals series 5–2

Stanley Cup Finals
March 21   Canadiens 2 at Victoria 5
March 23   Canadiens 1 at Victoria 3*
March 27   Canadiens 4 at Victoria 2
March 30   Canadiens 1 at Victoria 6
Victoria won best-of-five finals 3–1

* played at Vancouver

1925–26

	GP	W	L	T	GF	GA	PTS
Ottawa	36	24	8	4	77	42	52
Maroons	36	20	11	5	91	73	45
Pirates	36	19	16	1	82	70	39
Boston	36	17	15	4	92	85	38
Americans	36	12	20	4	68	89	28
St. Pats	36	12	21	3	92	114	27
Canadiens	36	11	24	1	79	108	23

NHL Finals

March 25   Ottawa 1 at Maroons 1
March 27   Maroons 1 at Ottawa 0 [Benedict]
Maroons win two-game total-goals finals 2–1

Stanley Cup Finals

March 30   Victoria 0 at Maroons 3 [Benedict]
April 1   Victoria 0 at Maroons 3 [Benedict]
April 3   Victoria 3 at Maroons 2
April 6   Victoria 0 at Maroons 2 [Benedict]
Maroons won best-of-five finals 3–1

1926–27

Canadian Division

	GP	W	L	T	GF	GA	PTS
Ottawa	44	30	10	4	86	69	64
Canadiens	44	28	14	2	99	67	58
Maroons	44	20	20	4	71	68	44
Americans	44	17	25	2	82	91	36
Toronto*	44	15	24	5	79	94	35

American Division

Rangers	44	25	13	6	95	72	56
Boston	44	21	20	3	97	89	45
Chicago	44	19	22	3	115	116	41
Pirates	44	15	26	3	79	108	33
Cougars	44	12	28	4	76	105	28

* on February 14, 1927, the St. Pats changed their name to Maple Leafs

Stanley Cup Finals

April 7	Ottawa 0 at Boston 0* [Connell/Winkler]
April 9	Ottawa 3 at Boston 1
April 11	Boston 1 at Ottawa 1**
April 13	Boston 1 at Ottawa 3

Ottawa won best-of-five finals 2–0–2

* two 10-minute overtime periods
** one 20-minute overtime period

1927–28

Canadian Division

	GP	W	L	T	GF	GA	PTS
Canadiens	44	26	11	7	116	48	59
Maroons	44	24	14	6	96	77	54
Ottawa	44	20	14	10	78	57	50
Toronto	44	18	18	8	89	88	44
Americans	44	11	27	6	63	128	28

American Division

Boston	44	20	13	11	77	70	51
Rangers	44	19	16	9	94	79	47
Pirates	44	19	17	8	67	76	46
Cougars	44	19	19	6	88	79	44
Chicago	44	7	34	3	68	134	17

* overtime limited to 10 minutes of sudden-death; forward passing now allowed in defending zone

Finals

April 5	Rangers 0 at Maroons 2 [Benedict]
April 7	Rangers 2 at Maroons 1 (Frank Boucher 7:05 OT)
April 10	Rangers 0 at Maroons 2 [Benedict]
April 12	Rangers 1 at Maroons 0 [Miller]
April 14	Rangers 2 at Maroons 1

Rangers won best-of-five finals 3–2

1928–29

Canadian Division

	GP	W	L	T	GF	GA	PTS
Canadiens	44	22	7	15	71	43	59
Americans	44	19	13	12	53	53	50
Toronto	44	21	18	5	85	69	47
Ottawa	44	14	17	13	54	67	41
Maroons	44	15	20	9	67	65	39

American Division

Boston	44	26	13	5	89	52	57
Rangers	44	21	13	10	72	65	52
Cougars	44	19	16	9	72	63	47
Pirates	44	9	27	8	46	80	26
Chicago	44	7	29	8	33	85	22

* overtime set at 10 minutes without sudden-death; passing allowed into, but not within, the offensive zone

* the two division winners played a best-of-five and the two second place teams and third-place teams played two-game total-goals series. Those two winners then played to see who would play the winner of the two division champions' series.

Stanley Cup Finals
March 28   Rangers 0 at Boston 2 [Thompson]
March 29   Boston 2 at Rangers 1
Boston won best-of-three finals 2–0

1929–30

Canadian Division

	GP	W	L	T	GF	GA	PTS
Maroons	44	23	16	5	141	114	51
Canadiens	44	21	14	9	142	114	51
Ottawa	44	21	15	8	138	118	50
Toronto	44	17	21	6	116	124	40
Americans	44	14	25	5	113	161	33

American Division

	GP	W	L	T	GF	GA	PTS
Boston	44	38	5	1	179	98	77
Chicago	44	21	18	5	117	111	47
Rangers	44	17	17	10	136	143	44
Falcons	44	14	24	6	117	133	34
Pirates	44	5	36	3	102	185	13

* forward passing allowed in all three zones, producing twice the number of goals this season over last

Stanley Cup Finals
April 1   Canadiens 3 at Boston 0 [Hainsworth]
April 3   Boston 3 at Canadiens 4
Canadiens won best-of-three finals 2–0

1930–31

Canadian Division

	GP	W	L	T	GF	GA	PTS
Canadiens	44	26	10	8	129	89	60
Toronto	44	22	13	9	118	99	53
Maroons	44	20	18	6	105	106	46
Americans	44	18	16	10	76	74	46
Ottawa	44	10	30	4	91	142	24

American Division

	GP	W	L	T	GF	GA	PTS
Boston	44	28	10	6	143	90	62
Chicago	44	24	17	3	108	78	51
Rangers	44	19	16	9	106	87	47
Falcons	44	16	21	7	102	105	39
Quakers	44	4	36	4	76	184	12

Stanley Cup Finals

April 3	Canadiens 2 at Chicago 1
April 5	Canadiens 1 at Chicago 2 (24:50 OT)
April 9	Chicago 3 at Canadiens 2 (53:50 OT)
April 11	Chicago 2 at Canadiens 4
April 14	Chicago 0 at Canadiens 2 [Hainsworth]

Canadiens won best-of-five finals 3–2

1931–32

Canadian Division

	GP	W	L	T	GF	GA	PTS
Canadiens	48	25	16	7	128	111	57
Toronto	48	23	18	7	155	127	53
Maroons	48	19	22	7	142	139	45
Americans	48	16	24	8	95	142	40

American Division

Rangers	48	23	17	8	134	112	54
Chicago	48	18	19	11	86	101	47
Falcons	48	18	20	10	95	108	46
Boston	48	15	21	12	122	117	42

Stanley Cup Finals

April 5	Toronto 6 at Rangers 4
April 7	Toronto 6 at Rangers 2*
April 9	Rangers 4 at Toronto 6

Toronto won best-of-five finals 3–0

* played at Boston because Madison Square Garden unavailable April 7 because of circus. Because of the scores in the finals (6–4, 6–2, 6–4) this series has long been dubbed the "Tennis Series"

* all members of this Toronto team were given gold coins by Conn Smythe as lifetime passes to the Gardens

1932–33
Canadian Division

	GP	W	L	T	GF	GA	PTS
Toronto	48	24	18	6	119	111	54
Maroons	48	22	20	6	135	119	50
Canadiens	48	18	25	5	92	115	41
Americans	48	15	22	11	91	118	41
Ottawa	48	11	27	10	88	131	32

American Division

Boston	48	25	15	8	124	88	58
Detroit	48	25	15	8	111	93	58
Rangers	48	23	17	8	135	107	54
Chicago	48	16	20	12	88	101	44

Stanley Cup Finals

April 4	Toronto 1 at Rangers 5
April 8	Rangers 3 at Toronto 1
April 11	Rangers 2 at Toronto 3
April 13	Rangers 1 at Toronto 0 (Bill Cook 7:33 OT) [Aitkenhead]

Rangers won best-of-five finals 3–1

1933–34

Canadian Division

	GP	W	L	T	GF	GA	PTS
Toronto	48	26	13	9	174	119	61
Canadiens	48	22	20	6	99	101	50
Maroons	48	19	18	11	117	122	49
Americans	48	15	23	10	104	132	40
Ottawa	48	13	29	6	115	143	32

American Division

	GP	W	L	T	GF	GA	PTS
Detroit	48	24	14	10	113	98	58
Chicago	48	20	17	11	88	83	51
Rangers	48	21	19	8	120	113	50
Boston	48	18	25	5	111	130	41

Stanley Cup Finals

April 3	Chicago 2 at Detroit 1 (Paul Thompson 21:10 OT)
April 5	Chicago 4 at Detroit 1
April 8	Detroit 5 at Chicago 2
April 10	Detroit 0 at Chicago 1 (Mush March 30:05 OT) [Gardiner]

Chicago won best-of-five finals 3–1

1934–35

Canadian Division

	GP	W	L	T	GF	GA	PTS
Toronto	48	30	14	4	157	111	64
Maroons	48	24	19	5	123	92	53
Canadiens	48	19	23	6	110	145	44
Americans	48	12	27	9	100	142	33
Eagles	48	11	31	6	86	144	28

American Division

	GP	W	L	T	GF	GA	PTS
Boston	48	26	16	6	129	112	58
Chicago	48	26	17	5	118	88	57
Rangers	48	22	20	6	137	139	50
Detroit	48	19	22	7	127	114	45

Stanley Cup Finals

April 4   Maroons 3 at Toronto 2 (Dave Trottier 5:28 OT)
April 6   Maroons 3 at Toronto 1
April 9   Toronto 1 at Maroons 4
Maroons won best-of-five finals 3–0

1935–36

Canadian Division

	GP	W	L	T	GF	GA	PTS
Maroons	48	22	16	10	114	106	54
Toronto	48	23	19	6	126	106	52
Americans	48	16	25	7	109	122	39
Canadiens	48	11	26	11	82	123	33

American Division

	GP	W	L	T	GF	GA	PTS
Detroit	48	24	16	8	124	103	56
Boston	48	22	20	6	92	83	50
Chicago	48	21	19	8	93	92	50
Rangers	48	19	17	12	91	96	50

Stanley Cup Finals

April 5	Toronto 1 at Detroit 3
April 7	Toronto 4 at Detroit 9
April 9	Detroit 3 at Toronto 4 (Buzz Boll 0:31 OT)
April 11	Detroit 3 at Toronto 2

Detroit won best-of-five finals 3–1

1936–37

Canadian Division

	GP	W	L	T	GF	GA	PTS
Canadiens	48	24	18	6	115	111	54
Maroons	48	22	17	9	126	110	53
Toronto	48	22	21	5	119	115	49
Americans	48	15	29	4	122	161	34

American Division

	GP	W	L	T	GF	GA	PTS
Detroit	48	25	14	9	128	102	59
Boston	48	23	18	7	120	110	53
Rangers	48	19	20	9	117	106	47
Chicago	48	14	27	7	99	131	35

Stanley Cup Finals

April 6	Detroit 1 at Rangers 5
April 8	Rangers 2 at Detroit 4
April 11	Rangers 1 at Detroit 0 [Kerr]
April 13	Rangers 0 at Detroit 1 [Robertson]
April 15	Rangers 0 at Detroit 3 [Robertson]

Detroit won best-of-five finals 3–2

1937–38

Canadian Division

	GP	W	L	T	GF	GA	PTS
Toronto	48	24	15	9	151	127	57
Americans	48	19	18	11	110	111	49
Canadiens	48	18	17	13	123	128	49
Maroons	48	12	30	6	101	149	30

American Division

	GP	W	L	T	GF	GA	PTS
Boston	48	30	11	7	142	89	67
Rangers	48	27	15	6	149	96	60
Chicago	48	14	25	9	97	139	37
Detroit	48	12	25	11	99	133	35

Stanley Cup Finals

April 5	Chicago 3 at Toronto 1
April 7	Chicago 1 at Toronto 5
April 10	Toronto 1 at Chicago 2
April 12	Toronto 1 at Chicago 4

Chicago won best-of-five finals 3–1

1938–39

	GP	W	L	T	GF	GA	PTS
Boston	48	36	10	2	156	76	74
Rangers	48	26	16	6	149	105	58
Toronto	48	19	20	9	114	107	47
Americans	48	17	21	10	119	157	44
Detroit	48	18	24	6	107	128	42
Canadiens	48	15	24	9	115	146	39
Chicago	48	12	28	8	91	132	32

* only the last-place team did not qualify for the playoffs under the new one-division, 7-team format. The first- and second-place team played a best-of-seven to advance to the finals. The second played third and fourth played fifth in best-of-three, the two winners playing another best-of-three to advance to the finals.

Stanley Cup Finals

April 6	Toronto 1 at Boston 2
April 9	Toronto 3 at Boston 2 (Doc Romnes 10:38 OT)
April 11	Boston 3 at Toronto 1
April 13	Boston 2 at Toronto 0 [Brimsek]
April 16	Toronto 1 at Boston 3

Boston won best-of-seven finals 4–1

1939–40

	GP	W	L	T	GF	GA	PTS
Boston	48	31	12	5	170	98	67
Rangers	48	27	11	10	136	77	64
Toronto	48	25	17	6	134	110	56
Chicago	48	23	19	6	112	120	52
Detroit	48	16	26	6	90	126	38
Americans	48	15	29	4	106	140	34
Canadiens	48	10	33	5	90	167	25

Stanley Cup Finals

April 2	Toronto 1 at Rangers 2 (Alf Pike 15:30 OT)
April 3	Toronto 2 at Rangers 6
April 6	Rangers 1 at Toronto 2
April 9	Rangers 0 at Toronto 3 [Broda]
April 11	Rangers 2 at Toronto 1 (Muzz Patrick 31:43 OT)*
April 13	Rangers 3 at Toronto 2 (Bryan Hextall 2:07 OT)

Rangers won best-of-seven finals 4–2

* game could not be played at Madison Square Garden as it was previously
  booked for the circus

1940–41

	GP	W	L	T	GF	GA	PTS
Boston	48	27	8	13	168	102	67
Toronto	48	28	14	6	145	99	62
Detroit	48	21	16	11	112	102	53
Rangers	48	21	19	8	143	125	50
Chicago	48	16	25	7	112	139	39
Canadiens	48	16	26	6	121	147	38
Americans	48	8	29	11	99	186	27

Stanley Cup Finals

April 6	Detroit 2 at Boston 3
April 8	Detroit 1 at Boston 2
April 10	Boston 4 at Detroit 2
April 12	Boston 3 at Detroit 1

Boston won best-of-seven finals 4-0

1941–42

	GP	W	L	T	GF	GA	PTS
Rangers	48	29	17	2	177	143	60
Toronto	48	27	18	3	158	136	57
Boston	48	25	17	6	160	118	56
Chicago	48	22	23	3	145	155	47
Detroit	48	19	25	4	140	147	42
Canadiens	48	18	27	3	134	173	39
Brooklyn	48	16	29	3	133	175	35

Stanley Cup Finals

April 4	Detroit 3 at Toronto 2
April 7	Detroit 4 at Toronto 2
April 9	Toronto 2 at Detroit 5

April 12   Toronto 4 at Detroit 3
April 14   Detroit 3 at Toronto 9
April 16   Toronto 3 at Detroit 0 [Broda]
April 18   Detroit 1 at Toronto 3
Toronto won best-of-seven finals 4–3

* only time in NHL history that a team has trailed 3–0 in the finals and won the Stanley Cup

1942–43

	GP	W	L	T	GF	GA	PTS
Detroit	50	25	14	11	169	124	61
Boston	50	24	17	9	195	176	57
Toronto	50	22	19	9	198	159	53
Canadiens	50	19	19	12	181	191	50
Chicago	50	17	18	15	179	180	49
Rangers	50	11	31	8	161	253	30

* because of wartime restrictions on train schedules overtime was eliminated as of November 21, 1942
* the top four teams qualified for the playoffs in the six-team league, and both rounds were best-of-seven

Stanley Cup Finals

April 1   Boston 2 at Detroit 6
April 4   Boston 3 at Detroit 4
April 7   Detroit 4 at Boston 0 [Mowers]
April 8   Detroit 2 at Boston 0 [Mowers]
Detroit won best-of-seven finals 4–0

1943–44

	GP	W	L	T	GF	GA	PTS
Canadiens	50	38	5	7	234	109	83
Detroit	50	26	18	6	214	177	58
Toronto	50	23	23	4	214	174	50
Chicago	50	22	23	5	178	187	49
Boston	50	19	26	5	223	268	43
Rangers	50	6	39	5	162	310	17

Stanley Cup Finals

April 4	Chicago 1 at Canadiens 5
April 6	Canadiens 3 at Chicago 1
April 9	Canadiens 3 at Chicago 2
April 13	Chicago 4 at Canadiens 5 (Toe Blake 9:12 OT)

Canadiens won best-of-seven finals 4–0

1944–45

	GP	W	L	T	GF	GA	PTS
Canadiens	50	38	8	4	228	121	80
Detroit	50	31	14	5	218	161	67
Toronto	50	24	22	4	183	161	52
Boston	50	16	30	4	179	219	36
Chicago	50	13	30	7	141	194	33
Rangers	50	11	29	10	154	247	32

Stanley Cup Finals

April 6	Toronto 1 at Detroit 0 [McCool]
April 8	Toronto 2 at Detroit 0 [McCool]
April 12	Detroit 0 at Toronto 1 [McCool]
April 14	Detroit 5 at Toronto 3
April 19	Toronto 0 at Detroit 2 [Lumley]
April 21	Detroit 1 at Toronto 0 (Ed Bruneteau 14:16 OT) [Lumley]
April 22	Toronto 2 at Detroit 1

Toronto won best-of-seven finals 4–3

1945–46

	GP	W	L	T	GF	GA	PTS
Canadiens	50	28	17	5	172	134	61
Boston	50	24	18	8	167	156	56
Chicago	50	23	20	7	200	178	53
Detroit	50	20	20	10	146	159	50
Toronto	50	19	24	7	174	185	45
Rangers	50	13	28	9	144	191	35

Stanley Cup Finals

March 30	Boston 3 at Canadiens 4 (Maurice Richard 9:08 OT)
April 2	Boston 2 at Canadiens 3 (Jimmy Peters 16:55 OT)
April 4	Canadiens 4 at Boston 2
April 7	Canadiens 2 at Boston 3 (Terry Reardon 15:13 OT)
April 9	Boston 3 at Canadiens 6

Canadiens won best-of-seven finals 4–1

1946–47

	GP	W	L	T	GF	GA	PTS
Canadiens	60	34	16	10	189	138	78
Toronto	60	31	19	10	209	172	72
Boston	60	26	23	11	190	175	63
Detroit	60	22	27	11	190	193	55
Rangers	60	22	32	6	167	186	50
Chicago	60	19	37	4	193	274	42

Stanley Cup Finals

April 8	Toronto 0 at Canadiens 6 [Durnan]
April 10	Toronto 4 at Canadiens 0 [Broda]
April 12	Canadiens 2 at Toronto 4
April 15	Canadiens 1 at Toronto 2 (Syl Apps 16:36 OT)
April 17	Toronto 1 at Canadiens 3
April 19	Toronto 1 at Canadiens 2

Toronto won best-of-seven finals 4–2

1947–48

	GP	W	L	T	GF	GA	PTS
Toronto	60	32	15	13	182	143	77
Detroit	60	30	18	12	187	148	72
Boston	60	23	24	13	167	168	59
Rangers	60	21	26	13	176	201	55
Canadiens	60	20	29	11	147	169	51
Chicago	60	20	34	6	195	225	46

Stanley Cup Finals

April 7   Detroit 3 at Toronto 5
April 10   Detroit 2 at Toronto 4
April 11   Toronto 2 at Detroit 0 [Broda]
April 14   Toronto 7 at Detroit 2
Toronto won best-of-seven finals 4–0

1948–49

	GP	W	L	T	GF	GA	PTS
Detroit	60	34	19	7	195	145	75
Boston	60	29	23	8	178	163	66
Canadiens	60	28	23	9	152	126	65
Toronto	60	22	25	13	147	161	57
Chicago	60	21	31	8	173	211	50
Rangers	60	18	31	11	133	172	47

Stanley Cup Finals

April 8   Toronto 3 at Detroit 2 (Joe Klukay 17:31 OT)
April 10   Toronto 3 at Detroit 1
April 13   Detroit 1 at Toronto 3
April 16   Detroit 1 at Toronto 3
Toronto won best-of-seven finals 4–0

1949–50

	GP	W	L	T	GF	GA	PTS
Detroit	70	37	19	14	229	164	88
Canadiens	70	29	22	19	172	150	77
Toronto	70	31	27	12	176	173	74
Rangers	70	28	31	11	170	189	67
Boston	70	22	32	16	198	228	60
Chicago	70	22	38	10	203	244	54

Stanley Cup Finals

April 11	Rangers 1 at Detroit 4
April 13	Detroit 1 Rangers 3*
April 15	Detroit 4 Rangers 0*[Lumley]
April 18	Rangers 4 at Detroit 3 (Don Raleigh 8:34 OT)
April 20	Rangers 2 at Detroit 1 (Don Raleigh 1:38 OT)
April 22	Rangers 4 at Detroit 5
April 23	Rangers 3 at Detroit 4 (Pete Babando 28:31 OT)**

Detroit won best-of-seven finals 4–3

* played at Toronto because Madison Square Garden was previously booked for the circus. Games 6 and 7 played in Detroit because league by-laws stipulated a Stanley Cup-winning game cannot be played on neutral ice.

** first time in history the Cup was won on an OT goal in game 7

1950–51

	GP	W	L	T	GF	GA	PTS
Detroit	70	44	13	13	236	139	101
Toronto	70	41	16	13	212	138	95
Canadiens	70	25	30	15	173	184	65
Boston	70	22	30	18	178	197	62
Rangers	70	20	29	21	169	201	61
Chicago	70	13	47	10	171	280	36

Stanley Cup Finals

April 11	Canadiens 2 at Toronto 3 (Sid Smith 5:51 OT)
April 14	Canadiens 3 at Toronto 2 (Maurice Richard 2:55 OT)
April 17	Toronto 2 at Canadiens 1 (Ted Kennedy 4:47 OT)
April 19	Toronto 3 at Canadiens 2 (Harry Watson 5:15 OT)
April 21	Canadiens 2 at Toronto 3 (Bill Barilko 2:53 OT)

Toronto won best-of-seven finals 4–1

1951–52

	GP	W	L	T	GF	GA	PTS
Detroit	70	44	14	12	215	133	100
Canadiens	70	34	26	10	195	164	78
Toronto	70	29	25	16	168	157	74
Boston	70	25	29	16	162	176	66
Rangers	70	23	34	13	192	219	59
Chicago	70	17	44	9	158	241	43

Stanley Cup Finals

April 10	Detroit 3 at Canadiens 1
April 12	Detroit 2 at Canadiens 1
April 13	Canadiens 0 at Detroit 3 [Sawchuk]
April 15	Canadiens 0 at Detroit 3 [Sawchuk]

Detroit won best-of-seven finals 4–0

1952–53

	GP	W	L	T	GF	GA	PTS
Detroit	70	36	16	18	222	133	90
Canadiens	70	28	23	19	155	148	75
Boston	70	28	29	13	152	172	69
Chicago	70	27	28	15	169	175	69
Toronto	70	27	30	13	156	167	67
Rangers	70	17	37	16	152	211	50

Stanley Cup Finals

April 9   Boston 2 at Canadiens 4
April 11   Boston 4 at Canadiens 1
April 12   Canadiens 3 at Boston 0 [McNeil]
April 14   Canadiens 7 at Boston 3
April 16   Boston 0 at Canadiens 1 (Elmer Lach 1:22 OT) [McNeil]

Canadiens won best-of-seven finals 4–1

1953–54

	GP	W	L	T	GF	GA	PTS
Detroit	70	37	19	14	191	132	88
Canadiens	70	35	24	11	195	141	81
Toronto	70	32	24	14	152	131	78
Boston	70	32	28	10	177	181	74
Rangers	70	29	31	10	161	182	68
Chicago	70	12	51	7	133	242	31

Stanley Cup Finals

April 4   Canadiens 1 at Detroit 3
April 6   Canadiens 3 at Detroit 1
April 8   Detroit 5 at Canadiens 2
April 10   Detroit 2 at Canadiens 0 [Sawchuk]
April 11   Canadiens 1 at Detroit 0 (Ken Mosdell 5:45 OT) [McNeil]
April 13   Detroit 1 at Canadiens 4
April 16   Canadiens 1 at Detroit 2 (Tony Leswick 4:29 OT)

Detroit won best-of-seven finals 4–3

1954–55

	GP	W	L	T	GF	GA	PTS
Detroit	70	42	17	11	204	134	95
Canadiens	70	41	18	11	228	157	93
Toronto	70	24	24	22	147	135	70
Boston	70	23	26	21	169	188	67
Rangers	70	17	35	18	150	210	52
Chicago	70	13	40	17	161	235	43

Stanley Cup Finals

April 3   Canadiens 2 at Detroit 4
April 5   Canadiens 1 at Detroit 7
April 7   Detroit 2 at Canadiens 4
April 9   Detroit 3 at Canadiens 5
April 10   Canadiens 1 at Detroit 5
April 12   Detroit 3 at Canadiens 6
April 14   Canadiens 1 at Detroit 3

Detroit won best-of-seven finals 4–3

1955–56

	GP	W	L	T	GF	GA	PTS
Canadiens	70	45	15	10	222	131	100
Detroit	70	30	24	16	183	148	76
Rangers	70	32	28	10	204	203	74
Toronto	70	24	33	13	153	181	61
Boston	70	23	34	13	147	185	59
Chicago	70	19	39	12	155	216	50

Stanley Cup Finals

March 31   Detroit 4 at Canadiens 6
April 3   Detroit 1 at Canadiens 5
April 5   Canadiens 1 at Detroit 3
April 8   Canadiens 3 at Detroit 0 [Plante]
April 10   Detroit 1 at Canadiens 3

Canadiens won best-of-seven finals 4–1

1956–57

	GP	W	L	T	GF	GA	PTS
Detroit	70	38	20	12	198	157	88
Canadiens	70	35	23	12	210	155	82
Boston	70	34	24	12	195	174	80
Rangers	70	26	30	14	184	227	66
Toronto	70	21	34	15	174	192	57
Chicago	70	16	39	15	169	225	47

* penalized player allowed to return to the ice after a power-play goal has been scored by the opposition

Stanley Cup Finals
April 6   Boston 1 at Canadiens 5
April 9   Boston 0 at Canadiens 1 [Plante]
April 11   Canadiens 4 at Boston 2
April 14   Canadiens 0 at Boston 2 [Simmons]
April 16   Boston 1 at Canadiens 5
Canadiens won best-of-seven finals 4–1

1957–58

	GP	W	L	T	GF	GA	PTS
Canadiens	70	43	17	10	250	158	96
Rangers	70	32	25	13	195	188	77
Detroit	70	29	29	12	176	207	70
Boston	70	27	28	15	199	194	69
Chicago	70	24	39	7	163	202	55
Toronto	70	21	38	11	192	226	53

Stanley Cup Finals
April 8   Boston 1 at Canadiens 2
April 10   Boston 5 at Canadiens 2
April 13   Canadiens 3 at Boston 0 [Plante]
April 15   Canadiens 1 at Boston 3
April 17   Boston 2 at Canadiens 3 (Maurice Richard 5:45 OT)

April 20   Canadiens 5 at Boston 3
Canadiens won best-of-seven finals 4–2

1958–59

	GP	W	L	T	GF	GA	PTS
Canadiens	70	39	18	13	258	158	91
Boston	70	32	29	9	205	215	73
Chicago	70	28	29	13	197	208	69
Toronto	70	27	32	11	189	201	65
Rangers	70	26	32	12	201	217	64
Detroit	70	25	37	8	167	218	58

Stanley Cup Finals

April 9   Toronto 3 at Canadiens 5
April 11   Toronto 1 at Canadiens 3
April 14   Canadiens 2 at Toronto 3 (Dick Duff 10:06 OT)
April 16   Canadiens 3 at Toronto 2
April 18   Toronto 3 at Canadiens 5
Canadiens won best-of-seven finals 4–1

1959–60

	GP	W	L	T	GF	GA	PTS
Canadiens	70	40	18	12	255	178	92
Toronto	70	35	26	9	199	195	79
Chicago	70	28	29	13	191	180	69
Detroit	70	26	29	15	186	197	67
Boston	70	28	34	8	220	241	64
Rangers	70	17	38	15	187	247	49

Stanley Cup Finals

April 7   Toronto 2 at Canadiens 4
April 9   Toronto 1 at Canadiens 2
April 12   Canadiens 5 at Toronto 2
April 14   Canadiens 4 at Toronto 0 [Plante]
Canadiens won best-of-seven finals 4–0

1960–61

	GP	W	L	T	GF	GA	PTS
Canadiens	70	41	19	10	254	188	92
Toronto	70	39	19	12	234	176	90
Chicago	70	29	24	17	198	180	75
Detroit	70	25	29	16	195	215	66
Rangers	70	22	38	10	204	248	54
Boston	70	15	42	13	176	254	43

Stanley Cup Finals

April 6   Detroit 2 at Chicago 3
April 8   Chicago 1 at Detroit 3
April 10   Detroit 1 at Chicago 3
April 12   Chicago 1 at Detroit 2
April 14   Detroit 3 at Chicago 6
April 16   Chicago 5 at Detroit 1
Chicago won best-of-seven finals 4–2

1961–62

	GP	W	L	T	GF	GA	PTS
Canadiens	70	42	14	14	259	166	98
Toronto	70	37	22	11	232	180	85
Chicago	70	31	26	13	217	186	75
Rangers	70	26	32	12	195	207	64
Detroit	70	23	33	14	184	219	60
Boston	70	15	47	8	177	306	38

Stanley Cup Finals

April 10   Chicago 1 at Toronto 4
April 12   Chicago 2 at Toronto 3
April 15   Toronto 0 at Chicago 3 [Hall]
April 17   Toronto 1 at Chicago 4
April 19   Chicago 4 at Toronto 8
April 22   Toronto 2 at Chicago 1
Toronto won best-of-seven finals 4–2

1962–63

	GP	W	L	T	GF	GA	PTS
Toronto	70	35	23	12	221	180	82
Chicago	70	32	21	17	194	178	81
Canadiens	70	28	19	23	225	183	79
Detroit	70	32	25	13	200	194	77
Rangers	70	22	36	12	211	233	56
Boston	70	14	39	17	198	281	45

Stanley Cup Finals
April 9   Detroit 2 at Toronto 4
April 11   Detroit 2 at Toronto 4
April 14   Toronto 2 at Detroit 3
April 16   Toronto 4 at Detroit 2
April 18   Detroit 1 at Toronto 3
Toronto won best-of-seven finals 4–1

1963–64

	GP	W	L	T	GF	GA	PTS
Canadiens	70	36	21	13	209	167	85
Chicago	70	36	22	12	218	169	84
Toronto	70	33	25	12	192	172	78
Detroit	70	30	29	11	191	204	71
Rangers	70	22	38	10	186	242	54
Boston	70	18	40	12	170	212	48

Stanley Cup Finals
April 11   Detroit 2 at Toronto 3
April 14   Detroit 4 at Toronto 3 (Larry Jeffrey 7:52 OT)
April 16   Toronto 3 at Detroit 4
April 18   Toronto 4 at Detroit 2
April 21   Detroit 2 at Toronto 1
April 23   Toronto 4 at Detroit 3 (Bobby Baun 1:43 OT)
April 25   Detroit 0 at Toronto 4 [Bower]
Toronto won best-of-seven finals 4–3

1964–65

	GP	W	L	T	GF	GA	PTS
Detroit	70	40	23	7	224	175	87
Canadiens	70	36	23	11	211	185	83
Chicago	70	34	28	8	224	176	76
Toronto	70	30	26	14	204	173	74
Rangers	70	20	38	12	179	246	52
Boston	70	21	43	6	166	253	48

Stanley Cup Finals

April 17	Chicago 2 at Canadiens 3
April 20	Chicago 0 at Canadiens 2 [Worsley]
April 22	Canadiens 1 at Chicago 3
April 25	Canadiens 1 at Chicago 5
April 27	Chicago 0 at Canadiens 6 [Hodge]
April 29	Canadiens 1 at Chicago 2
May 1	Chicago 0 at Canadiens 4 [Worsley]

Canadiens won best-of-seven finals 4–3

1965–66

	GP	W	L	T	GF	GA	PTS
Canadiens	70	41	21	8	239	173	90
Chicago	70	37	25	8	240	187	82
Toronto	70	34	25	11	208	187	79
Detroit	70	31	27	12	221	194	74
Boston	70	21	43	6	174	275	48
Rangers	70	18	41	11	195	261	47

Stanley Cup Finals

April 24	Detroit 3 at Canadiens 2
April 26	Detroit 5 at Canadiens 2
April 28	Canadiens 4 at Detroit 2
May 1	Canadiens 2 at Detroit 1

May 3   Detroit 1 at Canadiens 5
May 5   Canadiens 3 at Detroit 2 (Henri Richard 2:20 OT)
Canadiens won best-of-seven finals 4–2

1966–67

	GP	W	L	T	GF	GA	PTS
Chicago	70	41	17	12	264	170	94
Canadiens	70	32	25	13	202	188	77
Toronto	70	32	27	11	204	211	75
Rangers	70	30	28	12	188	189	72
Detroit	70	27	39	4	212	241	58
Boston	70	17	43	10	182	253	44

Stanley Cup Finals

April 20   Toronto 2 at Canadiens 6
April 22   Toronto 3 at Canadiens 0 [Bower]
April 25   Canadiens 2 at Toronto 3 (Bob Pulford 28:26 OT)
April 27   Canadiens 6 at Toronto 2
April 29   Toronto 4 at Canadiens 1
May 2   Canadiens 1 at Toronto 3
Toronto won best-of-seven finals 4–2

1967–68

East Division

	GP	W	L	T	GF	GA	PTS
Canadiens	74	42	22	10	236	167	94
Rangers	74	39	23	12	226	183	90
Boston	74	37	27	10	259	216	84
Chicago	74	32	26	16	212	222	80
Toronto	74	33	31	10	209	176	76
Detroit	74	27	35	12	245	257	66

West Division

Philadelphia	74	31	32	11	173	179	73
Los Angeles	74	31	33	10	200	224	72
St. Louis	74	27	31	16	177	191	70
North Stars	74	27	32	15	191	226	69
Pittsburgh	74	27	34	13	195	216	67
Oakland	74	15	42	17	153	219	47

* top four teams in each division qualified for the playoffs

Stanley Cup Finals

May 5	Canadiens 3 at St. Louis 2 (Jacques Lemaire 1:41 OT)
May 7	Canadiens 1 at St. Louis 0 [Worsley]
May 9	St. Louis 3 at Canadiens 4 (Bobby Rousseau 1:13 OT)
May 11	St. Louis 2 at Canadiens 3

Canadiens won best-of-seven finals 4–0

1968–69

East Division

	GP	W	L	T	GF	GA	PTS
Canadiens	76	46	19	11	271	202	103
Boston	76	42	18	16	303	221	100
Rangers	76	41	26	9	231	196	91
Toronto	76	35	26	15	234	217	85
Detroit	76	33	31	12	239	221	78
Chicago	76	34	33	9	280	246	77

West Division

St. Louis	76	37	25	14	204	157	88
Oakland	76	29	36	11	219	251	69
Philadelphia	76	20	35	21	174	225	61
Los Angeles	76	24	42	10	185	260	58
Pittsburgh	76	20	45	11	189	252	51
North Stars	76	18	43	15	189	270	51

Stanley Cup Finals

April 27   St. Louis 1 at Canadiens 3
April 29   St. Louis 1 at Canadiens 3
May 1   Canadiens 4 at St. Louis 0 [Vachon]
May 4   Canadiens 2 at St. Louis 1
Canadiens won best-of-seven finals 4–0

1969–70

East Division

	GP	W	L	T	GF	GA	PTS
Chicago	76	45	22	9	250	170	99
Boston	76	40	17	19	277	216	99
Detroit	76	40	21	15	246	199	95
Rangers	76	38	22	16	246	189	92
Canadiens	76	38	22	16	244	201	92
Toronto	76	29	34	13	222	242	71

West Division

	GP	W	L	T	GF	GA	PTS
St. Louis	76	37	27	12	224	179	86
Pittsburgh	76	26	38	12	182	238	64
North Stars	76	19	35	22	224	257	60
Oakland	76	22	40	14	169	243	58
Philadelphia	76	17	35	24	197	225	58
Los Angeles	76	14	52	10	168	290	38

Stanley Cup Finals

May 3   Boston 6 at St. Louis 1
May 5   Boston 6 at St. Louis 2
May 7   St. Louis 1 at Boston 4
May 10   St. Louis 3 at Boston 4 (Bobby Orr 0:40 OT)
Boston won best-of-seven finals 4–0

1970–71

East Division

	GP	W	L	T	GF	GA	PTS
Boston	78	57	14	7	399	207	121
Rangers	78	49	18	11	259	177	109
Canadiens	78	42	23	13	291	216	97
Toronto	78	37	33	8	248	211	82
Buffalo	78	24	39	15	217	291	63
Vancouver	78	24	46	8	229	296	56
Detroit	78	22	45	11	209	308	55

West Division

	GP	W	L	T	GF	GA	PTS
Chicago	78	49	20	9	277	184	107
St. Louis	78	34	25	19	223	208	87
Philadelphia	78	28	33	17	207	225	73
North Stars	78	28	34	16	191	223	72
Los Angeles	78	25	40	13	239	303	63
Pittsburgh	78	21	37	20	221	240	62
California	78	20	53	5	199	320	45

Stanley Cup Finals

May 4	Canadiens 1 at Chicago 2 (Jim Pappin 21:11 OT)
May 6	Canadiens 3 at Chicago 5
May 9	Chicago 2 at Canadiens 4
May 11	Chicago 2 at Canadiens 5
May 13	Canadiens 0 at Chicago 2 [Esposito]
May 16	Chicago 3 at Canadiens 4
May 18	Canadiens 3 at Chicago 2

Canadiens won best-of-seven finals 4–3

1971–72

East Division

	GP	W	L	T	GF	GA	PTS
Boston	78	54	13	11	330	204	119
Rangers	78	48	17	13	317	192	109
Canadiens	78	46	16	16	307	205	108
Toronto	78	33	31	14	209	208	80
Detroit	78	33	35	10	261	262	76
Buffalo	78	16	43	19	203	289	51
Vancouver	78	20	50	8	203	297	48

West Division

	GP	W	L	T	GF	GA	PTS
Chicago	78	46	17	15	256	166	107
North Stars	78	37	29	12	212	191	86
St. Louis	78	28	39	11	208	247	67
Pittsburgh	78	26	38	14	220	258	66
Philadelphia	78	26	38	14	200	236	66
California	78	21	39	18	216	288	60
Los Angeles	78	20	49	9	206	305	49

Stanley Cup Finals

April 30	Rangers 5 at Boston 6
May 2	Rangers 1 at Boston 2
May 4	Boston 2 at Rangers 5
May 7	Boston 3 at Rangers 2
May 9	Rangers 3 at Boston 2
May 11	Boston 3 at Rangers 0 [Johnston]

Boston won best-of-seven finals 4–2

1972–73

East Division

	GP	W	L	T	GF	GA	PIM	PTS
Canadiens	78	52	10	16	329	184	783	120
Boston	78	51	22	5	330	235	1097	107
Rangers	78	47	23	8	297	208	765	102
Buffalo	78	37	27	14	257	219	940	88
Detroit	78	37	29	12	265	243	893	86
Toronto	78	27	41	10	247	279	716	64
Vancouver	78	22	47	9	233	339	943	53
Islanders	78	12	60	6	170	347	881	30

West Division

	GP	W	L	T	GF	GA	PIM	PTS
Chicago	78	42	27	9	284	225	864	93
Philadelphia	78	37	30	11	296	256	1756	85
North Stars	78	37	30	11	254	230	881	85
St. Louis	78	32	34	12	233	251	1195	76
Pittsburgh	78	32	37	9	257	265	866	73
Los Angeles	78	31	36	11	232	245	888	73
Flames	78	25	38	15	191	239	852	65
California	78	16	46	16	213	323	840	48

Stanley Cup Finals

April 29   Chicago 3 at Canadiens 8
May 1   Chicago 1 at Canadiens 4
May 3   Canadiens 4 at Chicago 7
May 6   Canadiens 4 at Chicago 0 [Dryden]
May 8   Chicago 8 at Canadiens 7
May 10   Canadiens 6 at Chicago 4
Canadiens won best-of-seven finals 4–2

1973–74

East Division

	GP	W	L	T	GF	GA	PTS
Boston	78	52	17	9	349	221	113
Canadiens	78	45	24	9	293	240	99
Rangers	78	40	24	14	300	251	94
Toronto	78	35	27	16	274	230	86
Buffalo	78	32	34	12	242	250	76
Detroit	78	29	39	10	255	319	68
Vancouver	78	24	43	11	224	296	59
Islanders	78	19	41	18	182	247	56

West Division

	GP	W	L	T	GF	GA	PTS
Philadelphia	78	50	16	12	273	164	112
Chicago	78	41	14	23	272	164	105
Los Angeles	78	33	33	12	233	231	78
Flames	78	30	34	14	214	238	74
Pittsburgh	78	28	41	9	242	273	65
St. Louis	78	26	40	12	206	248	64
North Stars	78	23	38	17	235	275	63
California	78	13	55	10	195	342	36

Stanley Cup Finals

May 7 Philadelphia 2 at Boston 3
May 9 Philadelphia 3 at Boston 2 (Bobby Clarke 12:01 OT)
May 12 Boston 1 at Philadelphia 4
May 14 Boston 2 at Philadelphia 4
May 16 Philadelphia 1 at Boston 5
May 19 Boston 0 at Philadelphia 1 [Parent]
Philadelphia won best-of-seven finals 4–2

1974–75

PRINCE OF WALES CONFERENCE
Adams Division

	GP	W	L	T	GF	GA	PTS
Buffalo	80	49	16	15	354	240	113
Boston	80	40	26	14	345	245	94
Toronto	80	31	33	16	280	309	78
California	80	19	48	13	212	316	51

Norris Division

Canadiens	80	47	14	19	374	225	113
Los Angeles	80	42	17	21	269	185	105
Pittsburgh	80	37	28	15	326	289	89
Detroit	80	23	45	12	259	335	58
Washington	80	8	67	5	181	446	21

CLARENCE CAMPBELL CONFERENCE
Patrick Division

Philadelphia	80	51	18	11	293	181	113
Rangers	80	37	29	14	319	276	88
Islanders	80	33	25	22	264	221	88
Flames	80	34	31	15	243	233	83

Smythe Division

Vancouver	80	38	32	10	271	254	86
St. Louis	80	35	31	14	269	267	84
Chicago	80	37	35	8	268	241	82
North Stars	80	23	50	7	221	341	53
Kansas City	80	15	54	11	184	328	41

* the top three teams in each division qualified for the playoffs. The four division champions received byes to the second round and all second- and third-place clubs were seeded 1–8 by points, #1 playing # 8, #2 and #7, etc. The first round was best-of-three, the subsequent rounds best-of-seven.

Stanley Cup Finals

May 15	Buffalo 1 at Philadelphia 4
May 18	Buffalo 1 at Philadelphia 2
May 20	Philadelphia 4 at Buffalo 5 (Rene Robert 18:29 OT)
May 22	Philadelphia 2 at Buffalo 4
May 25	Buffalo 1 at Philadelphia 5
May 27	Philadelphia 2 at Buffalo 0 [Parent]

Philadelphia won best-of-seven finals 4–2

1975–76

PRINCE OF WALES CONFERENCE

Adams Division

	GP	W	L	T	GF	GA	PTS
Boston	80	48	15	17	313	237	113
Buffalo	80	46	21	13	339	240	105
Toronto	80	34	31	15	294	276	83
California	80	27	42	11	250	278	65

Norris Division

Canadiens	80	58	11	11	337	174	127
Los Angeles	80	38	33	9	263	265	85
Pittsburgh	80	35	33	12	339	303	82
Detroit	80	26	44	10	226	300	62
Washington	80	11	59	10	224	394	32

CLARENCE CAMPBELL CONFERENCE

Patrick Division

Philadelphia	80	51	13	16	348	209	118
Islanders	80	42	21	17	297	190	101
Flames	80	35	33	12	262	237	82
Rangers	80	29	42	9	262	333	67

Smythe Division

Chicago	80	32	30	18	254	261	82
Vancouver	80	33	32	15	271	272	81
St. Louis	80	29	37	14	249	290	72
North Stars	80	20	53	7	195	303	47
Kansas City	80	12	56	12	190	351	36

Stanley Cup Finals

May 9	Philadelphia 3 at Canadiens 4
May 11	Philadelphia 1 at Canadiens 2
May 13	Canadiens 3 at Philadelphia 2
May 16	Canadiens 5 at Philadelphia 3

Canadiens won best-of-seven finals 4–0

1976–77

PRINCE OF WALES CONFERENCE

Adams Division

	GP	W	L	T	GF	GA	PTS
Boston	80	49	23	8	312	240	106
Buffalo	80	48	24	8	301	220	104
Toronto	80	33	32	15	301	285	81
Cleveland	80	25	42	13	240	292	63

Norris Division

Canadiens	80	60	8	12	387	171	132
Los Angeles	80	34	31	15	271	241	83
Pittsburgh	80	34	33	13	240	252	81
Washington	80	24	42	14	221	307	62
Detroit	80	16	55	9	183	309	41

CLARENCE CAMPBELL CONFERENCE

Patrick Division

Philadelphia	80	48	16	16	323	213	112
Islanders	80	47	21	12	288	193	106
Flames	80	34	34	12	264	265	80
Rangers	80	29	37	14	272	310	64

Smythe Division

St. Louis	80	32	39	9	239	276	73
North Stars	80	23	39	18	240	310	64
Chicago	80	26	43	11	240	298	63
Vancouver	80	25	42	13	235	294	63
Rockies	80	20	46	14	226	307	54

Stanley Cup Finals

May 7	Boston 3 at Canadiens 7
May 10	Boston 0 at Canadiens 3 [Dryden]
May 12	Canadiens 4 at Boston 2
May 14	Canadiens 2 at Boston 1

Canadiens won best-of-seven finals 4–0

1977–78

PRINCE OF WALES CONFERENCE

Adams Division

	GP	W	L	T	GF	GA	PTS
Boston	80	51	18	11	333	218	113
Buffalo	80	44	19	17	288	215	105
Toronto	80	41	29	10	271	237	92
Cleveland	80	22	45	13	230	325	57

Norris Division

Canadiens	80	59	10	11	359	183	129
Detroit	80	32	34	14	252	266	78
Los Angeles	80	31	34	15	243	245	77
Pittsburgh	80	25	37	18	254	321	68
Washington	80	17	49	14	195	321	48

CLARENCE CAMPBELL CONFERENCE

Patrick Division

Islanders	80	48	17	15	334	210	111
Philadelphia	80	45	20	15	296	200	105
Flames	80	34	27	19	274	252	87
Rangers	80	30	37	13	279	280	73

Smythe Division

Chicago	80	32	29	19	230	220	83
Rockies	80	19	40	21	257	305	59
Vancouver	80	20	43	17	239	320	57
St. Louis	80	20	47	13	195	304	53
North Stars	80	18	53	9	218	325	45

* all 1st- and 2nd-place teams qualified for playoffs and the next best four regardless of division also qualified

Stanley Cup Finals

May 13	Boston 1 at Canadiens 4
May 16	Boston 2 at Canadiens 3 (Guy Lafleur 13:09 OT)
May 18	Canadiens 0 at Boston 4 [Cheevers]
May 21	Canadiens 3 at Boston 4 (Bobby Schmautz 6:22 OT)
May 23	Boston 1 at Canadiens 4
May 25	Canadiens 4 at Boston 1

Canadiens won best-of-seven finals 4–2

1978–79

PRINCE OF WALES CONFERENCE

Adams Division

	GP	W	L	T	GF	GA	PTS
Boston	80	43	23	14	316	270	100
Buffalo	80	36	28	16	280	263	88
Toronto	80	34	33	13	267	252	81
North Stars	80	28	40	12	257	289	68

Norris Division

Canadiens	80	52	17	11	337	204	115
Pittsburgh	80	36	31	13	281	279	85
Los Angeles	80	34	34	12	292	286	80
Washington	80	24	41	15	273	338	63
Detroit	80	23	41	16	252	295	62

CLARENCE CAMPBELL CONFERENCE

Patrick Division

Islanders	80	51	15	14	358	214	116
Philadelphia	80	40	25	15	281	248	95
Rangers	80	40	29	11	316	292	91
Flames	80	41	31	8	327	280	90

Smythe Division

Chicago	80	29	36	15	244	277	73
Vancouver	80	25	42	13	217	291	63
St. Louis	80	18	50	12	249	348	48
Rockies	80	15	53	12	210	331	42

Stanley Cup Finals

May 13	Rangers 4 at Canadiens 1
May 15	Rangers 2 at Canadiens 6
May 17	Canadiens 4 at Rangers 1

May 19   Canadiens 4 at Rangers 3 (Serge Savard 7:25 OT)
May 21   Rangers 1 at Canadiens 4
Canadiens won best-of-seven finals 4–1

1979–80

PRINCE OF WALES CONFERENCE

Adams Division

	GP	W	L	T	GF	GA	PTS
Buffalo	80	47	17	16	318	201	110
Boston	80	46	21	13	310	234	105
North Stars	80	36	28	16	311	253	88
Toronto	80	35	40	5	304	327	75
Quebec	80	25	44	11	248	313	61

Norris Division

Canadiens	80	47	20	13	328	240	107
Los Angeles	80	30	36	14	290	313	74
Pittsburgh	80	30	37	13	251	303	73
Hartford	80	27	34	19	303	312	73
Detroit	80	26	43	11	268	306	63

CLARENCE CAMPBELL CONFERENCE

Patrick Division

Philadelphia	80	48	12	20	327	254	116
Islanders	80	39	28	13	281	247	91
Rangers	80	38	32	10	308	284	86
Flames	80	35	32	13	282	269	83
Washington	80	27	40	13	261	293	67

Smythe Division

Chicago	80	34	27	19	241	250	87
St. Louis	80	34	34	12	266	278	80
Vancouver	80	27	37	16	256	281	70
Edmonton	80	28	39	13	301	322	69
Winnipeg	80	20	49	11	214	314	51
Rockies	80	19	48	13	234	308	51

* top four teams in each division qualified for the playoffs

Stanley Cup Finals

May 13	Islanders 4 at Philadelphia 3 (Denis Potvin 4:07 OT)
May 15	Islanders 3 at Philadelphia 8
May 17	Philadelphia 2 at Islanders 6
May 19	Philadelphia 2 at Islanders 5
May 22	Islanders 3 at Philadelphia 6
May 24	Philadelphia 4 at Islanders 5 (Bob Nystrom 7:11 OT)

Islanders won best-of-seven finals 4–2

1980–81

PRINCE OF WALES CONFERENCE

Adams Division

	GP	W	L	T	GF	GA	PTS
Buffalo	80	39	20	21	327	250	99
Boston	80	37	30	13	316	272	87
North Stars	80	35	28	17	291	263	87
Quebec	80	30	32	18	314	318	78
Toronto	80	28	37	15	322	367	71

Norris Division

Canadiens	80	45	22	13	332	232	103
Los Angeles	80	43	24	13	337	290	99
Pittsburgh	80	30	37	13	302	345	73
Hartford	80	21	41	18	292	372	60
Detroit	80	19	43	18	252	339	56

CLARENCE CAMPBELL CONFERENCE

Patrick Division

Islanders	80	48	18	14	355	260	110
Philadelphia	80	41	24	15	313	249	97
Calgary	80	39	27	14	329	298	92
Rangers	80	30	36	14	312	317	74
Washington	80	26	36	18	286	317	70

Smythe Division

St. Louis	80	45	18	17	352	281	107
Chicago	80	31	33	16	304	315	78
Vancouver	80	28	32	20	289	301	76
Edmonton	80	29	35	16	328	327	74
Rockies	80	22	45	13	258	344	57
Winnipeg	80	9	57	14	246	400	32

Stanley Cup Finals

May 12	North Stars 3 at Islanders 6
May 14	North Stars 3 at Islanders 6
May 17	Islanders 7 at North Stars 5
May 19	Islanders 2 at North Stars 4
May 21	North Stars 1 at Islanders 5

Islanders won best-of-seven finals 4–1

1981–82

CLARENCE CAMPBELL CONFERENCE
Norris Division

	GP	W	L	T	GF	GA	PTS
North Stars	80	37	23	20	346	288	94
Winnipeg	80	33	33	14	319	332	80
St. Louis	80	32	40	8	315	349	72
Chicago	80	30	38	12	332	363	72
Toronto	80	20	44	16	298	380	56
Detroit	80	21	47	12	270	351	54

Smythe Division

Edmonton	80	48	17	15	417	295	111
Vancouver	80	30	33	17	290	286	77
Calgary	80	29	34	17	334	345	75
Los Angeles	80	24	41	15	314	369	63
Rockies	80	18	49	13	241	362	49

PRINCE OF WALES CONFERENCE
Adams Division

Canadiens	80	46	17	17	360	223	109
Boston	80	43	27	10	323	285	96
Buffalo	80	39	26	15	307	273	93
Quebec	80	33	31	16	356	345	82
Hartford	80	21	41	18	264	351	60

Patrick Division

Islanders	80	54	16	10	385	250	118
Rangers	80	39	27	14	316	306	92
Philadelphia	80	38	31	11	325	313	87
Pittsburgh	80	31	36	13	310	337	75
Washington	80	26	41	13	319	338	65

Stanley Cup Finals

May 8	Vancouver 5 at Islanders 6 (Mike Bossy 19:58 OT)
May 11	Vancouver 4 at Islanders 6
May 13	Islanders 3 at Vancouver 0 [Smith]
May 16	Islanders 3 at Vancouver 1

Islanders won best-of-seven finals 4–0

1982–83

CLARENCE CAMPBELL CONFERENCE

Norris Division

	GP	W	L	T	GF	GA	PTS
Chicago	80	47	23	10	338	268	104
North Stars	80	40	24	16	321	290	96
Toronto	80	28	40	12	293	330	68
St. Louis	80	25	40	15	285	316	65
Detroit	80	21	44	15	263	344	57

Smythe Division

	GP	W	L	T	GF	GA	PTS
Edmonton	80	47	21	12	424	315	106
Calgary	80	32	34	14	321	317	78
Vancouver	80	30	35	15	303	309	75
Winnipeg	80	33	39	8	311	333	74
Los Angeles	80	27	41	12	308	365	66

PRINCE OF WALES CONFERENCE

Adams Division

	GP	W	L	T	GF	GA	PTS
Boston	80	50	20	10	327	228	110
Canadiens	80	42	24	14	350	286	98
Buffalo	80	38	29	13	318	285	89
Quebec	80	34	34	12	343	336	80
Hartford	80	19	54	7	261	403	45

Patrick Division

Philadelphia	80	49	23	8	326	240	106
Islanders	80	42	26	12	302	226	96
Washington	80	39	25	16	306	283	94
Rangers	80	35	35	10	306	287	80
New Jersey	80	17	49	14	230	338	48
Pittsburgh	80	18	53	9	257	394	45

Stanley Cup Finals

May 10	Islanders 2 at Edmonton 0 [Smith]
May 12	Islanders 6 at Edmonton 3
May 14	Edmonton 1 at Islanders 5
May 17	Edmonton 2 at Islanders 4

Islanders won best-of-seven finals 4–0

1983–84

CLARENCE CAMPBELL CONFERENCE

Norris Division

	GP	W	L	T	GF	GA	PTS
North Stars	80	39	31	10	345	344	88
St. Louis	80	32	41	7	293	316	71
Detroit	80	31	42	7	298	323	69
Chicago	80	30	42	8	277	311	68
Toronto	80	26	45	9	303	387	61

Smythe Division

Edmonton	80	57	18	5	446	314	119
Calgary	80	34	32	14	311	314	82
Vancouver	80	32	39	9	306	328	73
Winnipeg	80	31	38	11	340	374	73
Los Angeles	80	23	44	13	309	376	59

PRINCE OF WALES CONFERENCE

Adams Division

Boston	80	49	25	6	336	261	104
Buffalo	80	48	25	7	315	257	103
Quebec	80	42	28	10	360	278	94
Canadiens	80	35	40	5	286	295	75
Hartford	80	28	42	10	288	320	66

Patrick Division

Islanders	80	50	26	4	357	269	104
Washington	80	48	27	5	308	226	101
Philadelphia	80	44	26	10	350	290	98
Rangers	80	42	29	9	314	304	93
New Jersey	80	17	56	7	231	350	41
Pittsburgh	80	16	58	6	254	390	38

* five-minute sudden-death overtime introduced for regular-season games

Stanley Cup Finals

May 10	Edmonton 1 at Islanders 0 [Fuhr]
May 12	Edmonton 1 at Islanders 6
May 15	Islanders 2 at Edmonton 7
May 17	Islanders 2 at Edmonton 7
May 19	Islanders 2 at Edmonton 5

Edmonton won best-of-seven finals 4–1

1984–85

CLARENCE CAMPBELL CONFERENCE
Norris Division

	GP	W	L	T	GF	GA	PTS
St. Louis	80	37	31	12	299	288	86
Chicago	80	38	35	7	309	299	83
Detroit	80	27	41	12	313	357	66
North Stars	80	25	43	12	268	321	62
Toronto	80	20	52	8	253	358	48

Smythe Division

	GP	W	L	T	GF	GA	PTS
Edmonton	80	49	20	11	401	298	109
Winnipeg	80	43	27	10	358	332	96
Calgary	80	41	27	12	363	302	94
Los Angeles	80	34	32	14	339	326	82
Vancouver	80	25	46	9	284	401	59

PRINCE OF WALES CONFERENCE
Adams Division

	GP	W	L	T	GF	GA	PTS
Canadiens	80	41	27	12	309	262	94
Quebec	80	41	30	9	323	275	91
Buffalo	80	38	28	14	290	237	90
Boston	80	36	34	10	303	287	82
Hartford	80	30	41	9	268	318	69

Patrick Division

	GP	W	L	T	GF	GA	PTS
Philadelphia	80	53	20	7	348	241	113
Washington	80	46	25	9	322	240	101
Islanders	80	40	34	6	345	312	86
Rangers	80	26	44	10	295	345	62
New Jersey	80	22	48	10	264	346	54
Pittsburgh	80	24	51	5	276	385	53

Stanley Cup Finals

May 21	Edmonton 1 at Philadelphia 4
May 23	Edmonton 3 at Philadelphia 1
May 25	Philadelphia 3 at Edmonton 4
May 28	Philadelphia 3 at Edmonton 5
May 30	Philadelphia 3 at Edmonton 8

Edmonton won best-of-seven finals 4–1

1985–86

CLARENCE CAMPBELL CONFERENCE

Norris Division

	GP	W	L	T	GF	GA	PTS
Chicago	80	39	33	8	351	349	86
North Stars	80	38	33	9	327	305	85
St. Louis	80	37	34	9	302	291	83
Toronto	80	25	48	7	311	386	57
Detroit	80	17	57	6	266	415	40

Smythe Division

	GP	W	L	T	GF	GA	PTS
Edmonton	80	56	17	7	426	310	119
Calgary	80	40	31	9	354	315	89
Winnipeg	80	26	47	7	295	372	59
Vancouver	80	23	44	13	282	333	59
Los Angeles	80	23	49	8	284	389	54

PRINCE OF WALES CONFERENCE

Adams Division

	GP	W	L	T	GF	GA	PTS
Quebec	80	43	31	6	330	289	92
Canadiens	80	40	33	7	330	280	87
Boston	80	37	31	12	311	288	86
Hartford	80	40	36	4	332	302	84
Buffalo	80	37	37	6	296	291	80

Patrick Division

Philadelphia	80	53	23	4	335	241	110
Washington	80	50	23	7	315	272	107
Islanders	80	39	29	12	327	284	90
Rangers	80	36	38	6	280	276	78
Pittsburgh	80	34	38	8	313	305	76
New Jersey	80	28	49	3	300	374	59

Stanley Cup Finals

May 16	Canadiens 2 at Calgary 5
May 18	Canadiens 3 at Calgary 2 (Brian Skrudland 0:09 OT)
May 20	Calgary 3 at Canadiens 5
May 22	Calgary 0 at Canadiens 1 [Roy]
May 24	Canadiens 4 at Calgary 3

Canadiens won best-of-seven finals 4–1

1986–87

CLARENCE CAMPBELL CONFERENCE

Norris Division

	GP	W	L	T	GF	G	PTS
St. Louis	80	32	33	15	281	293	79
Detroit	80	34	36	10	260	274	78
Chicago*	80	29	37	14	290	310	72
Toronto	80	32	42	6	286	319	70
North Stars	80	30	40	10	296	314	70

Smythe Division

Edmonton	80	50	24	6	372	284	106
Calgary	80	46	31	3	318	289	95
Winnipeg	80	40	32	8	279	271	88
Los Angeles	80	31	41	8	318	341	70
Vancouver	80	29	43	8	282	314	66

PRINCE OF WALES CONFERENCE

Adams Division

Hartford	80	43	30	7	287	270	93
Canadiens	80	41	29	10	277	241	92
Boston	80	39	34	7	301	276	85
Quebec	80	31	39	10	267	276	72
Buffalo	80	28	44	8	280	308	64

Patrick Division

Philadelphia	80	46	26	8	310	245	100
Washington	80	38	32	10	285	278	86
Islanders	80	35	33	12	279	281	82
Rangers	80	34	38	8	307	323	76
Pittsburgh	80	30	38	12	297	290	72
New Jersey	80	29	45	6	293	368	64

* Chicago changed spelling of nickname from Black Hawks to Blackhawks at start of season

Stanley Cup Finals

May 17	Philadelphia 2 at Edmonton 4
May 20	Philadelphia 2 at Edmonton 3 (Jari Kurri 6:50 OT)
May 22	Edmonton 3 at Philadelphia 5
May 24	Edmonton 4 at Philadelphia 1
May 26	Philadelphia 4 at Edmonton 3
May 28	Edmonton 2 at Philadelphia 3
May 31	Philadelphia 1 at Edmonton 3

Edmonton won best-of-seven finals 4–3

1987–88

CLARENCE CAMPBELL CONFERENCE

Norris Division

	GP	W	L	T	GF	GA	PTS
Detroit	80	41	28	11	322	269	93
St. Louis	80	34	38	8	278	294	76
Chicago	80	30	41	9	284	326	69
Toronto	80	21	49	10	273	345	52
North Stars	80	19	48	13	242	349	51

Smythe Division

Calgary	80	48	23	9	397	305	105
Edmonton	80	44	25	11	363	288	99
Winnipeg	80	33	36	11	292	310	77
Los Angeles	80	30	42	8	318	359	68
Vancouver	80	25	46	9	272	320	59

PRINCE OF WALES CONFERENCE

Adams Division

Canadiens	80	45	22	13	298	238	103
Boston	80	44	30	6	300	251	94
Buffalo	80	37	32	11	283	305	85
Hartford	80	35	38	7	249	267	77
Quebec	80	32	43	5	271	306	69

Patrick Division

Islanders	80	39	31	10	308	267	88
Washington	80	38	33	9	281	249	85
Philadelphia	80	38	33	9	292	282	85
New Jersey	80	38	36	6	295	296	82
Rangers	80	36	34	10	300	283	82
Pittsburgh	80	36	35	9	319	316	81

Stanley Cup Finals

May 18	Boston 1 at Edmonton 2
May 20	Boston 2 at Edmonton 4
May 22	Edmonton 6 at Boston 3
May 24	Edmonton 3 at Boston 3*
May 26	Boston 3 at Edmonton 6

Edmonton won best-of-seven finals 4–0

* game suspended because of power failure but statistics counted (if necessary, this game would have been made up at the end of the series)

1988–89
CLARENCE CAMPBELL CONFERENCE
Norris Division

	GP	W	L	T	GF	GA	PTS
Detroit	80	34	34	12	313	316	80
St. Louis	80	33	35	12	275	285	78
North Stars	80	27	37	16	258	278	70
Chicago	80	27	41	12	297	335	66
Toronto	80	28	46	6	259	342	62

Smythe Division

Calgary	80	54	17	9	354	226	117
Los Angeles	80	42	31	7	376	335	91
Edmonton	80	38	34	8	325	306	84
Vancouver	80	33	39	8	251	253	74
Winnipeg	80	26	42	12	300	355	64

PRINCE OF WALES CONFERENCE
Adams Division

Canadiens	80	53	18	9	315	218	115
Boston	80	37	29	14	289	256	88
Buffalo	80	38	35	7	291	299	83
Hartford	80	37	38	5	299	290	79
Quebec	80	27	46	7	269	342	61

Patrick Division

Washington	80	41	29	10	305	259	92
Pittsburgh	80	40	33	7	347	349	87
Rangers	80	37	35	8	310	307	82
Philadelphia	80	36	36	8	307	285	80
New Jersey	80	27	41	12	281	325	66
Islanders	80	28	47	5	265	325	61

Stanley Cup Finals

May 14	Canadiens 2 at Calgary 3
May 17	Canadiens 4 at Calgary 2
May 19	Calgary 3 at Canadiens 4 (Ryan Walter 38:08 OT)
May 21	Calgary 4 at Canadiens 2
May 23	Canadiens 2 at Calgary 3
May 25	Calgary 4 at Canadiens 2

Calgary won best-of-seven finals 4–2

1989–90

CLARENCE CAMPBELL CONFERENCE

Norris Division

	GP	W	L	T	GF	GA	PTS
Chicago	80	41	33	6	316	294	88
St. Louis	80	37	34	9	295	279	83
Toronto	80	38	38	4	337	358	80
North Stars	80	36	40	4	284	291	76
Detroit	80	28	38	14	288	323	70

Smythe Division

Calgary	80	42	23	15	348	265	99
Edmonton	80	38	28	14	315	283	90
Winnipeg	80	37	32	11	298	290	85
Los Angeles	80	34	39	7	338	337	75
Vancouver	80	25	41	14	245	306	64

PRINCE OF WALES CONFERENCE

Adams Division

Boston	80	46	25	9	289	232	101
Buffalo	80	45	27	8	286	248	98
Canadiens	80	41	28	11	288	234	93
Hartford	80	38	33	9	275	268	85
Quebec	80	12	61	7	240	407	31

Patrick Division

Rangers	80	36	31	13	279	267	85
New Jersey	80	37	34	9	295	288	83
Washington	80	36	38	6	284	275	78
Islanders	80	31	38	11	281	288	73
Pittsburgh	80	32	40	8	318	359	72
Philadelphia	80	30	39	11	290	297	71

Stanley Cup Finals

May 15	Edmonton 3 at Boston 2 (Petr Klima 55:13 OT)
May 18	Edmonton 7 at Boston 2
May 20	Boston 2 at Edmonton 1
May 22	Boston 1 at Edmonton 5
May 24	Edmonton 4 at Boston 1

Edmonton won best-of-seven finals 4–1

1990–91

CLARENCE CAMPBELL CONFERENCE

Norris Division

	GP	W	L	T	GF	GA	PTS
Chicago	80	49	23	8	284	211	106
St. Louis	80	47	22	11	310	250	105
Detroit	80	34	38	8	273	298	76
North Stars	80	27	39	14	256	266	68
Toronto	80	23	46	11	241	318	57

Smythe Division

Los Angeles	80	46	24	10	340	254	102
Calgary	80	46	26	8	344	263	100
Edmonton	80	37	37	6	272	272	80
Vancouver	80	28	43	9	243	315	65
Winnipeg	80	26	43	11	260	288	63

PRINCE OF WALES CONFERENCE
Adams Division

Boston	80	44	24	12	299	264	100
Canadiens	80	39	30	11	273	249	89
Buffalo	80	31	30	19	292	278	81
Hartford	80	31	38	11	238	276	73
Quebec	80	16	50	14	236	354	46

Patrick Division

Pittsburgh	80	41	33	6	342	305	88
Rangers	80	36	31	13	297	265	85
Washington	80	37	36	7	258	258	81
New Jersey	80	32	33	15	272	264	79
Philadelphia	80	33	37	10	252	267	76
Islanders	80	25	45	10	223	290	60

Stanley Cup Finals

May 15	Minnesota 5 at Pittsburgh 4
May 17	Minnesota 1 at Pittsburgh 4
May 19	Pittsburgh 1 at Minnesota 3
May 21	Pittsburgh 5 at Minnesota 3
May 23	Minnesota 4 at Pittsburgh 6
May 25	Pittsburgh 8 at Minnesota 0 [Barrasso]

Pittsburgh won best-of-seven finals 4–2

1991–92
CLARENCE CAMPBELL CONFERENCE
Norris Division

	GP	W	L	T	GF	GA	PTS
Detroit	80	43	25	12	320	256	98
Chicago	80	36	29	15	257	236	87
St. Louis	80	36	33	11	279	266	83
North Stars	80	32	42	6	246	278	70
Toronto	80	30	43	7	234	294	67

Smythe Division

Vancouver	80	42	26	12	285	250	96
Los Angeles	80	35	31	14	287	296	84
Edmonton	80	36	34	10	295	297	82
Winnipeg	80	33	32	15	251	244	81
Calgary	80	31	37	12	296	305	74
San Jose	80	17	58	5	219	359	39

PRINCE OF WALES CONFERENCE
Adams Division

Canadiens	80	41	28	11	267	207	93
Boston	80	36	32	12	270	275	84
Buffalo	80	31	37	12	289	299	74
Hartford	80	26	41	13	247	283	65
Quebec	80	20	48	12	255	318	52

Patrick Division

Rangers	80	50	25	5	321	246	105
Washington	80	45	27	8	330	275	98
Pittsburgh	80	39	32	9	343	308	87
New Jersey	80	38	31	11	289	259	87
Islanders	80	34	35	11	291	299	79
Philadelphia	80	32	37	11	252	273	75

Stanley Cup Finals

May 26	Chicago 4 at Pittsburgh 5
May 28	Chicago 1 at Pittsburgh 3
May 30	Pittsburgh 1 at Chicago 0 [Barrasso]
June 1	Pittsburgh 6 at Chicago 5

Pittsburgh won best-of-seven finals 4–0

1992–93

CLARENCE CAMPBELL CONFERENCE
Norris Division

	GP	W	L	T	GF	GA	PTS
Chicago	84	47	25	12	279	230	106
Detroit	84	47	28	9	369	280	103
Toronto	84	44	29	11	288	241	99
St. Louis	84	37	36	11	282	278	85
North Stars	84	36	38	10	272	293	82
Tampa Bay	84	23	54	7	245	332	53

Smythe Division

	GP	W	L	T	GF	GA	PTS
Vancouver	84	46	29	9	346	278	101
Calgary	84	43	30	11	322	282	97
Los Angeles	84	39	35	10	338	340	88
Winnipeg	84	40	37	7	322	320	87
Edmonton	84	26	50	8	242	337	60
San Jose	84	11	71	2	218	414	24

PRINCE OF WALES CONFERENCE
Adams Division

	GP	W	L	T	GF	GA	PTS
Boston	84	51	26	7	332	268	109
Quebec	84	47	27	10	351	300	104
Canadiens	84	48	30	6	326	280	102
Buffalo	84	38	36	10	335	297	86
Hartford	84	26	52	6	284	369	58
Ottawa	84	10	70	4	202	395	24

Patrick Division

Pittsburgh	84	56	21	7	367	268	119
Washington	84	43	34	7	325	286	93
Islanders	84	40	37	7	335	297	87
New Jersey	84	40	37	7	308	299	87
Philadelphia	84	36	37	11	319	319	83
Rangers	84	34	39	11	304	308	79

Stanley Cup Finals

June 1	Los Angeles 4 at Canadiens 1
June 3	Los Angeles 2 at Canadiens 3 (Eric Desjardins 0:51 OT)
June 5	Canadiens 4 at Los Angeles 3 (John LeClair 0:34 OT)
June 7	Canadiens 3 at Los Angeles 2 (John LeClair 14:37 OT)
June 9	Los Angeles 1 at Canadiens 4

Canadiens won best-of-seven finals 4–1

1993–94

WESTERN CONFERENCE
Central Division

	GP	W	L	T	GF	GA	PTS
Detroit	84	46	30	8	356	275	100
Toronto	84	43	29	12	280	243	98
Dallas	84	42	29	13	286	265	97
St. Louis	84	40	33	11	270	283	91
Chicago	84	39	36	9	254	240	87
Winnipeg	84	24	51	9	245	344	57

Pacific Division

Calgary	84	42	29	13	302	256	97
Vancouver	84	41	40	3	279	276	85
San Jose	84	33	35	16	252	265	82
Anaheim	84	33	46	5	229	251	71
Los Angeles	84	27	45	12	294	322	66
Edmonton	84	25	45	14	261	305	64

EASTERN CONFERENCE

Northeast Division

Pittsburgh	84	44	27	13	299	285	101
Boston	84	42	29	13	289	252	97
Canadiens	84	41	29	14	283	248	96
Buffalo	84	43	32	9	282	218	95
Quebec	84	34	42	8	277	292	76
Hartford	84	27	48	9	227	288	63
Ottawa	84	14	61	9	201	397	37

Atlantic Division

Rangers	84	52	24	8	299	231	112
New Jersey	84	47	25	12	306	220	106
Washington	84	39	35	10	277	263	88
Islanders	84	36	36	12	282	264	84
Florida	84	33	34	17	233	233	83
Philadelphia	84	35	39	10	294	314	80
Tampa Bay	84	30	43	11	224	251	71

* the top eight teams in each conference qualified for the playoffs

Stanley Cup Finals

May 31	Vancouver 3 at Rangers 2 (Greg Adams 19:26 OT)
June 2	Vancouver 1 at Rangers 3
June 4	Rangers 5 at Vancouver 1
June 7	Rangers 4 at Vancouver 2
June 9	Vancouver 6 at Rangers 3
June 11	Rangers 1 at Vancouver 4
June 14	Vancouver 2 at Rangers 3

Rangers won best-of-seven finals 4–3

1994–95

WESTERN CONFERENCE
Central Division
	GP	W	L	T	GF	GA	PTS
Detroit	48	33	11	4	180	117	70
St. Louis	48	28	15	5	178	135	61
Chicago	48	24	19	5	156	115	53
Toronto	48	21	19	8	135	146	50
Dallas	48	17	23	8	136	135	42
Winnipeg	48	16	25	7	157	177	39

Pacific Division
	GP	W	L	T	GF	GA	PTS
Calgary	48	24	17	7	163	135	55
Vancouver	48	18	18	12	153	148	48
San Jose	48	19	25	4	129	161	42
Los Angeles	48	16	23	9	142	174	41
Edmonton	48	17	27	4	136	183	38
Anaheim	48	16	27	5	125	164	37

EASTERN CONFERENCE
Northeast Division
	GP	W	L	T	GF	GA	PTS
Quebec	48	30	13	5	185	134	65
Pittsburgh	48	29	16	3	181	158	61
Boston	48	27	18	3	150	127	57
Buffalo	48	22	19	7	130	119	51
Hartford	48	19	24	5	127	141	43
Canadiens	48	18	23	7	125	148	43
Ottawa	48	9	34	5	116	174	23

Atlantic Division

Philadelphia	48	28	16	4	150	132	60
New Jersey	48	22	18	8	136	121	52
Washington	48	22	18	8	136	120	52
Rangers	48	22	23	3	139	134	47
Florida	48	20	22	6	115	127	46
Tampa Bay	48	17	28	3	120	144	37
Islanders	48	15	28	5	126	158	35

Stanley Cup Finals

June 17	New Jersey 2 at Detroit 1
June 20	New Jersey 4 at Detroit 2
June 22	Detroit 2 at New Jersey 5
June 24	Detroit 2 at New Jersey 5

New Jersey won best-of-seven finals 4–0

1995–96

WESTERN CONFERENCE

Central Division

	GP	W	L	T	GF	GA	PTS
Detroit	82	62	13	7	325	181	131
Chicago	82	40	28	14	273	220	94
Toronto	82	34	36	12	247	252	80
St. Louis	82	32	34	16	219	248	80
Winnipeg	82	36	40	6	275	291	78
Dallas	82	26	42	14	227	280	66

Pacific Division

Colorado	82	47	25	10	326	240	104
Calgary	82	34	37	11	241	240	79
Vancouver	82	32	35	15	278	278	79
Anaheim	82	35	39	8	234	247	78
Edmonton	82	30	44	8	240	304	68
Los Angeles	82	24	40	18	256	302	66
San Jose	82	20	55	7	252	357	47

EASTERN CONFERENCE

Northeast Division

Pittsburgh	82	49	29	4	362	284	102
Boston	82	40	31	11	282	269	91
Canadiens	82	40	32	10	265	248	90
Hartford	82	34	39	9	237	259	77
Buffalo	82	33	42	7	247	262	73
Ottawa	82	18	59	5	191	291	41

Atlantic Division

Philadelphia	82	45	24	13	282	208	103
Rangers	82	41	27	14	272	237	96
Florida	82	41	31	10	254	234	92
Washington	82	39	32	11	234	204	89
Tampa Bay	82	38	32	12	238	248	88
New Jersey	82	37	33	12	215	202	86
Islanders	82	22	50	10	229	315	54

Stanley Cup Finals

June 4	Florida 1 at Colorado 3
June 6	Florida 1 at Colorado 8
June 8	Colorado 3 at Florida 2
June 10	Colorado 1 at Florida 0 (Uwe Krupp 44:31 OT) [Roy]

Colorado won best-of seven finals 4–0

1996-97

WESTERN CONFERENCE
Central Division

	GP	W	L	T	GF	GA	PTS
Dallas	82	48	26	8	252	198	104
Detroit	82	38	26	18	253	197	94
Phoenix	82	38	37	7	240	243	83
St. Louis	82	36	35	11	236	239	83
Chicago	82	34	35	13	223	210	81
Toronto	82	30	44	8	230	273	68

Pacific Division

	GP	W	L	T	GF	GA	PTS
Colorado	82	49	24	9	277	205	107
Anaheim	82	36	33	13	245	233	85
Edmonton	82	36	37	9	252	247	81
Vancouver	82	35	40	7	257	273	77
Calgary	82	32	41	9	214	239	73
Los Angeles	82	28	43	11	214	268	67
San Jose	82	27	47	8	211	278	62

EASTERN CONFERENCE
Northeast Division

	GP	W	L	T	GF	GA	PTS
Buffalo	82	40	30	12	237	208	92
Pittsburgh	82	38	36	8	285	280	84
Ottawa	82	31	36	15	226	234	77
Canadiens	82	31	36	15	249	276	77
Hartford	82	32	39	11	226	256	75
Boston	82	26	47	9	234	300	61

Atlantic Division

New Jersey	82	45	23	14	231	182	104
Philadelphia	82	45	24	13	274	217	103
Florida	82	35	28	19	221	201	89
Rangers	82	38	34	10	258	231	86
Washington	82	33	40	9	214	231	75
Tampa Bay	82	32	40	10	217	247	74
Islanders	82	29	41	12	240	250	70

Stanley Cup Finals

May 31	Detroit 4 at Philadelphia 2
June 3	Detroit 4 at Philadelphia 2
June 5	Philadelphia 1 at Detroit 6
June 7	Philadelphia 1 at Detroit 2

Detroit won best-of-seven finals 4–0

1997–98

WESTERN CONFERENCE

Central Division

	GP	W	L	T	GF	GA	PTS
Dallas	82	49	22	11	242	167	109
Detroit	82	44	23	15	250	196	103
St. Louis	82	45	29	8	256	204	98
Phoenix	82	35	35	12	224	227	82
Chicago	82	30	39	13	192	199	73
Toronto	82	30	43	9	194	237	69

Pacific Division

Colorado	82	39	26	17	231	205	95
Los Angeles	82	38	33	11	227	225	87
Edmonton	82	35	37	10	215	224	80
San Jose	82	34	38	10	210	216	78
Calgary	82	26	41	15	217	252	67
Anaheim	82	26	43	13	205	261	65
Vancouver	82	25	43	14	224	273	64

EASTERN CONFERENCE

Northeast Division

Pittsburgh	82	40	24	18	228	188	98
Boston	82	39	30	13	221	194	91
Buffalo	82	36	29	17	211	187	89
Canadiens	82	37	32	13	235	208	87
Ottawa	82	34	33	15	193	20	83
Carolina	82	33	41	8	200	219	74

Atlantic Division

New Jersey	82	48	23	11	225	166	107
Philadelphia	82	42	29	11	242	193	95
Washington	82	40	30	12	219	202	92
Islanders	82	30	41	11	212	225	71
Rangers	82	25	39	18	197	231	68
Florida	82	24	43	15	203	256	63
Tampa Bay	82	17	55	10	151	269	44

Stanley Cup Finals

June 9	Washington 1 at Detroit 2
June 11	Washington 4 at Detroit 5 (Kris Draper 15:24 OT)
June 13	Detroit 2 at Washington 1
June 16	Detroit 4 at Washington 1

Detroit won best-of-seven finals 4–0

1998–99

EASTERN CONFERENCE
Northeast Division

	GP	W	L	T	GF	GA	PTS
Ottawa	82	44	23	15	239	179	103
Toronto	82	45	30	7	268	231	97
Boston	82	39	30	13	214	181	91
Buffalo	82	37	28	17	207	175	91
Canadiens	82	32	39	11	184	209	75

Atlantic Division

	GP	W	L	T	GF	GA	PTS
New Jersey	82	47	24	11	248	196	105
Philadelphia	82	37	26	19	231	196	93
Pittsburgh	82	38	30	14	242	225	90
Rangers	82	33	38	11	217	227	77
Islanders	82	24	48	10	194	244	58

Southeast Division

	GP	W	L	T	GF	GA	PTS
Carolina	82	34	30	18	210	202	86
Florida	82	30	34	18	210	228	78
Washington	82	31	45	6	200	218	68
Tampa Bay	82	19	54	9	179	292	47

WESTERN CONFERENCE
Central Division

	GP	W	L	T	GF	GA	PTS
Detroit	82	43	32	7	245	202	93
St. Louis	82	37	32	13	237	209	87
Chicago	82	29	41	12	202	248	70
Nashville	82	28	47	7	190	261	63

Pacific Division

Dallas	82	51	19	12	236	168	114
Phoenix	82	39	31	12	205	197	90
Anaheim	82	35	34	13	215	206	83
San Jose	82	31	33	18	196	191	80
Los Angeles	82	32	45	5	189	222	69

Northwest Division

Colorado	82	44	28	10	239	205	98
Edmonton	82	33	37	12	230	226	78
Calgary	82	30	40	12	211	234	72
Vancouver	82	23	47	12	192	258	58

Stanley Cup Finals

June 8	Buffalo 3 at Dallas 2 (Jason Woolley 15:30 OT)
June 10	Buffalo 2 at Dallas 4
June 12	Dallas 2 at Buffalo 1
June 15	Dallas 1 at Buffalo 2
June 17	Buffalo 0 at Dallas 2 [Belfour]
June 19	Dallas 2 at Buffalo 1 (Brett Hull 54:51 OT)

Dallas won best-of-seven finals 4–2

1999–2000

EASTERN CONFERENCE

Northeast Division

	GP	W	L	T	OTL	GF	GA	PTS
Toronto	82	45	30	7	3	246	222	100
Ottawa	82	41	30	11	2	244	210	95
Buffalo	82	35	36	11	4	213	204	85
Canadiens	82	35	38	9	4	196	194	83
Boston	82	24	39	19	6	210	248	73

Atlantic Division

Philadelphia	82	45	25	12	3	237	179	105
New Jersey	82	45	29	8	5	251	203	103
Pittsburgh	82	37	37	8	6	241	236	88
Rangers	82	29	42	12	3	218	246	73
Islanders	82	24	49	9	1	194	275	58

Southeast Division

Washington	82	44	26	12	2	227	194	102
Florida	82	43	33	6	6	244	209	98
Carolina	82	37	35	10	0	217	216	84
Tampa Bay	82	19	54	9	7	204	309	54
Atlanta	82	14	61	7	4	170	313	39

WESTERN CONFERENCE

Central Division

St. Louis	82	51	20	11	1	248	165	114
Detroit	82	48	24	10	2	278	210	108
Chicago	82	33	39	10	2	242	245	78
Nashville	82	28	47	7	7	199	240	70

Northwest Division

Colorado	82	42	29	11	1	233	201	96
Edmonton	82	32	34	16	8	226	212	88
Vancouver	82	30	37	15	8	227	237	83
Calgary	82	31	41	10	5	211	256	77

Pacific Division

Dallas	82	43	29	10	6	211	184	102
Los Angeles	82	39	31	12	4	245	228	94
Phoenix	82	39	35	8	4	232	228	90
San Jose	82	35	37	10	7	225	214	87
Anaheim	82	34	36	12	3	217	227	83

Stanley Cup Finals

May 30	Dallas 3 at New Jersey 7
June 1	Dallas 2 at New Jersey 1
June 3	New Jersey 2 at Dallas 1
June 5	New Jersey 3 at Dallas 1
June 8	Dallas 1 at New Jersey 0 (Mike Modano 46:21 OT) [Belfour]
June 10	New Jersey 2 at Dallas 1 (Jason Arnott 28:20 OT)

New Jersey won best-of-seven finals 4–2

2000–01

EASTERN CONFERENCE

Northeast Division

	GP	W	L	T	OTL	GF	GA	PTS
Ottawa	82	48	21	9	4	274	205	109
Buffalo	82	46	30	5	1	218	184	98
Toronto	82	37	29	11	5	232	207	90
Boston	82	36	30	8	8	227	249	88
Montreal	82	28	40	8	6	206	232	70

Atlantic Division

	GP	W	L	T	OTL	GF	GA	PTS
New Jersey	82	48	19	12	3	295	195	111
Philadelphia	82	43	25	11	3	240	207	100
Pittsburgh	82	42	28	9	3	281	256	96
Rangers	82	33	43	5	1	250	290	72
Islanders	82	21	51	7	3	185	268	52

Southeast Division

	GP	W	L	T	OTL	GF	GA	PTS
Washington	82	41	27	10	4	233	211	96
Carolina	82	38	32	9	3	212	225	88
Florida	82	22	38	13	9	200	246	66
Atlanta	82	23	45	12	2	211	289	60
Tampa Bay	82	24	47	6	5	201	280	59

WESTERN CONFERENCE
Central Division

Detroit	82	49	20	9	4	253	202	111
St. Louis	82	43	22	12	5	249	195	103
Nashville	82	34	36	9	3	186	200	80
Chicago	82	29	40	8	5	210	246	71
Columbus	82	28	39	9	6	190	233	71

Northwest Division

Colorado	82	52	16	10	4	270	192	118
Edmonton	82	39	28	12	3	243	222	93
Vancouver	82	36	28	11	7	239	238	90
Calgary	82	27	36	15	4	197	236	73
Minnesota	82	25	39	13	5	168	210	68

Pacific Division

Dallas	82	48	24	8	2	241	187	106
San Jose	82	40	27	12	3	217	192	95
Los Angeles	82	38	28	13	3	252	228	92
Phoenix	82	35	27	17	3	214	212	90
Anaheim	82	25	41	11	5	188	245	66

Stanley Cup Finals

May 26	New Jersey 0 at Colorado 5 [Roy]
May 29	New Jersey 2 at Colorado 1
May 31	Colorado 3 at New Jersey 1
June 2	Colorado 2 at New Jersey 3
June 4	New Jersey 4 at Colorado 1
June 7	Colorado 4 at New Jersey 0 [Roy]
June 9	New Jersey 1 at Colorado 3

Colorado won best-of-seven finals 4–3

2001–02

EASTERN CONFERENCE
Northeast Division

	GP	W	L	T	OTL	GF	GA	PTS
Boston	82	43	24	6	9	236	201	101
Toronto	82	43	25	10	4	249	207	100
Ottawa	82	39	27	9	7	243	208	94
Montreal	82	36	31	12	3	207	209	87
Buffalo	82	35	35	11	1	213	200	82

Atlantic Division

Philadelphia	82	42	27	10	3	234	192	97
Islanders	82	42	28	8	4	239	220	96
New Jersey	82	41	28	9	4	205	187	95
Rangers	82	36	38	4	4	227	258	80
Pittsburgh	82	28	41	8	5	198	249	69

Southeast Division

Carolina	82	35	26	16	5	217	217	91
Washington	82	36	33	11	2	228	240	85
Tampa Bay	82	27	40	11	4	178	219	69
Florida	82	22	44	10	6	180	250	60
Atlanta	82	19	47	11	5	187	288	54

WESTERN CONFERENCE
Central Division

Detroit	82	51	17	10	4	251	187	116
St. Louis	82	43	27	8	4	227	188	98
Chicago	82	41	27	13	1	216	207	96
Nashville	82	28	41	13	0	196	230	69
Columbus	82	22	47	8	5	164	255	57

Pacific Division

San Jose	82	44	27	8	3	248	199	99
Phoenix	82	40	27	9	6	228	210	95
Los Angeles	82	40	27	11	4	214	190	95
Dallas	82	36	28	13	5	215	213	90
Anaheim	82	29	42	8	3	175	198	69

Northwest Division

Colorado	82	42	28	8	1	212	169	99
Vancouver	82	42	30	7	3	254	211	94
Edmonton	82	38	28	12	4	205	182	92
Calgary	82	32	35	12	3	201	220	79
Minnesota	82	26	35	12	9	195	238	73

Stanley Cup Finals

June 4	Carolina 3 at Detroit 2
June 6	Carolina 1 at Detroit 3
June 8	Detroit 3 at Carolina 2
June 10	Detroit 3 at Carolina 0
June 13	Carolina 1 at Detroit 3

Detroit won best-of-seven finals 4–1

2002–03

EASTERN CONFERENCE

Northeast Division

	GP	W	L	T	OTL	GF	GA	PTS
Ottawa	82	52	21	8	1	263	182	113
Toronto	82	44	28	7	3	236	208	98
Boston	82	36	31	11	4	245	237	87
Montreal	82	30	35	8	9	206	234	77
Buffalo	82	27	37	10	8	190	219	72

Atlantic Division

New Jersey	82	46	20	10	6	216	166	108
Philadelphia	82	45	20	13	4	211	166	107
Islanders	82	35	34	11	2	224	231	83
Rangers	82	32	36	10	4	210	231	78
Pittsburgh	82	27	44	6	5	189	255	65

Southeast Division

Tampa Bay	82	36	25	16	5	219	210	93
Washington	82	39	29	8	6	224	220	92
Atlanta	82	31	39	7	5	226	284	74
Florida	82	24	36	13	9	176	237	70
Carolina	82	22	43	11	6	171	240	61

WESTERN CONFERENCE

Central Division

Detroit	82	48	20	10	4	269	203	110
St. Louis	82	41	24	11	6	253	222	99
Chicago	82	30	33	13	6	207	226	79
Nashville	82	27	35	13	7	183	206	74
Columbus	82	29	42	8	3	213	263	69

Pacific Division

Dallas	82	46	17	15	4	245	169	111
Anaheim	82	40	27	9	6	203	193	95
Los Angeles	82	33	37	6	6	203	221	78
Phoenix	82	31	35	11	5	204	230	78
San Jose	82	28	37	9	8	214	239	73

Northwest Division

Colorado	82	42	19	13	8	251	194	105
Vancouver	82	45	23	13	1	264	208	104
Minnesota	82	42	29	10	1	198	178	95
Edmonton	82	36	26	11	9	231	230	92
Calgary	82	29	36	13	4	186	228	75

Stanley Cup Finals

May 27	Anaheim 0 at New Jersey 3 [Brodeur]
May 29	Anaheim 0 at New Jersey 3 [Brodeur]
May 31	New Jersey 2 at Anaheim 3 (Ruslan Salei 6:59 OT)
June 2	New Jersey 0 at Anaheim 1 (Steve Thomas 0:39 OT) [Giguere]
June 5	Anaheim 3 at New Jersey 6
June 7	New Jersey 2 at Anaheim 5
June 9	Anaheim 0 at New Jersey 3 [Brodeur]

New Jersey won best-of-seven finals 4–3

2003–04

EASTERN CONFERENCE

Atlantic Division

	GP	W	L	T	OTL	PTS	GF	GA
Philadelphia	82	40	21	15	6	101	229	186
New Jersey	82	43	25	12	2	100	213	164
Islanders	82	38	29	11	4	91	237	210
Rangers	82	27	40	7	8	69	206	250
Pittsburgh	82	23	47	8	4	58	190	303

Northeast Division

	GP	W	L	T	OTL	PTS	GF	GA
Boston	82	41	19	15	7	104	209	188
Toronto	82	45	24	10	3	103	242	204
Ottawa	82	43	23	10	6	102	262	189
Montreal	82	41	30	7	4	93	208	192
Buffalo	82	37	34	7	4	85	220	221

Southeast Division

Tampa Bay	82	46	22	8	6	106	245	192
Atlanta	82	33	37	8	4	78	214	243
Carolina	82	28	34	14	6	76	172	209
Florida	82	28	35	15	4	75	188	221
Washington	82	23	46	10	3	59	186	253

WESTERN CONFERENCE

Central Division

Detroit	82	48	21	11	2	109	255	189
St. Louis	82	39	30	11	2	91	191	198
Nashville	82	38	29	11	4	91	216	217
Columbus	82	25	45	8	4	62	177	238
Chicago	82	20	43	11	8	59	188	259

Northwest Division

Vancouver	82	43	24	10	5	101	235	194
Colorado	82	40	22	13	7	100	236	198
Calgary	82	42	30	7	3	94	200	176
Edmonton	82	36	29	12	5	89	221	208
Minnesota	82	30	29	20	3	83	188	183

Pacific Division

San Jose	82	43	21	12	6	104	219	183
Dallas	82	41	26	13	2	97	194	175
Los Angeles	82	28	29	16	9	81	205	217
Anaheim	82	29	35	10	8	76	184	213
Phoenix	82	22	36	18	6	68	188	245

Note: overtime losses (OTL) are worth one point in the standings and are not included in the loss column (L)

Stanley Cup Finals

May 25	Calgary 4 at Tampa Bay 1
May 27	Calgary 1 at Tampa Bay 4
May 29	Tampa Bay 0 at Calgary 3 [Kiprusoff]
May 31	Tampa Bay 1 at Calgary 0 (Richards 2:48 1st) [Khabibulin]
June 3	Calgary 3 at Tampa Bay 2 (Saprykin 14:40 OT)
June 5	Tampa Bay 3 at Calgary 2 (St. Louis 20:33 OT)
June 7	Calgary 1 at Tampa Bay 2

Tampa Bay won best-of-seven finals 4–3

Note: 2004–05 no season

2005–06

EASTERN CONFERENCE

Northeast Division	GP	W	L	OTL	SOL	GF	GA	P
Ottawa	82	52	21	3	6	314	211	113
Buffalo	82	52	24	1	5	281	239	110
Canadiens	82	42	31	6	3	243	247	93
Toronto	82	41	33	1	7	257	270	90
Boston	82	29	37	8	8	230	266	74

Atlantic Division								
New Jersey	82	46	27	5	4	242	229	101
Philadelphia	82	45	26	5	6	267	259	101
Rangers	82	44	26	8	4	257	215	100
Islanders	82	36	40	3	3	230	278	78
Pittsburgh	82	22	46	8	6	244	316	58

Southeast Division								
Carolina	82	52	22	6	2	294	260	112
Tampa Bay	82	43	33	2	4	252	260	92

	GP	W	L	OTL	SOL	GF	GA	P
Atlanta	82	41	33	3	5	281	275	90
Florida	82	37	34	6	5	240	257	85
Washington	82	29	41	6	6	237	306	70

WESTERN CONFERENCE

Central Division	GP	W	L	OTL	SOL	GF	GA	P
Detroit	82	58	16	5	3	305	209	124
Nashville	82	49	25	5	3	259	227	106
Columbus	82	35	43	1	3	223	279	74
Chicago	82	26	43	7	6	211	285	65
St. Louis	82	21	46	6	9	197	292	57

Northwest Division								
Calgary	82	46	25	4	7	218	200	103
Colorado	82	43	30	3	6	283	257	95
Edmonton	82	41	28	4	9	256	251	95
Vancouver	82	42	32	4	4	256	255	92
Minnesota	82	38	36	5	3	231	215	84

Pacific Division								
Dallas	82	53	23	5	1	265	218	112
San Jose	82	44	27	4	7	266	242	99
Anaheim	82	43	27	5	7	254	229	98
Los Angeles	82	42	35	4	1	249	270	89
Phoenix	82	38	39	2	3	246	271	81

Stanley Cup Finals

June 5	Edmonton 4 at Carolina 5
June 7	Edmonton 0 at Carolina 5 [Ward]
June 10	Carolina 1 at Edmonton 2
June 12	Carolina 2 at Edmonton 1
June 14	Edmonton 4 at Carolina 3 (Pisani 3:31 OT)]
June 17	Carolina 0 at Edmonton 4 [Ward]

June 19   Edmonton 1 at Carolina 3
Carolina won best-of-seven finals 4–3

2006–07

EASTERN CONFERENCE

Atlantic Division	GP	W	L	OT	GF	GA	P
New Jersey	82	49	24	9	216	201	107
Pittsburgh	82	47	24	11	277	246	105
Rangers	82	42	30	10	242	216	94
Islanders	82	40	30	12	248	240	92
Philadelphia	82	22	48	12	214	303	56

Northeast Division							
Buffalo	82	53	22	7	308	242	113
Ottawa	82	48	25	9	288	222	105
Toronto	82	40	31	11	258	269	91
Canadiens	82	42	34	6	245	256	90
Boston	82	35	41	6	219	289	76

Southeast Division							
Atlanta	82	43	28	11	246	245	97
Tampa Bay	82	44	33	5	253	261	93
Carolina	82	40	34	8	241	253	88
Florida	82	35	31	16	247	257	86
Washington	82	28	40	14	235	286	70

WESTERN CONFERENCE

Central Division							
Detroit	82	50	19	13	254	199	113
Nashville	82	51	23	8	272	212	110
St. Louis	82	34	35	13	214	254	81
Columbus	82	33	42	7	201	249	73
Chicago	82	31	42	9	201	258	71

Northwest Division

Vancouver	82	49	26	7	222	201	105
Minnesota	82	48	26	8	235	191	104
Calgary	82	43	29	10	258	226	96
Colorado	82	44	31	7	272	251	95
Edmonton	82	32	43	7	195	248	71

Pacific Division

Anaheim	82	48	20	14	258	208	110
San Jose	82	51	26	5	258	199	107
Dallas	82	50	25	7	226	197	107
Los Angeles	82	27	41	14	227	283	68
Phoenix	82	31	46	5	216	284	67

Stanley Cup Finals

May 28	Ottawa 2 at Anaheim 3
May 30	Ottawa 0 at Anaheim 1 (Pahlsson 14:15 3rd) [Giguere]
June 2	Anaheim 3 at Ottawa 5
June 4	Anaheim 3 at Ottawa 2
June 6	Ottawa 2 at Anaheim 6

Anaheim won best-of-seven 4–1

2007–08

EASTERN CONFERENCE

Northeast Division	GP	W	L	OT	GF	GA	P
Canadiens	82	47	25	10	262	222	104
Ottawa	82	43	31	8	261	247	94
Boston	82	41	29	12	212	222	94
Buffalo	82	39	31	12	255	242	90
Toronto	82	36	35	11	231	260	83

Atlantic Division	GP	W	L	OT	GF	GA	P
Pittsburgh	82	47	27	8	247	216	102
New Jersey	82	46	29	7	206	197	99
Rangers	82	42	27	13	213	199	97
Philadelphia	82	42	29	11	248	233	95
Islanders	82	35	38	9	194	243	79
Southeast Division							
Washington	82	43	31	8	242	231	94
Carolina	82	43	33	6	252	249	92
Florida	82	38	35	9	216	226	85
Atlanta	82	34	40	8	216	272	76
Tampa Bay	82	31	42	9	223	267	71
WESTERN CONFERENCE							
Central Division							
Detroit	82	54	21	7	257	184	115
Nashville	82	41	32	9	230	229	91
Chicago	82	40	34	8	239	235	88
Columbus	82	34	36	12	193	218	80
St. Louis	82	33	36	13	205	237	79
Northwest Division							
Minnesota	82	44	28	10	223	218	98
Colorado	82	44	31	7	231	219	95
Calgary	82	42	30	10	229	227	94
Edmonton	82	41	35	6	235	251	88
Vancouver	82	39	33	10	213	215	88
Pacific Division							
San Jose	82	49	23	10	222	193	108
Anaheim	82	47	27	8	205	191	102
Dallas	82	45	30	7	242	207	97
Phoenix	82	38	37	7	214	231	83
Los Angeles	82	32	43	7	231	266	71

Stanley Cup Finals

Detroit vs. Pittsburgh

May 24	Pittsburgh 0 at Detroit 4 [Osgood]
May 26	Pittsburgh 0 at Detroit 3 [Osgood]
May 28	Detroit 2 at Pittsburgh 3
May 31	Detroit 2 at Pittsburgh 1
June 2	Pittsburgh 4 at Detroit 3 (Sykora 49:57 OT)
June 4	Detroit 3 at Pittsburgh 2

Detroit won best of seven 4–2

2008–09

EASTERN CONFERENCE

Northeast Division	GP	W	L	OT	GF	GA	Pts
Boston	82	53	19	10	274	196	116
Montreal	82	41	30	11	249	247	93
Buffalo	82	41	32	9	250	234	91
Ottawa	82	36	35	11	217	237	83
Toronto	82	34	35	13	250	293	81

Southeast Division	GP	W	L	OT	GF	GA	Pts
Washington	82	50	24	8	272	245	108
Carolina	82	45	30	7	239	226	97
Florida	82	41	30	11	234	231	93
Atlanta	82	35	41	6	257	280	76
Tampa Bay	82	24	40	18	210	279	66

Atlantic Division	GP	W	L	OT	GF	GA	Pts
New Jersey	82	51	27	4	244	209	106
Pittsburgh	82	45	28	9	264	239	99
Philadelphia	82	44	27	11	264	238	99
NY Rangers	82	43	30	9	210	218	95
NY Islanders	82	26	47	9	201	279	61

WESTERN CONFERENCE
Central Division

Detroit	82	51	21	10	295	244	112
Chicago	82	46	24	12	264	216	104
St. Louis	82	41	31	10	233	233	92
Columbus	82	41	31	10	226	230	92
Nashville	82	40	34	8	213	233	88

Northwest Division

Vancouver	82	45	27	10	246	220	100
Calgary	82	46	30	6	254	248	98
Minnesota	82	40	33	9	219	200	89
Edmonton	82	38	35	9	234	248	85
Colorado	82	32	45	5	199	257	69

Pacific Division

San Jose	82	53	18	11	257	204	117
Anaheim	82	42	33	7	245	238	91
Dallas	82	36	35	11	230	257	83
Phoenix	82	36	39	7	208	252	79
Los Angeles	82	34	37	11	207	234	79

STANLEY CUP FINAL

May 30	Pittsburgh 1 at Detroit 3
May 31	Pittsburgh 1 at Detroit 3
June 2	Detroit 2 at Pittsburgh 4
June 4	Detroit 2 at Pittsburgh 4
June 6	Pittsburgh 0 at Detroit 5 [Osgood]
June 9	Detroit 1 at Pittsburgh 2
June 12	Pittsburgh 2 at Detroit 1

Pittsburgh won best-of-seven finals 4–3

NHL AWARDS

Art Ross Trophy

1917–18	Joe Malone	Montreal Canadiens (48 points)
1918–19	Newsy Lalonde	Montreal Canadiens (32 points)
1919–20	Joe Malone	Quebec Bulldogs (49 points)
1920–21	Newsy Lalonde	Montreal Canadiens (43 points)
1921–22	Punch Broadbent	Ottawa Senators (46 points)
1922–23	Babe Dye	Toronto St. Pats (37 points)
1923–24	Cy Denneny	Ottawa Senators (24 points)
1924–25	Babe Dye	Toronto St. Pats (46 points)
1925–26	Nels Stewart	Montreal Maroons (42 points)
1926–27	Bill Cook	New York Rangers (37 points)
1927–28	Howie Morenz	Montreal Canadiens (51 points)
1928–29	Ace Bailey	Toronto Maple Leafs (32 points)
1929–30	Cooney Weiland	Boston Bruins (73 points)
1930–31	Howie Morenz	Montreal Canadiens (51 points)
1931–32	Busher Jackson	Toronto Maple Leafs (53 points)
1932–33	Bill Cook	New York Rangers (50 points)
1933–34	Charlie Conacher	Toronto Maple Leafs (52 points)
1934–35	Charlie Conacher	Toronto Maple Leafs (57 points)
1935–36	Sweeney Schriner	New York Americans (45 points)
1936–37	Sweeney Schriner	New York Americans (46 points)
1937–38	Gordie Drillon	Toronto Maple Leafs (52 points)
1938–39	Toe Blake	Montreal Canadiens (47 points)
1939–40	Milt Schmidt	Boston Bruins (52 points)
1940–41	Bill Cowley	Boston Bruins (62 points)
1941–42	Bryan Hextall	New York Rangers (56 points)
1942–43	Doug Bentley	Chicago Black Hawks (73 points)
1943–44	Herb Cain	Boston Bruins (82 points)
1944–45	Elmer Lach	Montreal Canadiens (80 points)
1945–46	Max Bentley	Chicago Black Hawks (61 points)

1947–48	Elmer Lach	Montreal Canadiens (61 points)
1948–49	Roy Conacher	Chicago Black Hawks (68 points)
1949–50	Ted Lindsay	Detroit Red Wings (78 points)
1950–51	Gordie Howe	Detroit Red Wings (86 points)
1951–52	Gordie Howe	Detroit Red Wings (86 points)
1952–53	Gordie Howe	Detroit Red Wings (95 points)
1953–54	Gordie Howe	Detroit Red Wings (81 points)
1954–55	Bernie Geoffrion	Montreal Canadiens (75 points)
1955–56	Jean Beliveau	Montreal Canadiens (88 points)
1956–57	Gordie Howe	Detroit Red Wings (89 points)
1957–58	Dickie Moore	Montreal Canadiens (84 points)
1958–59	Dickie Moore	Montreal Canadiens (96 points)
1959–60	Bobby Hull	Chicago Black Hawks (81 points)
1960–61	Bernie Geoffrion	Montreal Canadiens (95 points)
1961–62	Bobby Hull	Chicago Black Hawks (84 points)
1962–63	Gordie Howe	Detroit Red Wings (86 points)
1963–64	Stan Mikita	Chicago Black Hawks (89 points)
1964–65	Stan Mikita	Chicago Black Hawks (87 points)
1965–66	Bobby Hull	Chicago Black Hawks (97 points)
1966–67	Stan Mikita	Chicago Black Hawks (97 points)
1967–68	Stan Mikita	Chicago Black Hawks (87 points)
1968–69	Phil Esposito	Boston Bruins (126 points)
1969–70	Bobby Orr	Boston Bruins (120 points)
1970–71	Phil Esposito	Boston Bruins (152 points)
1971–72	Phil Esposito	Boston Bruins (133 points)
1972–73	Phil Esposito	Boston Bruins (130 points)
1973–74	Phil Esposito	Boston Bruins (145 points)
1974–75	Bobby Orr	Boston Bruins (135 points)
1975–76	Guy Lafleur	Montreal Canadiens (125 points)
1976–77	Guy Lafleur	Montreal Canadiens (136 points)
1977–78	Guy Lafleur	Montreal Canadiens (132 points)
1978–79	Bryan Trottier	New York Islanders (134 points)
1979–80	Marcel Dionne	Los Angeles Kings (137 points)
1980–81	Wayne Gretzky	Edmonton Oilers (164 points)

1981–82	Wayne Gretzky	Edmonton Oilers (212 points)
1982–83	Wayne Gretzky	Edmonton Oilers (196 points)
1983–84	Wayne Gretzky	Edmonton Oilers (205 points)
1984–85	Wayne Gretzky	Edmonton Oilers (208 points)
1985–86	Wayne Gretzky	Edmonton Oilers (215 points)
1986–87	Wayne Gretzky	Edmonton Oilers (183 points)
1987–88	Mario Lemieux	Pittsburgh Penguins (168 points)
1988–89	Mario Lemieux	Pittsburgh Penguins (199 points)
1989–90	Wayne Gretzky	Los Angeles Kings (142 points)
1990–91	Wayne Gretzky	Los Angeles Kings (163 points)
1991–92	Mario Lemieux	Pittsburgh Penguins (131 points)
1992–93	Mario Lemieux	Pittsburgh Penguins (160 points)
1993–94	Wayne Gretzky	Los Angeles Kings (130 points)
1994–95	Jaromir Jagr	Pittsburgh Penguins (70 points)
1995–96	Mario Lemieux	Pittsburgh Penguins (161 points)
1996–97	Mario Lemieux	Pittsburgh Penguins (122 points)
1997–98	Jaromir Jagr	Pittsburgh Penguins (102 points)
1998–99	Jaromir Jagr	Pittsburgh Penguins (127 points)
1999–00	Jaromir Jagr	Pittsburgh Penguins (96 points)
2000–01	Jaromir Jagr	Pittsburgh Penguins (121 points)
2001–02	Jarome Iginla	Calgary Flames (96 points)
2002–03	Peter Forsberg	Colorado Avalanche (106 points)
2003–04	Martin St. Louis	Tampa Bay Lightning (94 points)
2004–05	no winner	
2005–06	Joe Thornton	Boston Bruins/San Jose Sharks (125 points)
2006–07	Sidney Crosby	Pittsburgh Penguins (120 points)
2007–08	Alexander Ovechkin	Washington Capitals (112 points)
2008–09	Evgeni Malkin	Pittsburgh Penguins (113 points)
2009–10	Henrik Sedin	Vancouver Canucks (112 points)

Hart Trophy

1923–24	Frank Nighbor	Ottawa Senators
1924–25	Billy Burch	Hamilton Tigers

1925–26	Nels Stewart	Montreal Maroons
1926–27	Herb Gardiner	Montreal Canadiens
1927–28	Howie Morenz	Montreal Canadiens
1928–29	Roy Worters	New York Americans
1929–30	Nels Stewart	Montreal Maroons
1930–31	Howie Morenz	Montreal Canadiens
1931–32	Howie Morenz	Montreal Canadiens
1932–33	Eddie Shore	Boston Bruins
1933–34	Aurel Joliat	Montreal Canadiens
1934–35	Eddie Shore	Boston Bruins
1935–36	Eddie Shore	Boston Bruins
1936–37	Babe Siebert	Montreal Canadiens
1937–38	Eddie Shore	Boston Bruins
1938–39	Toe Blake	Montreal Canadiens
1939–40	Ebbie Goodfellow	Detroit Red Wings
1940–41	Bill Cowley	Boston Bruins
1941–42	Tom Anderson	Brooklyn Americans
1942–43	Bill Cowley	Boston Bruins
1943–44	Babe Pratt	Toronto Maple Leafs
1944–45	Elmer Lach	Montreal Canadiens
1945–46	Max Bentley	Chicago Black Hawks
1946–47	Maurice Richard	Montreal Canadiens
1947–48	Buddy O'Connor	New York Rangers
1948–49	Sid Abel	Detroit Red Wings
1949–50	Chuck Rayner	New York Rangers
1950–51	Milt Schmidt	Boston Bruins
1951–52	Gordie Howe	Detroit Red Wings
1952–53	Gordie Howe	Detroit Red Wings
1953–54	Al Rollins	Chicago Black Hawks
1954–55	Ted Kennedy	Toronto Maple Leafs
1955–56	Jean Beliveau	Montreal Canadiens
1956–57	Gordie Howe	Detroit Red Wings
1957–58	Gordie Howe	Detroit Red Wings
1958–59	Andy Bathgate	New York Rangers

1959–60	Gordie Howe	Detroit Red Wings
1960–61	Bernie Geoffrion	Montreal Canadiens
1961–62	Jacques Plante	Montreal Canadiens
1962–63	Gordie Howe	Detroit Red Wings
1963–64	Jean Beliveau	Montreal Canadiens
1964–65	Bobby Hull	Chicago Black Hawks
1965–66	Bobby Hull	Chicago Black Hawks
1966–67	Stan Mikita	Chicago Black Hawks
1967–68	Stan Mikita	Chicago Black Hawks
1968–69	Phil Esposito	Boston Bruins
1969–70	Bobby Orr	Boston Bruins
1970–71	Bobby Orr	Boston Bruins
1971–72	Bobby Orr	Boston Bruins
1972–73	Bobby Clarke	Philadelphia Flyers
1973–74	Phil Esposito	Boston Bruins
1974–75	Bobby Clarke	Philadelphia Flyers
1975–76	Bobby Clarke	Philadelphia Flyers
1976–77	Guy Lafleur	Montreal Canadiens
1977–78	Guy Lafleur	Montreal Canadiens
1978–79	Bryan Trottier	New York Islanders
1979–80	Wayne Gretzky	Edmonton Oilers
1980–81	Wayne Gretzky	Edmonton Oilers
1981–82	Wayne Gretzky	Edmonton Oilers
1982–83	Wayne Gretzky	Edmonton Oilers
1983–84	Wayne Gretzky	Edmonton Oilers
1984–85	Wayne Gretzky	Edmonton Oilers
1985–86	Wayne Gretzky	Edmonton Oilers
1986–87	Wayne Gretzky	Edmonton Oilers
1987–88	Mario Lemieux	Pittsburgh Penguins
1988–89	Wayne Gretzky	Edmonton Oilers
1989–90	Mark Messier	Edmonton Oilers
1990–91	Brett Hull	St. Louis Blues
1991–92	Mark Messier	New York Rangers
1992–93	Mario Lemieux	Pittsburgh Penguins

1993–94	Sergei Fedorov	Detroit Red Wings
1994–95	Eric Lindros	Philadelphia Flyers
1995–96	Mario Lemieux	Pittsburgh Penguins
1996–97	Dominik Hasek	Buffalo Sabres
1997–98	Dominik Hasek	Buffalo Sabres
1998–99	Jaromir Jagr	Pittsburgh Penguins
1999–00	Chris Pronger	St. Louis Blues
2000–01	Joe Sakic	Colorado Avalanche
2001–02	Jose Theodore	Montreal Canadiens
2002–03	Peter Forsberg	Colorado Avalanche
2003–04	Martin St. Louis	Tampa Bay Lightning
2004–05	*no winner*	
2005–06	Joe Thornton	Boston Bruins/San Jose Sharks
2006–07	Sidney Crosby	Pittsburgh Penguins
2007–08	Alexander Ovechkin	Washington Capitals
2008–09	Alexander Ovechkin	Washington Capitals
2009–10	Henrik Sedin	Vancouver Canucks

Lady Byng Trophy

1924–25	Frank Nighbor	Ottawa Senators
1925–26	Frank Nighbor	Ottawa Senators
1926–27	Billy Burch	New York Americans
1927–28	Frank Boucher	New York Rangers
1928–29	Frank Boucher	New York Rangers
1929–30	Frank Boucher	New York Rangers
1930–31	Frank Boucher	New York Rangers
1931–32	Joe Primeau	Toronto Maple Leafs
1932–33	Frank Boucher	New York Rangers
1933–34	Frank Boucher	New York Rangers
1934–35	Frank Boucher	New York Rangers
1935–36	Doc Romnes	Chicago Black Hawks
1936–37	Marty Barry	Detroit Red Wings
1937–38	Gordie Drillon	Toronto Maple Leafs
1938–39	Clint Smith	New York Rangers

1939–40	Bobby Bauer	Boston Bruins
1940–41	Bobby Bauer	Boston Bruins
1941–42	Syl Apps	Toronto Maple Leafs
1942–43	Max Bentley	Chicago Black Hawks
1943–44	Clint Smith	Chicago Black Hawks
1944–45	Bill Mosienko	Chicago Black Hawks
1945–46	Toe Blake	Montreal Canadiens
1946–47	Bobby Bauer	Boston Bruins
1947–48	Buddy O'Connor	New York Rangers
1948–49	Bill Quackenbush	Detroit Red Wings
1949–50	Edgar Laprade	New York Rangers
1950–51	Red Kelly	Detroit Red Wings
1951–52	Sid Smith	Toronto Maple Leafs
1952–53	Red Kelly	Detroit Red Wings
1953–54	Red Kelly	Detroit Red Wings
1954–55	Sid Smith	Toronto Maple Leafs
1955–56	Dutch Reibel	Detroit Red Wings
1956–57	Andy Hebenton	New York Rangers
1957–58	Camille Henry	New York Rangers
1958–59	Alex Delvecchio	Detroit Red Wings
1959–60	Don McKenney	Boston Bruins
1960–61	Red Kelly	Toronto Maple Leafs
1961–62	Dave Keon	Toronto Maple Leafs
1962–63	Dave Keon	Toronto Maple Leafs
1963–64	Kenny Wharram	Chicago Black Hawks
1964–65	Bobby Hull	Chicago Black Hawks
1965–66	Alex Delvecchio	Detroit Red Wings
1966–67	Stan Mikita	Chicago Black Hawks
1967–68	Stan Mikita	Chicago Black Hawks
1968–69	Alex Delvecchio	Detroit Red Wings
1969–70	Phil Goyette	St. Louis Blues
1970–71	John Bucyk	Boston Bruins
1971–72	Jean Ratelle	New York Rangers
1972–73	Gilbert Perreault	Buffalo Sabres

1973–74	John Bucyk	Boston Bruins
1974–75	Marcel Dionne	Detroit Red Wings
1975–76	Jean Ratelle	New York Rangers/Boston Bruins
1976–77	Marcel Dionne	Los Angeles Kings
1977–78	Butch Goring	Los Angeles Kings
1978–79	Bob MacMillan	Atlanta Flames
1979–80	Wayne Gretzky	Edmonton Oilers
1980–81	Rick Kehoe	Pittsburgh Penguins
1981–82	Rick Middleton	Boston Bruins
1982–83	Mike Bossy	New York Islanders
1983–84	Mike Bossy	New York Islanders
1984–85	Jari Kurri	Edmonton Oilers
1985–86	Mike Bossy	New York Islanders
1986–87	Joe Mullen	Calgary Flames
1987–88	Mats Naslund	Montreal Canadiens
1988–89	Joe Mullen	Calgary Flames
1989–90	Brett Hull	St. Louis Blues
1990–91	Wayne Gretzky	Los Angeles Kings
1991–92	Wayne Gretzky	Los Angeles Kings
1992–93	Pierre Turgeon	New York Islanders
1993–94	Wayne Gretzky	Los Angeles Kings
1994–95	Ron Francis	Pittsburgh Penguins
1995–96	Paul Kariya	Mighty Ducks of Anaheim
1996–97	Paul Kariya	Mighty Ducks of Anaheim
1997–98	Ron Francis	Pittsburgh Penguins
1998–99	Wayne Gretzky	New York Rangers
1999–00	Pavol Demitra	St. Louis Blues
2000–01	Joe Sakic	Colorado Avalanche
2001–02	Ron Francis	Carolina Hurricanes
2002–03	Alexander Mogilny	Toronto Maple Leafs
2003–04	Brad Richards	Tampa Bay Lightning
2004–05	*no winner*	
2005–06	Pavel Datsyuk	Detroit Red Wings
2006–07	Pavel Datsyuk	Detroit Red Wings
2007–08	Pavel Datsyuk	Detroit Red Wings

| 2008–09 | Pavel Datsyuk | Detroit Red Wings |
| 2009–10 | Martin St. Louis | Tampa Bay Lightning |

Vezina Trophy

1926–27	George Hainsworth	Montreal Canadiens (1.47 GAA)
1927–28	George Hainsworth	Montreal Canadiens (1.05 GAA)
1928–29	George Hainsworth	Montreal Canadiens (0.92 GAA)
1929–30	Tiny Thompson	Boston Bruins (2.19 GAA)
1930–31	Roy Worters	New York Americans (1.61 GAA)
1931–32	Charlie Gardiner	Chicago Black Hawks (1.85 GAA)
1932–33	Tiny Thompson	Boston Bruins (1.76 GAA)
1933–34	Charlie Gardiner	Chicago Black Hawks (1.63 GAA)
1934–35	Lorne Chabot	Chicago Black Hawks (1.80 GAA)
1935–36	Tiny Thompson	Boston Bruins (1.68 GAA)
1936–37	Normie Smith	Detroit Red Wings (2.05 GAA)
1937–38	Tiny Thompson	Boston Bruins (1.80 GAA)
1938–39	Frank Brimsek	Boston Bruins (1.56 GAA)
1939–40	Dave Kerr	New York Rangers (1.54 GAA)
1940–41	Turk Broda	Toronto Maple Leafs (2.00 GAA)
1941–42	Frank Brimsek	Boston Bruins (2.35 GAA)
1942–43	Johnny Mowers	Detroit Red Wings (2.47 GAA)
1943–44	Bill Durnan	Montreal Canadiens (2.18 GAA)
1944–45	Bill Durnan	Montreal Canadiens (2.42 GAA)
1945–46	Bill Durnan	Montreal Canadiens (2.60 GAA)
1946–47	Bill Durnan	Montreal Canadiens (2.30 GAA)
1947–48	Turk Broda	Toronto Maple Leafs (2.38 GAA)
1948–49	Bill Durnan	Montreal Canadiens (2.10 GAA)
1949–50	Bill Durnan	Montreal Canadiens (2.20 GAA)
1950–51	Al Rollins	Toronto Maple Leafs (1.77 GAA)
1951–52	Terry Sawchuk	Detroit Red Wings (1.90 GAA)
1952–53	Terry Sawchuk	Detroit Red Wings (1.90 GAA)
1953–54	Harry Lumley	Toronto Maple Leafs (1.86 GAA)
1954–55	Terry Sawchuk	Detroit Red Wings (1.96 GAA)
1955–56	Jacques Plante	Montreal Canadiens (1.86 GAA)
1956–57	Jacques Plante	Montreal Canadiens (2.00 GAA)

1957–58	Jacques Plante	Montreal Canadiens (2.11 GAA)
1958–59	Jacques Plante	Montreal Canadiens (2.16 GAA)
1959–60	Jacques Plante	Montreal Canadiens (2.54 GAA)
1960–61	Johnny Bower	Toronto Maple Leafs (2.50 GAA)
1961–62	Jacques Plante	Montreal Canadiens (2.37 GAA)
1962–63	Glenn Hall	Chicago Black Hawks (2.47 GAA)
1963–64	Charlie Hodge	Montreal Canadiens (2.26 GAA)
1964–65	Terry Sawchuk	Toronto Maple Leafs (2.56 GAA)
	Johnny Bower	Toronto Maple Leafs (2.38 GAA)
1965–66	Gump Worsley	Montreal Canadiens (2.36 GAA)
	Charlie Hodge	Montreal Canadiens (2.58 GAA)
1966–67	Glenn Hall	Chicago Black Hawks (2.38 GAA)
	Denis DeJordy	Chicago Black Hawks (2.46 GAA)
1967–68	Gump Worsley	Montreal Canadiens (1.98 GAA)
	Rogie Vachon	Montreal Canadiens (2.48 GAA)
1968–69	Jacques Plante	St. Louis Blues (1.96 GAA)
	Glenn Hall	St. Louis Blues (2.17 GAA)
1969–70	Tony Esposito	Chicago Black Hawks (2.17 GAA)
1970–71	Ed Giacomin	New York Rangers (2.16 GAA)
	Gilles Villemure	New York Rangers (2.30 GAA)
1971–72	Tony Esposito	Chicago Black Hawks (1.77 GAA)
	Gary Smith	Chicago Black Hawks (2.42 GAA)
1972–73	Ken Dryden	Montreal Canadiens (2.26 GAA)
1973–74	Bernie Parent	Philadelphia Flyers (1.89 GAA)
	Tony Esposito	Chicago Black Hawks (2.04 GAA)
1974–75	Bernie Parent	Philadelphia Flyers (2.03 GAA)
1975–76	Ken Dryden	Montreal Canadiens (2.03 GAA)
1976–77	Ken Dryden	Montreal Canadiens (2.14 GAA)
	Michel Larocque	Montreal Canadiens (2.09 GAA)
1977–78	Ken Dryden	Montreal Canadiens (2.05 GAA)
	Michel Larocque	Montreal Canadiens (2.67 GAA)
1978–79	Ken Dryden	Montreal Canadiens (2.30 GAA)
	Michel Larocque	Montreal Canadiens (2.84 GAA)
1979–80	Bob Sauve	Buffalo Sabres (2.36 GAA)

	Don Edwards	Buffalo Sabres (2.57 GAA)
1980–81	Richard Sevigny	Montreal Canadiens (2.40 GAA)
	Denis Herron	Montreal Canadiens (3.50 GAA)
	Michel Larocque	Montreal Canadiens (3.03 GAA)
1981–82	Billy Smith	New York Islanders (2.97 GAA)
1982–83	Pete Peeters	Boston Bruins (2.36 GAA)
1983–84	Tom Barrasso	Buffalo Sabres (2.84 GAA)
1984–85	Pelle Lindbergh	Philadelphia Flyers (3.02 GAA)
1985–86	John Vanbiesbrouck	New York Rangers (3.32 GAA)
1986–87	Ron Hextall	Philadelphia Flyers (3.00 GAA)
1987–88	Grant Fuhr	Edmonton Oilers (3.43 GAA)
1988–89	Patrick Roy	Montreal Canadiens (2.47 GAA)
1989–90	Patrick Roy	Montreal Canadiens (2.53 GAA)
1990–91	Ed Belfour	Chicago Blackhawks (2.47 GAA)
1991–92	Patrick Roy	Montreal Canadiens (2.36 GAA)
1992–93	Ed Belfour	Chicago Blackhawks (2.59 GAA)
1993–94	Dominik Hasek	Buffalo Sabres (1.95 GAA)
1994–95	Dominik Hasek	Buffalo Sabres (2.11 GAA)
1995–96	Jim Carey	Washington Capitals (2.26 GAA)
1996–97	Dominik Hasek	Buffalo Sabres (2.27 GAA)
1997–98	Dominik Hasek	Buffalo Sabres (2.09 GAA)
1998–99	Dominik Hasek	Buffalo Sabres (1.87 GAA)
1999–00	Olaf Kolzig	Washington Capitals (2.24 GAA)
2000–01	Dominik Hasek	Buffalo Sabres (2.11 GAA)
2001–02	Jose Theodore	Montreal Canadiens (2.11 GAA)
2002–03	Martin Brodeur	New Jersey Devils (2.02 GAA)
2003–04	Martin Brodeur	New Jersey Devils (2.62 GAA)
2004–05	*no winner*	
2005–06	Miikka Kiprusoff	Calgary Flames (2.07 GAA)
2006–07	Martin Brodeur	New Jersey Devils (2.18 GAA)
2007–08	Martin Brodeur	New Jersey Devils (2.17 GAA)
2008–09	Tim Thomas	Boston Bruins (2.10 GAA)
2009–10	Ryan Miller	Buffalo Sabres (2.22 GAA)

Calder Memorial Trophy

1932–33	Carl Voss	Detroit Red Wings
1933–34	Russ Blinco	Montreal Maroons
1934–35	Sweeney Schriner	New York Americans
1935–36	Mike Karakas	Chicago Black Hawks
1936–37	Syl Apps	Toronto Maple Leafs
1937–38	Cully Dahlstrom	Chicago Black Hawks
1938–39	Frank Brimsek	Boston Bruins
1939–40	Kilby MacDonald	New York Rangers
1940–41	John Quilty	Montreal Canadiens
1941–42	Grant Warwick	New York Rangers
1942–43	Gaye Stewart	Toronto Maple Leafs
1943–44	Gus Bodnar	Toronto Maple Leafs
1944–45	Frank McCool	Toronto Maple Leafs
1945–46	Edgar Laprade	New York Rangers
1946–47	Howie Meeker	Toronto Maple Leafs
1947–48	Jim McFadden	Detroit Red Wings
1948–49	Pentti Lund	New York Rangers
1949–50	Jack Gelineau	Boston Bruins
1950–51	Terry Sawchuk	Detroit Red Wings
1951–52	Bernie Geoffrion	Montreal Canadiens
1952–53	Gump Worsley	New York Rangers
1953–54	Camille Henry	New York Rangers
1954–55	Ed Litzenberger	Chicago Black Hawks
1955–56	Glenn Hall	Detroit Red Wings
1956–57	Larry Regan	Boston Bruins
1957–58	Frank Mahovlich	Toronto Maple Leafs
1958–59	Ralph Backstrom	Montreal Canadiens
1959–60	Bill Hay	Chicago Black Hawks
1960–61	Dave Keon	Toronto Maple Leafs
1961–62	Bobby Rousseau	Montreal Canadiens
1962–63	Kent Douglas	Toronto Maple Leafs
1963–64	Jacques Laperriere	Montreal Canadiens
1964–65	Roger Crozier	Detroit Red Wings

1965–66	Brit Selby	Toronto Maple Leafs
1966–67	Bobby Orr	Boston Bruins
1967–68	Derek Sanderson	Boston Bruins
1968–69	Danny Grant	Minnesota North Stars
1969–70	Tony Esposito	Chicago Black Hawks
1970–71	Gilbert Perreault	Buffalo Sabres
1971–72	Ken Dryden	Montreal Canadiens
1972–73	Steve Vickers	New York Rangers
1973–74	Denis Potvin	New York Islanders
1974–75	Eric Vail	Atlanta Flames
1975–76	Bryan Trottier	New York Islanders
1976–77	Willi Plett	Atlanta Flames
1977–78	Mike Bossy	New York Islanders
1978–79	Bobby Smith	Minnesota North Stars
1979–80	Raymond Bourque	Boston Bruins
1980–81	Peter Stastny	Quebec Nordiques
1981–82	Dale Hawerchuk	Winnipeg Jets
1982–83	Steve Larmer	Chicago Black Hawks
1983–84	Tom Barrasso	Buffalo Sabres
1984–85	Mario Lemieux	Pittsburgh Penguins
1985–86	Gary Suter	Calgary Flames
1986–87	Luc Robitaille	Los Angeles Kings
1987–88	Joe Nieuwendyk	Calgary Flames
1988–89	Brian Leetch	New York Rangers
1989–90	Sergei Makarov	Calgary Flames
1990–91	Ed Belfour	Chicago Blackhawks
1991–92	Pavel Bure	Vancouver Canucks
1992–93	Teemu Selanne	Winnipeg Jets
1993–94	Martin Brodeur	New Jersey Devils
1994–95	Peter Forsberg	Quebec Nordiques
1995–96	Daniel Alfredsson	Ottawa Senators
1996–97	Bryan Berard	New York Islanders
1997–98	Sergei Samsonov	Boston Bruins
1998–99	Chris Drury	Colorado Avalanche

1999–00	Scott Gomez	New Jersey Devils
2000–01	Evgeni Nabokov	San Jose Sharks
2001–02	Danny Heatley	Atlanta Thrashers
2002–03	Barret Jackman	St. Louis Blues
2003–04	Andrew Raycroft	Boston Bruins
2004–05	*no winner*	
2005–06	Alexander Ovechkin	Washington Capitals
2006–07	Evgeni Malkin	Pittsburgh Penguins
2007–08	Patrick Kane	Chicago Blackhawks
2008–09	Steve Mason	Columbus Blue Jackets
2009–10	Tyler Myers	Buffalo Sabres

James Norris Trophy

1953–54	Red Kelly	Detroit Red Wings
1954–55	Doug Harvey	Montreal Canadiens
1955–56	Doug Harvey	Montreal Canadiens
1956–57	Doug Harvey	Montreal Canadiens
1957–58	Doug Harvey	Montreal Canadiens
1958–59	Tom Johnson	Montreal Canadiens
1959–60	Doug Harvey	Montreal Canadiens
1960–61	Doug Harvey	Montreal Canadiens
1961–62	Doug Harvey	Montreal Canadiens
1962–63	Pierre Pilote	Chicago Black Hawks
1963–64	Pierre Pilote	Chicago Black Hawks
1964–65	Pierre Pilote	Chicago Black Hawks
1965–66	Jacques Laperriere	Montreal Canadiens
1966–67	Harry Howell	New York Rangers
1967–68	Bobby Orr	Boston Bruins
1968–69	Bobby Orr	Boston Bruins
1969–70	Bobby Orr	Boston Bruins
1970–71	Bobby Orr	Boston Bruins
1971–72	Bobby Orr	Boston Bruins
1972–73	Bobby Orr	Boston Bruins
1973–74	Bobby Orr	Boston Bruins

1974–75	Bobby Orr	Boston Bruins
1975–76	Denis Potvin	New York Islanders
1976–77	Larry Robinson	Montreal Canadiens
1977–78	Denis Potvin	New York Islanders
1978–79	Denis Potvin	New York Islanders
1979–80	Larry Robinson	Montreal Canadiens
1980–81	Randy Carlyle	Pittsburgh Penguins
1981–82	Doug Wilson	Chicago Black Hawks
1982–83	Rod Langway	Washington Capitals
1983–84	Rod Langway	Washington Capitals
1984–85	Paul Coffey	Edmonton Oilers
1985–86	Paul Coffey	Edmonton Oilers
1986–87	Raymond Bourque	Boston Bruins
1987–88	Raymond Bourque	Boston Bruins
1988–89	Chris Chelios	Montreal Canadiens
1989–90	Raymond Bourque	Boston Bruins
1990–91	Raymond Bourque	Boston Bruins
1991–92	Brian Leetch	New York Rangers
1992–93	Chris Chelios	Chicago Blackhawks
1993–94	Raymond Bourque	Boston Bruins
1994–95	Paul Coffey	Detroit Red Wings
1995–96	Chris Chelios	Chicago Blackhawks
1996–97	Brian Leetch	New York Rangers
1997–98	Rob Blake	Los Angeles Kings
1998–99	Al MacInnis	St. Louis Blues
1999–00	Chris Pronger	St. Louis Blues
2000–01	Nicklas Lidstrom	Detroit Red Wings
2001–02	Nicklas Lidstrom	Detroit Red Wings
2002–03	Nicklas Lidstrom	Detroit Red Wings
2003–04	Scott Niedermayer	New Jersey Devils
2004–05	*no winner*	
2005–06	Nicklas Lidstrom	Detroit Red Wings
2006–07	Nicklas Lidstrom	Detroit Red Wings
2007–08	Nicklas Lidstrom	Detroit Red Wings

| 2008–09 | Zdeno Chara | Boston Bruins |
| 2009–10 | Duncan Keith | Chicago Blackhawks |

Lester Patrick Trophy

1965–66	Jack Adams
1966–67	Gordie Howe
	Charles F. Adams
	James Norris, Sr.
1967–68	Tommy Lockhart
	Walter A. Brown
	Gen. John R. Kilpatrick
1968–69	Bobby Hull
	Ed Jeremiah
1969–70	Eddie Shore
	Jim Hendy
1970–71	Bill Jennings
	John B. Sollenberger
	Terry Sawchuk
1971–72	Clarence Campbell
	John A. Kelly
	Cooney Weiland
	James D. Norris
1972–73	Walter Bush, Jr.
1973–74	Alex Delvecchio
	Murray Murdoch
	Weston W. Adams Sr.
	Charles L. Crovat
1974–75	Donald M. Clark
	Bill Chadwick
	Tommy Ivan
1975–76	Stan Mikita
	George Leader
	Bruce A. Norris

1976–77	Johnny Bucyk
	Murray Armstrong
	John Mariucci
1977–78	Phil Esposito
	Tom Fitzgerald
	William T. Tutt
	Bill Wirtz
1978–79	Bobby Orr
1979–80	Bobby Clarke
	Ed Snider
	Fred Shero
	1980 U.S. Olympic Hockey Team
1980–81	Charles M. Schulz
1981–82	Emile Francis
1982–83	Bill Torrey
1983–84	John A. Ziegler Jr.
	Art Ross
1984–85	Jack Butterfield
	Arthur M. Wirtz
1985–86	John MacInnes
	Jack Riley
1986–87	Hobey Baker
	Frank Mathers
1987–88	Keith Allen
	Fred Cusick
	Bob Johnson
1988–89	Dan Kelly
	Lou Nanne
	Lynn Patrick
	Bud Poile
1989–90	Len Ceglarski
1990–91	Rod Gilbert
	Mike Ilitch

1991–92	Al Arbour
	Art Berglund
	Lou Lamoriello
1992–93	Frank Boucher
	Red Dutton
	Bruce McNall
	Gil Stein
1993–94	Wayne Gretzky
	Robert Ridder
1994–95	Joe Mullen
	Brian Mullen
	Bob Fleming
1995–96	George Gund
	Ken Morrow
	Milt Schmidt
1996–97	Seymour H. Knox III
	Bill Cleary
	Pat LaFontaine
1997–98	Peter Karmanos
	Neal Broten
	John Mayasich
	Max McNab
1998–99	Harry Sinden
	1998 U.S. Olympic Women's Hockey Team
1999–00	Mario Lemieux
	Craig Patrick
	Lou Vairo
2000–01	Scotty Bowman
	David Poile
	Gary Bettman
2001–02	1960 U.S. Olympic Team
	Herb Brooks
	Larry Pleau

2002–03	Ray Bourque	
	Ron DeGregorio	
	Willie O'Ree	
2003–04	Mike Emrick	
	John Davidson	
	Ray Miron	
2004–05	*none*	
2005–06	Red Berenson	
	Marcel Dionne	
	Reed Larson	
	Glen Sonmor	
	Steve Yzerman	
2006–07	Brian Leetch	
	Cammi Granato	
	John Halligan	
	Stan Fischler	
2007–08	Brian Burke	
	Ted Lindsay	
	Phil Housley	
	Bob Naegele, Jr.	
2008–09	Mark Messier	
	Mike Richter	
	Jimmy Devellano	

Conn Smythe Trophy

* indicates played for losing team

1964–65	Jean Beliveau	Montreal Canadiens
1965–66	Roger Crozier*	Detroit Red Wings
1966–67	Dave Keon	Toronto Maple Leafs
1967–68	Glenn Hall*	St. Louis Blues
1968–69	Serge Savard	Montreal Canadiens
1969–70	Bobby Orr	Boston Bruins
1970–71	Ken Dryden	Montreal Canadiens
1971–72	Bobby Orr	Boston Bruins

1972–73	Yvan Cournoyer	Montreal Canadiens
1973–74	Bernie Parent	Philadelphia Flyers
1974–75	Bernie Parent	Philadelphia Flyers
1975–76	Reggie Leach*	Philadelphia Flyers
1976–77	Guy Lafleur	Montreal Canadiens
1977–78	Larry Robinson	Montreal Canadiens
1978–79	Bob Gainey	Montreal Canadiens
1979–80	Bryan Trottier	New York Islanders
1980–81	Butch Goring	New York Islanders
1981–82	Mike Bossy	New York Islanders
1982–83	Billy Smith	New York Islanders
1983–84	Mark Messier	Edmonton Oilers
1984–85	Wayne Gretzky	Edmonton Oilers
1985–86	Patrick Roy	Montreal Canadiens
1986–87	Ron Hextall	Philadelphia Flyers
1987–88	Wayne Gretzky	Edmonton Oilers
1988–89	Al MacInnis	Calgary Flames
1989–90	Bill Ranford	Edmonton Oilers
1990–91	Mario Lemieux	Pittsburgh Penguins
1991–92	Mario Lemieux	Pittsburgh Penguins
1992–93	Patrick Roy	Montreal Canadiens
1993–94	Brian Leetch	New York Rangers
1994–95	Claude Lemieux	New Jersey Devils
1995–96	Joe Sakic	Colorado Avalanche
1996–97	Mike Vernon	Detroit Red Wings
1997–98	Steve Yzerman	Detroit Red Wings
1998–99	Joe Nieuwendyk	Dallas Stars
1999–00	Scott Stevens	New Jersey Devils
2000–01	Patrick Roy	Colorado Avalanche
2001–02	Nicklas Lidstrom	Detroit Red Wings
2002–03	J-S Giguere*	Mighty Ducks of Anaheim
2003–04	Brad Richards	Tampa Bay Lightning
2004–05	*no winner*	
2005–06	Cam Ward	Carolina Hurricanes

2006–07	Scott Niedermayer	Anaheim Ducks
2007–08	Henrik Zetterberg	Detroit Red Wings
2008–09	Evgeni Malkin	Pittsburgh Penguins
2009–10	Jonathan Toews	Chicago Blackhawks

Bill Masterton Trophy

1967–68	Claude Provost	Montreal Canadiens
1968–69	Ted Hampson	Oakland Seals
1969–70	Pit Martin	Chicago Black Hawks
1970–71	Jean Ratelle	New York Rangers
1971–72	Bobby Clarke	Philadelphia Flyers
1972–73	Lowell MacDonald	Pittsburgh Penguins
1973–74	Henri Richard	Montreal Canadiens
1974–75	Don Luce	Buffalo Sabres
1975–76	Rod Gilbert	New York Rangers
1976–77	Ed Westfall	New York Islanders
1977–78	Butch Goring	Los Angeles Kings
1978–79	Serge Savard	Montreal Canadiens
1979–80	Al MacAdam	Minnesota North Stars
1980–81	Blake Dunlop	St. Louis Blues
1981–82	Glenn Resch	Colorado Rockies
1982–83	Lanny McDonald	Calgary Flames
1983–84	Brad Park	Detroit Red Wings
1984–85	Anders Hedberg	New York Rangers
1985–86	Charlie Simmer	Boston Bruins
1986–87	Doug Jarvis	Hartford Whalers
1987–88	Bob Bourne	Los Angeles Kings
1988–89	Tim Kerr	Philadelphia Flyers
1989–90	Gord Kluzak	Boston Bruins
1990–91	Dave Taylor	Los Angeles Kings
1991–92	Mark Fitzpatrick	New York Islanders
1992–93	Mario Lemieux	Pittsburgh Penguins
1993–94	Cam Neely	Boston Bruins
1994–95	Pat LaFontaine	Buffalo Sabres

1995–96	Gary Roberts	Calgary Flames
1996–97	Tony Granato	San Jose Sharks
1997–98	Jamie McLennan	St. Louis Blues
1998–99	John Cullen	Tampa Bay Lightning
1999–00	Ken Daneyko	New Jersey Devils
2000–01	Adam Graves	New York Rangers
2001–02	Saku Koivu	Montreal Canadiens
2002–03	Steve Yzerman	Detroit Red Wings
2003–04	Bryan Berard	Chicago Blackhawks
2004–05	*no winner*	
2005–06	Teemu Selanne	Mighty Ducks of Anaheim
2006–07	Phil Kessel	Boston Bruins
2007–08	Jason Blake	Toronto Maple Leafs
2008–09	Steve Sullivan	Nashville Predators
2009–10	Jose Theodore	Washington Capitals

Jack Adams Award

1973–74	Fred Shero	Philadelphia Flyers
1974–75	Bob Pulford	Los Angeles Kings
1975–76	Don Cherry	Boston Bruins
1976–77	Scotty Bowman	Montreal Canadiens
1977–78	Bobby Kromm	Detroit Red Wings
1978–79	Al Arbour	New York Islanders
1979–80	Pat Quinn	Philadelphia Flyers
1980–81	Red Berenson	St. Louis Blues
1981–82	Tom Watt	Winnipeg Jets
1982–83	Orval Tessier	Chicago Black Hawks
1983–84	Bryan Murray	Washington Capitals
1984–85	Mike Keenan	Philadelphia Flyers
1985–86	Glen Sather	Edmonton Oilers
1986–87	Jacques Demers	Detroit Red Wings
1987–88	Jacques Demers	Detroit Red Wings
1988–89	Pat Burns	Montreal Canadiens
1989–90	Bob Murdoch	Winnipeg Jets

1990–91	Brian Sutter	St. Louis Blues
1991–92	Pat Quinn	Vancouver Canucks
1992–93	Pat Burns	Toronto Maple Leafs
1993–94	Jacques Lemaire	New Jersey Devils
1994–95	Marc Crawford	Quebec Nordiques
1995–96	Scotty Bowman	Detroit Red Wings
1996–97	Ted Nolan	Buffalo Sabres
1997–98	Pat Burns	Boston Bruins
1998–99	Jacques Martin	Ottawa Senators
1999–00	Joel Quenneville	St. Louis Blues
2000–01	Bill Barber	Philadelphia Flyers
2001–02	Bob Francis	Phoenix Coyotes
2002–03	Jacques Lemaire	Minnesota Wild
2003–04	John Tortorella	Tampa Bay Lightning
2004–05	*no winner*	
2005–06	Lindy Ruff	Buffalo Sabres
2006–07	Alain Vigneault	Vancouver Canucks
2007–08	Bruce Boudreau	Washington Capitals
2008–09	Claude Julien	Boston Bruins
2009–10	Dave Tippett	Phoenix Coyotes

Lester B. Pearson Award

1970–71	Phil Esposito	Boston Bruins
1971–72	Jean Ratelle	New York Rangers
1972–73	Bobby Clarke	Philadelphia Flyers
1973–74	Phil Esposito	Boston Bruins
1974–75	Bobby Orr	Boston Bruins
1975–76	Guy Lafleur	Montreal Canadiens
1976–77	Guy Lafleur	Montreal Canadiens
1977–78	Guy Lafleur	Montreal Canadiens
1978–79	Marcel Dionne	Los Angeles Kings
1979–80	Marcel Dionne	Los Angeles Kings
1980–81	Mike Liut	St. Louis Blues
1981–82	Wayne Gretzky	Edmonton Oilers

1982–83	Wayne Gretzky	Edmonton Oilers
1983–84	Wayne Gretzky	Edmonton Oilers
1984–85	Wayne Gretzky	Edmonton Oilers
1985–86	Mario Lemieux	Pittsburgh Penguins
1986–87	Wayne Gretzky	Edmonton Oilers
1987–88	Mario Lemieux	Pittsburgh Penguins
1988–89	Steve Yzerman	Detroit Red Wings
1989–90	Mark Messier	Edmonton Oilers
1990–91	Brett Hull	St. Louis Blues
1991–92	Mark Messier	New York Rangers
1992–93	Mario Lemieux	Pittsburgh Penguins
1993–94	Sergei Fedorov	Detroit Red Wings
1994–95	Eric Lindros	Philadelphia Flyers
1995–96	Mario Lemieux	Pittsburgh Penguins
1996–97	Dominik Hasek	Buffalo Sabres
1997–98	Dominik Hasek	Buffalo Sabres
1998–99	Jaromir Jagr	Pittsburgh Penguins
1999–00	Jaromir Jagr	Pittsburgh Penguins
2000–01	Joe Sakic	Colorado Avalanche
2001–02	Jarome Iginla	Calgary Flames
2002–03	Markus Naslund	Vancouver Canucks
2003–04	Martin St. Louis	Tampa Bay Lightning
2004–05	*no winner*	
2005–06	Jaromir Jagr	New York Rangers
2006–07	Sidney Crosby	Pittsburgh Penguins
2007–08	Alexander Ovechkin	Washington Capitals
2008–09	Alexander Ovechkin	Washington Capitals

Ted Lindsay Award

(Formerly Lester B. Pearson Award)

| 2009–10 | Alexander Ovechkin | Washington Capitals |

Frank J. Selke Trophy

1977–78	Bob Gainey	Montreal Canadiens
1978–79	Bob Gainey	Montreal Canadiens
1979–80	Bob Gainey	Montreal Canadiens
1980–81	Bob Gainey	Montreal Canadiens
1981–82	Steve Kasper	Boston Bruins
1982–83	Bobby Clarke	Pittsburgh Penguins
1983–84	Doug Jarvis	Washington Capitals
1984–85	Craig Ramsay	Buffalo Sabres
1985–86	Troy Murray	Chicago Black Hawks
1986–87	Dave Poulin	Philadelphia Flyers
1987–88	Guy Carbonneau	Montreal Canadiens
1988–89	Guy Carbonneau	Montreal Canadiens
1989–90	Rick Meagher	St. Louis Blues
1990–91	Dirk Graham	Chicago Blackhawks
1991–92	Guy Carbonneau	Montreal Canadiens
1992–93	Doug Gilmour	Toronto Maple Leafs
1993–94	Sergei Fedorov	Detroit Red Wings
1994–95	Ron Francis	Pittsburgh Penguins
1995–96	Sergei Fedorov	Detroit Red Wings
1996–97	Michael Peca	Buffalo Sabres
1997–98	Jere Lehtinen	Dallas Stars
1998–99	Jere Lehtinen	Dallas Stars
1999–00	Steve Yzerman	Detroit Red Wings
2000–01	John Madden	New Jersey Devils
2001–02	Michael Peca	New York Islanders
2002–03	Jere Lehtinen	Dallas Stars
2003–04	Kris Draper	Detroit Red Wings
2004–05	*no winner*	
2005–06	Rod Brind'Amour	Carolina Hurricanes
2006–07	Rod Brind'Amour	Carolina Hurricanes
2007–08	Pavel Datsyuk	Detroit Red Wings
2008–09	Pavel Datsyuk	Detroit Red Wings
2009–10	Pavel Datsyuk	Detroit Red Wings

William M. Jennings Trophy

1981–82	Rick Wamsley & Denis Herron	Montreal Canadiens
1982–83	Rollie Melanson & Billy Smith	New York Islanders
1983–84	Al Jensen & Pat Riggin	Washington Capitals
1984–85	Tom Barrasso & Bob Sauve	Buffalo Sabres
1985–86	Bob Froese & Darren Jensen	Philadelphia Flyers
1986–87	Patrick Roy & Brian Hayward	Montreal Canadiens
1987–88	Patrick Roy & Brian Hayward	Montreal Canadiens
1988–89	Patrick Roy & Brian Hayward	Montreal Canadiens
1989–90	Andy Moog & Reggie Lemelin	Boston Bruins
1990–91	Ed Belfour	Chicago Blackhawks
1991–92	Patrick Roy	Montreal Canadiens
1992–93	Ed Belfour	Chicago Blackhawks
1993–94	Dominik Hasek & Grant Fuhr	Buffalo Sabres
1994–95	Ed Belfour	Chicago Blackhawks
1995–96	Chris Osgood & Mike Vernon	Detroit Red Wings
1996–97	Martin Brodeur & Mike Dunham	New Jersey Devils
1997–98	Martin Brodeur	New Jersey Devils
1998–99	Ed Belfour & Roman Turek	Dallas Stars
1999–00	Roman Turek	St. Louis Blues
2000–01	Dominik Hasek	Buffalo Sabres
2001–02	Patrick Roy	Colorado Avalanche
2002–03	Martin Brodeur	New Jersey Devils
	Roman Cechmanek	Philadelphia Flyers
	Robert Esche	Philadelphia Flyers
2003–04	Martin Brodeur	New Jersey Devils
2004–05	*no winner*	
2005–06	Miikka Kiprusoff	Calgary Flames
2006–07	Manny Fernandez & Niklas Backstrom	Minnesota Wild
2007–08	Chris Osgood & Dominik Hasek	Detroit Red Wings

2008–09	Tim Thomas &	
	Manny Fernandez	Boston Bruins
2009–10	Martin Brodeur	New Jersey Devils

King Clancy Memorial Trophy

1987–88	Lanny McDonald	Calgary Flames
1988–89	Bryan Trottier	New York Islanders
1989–90	Kevin Lowe	Edmonton Oilers
1990–91	Dave Taylor	Los Angeles Kings
1991–92	Raymond Bourque	Boston Bruins
1992–93	Dave Poulin	Boston Bruins
1993–94	Adam Graves	New York Rangers
1994–95	Joe Nieuwendyk	Calgary Flames
1995–96	Kris King	Winnipeg Jets
1996–97	Trevor Linden	Vancouver Canucks
1997–98	Kelly Chase	St. Louis Blues
1998–99	Rob Ray	Buffalo Sabres
1999–00	Curtis Joseph	Toronto Maple Leafs
2000–01	Shjon Podein	Colorado Avalanche
2001–02	Ron Francis	Carolina Hurricanes
2002–03	Brendan Shanahan	Detroit Red Wings
2003–04	Jarome Iginla	Calgary Flames
2004–05	*no winner*	
2005–06	Olaf Kolzig	Washington Capitals
2006–07	Saku Koivu	Montreal Canadiens
2007–08	Vincent Lecavalier	Tampa Bay Lightning
2008–09	Ethan Moreau	Edmonton Oilers
2009–10	Shane Doan	Phoenix Coyotes

Rocket Richard Trophy

1998–99	Teemu Selanne	Mighty Ducks of Anaheim (47 goals)
1999–00	Pavel Bure	Florida Panthers (58 goals)
2000–01	Pavel Bure	Florida Panthers (59 goals)
2001–02	Jarome Iginla	Calgary Flames (52 goals)

2002–03	Milan Hejduk	Colorado Avalanche (50 goals)
2003–04	Rick Nash	Columbus Blue Jackets (41 goals)
	Jarome Iginla	Calgary Flames (41 goals)
	Ilya Kovalchuk	Atlanta Thrashers (41 goals)
2004–05	*no winner*	
2005–06	Jonathan Cheechoo	San Jose Sharks (56 goals)
2006–07	Vincent Lacavalier	Tampa Bay Lightning (52 goals)
2007–08	Alexander Ovechkin	Washington Capitals (65 goals)
2008–09	Alexander Ovechkin	Washington Capitals (56 goals)
2009–10	Sidney Crosby	Pittsburgh Penguins (51 goals)
	Steve Stamkos	Tampa Bay Lightning (51 goals)

2010 HOCKEY HALL OF FAME ELECTIONS, JUNE 22, 2010

Induction Ceremonies, November 8, 2010

Player Inductees

Men
Dino Ciccarelli
An incredible success story, Ciccarelli retired in 1999 having scored 608 goals and exactly 1,200 points despite never having been drafted. In other words, no NHL wanted him at a time when any could have had him for the price of a draft selection. Nevertheless, Ciccarelli was an almost instant success at the highest level of play, being noted for his touch around the net. He wasn't a fancy stickhandler who could rush the puck the length of the ice, and he didn't have a booming shot, but he was more than willing to absorb punishment in front of the goal to scoop up rebounds and loose pucks, which he did extraordinarily well. He waited eight years to be inducted, during which time he was always the highest scorer not in the Hall of Fame.

Women
Angela James
Part of the inaugural group of three women inducted into the IIHF Hall of Fame two years earlier, James is making history as one of the first two to be inducted into the Hockey Hall of Fame this year. Called the Wayne Gretzky of women's hockey, she led Canada to gold medals in each of the first four official IIHF World Women's Championships, in 1990, 1992, 1994 and 1997. She had played at the unofficial event in 1987 but was cut just before women made history by participating at the Olympics, in Nagano in 1998. James was a pure scorer and powerful skater, an imposing threat with the puck and in the offensive end.

Catherine "Cammi" Granato

The leading scorer among American women, Granato was often James's key nemesis during the time their international careers overlapped. Granato was only 18 when she debuted at the 1990 World Women's Championship in Ottawa, and over the next 15 years she became the face of women's hockey in the U.S. She played in 11 World Women's Championships and Olympics, winning two gold medals and nine silver medals, all final games played against Canada. She retired in 2005 with 54 goals and 96 points in 54 games, second all-time only to Hayley Wickenheiser.

Builders
Jimmy Devellano

Devellano began his career as a scout with the St. Louis Blues more than 40 years ago, but he first rose to prominence with the New York Islanders in the early 1980s. His name is on the Stanley Cup in 1980 and 1981 in that capacity, and in 1982 he was the team's assistant general manager when it won for a third straight year. Devellano was wooed away to the Detroit Red Wings with the lure of a general manager's title, and he slowly became the best in the business. While the Red Wings were a weak team for many years, Devellano soon had Steve Yzerman as the cornerstone of the franchise. The Red Wings went on to win the Cup four times in 11 years (1997–2008), and Devellano deserves much of the credit for building a scouting staff second to none and having a savvy that few men could match.

Daryl "Doc" Seaman

A flying officer with the RCAF during the Second World War, Seaman was a co-founder of Bow Valley Industries in 1949, an oil and gas company, and became a wealthy man. His love of sports, however, was an important part of his life, and in 1980 he was one of six businessmen to buy the Atlanta Flames and move the team to Calgary. Later that decade he was integral to that city's successful hosting of the 1988 Olympic Winter Games, and the next year the Flames won their first, and still only, Stanley Cup. Seaman was made an Officer of the Order of Canada in 1992 and passed away early in 2009 after a lengthy battle with prostate cancer.

Other notable names eligible but not inducted: Joe Nieuwendyk, Pat Burns, Doug Gilmour, Pavel Bure, Eric Lindros, Adam Oates, Dave Andreychuk, Phil Housley, Fred Shero, Mark Howe, Sergei Makarov, Mike Vernon, Tom Barrasso, Arturs Irbe, Tommy Salo, Peter Bondra, Fredrik Olausson, Pierre Turgeon.

The Hockey Hall of Fame Selection Committee comprises Scotty Bowman, David Branch, Colin Campbell, John Davidson, Eric Duhatschek, Jan-Ake Edvinsson, Mike (Doc) Emrick, Michael Farber, Mike Gartner, Jim Gregory (co-chair), Dick Irvin, Lanny McDonald, Yvon Pedneault, Pat Quinn (co-chair), Serge Savard, Harry Sinden, Peter Stastny and Bill Torrey.

Hockey Hall of Fame Honoured Members

(member—category, year inducted)

Sid Abel—Player, 1969

Charles Adams—Builder, 1960

Jack Adams—Player, 1959

Weston Adams—Builder, 1972

Frank Ahearn—Builder, 1962

Bunny Ahearne—Builder, 1977

Sir Montagu Allan—Builder, 1945

Keith Allen—Builder, 1992

Glenn Anderson—Player, 2008

Syl Apps—Player, 1961

Al Arbour—Builder, 1996

George Armstrong—Player, 1975

Neil Armstrong—Official, 1991

John Ashley—Official, 1981

Ace Bailey—Player, 1975

Dan Bain—Player, 1945

Hobey Baker—Player, 1945

Harold Ballard—Builder, 1977

Bill Barber—Player, 1990

Marty Barry—Player, 1965

Andy Bathgate—Player, 1978

Bobby Bauer—Player, 1996

Father David Bauer—Builder, 1989

Jean Beliveau—Player, 1972

Clint Benedict—Player, 1965

Doug Bentley—Player, 1964

Max Bentley—Player, 1966

Jack Bickell—Builder, 1978

Toe Blake—Player, 1966

Leo Boivin—Player, 1986

Dickie Boon—Player, 1952

Mike Bossy—Player, 1991

Butch Bouchard—Player, 1966

Frank Boucher—Player, 1958

George Boucher—Player, 1960

Ray Bourque—Player, 2004

Johnny Bower—Player, 1976

Russell Bowie—Player, 1945

Scotty Bowman—Builder, 1991

Frank Brimsek—Player, 1966

Punch Broadbent—Player, 1962

Turk Broda—Player, 1967

Herb Brooks—Builder, 2006

George Brown—Builder, 1961

Walter Brown—Builder, 1962

Frank Buckland—Builder, 1975

Johnny Bucyk—Player, 1981

Billy Burch—Player, 1974

Walter Bush—Builder, 2000

Jack Butterfield—Builder, 1980

Frank Calder—Builder, 1947

Harry Cameron—Player, 1962

Angus Campbell—Builder, 1964

Clarence Campbell—Builder, 1966

Joe Cattarinich—Builder, 1977

Bill Chadwick—Official, 1964

Gerry Cheevers—Player, 1985

Ed Chynoweth—Builder, 2008

King Clancy—Player, 1958

Dino Ciccarelli—Player, 2010

Dit Clapper—Player, 1947

Bobby Clarke—Player, 1987

Sprague Cleghorn—Player, 1958

Paul Coffey—Player, 2004

Neil Colville—Player, 1967

Charlie Conacher—Player, 1961

Lionel Conacher—Player, 1994

Roy Conacher—Player, 1998

Alex Connell—Player, 1958

Bill Cook—Player, 1952

Bun Cook—Player, 1995

Murray Costello—Builder, 2005

Art Coulter—Player, 1974

Yvan Cournoyer—Player, 1982

Bill Cowley—Player, 1968

Rusty Crawford—Player, 1962

John D'Amico—Official, 1993

Leo Dandurand—Builder, 1963

Jack Darragh—Player, 1962

Scotty Davidson—Player, 1950

Hap Day—Player, 1961

Alex Delvecchio—Player, 1977

Cy Denneny—Player, 1959

Frank Dilio—Builder, 1964

Jimmy Devellano—Builder, 2010

Marcel Dionne—Player, 1992

Gord Drillon—Player, 1975

Graham Drinkwater—Player, 1950

Ken Dryden—Player, 1983

George Dudley—Builder, 1958

Dick Duff—Player, 2006

Woody Dumart—Player, 1992

Tommy Dunderdale—Player, 1974

James Dunn—Builder, 1968

Bill Durnan—Player, 1964

Red Dutton—Player, 1958

Babe Dye—Player, 1970

Chaucer Elliott—Official, 1961

Tony Esposito—Player, 1988

Phil Esposito—Player, 1984

Art Farrell—Player, 1965

Bernie Federko—Player, 2002

Slava Fetisov—Player, 2001

Fern Flaman—Player, 1990

Cliff Fletcher—Builder, 2004

Frank Foyston—Player, 1958

Emile Francis—Builder, 1982

Ron Francis—Player, 2007

Frank Fredrickson—Player, 1958

Grant Fuhr—Player, 2003

Bill Gadsby—Player, 1970

Bob Gainey—Player, 1992

Chuck Gardiner—Player, 1945

Herb Gardiner—Player, 1958

Jimmy Gardner—Player, 1962

Mike Gartner—Player, 2001

Bernie Geoffrion—Player, 1972

Eddie Gerard—Player, 1945

Ed Giacomin—Player, 1987

Dr. Jack Gibson—Builder, 1976

Rod Gilbert—Player, 1982

Clark Gillies—Player, 2002

Billy Gilmour—Player, 1962

Moose Goheen—Player, 1952

Ebbie Goodfellow—Player, 1963

Tommy Gorman—Builder, 1963

Michel Goulet—Player, 1998

Cammi Granato—Women, 2010

Mike Grant—Player, 1950

Shorty Green—Player, 1962

Jim Gregory—Builder, 2007

Wayne Gretzky—Player, 1999

Si Griffis—Player, 1950

Frank Griffiths—Builder, 1993

George Hainsworth—Player, 1961

Glenn Hall—Player, 1975

Joe Hall—Player, 1961

William Hanley—Builder, 1986

Doug Harvey—Player, 1973

Dale Hawerchuk—Player, 2001

Charles Hay—Builder, 1974

George Hay—Player, 1958

George Hayes—Official, 1988

Jim Hendy—Builder, 1968

Riley Hern—Player, 1962

Bobby Hewitson—Official, 1963

Foster Hewitt—Builder, 1965

William Hewitt—Builder, 1947

Bryan Hextall—Player, 1969

Harry Holmes—Player, 1972

Tom Hooper—Player, 1962

Red Horner—Player, 1965

Tim Horton—Player, 1977

Harley Hotchkiss—Builder, 2006

Gordie Howe—Player, 1972

Syd Howe—Player, 1965

Harry Howell—Player, 197

Bobby Hull—Player, 1983

Brett Hull—Player, 2009

Fred Hume—Builder, 1962

Bouse Hutton—Player, 1962

Harry Hyland—Player, 1962

Mike Ilitch—Builder, 2003

Punch Imlach—Builder, 1984

Mickey Ion—Official, 1961

Dick Irvin—Player, 1958

Tommy Ivan—Builder, 1974

Harvey Jackson—Player, 1971

Angela James—Women, 2010

William Jennings—Builder, 1975

Bob Johnson—Builder, 1992

Moose Johnson—Player, 1952

Ching Johnson—Player, 1958

Tom Johnson—Player, 1970

Aurel Joliat—Player, 1947

Gordon Juckes—Builder, 1979

Duke Keats—Player, 1958

Red Kelly—Player, 1969

Ted Kennedy—Player, 1966

Dave Keon—Player, 1986

Valeri Kharlamov—Player, 2005

Gen. John Reed Kilpatrick—
    Builder, 1960

Brian Kilrea—Builder, 2003

Seymour Knox—Builder, 1993

Jari Kurri—Player, 2001

Elmer Lach—Player, 1966

Guy Lafleur—Player, 1988

Pat LaFontaine—Player, 2003

Newsy Lalonde—Player, 1950

Rod Langway—Player, 2002

Lou Lamoriello—Builder, 2009

Jacques Laperriere—Player, 1987

Guy Lapointe—Player, 1993

Edgar Laprade—Player, 1993

Igor Larionov—Player, 2008

Jack Laviolette—Player, 1962

George Leader—Builder, 1969

Robert LeBel—Builder, 1970

Brian Leetch—Player, 2009

Hugh Lehman—Player, 1958

Jacques Lemaire—Player, 1984

Mario Lemieux—Player, 1997

Percy LeSueur—Player, 1961

Herbie Lewis—Player, 1989

Ted Lindsay—Player, 1966

Tommy Lockhart—Builder, 1965

Paul Loicq—Builder, 1961

Harry Lumley—Player, 1980

Al MacInnis—Player, 2007

Mickey MacKay—Player, 1952

Frank Mahovlich—Player, 1981

Joe Malone—Player, 1950

Sylvio Mantha—Player, 1960

John Mariucci—Builder, 1985

Jack Marshall—Player, 1965

Frank Mathers—Builder, 1992

Steamer Maxwell—Player, 1962

Lanny McDonald—Player, 1992

Frank McGee—Player, 1945

Billy McGimsie—Player, 1962

Major Frederic McLaughlin—
    Builder, 1963

George McNamara—Player, 1958

Mark Messier—Player, 2007

Stan Mikita—Player, 1983

Jake Milford—Builder, 1984

Hon. Hartland Molson—
Builder, 1973

Dickie Moore—Player, 1974

Paddy Moran—Player, 1958

Howie Morenz—Player, 1945

Scotty Morrison—Builder, 1999

Bill Mosienko—Player, 1965

Joe Mullen—Player, 2000

Larry Murphy—Player, 2004

Monsignor Athol Murray—
Builder, 1998

Cam Neely—Player, 2005

Roger Neilson—Builder, 2002

Francis Nelson—Builder, 1947

Frank Nighbor—Player, 1947

Reg Noble—Player, 1962

Bruce A. Norris—Builder, 1969

James Norris Jr.—Builder, 1962

James Norris Sr.—Builder, 1958

William Northey—Builder, 1947

Ambrose O'Brien—Builder, 1962

Buddy O'Connor—Player, 1988

Harry Oliver—Player, 1967

Bert Olmstead—Player, 1985

Brian O'Neill—Builder, 1994

Bobby Orr—Player, 1979

Fred Page—Builder, 1993

Bernie Parent—Player, 1984

Brad Park—Player, 1988

Craig Patrick—Builder, 2001

Frank Patrick—Builder, 1958

Lester Patrick—Player, 1947

Lynn Patrick—Player, 1980

Matt Pavelich—Official, 1987

Gilbert Perreault—Player, 1990

Tommy Phillips—Player, 1945

Allan Pickard—Builder, 1958

Pierre Pilote—Player, 1975

Rudy Pilous—Builder, 1985

Didier Pitre—Player, 1962

Jacques Plante—Player, 1978

Bud Poile—Builder, 1990

Sam Pollock—Builder, 1978

Denis Potvin—Player, 1991

Babe Pratt—Player, 1966

Joe Primeau—Player, 1963

Marcel Pronovost—Player, 1978

Bob Pulford—Player, 1991

Harvey Pulford—Player, 1945

Bill Quackenbush—Player, 1976

Frank Rankin—Player, 1961

Jean Ratelle—Player, 1985

Sen. Donat Raymond—
Builder, 1958

Chuck Rayner—Player, 1973

Ken Reardon—Player, 1966

Henri Richard—Player, 1979

Maurice Richard—Player, 1961

George Richardson—Player, 1950

Gordon Roberts—Player, 1971

John Ross Robertson—Builder, 1947

Claude Robinson—Builder, 1947

Larry Robinson—Player, 1995

Luc Robitaille—Player, 2009

Mike Rodden—Official, 1962

Art Ross—Player, 1945

Philip D. Ross—Builder, 1976

Patrick Roy—Player, 2006

Blair Russel—Player, 1965

Ernie Russell—Player, 1965

Jack Ruttan—Player, 1962

Dr. Gunther Sabetzki—
Builder, 1995

Borje Salming—Player, 1996

Glen Sather—Builder, 1997

Denis Savard—Player, 2000

Serge Savard—Player, 1986

Terry Sawchuk—Player, 1971

Fred Scanlan—Player, 1965

Ray Scapinello—Official, 2008

Milt Schmidt—Player, 1961

Sweeney Schriner—Player, 1962

Daryl "Doc" Seaman—Builder, 2010

Earl Seibert—Player, 1963

Oliver Seibert—Player, 1961

Frank Selke—Builder, 1960

Eddie Shore—Player, 1947

Steve Shutt—Player, 1993

Babe Siebert—Player, 1964

Joe Simpson—Player, 1962

Harry Sinden—Builder, 1983

Darryl Sittler—Player, 1989

Cooper Smeaton—Official, 1961

Alf Smith—Player, 1962

Billy Smith—Player, 1993

Clint Smith—Player, 1991

Frank Smith—Builder, 1962

Hooley Smith—Player, 1972

Tommy Smith—Player, 1973

Conn Smythe—Builder, 1958

Ed Snider—Builder, 1988

Allan Stanley—Player, 1981

Barney Stanley—Player, 1962

Peter Stastny—Player, 1998

Scott Stevens—Player, 2007

Jack Stewart—Player, 1964

Lord Stanley of Preston—
Builder, 1945

Nels Stewart—Player, 1962

Red Storey—Official, 1967

Bruce Stuart—Player, 1961

Hod Stuart—Player, 1945

Capt. James T. Sutherland—
Builder, 1947

Anatoli Tarasov—Builder, 1974

Cyclone Taylor—Player, 1947

Tiny Thompson—Player, 1959

Bill Torrey—Builder, 1995

Vladislav Tretiak—Player, 1989

Harry Trihey—Player, 1950

Bryan Trottier—Player, 1997

Lloyd Turner—Builder, 1958

William Tutt—Builder, 1978

Frank Udvari—Official, 1973

Norm Ullman—Player, 1982

Andy Van Hellemond—
Official, 1999

Georges Vezina—Player, 1945

Carl Voss—Builder, 1974

Fred Waghorne—Builder, 1961

Jack Walker—Player, 1960

Marty Walsh—Player, 1962

Harry E. Watson—Player, 1962

Harry Watson—Player, 1994

Cooney Weiland—Player, 1971

Harry Westwick—Player, 1962
Fred Whitcroft—Player, 1962
Phat Wilson—Player, 1962
Arthur Wirtz—Builder, 1971
Bill Wirtz—Builder, 1976

Gump Worsley—Player, 1980
Roy Worters—Player, 1969
Steve Yzerman—Player, 2009
John Ziegler—Builder, 1987

IIHF Hall of Fame
(name, nationality, year inducted)
° denotes Referee; * denotes Builder; all others are Players

°Quido Adamec (Czech Republic), 2005
*John "Bunny" Ahearne (Great Britain), 1997
Veniamin Alexandrov (Russia), 2007
*Ernest Aljancic, Sr. (Slovenia), 2002
Helmut Balderis (Latvia), 1998
Rudi Ball (Germany), 2004
*Father David Bauer (Canada), 1997
Art Berglund (USA), 2008
*Curt Berglund (Sweden), 2003
Sven Bergqvist (Sweden), 1999
Lars Bjorn (Sweden), 1998
Vsevolod Bobrov (Russia), 1997
Vladimir Bouzek (Czech Republic), 2007
Roger Bourbonnais (Canada), 1999
Philippe Bozon (France), 2008
*Herb Brooks (USA), 1999
*Walter Brown (USA), 1997

Vlastimil Bubnik (Czech Republic), 1997
*Mike Buckna (Canada), 2004
*Ludek Bukac (Czech Republic), 2007
Walter Bush, Jr. (USA), 2009
*Enrico Calcaterra (Italy), 1999
Ferdinand Cattini (Switzerland), 1998
Hans Cattini (Switzerland), 1998
Josef Cerny (Czech Republic), 2007
*Arkady Chernyshev (Russia), 1999
Bill Christian (USA), 1998
Bill Cleary (USA), 1997
Gerry Cosby (USA), 1997
Jim Craig (USA), 1999
Mike Curran (USA), 1999
°Ove Dahlberg (Sweden), 2004
Vitali Davydov (Russia), 2004
Igor Dimitriev (Russia), 2007
Hans Dobida (Austria), 2007

Jaroslav Drobny
   (Czechoslovakia), 1997
Vladimir Dzurilla (Slovakia), 1998
*Rudolf Eklow (Sweden), 1999
Carl Erhardt (Great Britain), 1998
*Rickard Fagerlund (Sweden), 2010
Slava Fetisov (Russia), 2005
Anatoli Firsov (Russia), 1998
Josef Golonka (Slovakia), 1998
Cammi Granato (USA), 2008
Wayne Gretzky (Canada), 2000
*Arne Grunander (Sweden), 1997
Henryk Gruth (Poland), 2006
*Bengt-Ake Gustafsson (Sweden),
   2003
Karel Gut (Czech Republic), 1998
Geraldine Heaney (Canada), 2008
Anders Hedberg (Sweden), 1997
Dieter Hegen (Germany), 2010
*Heinz Henschel (Germany), 2003
William Hewitt (Canada), 1998
Rudi Hiti (Slovenia), 2009
Ivan Hlinka (Czech Republic), 2002
Jiri Holecek (Czech Republic), 1998
Jiri Holik (Czech Republic), 1999
*Derek Holmes (Canada), 1999
Leif Holmqvist (Sweden), 1999
*Ladislav Horsky (Slovakia), 2004
Fran Huck (Canada), 1999
*Jorgen Hviid (Denmark), 2005
Arturs Irbe (Latvia), 2010
Gustav Jaenecke (Germany), 1998
Angela James (Canada), 2008
*Tore Johannessen (Norway), 1999

Mark Johnson (USA), 1999
Marshall Johnston (Canada), 1998
Tomas Jonsson (Sweden), 2000
Gord Juckes (Canada), 1997
Timo Jutila (Finland), 2003
°Yuri Karandin (Russia), 2004
Alexei Kasatonov (Russia), 2009
*Tsutomu Kawabuchi (Japan),
   2004
Matti Keinonen (Finland), 2002
Valeri Kharlamov (Russia), 1998
*Anatoli Khorozov (Ukraine),
   2006
Udo Kiessling (Germany), 2000
*Dave King (Canada), 2001
Jakob Kolliker (Switzerland), 2007
°Josef Kompalla (Germany), 2003
Viktor Konovalenko (Russia), 2007
*Vladimir Kostka (Czech
   Republic), 1997
Vladimir Krutov (Russia), 2010
Erich Kuhnhackl (Germany), 1997
Jari Kurri (Finland), 2000
Viktor Kuzkin (Russia), 2005
Jacques Lacarriere (France), 1998
Igor Larionov (Russia), 2008
*Bob Lebel (Canada), 1997
Mario Lemieux (Canada), 2008
*Harry Lindblad (Finland), 1999
Vic Lindquist (Canada), 1997
*Paul Loicq (Belgium), 1997
Konstantin Loktev (Russia), 2007
Hakan Loob (Sweden), 1998
*Cesar Luthi (Switzerland), 1998

Oldrich Machac (Czech Republic), 1999

Barry MacKenzie (Canada), 1999

Sergei Makarov (Russia), 2001

Josef Malecek (Czech Republic), 2003

Alexander Maltsev (Russia), 1999

*Louis Magnus (France), 1997

Pekka Marjamaki (Finland), 1998

Seth Martin (Canada), 1997

Vladimir Martinec (Czech Republic), 2001

John Mayasich (USA), 1997

Boris Mayorov (Russia), 1999

Jack McCartan (USA), 1998

Jack McLeod (Canada), 1999

Boris Mikhailov (Russia), 2000

Lou Nanne (USA), 2004

Mats Naslund (Sweden), 2005

Vaclav Nedomansky (Czech Republic), 1997

Riikka Nieminen-Valila (Finland), 2010

Kent Nilsson (Sweden), 2006

Nisse Nilsson (Sweden), 2002

Lasse Oksanen (Finland), 1999

Terry O'Malley (Canada), 1998

Eduard Pana (Romania), 1998

*Gyorgy Pasztor (Hungary), 2001

*Peter Patton (Great Britain), 2002

Esa Peltonen (Finland), 2007

Vladimir Petrov (Russia), 2006

Ronald Pettersson (Sweden), 2004

Frantisek Pospisil (Czech Republic), 1999

Sepp Puschnig (Austria), 1999

Alexander Ragulin (Russia), 1997

Hans Rampf (Germany), 2001

*Gord Renwick (Canada), 2002

*Bob Ridder (USA), 1998

*Jack Riley (USA), 1998

Thomas Rundquist (Sweden), 2007

*Gunther Sabetzki (Germany), 1997

Borje Salming (Sweden), 1998

Laszlo Schell (Hungary), 2009

Alois Schloder (Germany), 2005

Harry Sinden (Canada), 1997

Nikolai Sologubov (Russia), 2004

*Andrei Starovoitov (Russia), 1997

Vyacheslav Starshinov (Russia), 2007

*Jan Starsi (Slovakia), 1999

Peter Stastny (Slovakia), 2000

Ulf Sterner (Sweden), 2001

Roland Stoltz (Sweden), 1999

*Arne Stromberg (Sweden), 1998

*Goran Stubb (Finland), 2000

*Miroslav Subrt (Czech Republic), 2004

Jan Suchy (Czech Republic), 2009

*Anatoli Tarasov (Russia), 1997

Frantisek Tikal (Czech Republic), 2004

*Viktor Tikhonov (Russia), 1998

*Shoichi Tomita (Japan), 2006

Richard "Bibi" Torriani (Switzerland), 1997

Vladislav Tretiak (Russia), 1997

*Hal Trumble (USA), 1999

*Yoshiaki Tsutsumi (Japan), 1999

Sven Tumba (Sweden), 1997

*Thayer Tutt (USA), 2002
*Xaver Unsinn (Germany), 1998
*Lou Vairo (United States), 2010
Jorma Valtonen (Finland), 1999
Valeri Vasiliev (Russia), 1998
Juhani Wahlsten (Finland), 2006
*Walter Wasservogel (Austria), 1997
Harry Watson (Canada), 1998
°Unto Wiitala (Finland), 2003
Alexander Yakushev (Russia), 2003
Urpo Ylonen (Finland), 1997
*Vldimir Yurzinov (Russia), 2002
Vladimir Zabrodsky (Czech
    Republic), 1997
Joachim Ziesche (Germany), 1999

2010 WORLD JUNIOR (U20) CHAMPIONSHIP

Saskatoon/Regina, Canada, December 26, 2009–January 5, 2010

FINAL PLACING

GOLD MEDAL	United States
SILVER MEDAL	Canada
BRONZE MEDAL	Sweden
Fourth Place	Switzerland
Fifth Place	Finland
Sixth Place	Russia
Seventh Place	Czech Republic
Eighth Place	Slovakia
Ninth Place	Latvia
Tenth Place	Austria

All-Star Team

Goal   Benjamin Conz (SUI)
Defence   Alex Pietrangelo (CAN), John Carlson (USA)
Forward   Jordan Eberle (CAN), Derek Stepan (USA), Nino
    Niederreiter (SUI)

Directorate Awards

Best Goalie	Benjamin Conz (SUI)
Best Defenceman	Alex Pietrangelo (CAN)
Best Forward	Jordan Eberle (CAN)
Tournament MVP	Jordan Eberle (CAN)

FINAL STANDINGS

Preliminary Round
Group A (Saskatoon)

	GP	W	OTW	OTL	L	GF	GA	P
Canada	4	3	1	0	0	35	6	11
United States	4	3	0	1	0	26	9	10
Switzerland	4	2	0	0	2	11	15	6
Slovakia	4	1	0	0	3	14	22	3
Latvia	4	0	0	0	4	9	43	0

December 26	Canada 16/Latvia 0
December 26	United States 7/Slovakia 3
December 27	United States 3/Switzerland 0
December 27	Slovakia 8/Latvia 3
December 28	Canada 6/Switzerland 0
December 29	United States 12/Latvia 1
December 29	Canada 8/Slovakia 2
December 30	Switzerland 7/Latvia 5
December 31	Switzerland 4/Slovakia 1
December 31	Canada 5/United States 4 (5:00 OT/SO)

Group B (Regina)

	GP	W	OTW	OTL	L	GF	GA	P
Sweden	4	4	0	0	0	28	6	12
Russia	4	3	0	0	1	14	8	9
Finland	4	2	0	0	2	15	13	6
Czech Republic	4	1	0	0	3	13	20	3
Austria	4	0	0	0	4	7	30	0

December 26	Sweden 10/Czech Republic 1
December 26	Russia 6/Austria 2
December 27	Sweden 7/Austria 3
December 27	Finland 4/Czech Republic 3

December 28	Russia 2/Finland 0
December 29	Czech Republic 7/Austria 1
December 29	Sweden 4/Russia 1
December 30	Finland 10/Austria 1
December 31	Sweden 7/Finland 1
December 31	Russia 5/Czech Republic 2

Relegation Round (Saskatoon)

	GP	W	OTW	OTL	L	GF	GA	P
Czech Republic	3	3	0	0	0	22	5	9
Slovakia	3	2	0	0	1	13	10	6
Latvia	3	1	0	0	2	11	22	3
Austria	3	0	0	0	3	7	16	0

January 2	Slovakia 3/Austria 2
January 3	Czech Republic 10/Latvia 2
January 4	Czech Republic 5/Slovakia 2
January 4	Latvia 6/Austria 4

Playoffs (Saskatoon)
Quarterfinals

| January 2 | Switzerland 3/Russia 2 (OT) |
| January 2 | United States 6/Finland 2 |

Semifinals

| January 3 | Canada 6/Switzerland 1 |
| January 3 | United States 5/Sweden 2 |

Fifth-Place Game

| January 4 | Finland 4/Russia 3 |

Bronze Medal Game

| January 5 | Sweden 11/Switzerland 4 |

Gold Medal Game
January 5   United States 6 Canada 5 (OT)

Team Canada Statistics
(Willie Desjardins, coach)

#	Pos.		GP	G	A	P	Pim
14	F	Jordan Eberle	6	8	5	13	4
4	F	Taylor Hall	6	6	6	12	0
27	D	Alex Pietrangelo	6	3	9	12	14
7	F	Gabriel Bourque	6	3	6	9	4
20	F	Luke Adam	6	4	4	8	8
15	F	Brandon McMillan	6	4	4	8	0
9	F	Nazem Kadri	6	3	5	8	14
10	F	Brayden Schenn	6	2	6	8	4
6	D	Ryan Ellis	6	1	7	8	2
17	F	Brandon Kozun	6	3	4	7	0
19	F	Stefan Della Rovere	6	3	3	6	8
28	F	Patrice Cormier	6	2	3	5	4
26	F	Jordan Caron	6	0	4	4	6
5	D	Marco Scandella	6	1	2	3	2
3	D	Travis Hamonic	6	1	2	3	0
12	F	Adam Henrique	6	1	0	1	2
16	F	Greg Nemisz	6	1	0	1	0
22	D	Jared Cowen	6	0	1	1	2
2	D	Colten Teubert	6	0	1	1	0
24	D	Calvin de Haan	4	0	1	1	0
1	GK	Jake Allen	5	0	0	0	0
31	GK	Martin Jones	2	0	0	0	0

In Goal	GP	W-L	Mins	GA	SO	GAA
Jake Allen	5	3–0	291:23	10	2	2.06
Martin Jones	2	1–1	78:08	3	0	2.30

2011 WORLD JUNIOR (U20) CHAMPIONSHIP SCHEDULE

Buffalo/Lewiston, USA, December 26, 2010–January 5, 2011

Venues: HSBC Arena (Buffalo) and Dwyer Arena (Niagara University, Lewiston)

Group A: Finland, Germany, Slovakia, Switzerland, United States
Group B: Canada, Czech Republic, Norway, Russia, Sweden

December 26, 2010
Germany vs. Switzerland
Russia vs. Canada
Norway vs. Sweden
Finland vs. United States

December 27, 2010
Slovakia vs. Germany
Czech Republic vs. Norway
Switzerland vs. Finland
Canada vs. Czech Republic

December 28, 2010
Sweden vs. Russia
United States vs. Slovakia

December 29, 2010
Finland vs. Germany
Norway vs. Canada

December 30, 2010
Switzerland vs. Slovakia
Sweden vs. Czech Republic

Russia vs. Norway
Germany vs. United States

December 31, 2010
Slovakia vs. Finland
Canada vs. Sweden
Czech Republic vs. Russia
United States vs. Switzerland

January 1, 2011
No Games Scheduled

January 2, 2011
Quarterfinal 1
A4–B5 Relegation

January 2, 2011
Quarterfinal 2
B4–A5 Relegation

January 3, 2011
Semifinal 1
Semifinal 2

January 4, 2011
A5–B5 Relegation
Fifth-Place Game
A4–B4 Relegation

January 5, 2011
Bronze Medal Game
Gold Medal Game

2010 WORLD CHAMPIONSHIPS

Final Placing

GOLD MEDAL	Czech Republic
SILVER MEDAL	Russia
BRONZE MEDAL	Sweden
Fourth Place	Germany
Fifth Place	Switzerland
Sixth Place	Finland
Seventh Place	Canada
Eighth Place	Denmark
Ninth Place	Norway
Tenth Place	Belarus
Eleventh Place	Latvia
Twelfth Place	Slovakia
Thirteenth Place	United States
Fourteenth Place	France
Fifteenth Place	Italy
Sixteenth Place	Kazakhstan

All-Star Team

Goal: Dennis Endras (GER)

Defence: Petteri Nummelin (FIN), Christian Ehrhoff (GER)

Forward: Pavel Datsyuk (RUS), Evgeni Malkin (RUS), Magnus Paajarvi Svensson (SWE)

Directorate Awards

Best Goalie	Dennis Endras (GER)
Best Defenceman	Petteri Nummelin (FIN)
Best Forward	Pavel Datsyuk (RUS)
Tournament MVP	Dennis Endras (GER)

FINAL STANDINGS

Preliminary Round
Group A (Cologne)

	GP	W	OTW	OTL	L	GF	GA	P
Russia	3	3	0	0	0	10	3	9
Slovakia	3	2	0	0	1	10	6	6
Belarus	3	1	0	0	2	8	9	3
Kazakhstan	3	0	0	0	3	4	14	0

May 9	Belarus 5/Kazakhstan 2
May 9	Russia 3/Slovakia 1
May 11	Russia 4/Kazakhstan 1
May 11	Slovakia 4/Belarus 2
May 13	Russia 3/Belarus 1
May 13	Slovakia 5/Kazakhstan 1

Group B (Mannheim)

	GP	W	OTW	OTL	L	GF	GA	P
Switzerland	3	3	0	0	0	10	2	9
Canada	3	2	0	0	1	12	6	6
Latvia	3	1	0	0	2	7	11	3
Italy	3	0	0	0	3	3	13	0

May 8	Canada 5/Italy 1
May 8	Switzerland 3/Latvia 1
May 10	Switzerland 3/Italy 0
May 10	Canada 6/Latvia 1
May 12	Latvia 5/Italy 2
May 12	Switzerland 4/Canada 1

Group C (Mannheim)

	GP	W	OTW	OTL	L	GF	GA	P
Sweden	3	2	0	0	1	9	6	6
Czech Republic	3	2	0	0	1	10	6	6
Norway	3	2	0	0	1	10	8	6
France	3	0	0	0	3	5	14	0

May 9	Czech Republic 6/France 2
May 9	Sweden 5/Norway 2
May 11	Norway 3/Czech Republic 2
May 11	Sweden 3/France 2
May 13	Norway 5/France 1
May 13	Czech Republic 2/Sweden 1

Group D (Cologne)

	GP	W	OTW	OTL	L	GF	GA	P
Finland	3	2	0	0	1	5	6	6
Germany	3	1	1	0	1	5	3	5
Denmark	3	1	1	0	1	7	5	5
United States	3	0	0	2	1	4	7	2

May 7	Germany 2/United States 1 (OT)*
May 8	Denmark 4/Finland 1
May 10	Denmark 2/United States 1 (OT)
May 10	Finland 1/Germany 0
May 12	Germany 3/Denmark 1
May 12	Finland 3/United States 2

*played at Gelsenkirchen before a world-record crowd of 77,803

Relegation Round

	GP	W	OTW	OTL	L	GF	GA	P
United States	3	2	1	0	0	17	2	8
France	3	2	0	0	1	7	8	6
Italy	3	1	0	1	1	5	6	4
Kazakhstan	3	0	0	0	3	4	17	0

May 15	Cologne	United States 10/Kazakhstan 0
May 15	Mannheim	France 2/Italy 1
May 16	Cologne	United States 4/France 0
May 16	Mannheim	Italy 2/Kazakhstan 1
May 18	Cologne	United States 3/Italy 2 (OT)
May 18	Mannheim	France 5/Kazakhstan 3

Qualifying Round
Group E (Cologne)

	GP	W	OTW	OTL	L	GF	GA	P
Russia	5	5	0	0	0	20	5	15
Finland	5	3	0	0	2	9	11	9
Germany	5	2	0	1	2	8	8	7
Denmark	5	2	0	0	3	13	12	6
Belarus	5	1	1	0	3	7	11	5
Slovakia	5	1	0	0	4	8	18	3

May 14	Denmark 6/Slovakia 0
May 14	Finland 2/Belarus 0
May 15	Russia 3/Germany 2
May 16	Russia 6/Denmark 1
May 16	Belarus 2/Germany 1 (OT)
May 17	Finland 5/Slovakia 2
May 17	Belarus 2/Denmark 1
May 18	Germany 2/Slovakia 1
May 18	Russia 5/Finland 0

Group F (Mannheim)

	GP	W	OTW	OTL	L	GF	GA	P
Sweden	5	4	0	0	1	18	7	12
Switzerland	5	3	0	0	2	12	12	9
Czech Republic	5	3	0	0	2	12	10	9
Canada	5	2	0	0	3	22	12	6
Norway	5	2	0	0	3	9	26	6
Latvia	5	1	0	0	4	10	16	3

May 14	Canada 12/Norway 1
May 14	Sweden 4/Latvia 2
May 15	Switzerland 3/Czech Republic 2
May 16	Latvia 5/Norway 0
May 16	Sweden 3/Canada 1
May 17	Norway 3/Switzerland 2
May 17	Czech Republic 3/Latvia 1
May 18	Czech Republic 3/Canada 2
May 18	Sweden 5/Switzerland 0

PLAYOFFS
Quarterfinals

May 20	Cologne	Czech Republic 2/Finland 1 (SO)
May 20	Mannheim	Sweden 4/Denmark 2
May 20	Cologne	Russia 5/Canada 2
May 20	Mannheim	Germany 1/Switzerland 0

Semifinals

May 22	Mannheim	Czech Republic 3/Sweden 2 (SO)
May 22	Mannheim	Russia 2/Germany 1

Bronze Medal Game

May 23	Mannheim	Sweden 3/Germany 1

Gold Medal Game

May 23   Mannheim   Czech Republic 3/Russia 1

2009 VICTORIA CUP

Hallenstadion, Zurich, SWITZERLAND, September 29, 2009
Zurich Lions 2, Chicago Blackhawks 1

Backed by superb goaltending from 40-year-old Ari Sulander, the Zurich Lions beat the NHL's Blackhawks by a 2–1 score to reclaim the Victoria Cup. In 2008, the New York Rangers captured the inaugural edition of the series, which pits the NHL against Europe's best, with a 4–3 win over Metallurg Magnitogorsk.

And just as the Rangers rallied for victory the previous year, the Lions found themselves down a goal early in the game and had to fight back for the win. "I knew that if we just believed in ourselves, we'd have a chance," Sulander said after the game.

The Lions were not intimidated by Chicago's 9–2 pasting of HC Davos in the exhibition tuneup to this Victoria Cup, but still the Hawks had control of the game early on. Cam Barker's one-timer slipped under the arm of Sulander to give the visitors the early lead, but it was to be the only goal they'd score this night.

Zurich tied the game six minutes later on a great pass by Thibaut Monnet to spring Patrick Bartschi in alone on goalie Antti Niemi. Bartschi made a great move and roofed a backhand over the sprawling goalie to tie the score and send the home crowd into a frenzy of excitement.

Lukas Grauwiler got the game-winner in the middle period when he scooped in a loose puck after Niemi failed to control a shot from Cyrill Buhler. Bartschi got another great chance to make it 3–1 in the final period. First, he was hauled down by Brent Seabrook on a breakaway, but he was stopped on the penalty shot by Niemi when he tried to shoot instead of deke.

No matter. The Lions pulled off a significant upset against one of the NHL's most skilled and exciting young teams.

Victoria Cup Game
Lineups

Zurich—Goal: Ari Sulander, Lukas Flueler (DNP); Defence: Radoslav Suchy, Philippe Schelling, Mathias Seger, Daniel Schnyder, Patrick Geering, Andre Signoretti, Andri Stoffel; Forwards: Domenico Pittis, Peter Sejna, Mark Bastl, Jean-Guy Trudel, Jan Alston, Ryan Gardner, Thibaut Monnet, Patrick Bartschi, Blaine Down, Cyrill Buhler, Lukas Grauwiler, Oliver Kamber.

Chicago—Goal: Cristobal Huet, Antti Niemi (DNP); Defence: Duncan Keith, Brent Seabrook, Niklas Hjalmarsson, Brian Campbell, Brent Sopel, Cam Barker; Forwards: Jonathan Toews, Troy Brouwer, Patrick Kane, Patrick Sharp, Andrew Ladd, Dave Bolland, Dustin Byfuglien, Ben Eager, Tomas Kopecky, Jack Skille, Kris Versteeg, Colin Fraser, Radek Smolenak.

Game Summary
First Period
0–1   Chicago, Barker (Sharp) 6:13
1–1   Zurich, Bartschi (Monnet, Signoretti) 12:25
Penalties: Pittis (ZSC, 2:53), Pittis (ZSC, 14:11), Sharp (CHI, 15:17).

Second Period
2–1   Zurich, Grauwiler (Buhler) 14:44
Penalties: Down (ZSC, 7:59), Seger (ZSC, 9:34), Byfuglien (CHI, 9:34), Trudel (ZSC, 17:32).

Third Period
No scoring.
Penalties: Monnet (ZSC, 8:28), Byfuglien (CHI, 9:43), Skille (CHI, 13:16), Bastl (ZSC, 14:04), Bolland (CHI, 14:19).
Missed Penalty Shot: Bartschi (ZSC, 16:46)

In Goal
ZSC—Sulander
CHI—Huet

Shots on Goal

ZSC	7	6	9	22
CHI	11	12	12	35

Referees—Dan Marouelli (CAN) & Vyacheslav Bulanov (RUS)
Linesmen—Tim Nowak (USA) & Frantisek Kalivoda (CZE)

Attendance: 9,744

PRO CLASSICS RESULTS

1972 Summit Series
Canada/Moscow, September 2–28, 1972

	GP	W	L	T	GF	GA	P
Canada	8	4	3	1	31	32	9
Soviet Union	8	3	4	1	32	31	7

Results

Game 1	September 2	Montreal	Soviet Union 7/Canada 3
Game 2	September 4	Toronto	Canada 4/Soviet Union 1
Game 3	September 6	Winnipeg	Canada 4/Soviet Union 4
Game 4	September 8	Vancouver	Soviet Union 5/Canada 3

Exhibition	September 16	Stockholm	Canada 4/Swedish Nationals 1
Exhibition	September 17	Stockholm	Canada 4/Swedish Nationals 4

Game 5	September 22	Moscow	Soviet Union 5/Canada 4
Game 6	September 24	Moscow	Canada 3/Soviet Union 2
Game 7	September 26	Moscow	Canada 4/Soviet Union 3
Game 8	September 28	Moscow	Canada 6/Soviet Union 5

(Paul Henderson scores series winner at 19:26 of 3rd)

Exhibition	September 30	Prague	Canada 3/Czech Nationals 3

1976 Canada Cup
Canada, September 2–15, 1976
Series MVP: Bobby Orr (Canada)

Team MVPs
Canada	Rogie Vachon
Czechoslovakia	Milan Novy
Soviet Union	Alexander Maltsev
Sweden	Borje Salming
United States	Robbie Ftorek
Finland	Matti Hagman

Final Standings Round Robin
	GP	W	L	T	GF	GA	P
Canada	5	4	1	0	22	6	8
Czechoslovakia	5	3	1	1	19	9	7
Soviet Union	5	2	2	1	23	14	5
Sweden	5	2	2	1	16	18	5
United States	5	1	3	1	14	21	3
Finland	5	1	4	0	16	42	2

Results
September 2	Ottawa	Canada 11/Finland 2
September 3	Toronto	Sweden 5/United States 2
	Montreal	Czechoslovakia 5/Soviet Union 3
September 5	Montreal	Canada 4/United States 2
	Montreal	Soviet Union 3/Sweden 3
	Toronto	Czechoslovakia 8/Finland 0
September 7	Toronto	Canada 4/Sweden 0
	Montreal	Soviet Union 11/Finland 3
	Philadelphia	Czechoslovakia 4/United States 4
September 9	Montreal	Czechoslovakia 1/Canada 0
	Winnipeg	Finland 8/Sweden 6

	Philadelphia	Soviet Union 5/United States 0
September 11	Toronto	Canada 3/Soviet Union 1
	Quebec City	Sweden 2/Czechoslovakia 1
	Montreal	United States 6/Finland 3

FINALS (best two-of-three)

September 13	Toronto	Canada 6/Czechoslovakia 0
September 15	Montreal	Canada 5/Czechoslovakia 4
		(Sittler 11:33 OT)

1981 Canada Cup
Canada, September 1–13, 1981
Tournament MVP: Vladislav Tretiak
Team Canada MVP: Mike Bossy

All-Star Team

Goal	Vladislav Tretiak (Soviet Union)
Defence	Alexei Kasatonov (Soviet Union)
	Arnold Kadlec (Czechoslovakia)
Forward	Gil Perreault (Canada)
	Mike Bossy (Canada)
	Sergei Shepelev (Soviet Union)

Final Standings Round Robin

	GP	W	L	T	GF	GA	P
Canada	5	4	0	1	32	13	9
Soviet Union	5	3	1	1	20	13	7
Czechoslovakia	5	2	1	2	21	13	6
United States	5	2	2	1	17	19	5
Sweden	5	1	4	0	13	20	2
Finland	5	0	4	1	6	31	1

Results

September 1	Edmonton	Canada 9/Finland 0
	Edmonton	United States 3/Sweden 1
	Winnipeg	Czechoslovakia 1/Soviet Union 1
September 3	Edmonton	Canada 8/United States 3
	Edmonton	Czechoslovakia 7/Finland 1
	Winnipeg	Soviet Union 6/Sweden 3
September 5	Winnipeg	Canada 4/Czechoslovakia 4
	Winnipeg	Sweden 5/Finland 0
	Edmonton	Soviet Union 4/United States 1
September 7	Montreal	Canada 4/Sweden 3
	Winnipeg	Soviet Union 6/Finland 1
	Montreal	United States 6/Czechoslovakia 2
September 9	Montreal	Canada 7/Soviet Union 3
	Ottawa	Czechoslovakia 7/Sweden 1
	Montreal	Finland 4/United States 4

Semifinals

| September 11 | Montreal | Canada 4/United States 1 |
| | Ottawa | Soviet Union 4/Czechoslovakia 1 |

Finals

| September 13 | Montreal | Soviet Union 8/Canada 1 |

1984 Canada Cup
Canada, September 1–18, 1984
Tournament MVP: John Tonelli

All-Star Team
Goal	Vladimir Myshkin (Soviet Union)
Defence	Paul Coffey (Canada)
	Rod Langway (United States)
Forward	Wayne Gretzky (Canada)
	John Tonelli (Canada)
	Sergei Makarov (Soviet Union)

Final Standings Round Robin
	GP	W	L	T	GF	GA	P
Soviet Union	5	5	0	0	22	7	10
United States	5	3	1	1	21	13	7
Sweden	5	3	2	0	15	16	6
Canada	5	2	2	1	23	18	5
West Germany	5	0	4	1	13	29	1
Czechoslovakia	5	0	4	1	10	21	1

Results
September 1	Montreal	Canada 7/West Germany 2
	Halifax	United States 7/Sweden 1
September 2	Montreal	Soviet Union 3/Czechoslovakia 0
September 3	Montreal	Canada 4/United States 4
September 4	London	Czechoslovakia 4/West Germany 4
	Calgary	Soviet Union 3/Sweden 2
September 6	Vancouver	Sweden 4/Canada 2
	Edmonton	Soviet Union 8/West Germany 1
	Buffalo	United States 3 /Czechoslovakia 2
September 8	Calgary	Canada 7/Czechoslovakia 2
	Calgary	Sweden 4/West Germany 2
	Edmonton	Soviet Union 2/United States 1

September 10	Edmonton	Soviet Union 6/Canada 3
	Vancouver	Sweden 4/Czechoslovakia 2
	Calgary	United States 6/West Germany 4

Semifinals

September 12	Edmonton	Sweden 9/United States 2
September 13	Calgary	Canada 3/Soviet Union 2
		(Bossy 12:29 OT)

Finals (best two-of-three)

| September 16 | Calgary | Canada 5/Sweden 2 |
| September 18 | Edmonton | Canada 6/Sweden 5 |

1987 Canada Cup
Canada, August 28–September 15, 1987

Tournament All-Star Team

Goal	Grant Fuhr (Canada)
Defence	Ray Bourque (Canada)
	Viacheslav Fetisov (Soviet Union)
Forward	Mario Lemieux (Canada)
	Wayne Gretzky (Canada)
	Vladimir Krutov (Soviet Union)

Final Standings Round Robin

	GP	W	L	T	GF	GA	P
Canada	5	3	0	2	19	13	8
Soviet Union	5	3	1	1	22	13	7
Sweden	5	3	2	0	17	14	6
Czechoslovakia	5	2	2	1	12	15	5
United States	5	2	3	0	13	14	4
Finland	5	0	5	0	9	23	0

Results

August 28	Calgary	Canada 4/Czechoslovakia 4
	Hartford	United States 4/Finland 1
August 29	Calgary	Sweden 5/Soviet Union 3
August 30	Hamilton	Canada 4/Finland 1
August 31	Regina	Soviet Union 4/Czechoslovakia 0
	Hamilton	United States 5/Sweden 2
September 2	Halifax	Soviet Union 7/Finland 4
	Hamilton	Canada 3/United States 2
	Regina	Sweden 4/Czechoslovakia 0
September 4	Hartford	Soviet Union 5/United States 1
	Sydney	Czechoslovakia 5/Finland 2
	Montreal	Canada 5/Sweden 3
September 6	Sydney	Sweden 3/Finland 1
	Sydney	Czechoslovakia 3/United States 1
	Hamilton	Canada 3/Soviet Union 3
September 8	Hamilton	Soviet Union 4/Sweden 2
	Montreal	Canada 5/Czechoslovakia 3

Finals (best two-of-three)

September 11	Montreal	Soviet Union 6/Canada 5 (Semak 5:33 OT)
September 13	Hamilton	Canada 6/Soviet Union 5 (Mario Lemieux 30:07 OT)
September 15	Hamilton	Canada 6/Soviet Union 5 (Lemieux scores winner at 18:34 of 3rd)

1991 Canada Cup

Canada, August 31–September 16, 1991

Tournament All-Star Team

Goal	Bill Ranford (Canada)
Defence	Al MacInnis (Canada)
	Chris Chelios (United States)

Forward   Wayne Gretzky (Canada)
          Jeremy Roenick (United States)
          Mats Sundin (Sweden)

Final Standings Round Robin

	GP	W	L	T	GF	GA	P
Canada	5	3	0	2	21	11	8
United States	5	4	1	0	19	15	8
Finland	5	2	2	1	10	13	5
Sweden	5	2	3	0	13	17	4
Soviet Union	5	1	3	1	14	14	3
Czechoslovakia	5	1	4	0	11	18	2

Results

August 31	Toronto	Canada 2/Finland 2
	Saskatoon	Czechoslovakia 5/Soviet Union 2
	Pittsburgh	United States 6/Sweden 3
September 2	Hamilton	Canada 6/United States 3
	Montreal	Sweden 3/Soviet Union 2
	Saskatoon	Finland 1/Czechoslovakia 0
September 5	Toronto	Canada 4/Sweden 1
	Hamilton	Soviet Union 6/Finland 1
	Detroit	United States 4/Czechoslovakia 2
September 7	Montreal	Canada 6/Czechoslovakia 2
	Toronto	Finland 3/Sweden 1
	Chicago	United States 2/Soviet Union 1
September 9	Quebec City	Canada 3/Soviet Union 3
	Toronto	Sweden 5/Czechoslovakia 2
	Chicago	United States 4/Finland 3

Semifinals

September 11	Hamilton	United States 7/Finland 3
September 12	Toronto	Canada 4/Sweden 0

Finals (best two-of-three)

September 14	Montreal	Canada 4/United States 1
September 16	Hamilton	Canada 4/United States 2

World Cup of Hockey 1996
Canada/Europe/United States, August 30–September 14, 1996

FINAL STANDINGS ROUND ROBIN
North American Pool

	GP	W	L	T	GF	GA	P
United States	3	3	0	0	19	8	6
Canada	3	2	1	0	11	10	4
Russia	3	1	2	0	12	14	2
Slovakia	3	0	3	0	9	19	0

European Pool

	GP	W	L	T	GF	GA	P
Sweden	3	3	0	0	14	3	6
Finland	3	2	1	0	17	11	4
Germany	3	1	2	0	11	15	2
Czech Republic	3	0	3	0	4	17	0

Results

August 26	Stockholm	Sweden 6/Germany 1
August 27	Helsinki	Finland 7/Czech Republic 3
August 28	Helsinki	Finland 8/Germany 3
	Prague	Sweden 3/Czech Republic 0
	Vancouver	Canada 5/Russia 3
August 31	Philadelphia	United States 5/Canada 3
	Garmisch	Germany 7/Czech Republic 1
	Montreal	Russia 7/Slovakia 4

September 1	Ottawa	Canada 3/Slovakia 2
	Stockholm	Sweden 5/Finland 2
September 2	New York	United States 5/Russia 2
September 3	New York	United States 9/Slovakia 3

Quarter-finals

| September 5 | Montreal | Canada 4/Germany 1 |
| September 6 | Ottawa | Russia 5/Finland 0 |

Semifinals

September 7	Philadelphia	Canada 3/Sweden 2
		(Fleury 39:47 OT)
September 8	Ottawa	United States 5/Russia 2

Finals (best two-of-three)

September 10	Philadelphia	Canada 4/United States 3
		(Yzerman 19:53 OT)
September 12	Montreal	United States 5/Canada 2
September 14	Montreal	United States 5/Canada 2

World Cup of Hockey 2004
August 30–September 14, 2004
Tournament MVP: Vincent Lecavalier (CAN)

All-Tournament Team

Goal	Martin Brodeur (CAN)
Defence	Adam Foote (CAN)
	Kimmo Timonen (FIN)
Forward	Vincent Lecavalier (CAN)
	Fredrik Modin (SWE)
	Saku Koivu (FIN)

PRELIMINARY ROUND STANDINGS
European Pool

	GP	W	L	T	GF	GA	P
Finland	3	2	0	1	11	4	5
Sweden	3	2	0	1	13	9	5
Czech Republic	3	1	2	0	10	10	2
Germany	3	0	3	0	4	15	0

August 30	Helsinki	Finland 4/Czech Republic 0
August 31	Stockholm	Sweden 5/Germany 2
September 1	Stockholm	Sweden 4/Czech Republic 3
September 2	Cologne	Finland 3/Germany 0
September 3	Prague	Czech Republic 7/Germany 2
September 4	Helsinki	Finland 4/Sweden 4 (5:00 OT)

North American Pool

	GP	W	L	T	GF	GA	P
Canada	3	3	0	0	10	3	6
Russia	3	2	1	0	9	6	4
USA	3	1	2	0	5	6	2
Slovakia	3	0	3	0	4	13	0

August 31	Montreal	Canada 2/USA 1
September 1	Montreal	Canada 5/Slovakia 1
September 2	St. Paul	Russia 3/USA 1
September 3	St. Paul	USA 3/Slovakia 1
September 4	Toronto	Canada 3/Russia 1
September 5	Toronto	Russia 5/Slovakia 2

Quarter-finals

September 6	Helsinki	Finland 2/Germany 1
September 7	Stockholm	Czech Republic 6/Sweden 1
September 7	St. Paul	USA 5/Russia 2

September 8   Toronto   Canada 5/Slovakia 1

Semifinals
September 11 St. Paul   Finland 2/USA 1
September 12 Toronto   Canada 4/Czech Republic 3
                           (Vincent Lecavalier 3:45 OT)

Finals
September 14 Toronto   Canada 3/Finland 2

WORLD CHAMPIONSHIPS, 1930–2009

January 31–February 10, 1930

Chamonix, France/Berlin, Germany/Vienna, Austria

GOLD MEDAL	Canada
SILVER MEDAL	Germany
BRONZE MEDAL	Switzerland
Fourth Place	Austria
Fifth Place	Poland
Sixth Place (tie)	Czechoslovakia
	France
	Hungary
	Japan
Tenth Place (tie)	Belgium
	Great Britain
	Italy

March 1–8, 1931

Krynica, Poland

GOLD MEDAL	Canada
SILVER MEDAL	United States
BRONZE MEDAL	Austria
Fourth Place	Poland
Fifth Place	Czechoslovakia
Sixth Place	Sweden
Seventh Place	Hungary
Eighth Place	Great Britain
Ninth Place	France
Tenth Place	Romania

February 18–26, 1933

Prague, Czechoslovakia

GOLD MEDAL	United States
SILVER MEDAL	Canada
BRONZE MEDAL	Czechoslovakia
Fourth Place	Austria
Fifth Place (tie)	Germany
	Switzerland
Seventh Place (tie)	Hungary
	Poland
Ninth Place	Romania
Tenth Place	Latvia
Eleventh Place	Italy
Twelfth Place	Belgium

February 3–11, 1934

Milan, Italy

GOLD MEDAL	Canada
SILVER MEDAL	United States
BRONZE MEDAL	Germany
Fourth Place	Switzerland
Fifth Place	Czechoslovakia
Sixth Place	Hungary
Seventh Place	Austria
Eighth Place	Great Britain
Ninth Place	Italy
Tenth Place	Romania
Eleventh Place	France
Twelfth Place	Belgium

January 19–27, 1935

Davos, Switzerland

GOLD MEDAL	Canada
SILVER MEDAL	Switzerland
BRONZE MEDAL	Great Britain
Fourth Place	Czechoslovakia
Fifth Place	Sweden
Sixth Place	Austria
Seventh Place	France
Eighth Place	Italy
Ninth Place	Germany
Tenth Place	Poland
Eleventh Place (tie)	Hungary
	Romania
Thirteenth Place	Latvia
Fourteenth Place	Belgium
	Netherlands

February 17–27, 1937

London, Great Britain

GOLD MEDAL	Canada
SILVER MEDAL	Great Britain
BRONZE MEDAL	Switzerland
Fourth Place	Germany
Fifth Place	Hungary
Sixth Place	Czechoslovakia
Seventh Place	France
Eighth Place	Poland
Ninth Place (tie)	Norway
	Romania
	Sweden

February 11–20, 1938

Prague, Czechoslovakia

GOLD MEDAL	Canada
SILVER MEDAL	Great Britain
BRONZE MEDAL	Czechoslovakia
Fourth Place	Germany
Fifth Place	Sweden
Sixth Place	Switzerland
Seventh Place (tie)	Hungary
	Poland
	United States
Tenth Place (tie)	Austria
	Latvia
	Lithuania
Thirteenth Place (tie)	Norway
	Romania

February 3–12, 1939

Basel/Zurich, Switzerland

GOLD MEDAL	Canada
SILVER MEDAL	United States
BRONZE MEDAL	Switzerland
Fourth Place	Czechoslovakia
Fifth Place	Germany
Sixth Place	Poland
Seventh Place	Hungary
Eighth Place	Great Britain
Ninth Place	Italy
Tenth Place	Latvia
Eleventh Place (tie)	Belgium
	Netherlands
Thirteenth Place	Finland
	Yugoslavia

February 15–23, 1947

Prague, Czechoslovakia

GOLD MEDAL	Czechoslovakia
SILVER MEDAL	Sweden
BRONZE MEDAL	Austria
Fourth Place	Switzerland
Fifth Place	United States
Sixth Place	Poland
Seventh Place	Romania
Eighth Place	Belgium

February 12–20, 1949

Stockholm, Sweden

GOLD MEDAL	Czechoslovakia
SILVER MEDAL	Canada
BRONZE MEDAL	United States
Fourth Place	Sweden
Fifth Place	Switzerland
Sixth Place	Austria
Seventh Place	Finland
Eighth Place	Norway
Ninth Place	Belgium
Tenth Place	Denmark

March 13–22, 1950

London, Great Britain

GOLD MEDAL	Canada
SILVER MEDAL	United States
BRONZE MEDAL	Switzerland
Fourth Place	Great Britain
Fifth Place	Sweden

Sixth Place   Norway
Seventh Place   Belgium
Eighth Place   Netherlands
Ninth Place   France

March 9–17, 1951

Paris, France

GOLD MEDAL   Canada
SILVER MEDAL   Sweden
BRONZE MEDAL   Switzerland
Fourth Place   Norway
Fifth Place   Great Britain
Sixth Place   United States
Seventh Place   Finland

March 6–15, 1953

Zurich/Basel, Switzerland

GOLD MEDAL   Sweden
SILVER MEDAL   West Germany
BRONZE MEDAL   Switzerland
Fourth Place   Czechoslovakia

February 26–March 7, 1954

Stockholm, Sweden

GOLD MEDAL   Soviet Union
SILVER MEDAL   Canada
BRONZE MEDAL   Sweden
Fourth Place   Czechoslovakia
Fifth Place   West Germany
Sixth Place   Finland
Seventh Place   Switzerland

Eighth Place   Norway

February 25–March 6, 1955

Düsseldorf, West Germany

GOLD MEDAL   Canada
SILVER MEDAL   Soviet Union
BRONZE MEDAL   Czechoslovakia
Fourth Place   United States
Fifth Place   Sweden
Sixth Place   West Germany
Seventh Place   Poland
Eighth Place   Switzerland
Ninth Place   Finland

February 24–March 5, 1957

Moscow, Soviet Union

GOLD MEDAL   Sweden
SILVER MEDAL   Soviet Union
BRONZE MEDAL   Czechoslovakia
Fourth Place   Finland
Fifth Place   West Germany
Sixth Place   Poland
Seventh Place   Austria
Eighth Place   Japan

To protest the suppression of the Hungarian revolution by Soviet forces, Canadian Prime Minister Louis St. Laurent refused to allow a Canadian team to travel to Moscow to play at the World Championships.

February 25–March 9, 1958

Oslo, Norway

GOLD MEDAL   Canada
SILVER MEDAL   Soviet Union
BRONZE MEDAL   Sweden

Fourth Place	Czechoslovakia
Fifth Place	United States
Sixth Place	Finland
Seventh Place	Norway
Eighth Place	Poland

March 9–15, 1959

Prague, Czechoslovakia

GOLD MEDAL	Canada
SILVER MEDAL	Soviet Union
BRONZE MEDAL	Czechoslovakia
Fourth Place	United States
Fifth Place	Sweden
Sixth Place	Finland
Seventh Place	West Germany
Eighth Place	Norway
Ninth Place	East Germany
Tenth Place	Italy
Eleventh Place	Poland
Twelfth Place	Switzerland
Thirteenth Place	Romania
Fourteenth Place	Hungary
Fifteenth Place	Austria

March 1–12, 1961

Geneva/Lausanne, Switzerland

GOLD MEDAL	Canada
SIVER MEDAL	Czechoslovakia
BRONZE MEDAL	Soviet Union
Fourth Place	Sweden
Fifth Place	East Germany
Sixth Place	United States

Seventh Place	Finland
Eighth Place	West Germany

May 8–18, 1962

Colorado Springs, United States

GOLD MEDAL	Sweden
SILVER MEDAL	Canada
BRONZE MEDAL	United States
Fourth Place	Finland
Fifth Place	Norway
Sixth Place	West Germany
Seventh Place	Switzerland
Eighth Place	Great Britain

March 7–17, 1963

Stockholm, Sweden

GOLD MEDAL	Soviet Union
SILVER MEDAL	Sweden
BRONZE MEDAL	Czechoslovakia
Fourth Place	Canada
Fifth Place	Finland
Sixth Place	East Germany
Seventh Place	West Germany
Eighth Place	United States

March 3–14, 1965

Tampere, Finland

GOLD MEDAL	Soviet Union
SILVER MEDAL	Czechoslovakia
BRONZE MEDAL	Sweden
Fourth Place	Canada

Fifth Place	East Germany
Sixth Place	United States
Seventh Place	Finland
Eighth Place	Norway

March 3–14, 1966

Ljubljana, Yugoslavia

GOLD MEDAL	Soviet Union
SILVER MEDAL	Czechoslovakia
BRONZE MEDAL	Canada
Fourth Place	Sweden
Fifth Place	East Germany
Sixth Place	United States
Seventh Place	Finland
Eighth Place	Poland

March 18–29, 1967

Vienna, Austria

GOLD MEDAL	Soviet Union
SILVER MEDAL	Sweden
BRONZE MEDAL	Canada
Fourth Place	Czechoslovakia
Fifth Place	United States
Sixth Place	Finland
Seventh Place	West Germany
Eighth Place	East Germany

March 15–30, 1969

Stockholm, Sweden

GOLD MEDAL	Soviet Union
SILVER MEDAL	Sweden

BRONZE MEDAL	Czechoslovakia
Fourth Place	Canada
Fifth Place	Finland
Sixth Place	United States

To protest the ineligibility of professionals from the World Championships according to IIHF rules, Canada did not compete in IIHF sanctioned tournaments from 1970 through 1976.

March 14–30, 1970

Stockholm, Sweden

GOLD MEDAL	Soviet Union
SILVER MEDAL	Sweden
BRONZE MEDAL	Czechoslovakia
Fourth Place	Finland
Fifth Place	East Germany
Sixth Place	Poland

March 19–April 3, 1971

Bern/Geneva, Switzerland

GOLD MEDAL	Soviet Union
SILVER MEDAL	Czechoslovakia
BRONZE MEDAL	Sweden
Fourth Place	Finland
Fifth Place	East Germany
Sixth Place	United States

April 7–22, 1972

Prague, Czechoslovakia

GOLD MEDAL	Czechoslovakia
SILVER MEDAL	Soviet Union
BRONZE MEDAL	Sweden

Fourth Place	Finland
Fifth Place	East Germany
Sixth Place	Switzerland

March 31–April 15, 1973

Moscow, Soviet Union

GOLD MEDAL	Soviet Union
SILVER MEDAL	Sweden
BRONZE MEDAL	Czechoslovakia
Fourth Place	Finland
Fifth Place	Poland
Sixth Place	East Germany

April 5–20, 1974

Helsinki, Finland

GOLD MEDAL	Soviet Union
SILVER MEDAL	Czechoslovakia
BRONZE MEDAL	Sweden
Fourth Place	Finland
Fifth Place	Poland
Sixth Place	East Germany

April 3–19, 1975

Munich/Düsseldorf, West Germany

GOLD MEDAL	Soviet Union
SILVER MEDAL	Czechoslovakia
BRONZE MEDAL	Sweden
Fourth Place	Finland
Fifth Place	Poland
Sixth Place	United States

April 8–25, 1976

Katowice, Poland

GOLD MEDAL	Czechoslovakia
SILVER MEDAL	Soviet Union
BRONZE MEDAL	Sweden
Fourth Place	United States
Fifth Place	Finland
Sixth Place	West Germany
Seventh Place	Poland
Eighth Place	East Germany

April 21–May 8, 1977

Vienna, Austria

GOLD MEDAL	Czechoslovakia
SILVER MEDAL	Sweden
BRONZE MEDAL	Soviet Union
Fourth Place	Canada
Fifth Place	Finland
Sixth Place	United States
Seventh Place	West Germany
Eighth Place	Romania

April 25–May 8, 1978

Prague, Czechoslovakia

GOLD MEDAL	Soviet Union
SILVER MEDAL	Czechoslovakia
BRONZE MEDAL	Canada
Fourth Place	Sweden
Fifth Place	West Germany
Sixth Place	USA
Seventh Place	Finland

Eighth Place   East Germany

April 14–27, 1979

Moscow, Soviet Union

GOLD MEDAL   Soviet Union
SILVER MEDAL   Czechoslovakia
BRONZE MEDAL   Sweden
Fourth Place   Canada
Fifth Place   Finland
Sixth Place   West Germany
Seventh Place   United States
Eighth Place   Poland

April 12–26, 1981

Gothenburg/Stockholm, Sweden

GOLD MEDAL   Soviet Union
SILVER MEDAL   Sweden
BRONZE MEDAL   Czechoslovakia
Fourth Place   Canada
Fifth Place   United States
Sixth Place   Finland
Seventh Place   West Germany
Eighth Place   Netherlands

April 15–29, 1982

Helsinki/Tampere, Finland

GOLD MEDAL   Soviet Union
SILVER MEDAL   Czechoslovakia
BRONZE MEDAL   Canada
Fourth Place   Sweden
Fifth Place   Finland

Sixth Place	West Germany
Seventh Place	Italy
Eighth Place	United States

April 16–May 2, 1983

Dortmund/Düsseldorf/Munich, West Germany

GOLD MEDAL	Soviet Union
SILVER MEDAL	Czechoslovakia
BRONZE MEDAL	Canada
Fourth Place	Sweden
Fifth Place	East Germany
Sixth Place	West Germany
Seventh Place	Finland
Eighth Place	Italy

April 17–May 3, 1985

Prague, Czechoslovakia

GOLD MEDAL	Czechoslovakia
SILVER MEDAL	Canada
BRONZE MEDAL	Soviet Union
Fourth Place	United States
Fifth Place	Finland
Sixth Place	Sweden
Seventh Place	East Germany
Eighth Place	West Germany

April 12–28, 1986

Moscow, Soviet Union

GOLD MEDAL	Soviet Union
SILVER MEDAL	Sweden
BRONZE MEDAL	Canada

Fourth Place	Finland
Fifth Place	Czechoslovakia
Sixth Place	United States
Seventh Place	East Germany
Eighth Place	Poland

April 17–May 3, 1987

Vienna, Austria

GOLD MEDAL	Sweden
SILVER MEDAL	Soviet Union
BRONZE MEDAL	Czechoslovakia
Fourth Place	Canada
Fifth Place	Finland
Sixth Place	West Germany
Seventh Place	United States
Eighth Place	Switzerland

April 15–May 1, 1989

Stockholm, Sweden

GOLD MEDAL	Soviet Union
SILVER MEDAL	Canada
BRONZE MEDAL	Czechoslovakia
Fourth Place	Sweden
Fifth Place	Finland
Sixth Place	United States
Seventh Place	West Germany
Eighth Place	Poland

April 16–May 2, 1990

Bern, Switzerland

| GOLD MEDAL | Soviet Union |

SILVER MEDAL	Sweden
BRONZE MEDAL	Czechoslovakia
Fourth Place	Canada
Fifth Place	United States
Sixth Place	Finland
Seventh Place	West Germany
Eighth Place	Norway

April 14–May 5, 1991

Helsinki, Finland

GOLD MEDAL	Sweden
SILVER MEDAL	Canada
BRONZE MEDAL	Soviet Union
Fourth Place	United States
Fifth Place	Finland
Sixth Place	Czechoslovakia
Seventh Place	Switzerland
Eight Place	Germany

April 28–May 10, 1992

Prague/Bratislava, Czechoslovakia

GOLD MEDAL	Sweden
SILVER MEDAL	Finland
BRONZE MEDAL	Czechoslovakia
Fourth Place	Switzerland
Fifth Place	Russia
Sixth Place	Germany
Seventh Place	United States
Eighth Place	Canada
Ninth Place	Italy
Tenth Place	Norway
Eleventh Place	France

Twelfth Place   Poland

April 18–May 2, 1993

Munich, Germany

GOLD MEDAL	Russia
SILVER MEDAL	Sweden
BRONZE MEDAL	Czech Republic
Fourth Place	Canada
Fifth Place	Germany
Sixth Place	United States
Seventh Place	Finland
Eighth Place	Italy
Ninth Place	Austria
Tenth Place	France
Eleventh Place	Norway
Twelfth Place	Switzerland

April 25–May 8, 1994

Bolzano, Italy

GOLD MEDAL	Canada
SILVER MEDAL	Finland
BRONZE MEDAL	Sweden
Fourth Place	United States
Fifth Place	Russia
Sixth Place	Italy
Seventh Place	Czech Republic
Eighth Place	Austria
Ninth Place	Germany
Tenth Place	France
Eleventh Place	Norway
Twelfth Place	Great Britain

April 23–May 7, 1995

Stockholm/Gavle, Sweden

GOLD MEDAL	Finland
SILVER MEDAL	Sweden
BRONZE MEDAL	Canada
Fourth Place	Czech Republic
Fifth Place	Russia
Sixth Place	United States
Seventh Place	Italy
Eighth Place	France
Ninth Place	Germany
Tenth Place	Norway
Eleventh Place	Austria
Twelfth Place	Switzerland

April 21–May 5, 1996

Vienna, Austria

GOLD MEDAL	Czech Republic
SILVER MEDAL	Canada
BRONZE MEDAL	United States
Fourth Place	Russia
Fifth Place	Finland
Sixth Place	Sweden
Seventh Place	Italy
Eighth Place	Germany
Ninth Place	Norway
Tenth Place	Slovakia
Eleventh Place	France
Twelfth Place	Austria

April 26–May 14, 1997

Helsinki/Tampere/Turku, Finland

GOLD MEDAL	Canada
SILVER MEDAL	Sweden
BRONZE MEDAL	Czech Republic
Fourth Place	Russia
Fifth Place	Finland
Sixth Place	United States
Seventh Place	Latvia
Eighth Place	Italy
Ninth Place	Slovakia
Tenth Place	France
Eleventh Place	Germany
Twelfth Place	Norway

May 1–17, 1998

Zurich, Switzerland

GOLD MEDAL	Sweden
SILVER MEDAL	Finland
BRONZE MEDAL	Czech Republic
Fourth Place	Switzerland
Fifth Place	Russia
Sixth Place	Canada
Seventh Place	Slovakia
Eighth Place	Belarus
Ninth Place	Latvia
Tenth Place	Italy
Eleventh Place	Germany
Twelfth Place	United States

May 1–16, 1999

Oslo/Hamar/Lillehammer, Norway

GOLD MEDAL	Czech Republic
SILVER MEDAL	Finland
BRONZE MEDAL	Sweden
Fourth Place	Canada
Fifth Place	Russia
Sixth Place	United States
Seventh Place	Slovakia
Eighth Place	Switzerland
Ninth Place	Belarus
Tenth Place	Austria
Eleventh Place	Latvia
Twelfth Place	Norway
Thirteenth Place	Italy
Fourteenth Place	Ukraine
Fifteenth Place	France
Sixteenth Place	Japan

April 29–May 14, 2000

St. Petersburg, Russia

GOLD MEDAL	Czech Republic
SILVER MEDAL	Slovakia
BRONZE MEDAL	Finland
Fourth Place	Canada
Fifth Place	United States
Sixth Place	Switzerland
Seventh Place	Sweden
Eighth Place	Latvia
Ninth Place	Belarus
Tenth Place	Norway
Eleventh Place	Russia

Twelfth Place	Italy
Thirteenth Place	Austria
Fourteenth Place	Ukraine
Fifteenth Place	France
Sixteenth Place	Japan

April 28–May 13, 2001

Hanover/Cologne/Nuremberg, Germany

GOLD MEDAL	Czech Republic
SILVER MEDAL	Finland
BRONZE MEDAL	Sweden
Fourth Place	United States
Fifth Place	Canada
Sixth Place	Russia
Seventh Place	Slovakia
Eighth Place	Germany
Ninth Place	Switzerland
Tenth Place	Ukraine
Eleventh Place	Austria
Twelfth Place	Italy
Thirteenth Place	Latvia
Fourteenth Place	Belarus
Fifteenth Place	Norway
Sixteenth Place	Japan

April 26–May 11, 2002

Gothenburg/Karlstad/Jonkoping, Sweden

GOLD MEDAL	Slovakia
SILVER MEDAL	Russia
BRONZE MEDAL	Sweden
Fourth Place	Finland
Fifth Place	Czech Republic

Sixth Place	Canada
Seventh Place	United States
Eighth Place	Germany
Ninth Place	Ukraine
Tenth Place	Switzerland
Eleventh Place	Latvia
Tweflth Place	Austria
Thirteenth Place	Slovenia
Fourteenth Place	Poland
Fifteenth Place	Italy
Sixteenth Place	Japan

April 27–May 11, 2003

Helsinki/Tampere/Turku, Finland

GOLD MEDAL	Canada
SILVER MEDAL	Sweden
BRONZE MEDAL	Slovakia
Fourth Place	Czech Republic
Fifth Place	Finland
Sixth Place	Germany
Seventh Place	Russia
Eighth Place	Switzerland
Ninth Place	Latvia
Tenth Place	Austria
Eleventh Place	Denmark
Twelfth Place	Ukraine
Thirteenth Place	United States
Fourteenth Place	Belarus
Fifteenth Place	Slovenia
Sixteenth Place	Japan

April 24–May 9, 2004

Prague/Ostrava, Czech Republic

GOLD MEDAL	Canada
SILVER MEDAL	Sweden
BRONZE MEDAL	United States
Fourth Place	Slovakia
Fifth Place	Czech Republic
Sixth Place	Finland
Seventh Place	Latvia
Eighth Place	Switzerland
Ninth Place	Germany
Tenth Place	Russia
Eleventh Place	Austria
Twelfth Place	Denmark
Thirteenth Place	Kazakhstan
Fourteenth Place	Ukraine
Fifteenth Place	Japan
Sixteenth Place	France

April 30–May 15, 2005

Vienna/Innsbruck, Austria

GOLD MEDAL	Czech Republic
SILVER MEDAL	Canada
BRONZE MEDAL	Russia
Fourth Place	Sweden
Fifth Place	Slovakia
Sixth Place	United States
Seventh Place	Finland
Eighth Place	Switzerland
Ninth Place	Latvia
Tenth Place	Belarus

Eleventh Place	Ukraine
Twelfth Place	Kazakhstan
Thirteenth Place	Slovenia
Fourteenth Place	Denmark
Fifteenth Place	Germany
Sixteenth Place	Austria

May 5–May 21, 2006

Riga, Latvia

GOLD MEDAL	Sweden
SILVER MEDAL	Czech Republic
BRONZE MEDAL	Finland
Fourth Place	Canada
Fifth Place	Russia
Sixth Place	Belarus
Seventh Place	United States
Eighth Place	Slovakia
Ninth Place	Switzerland
Tenth Place	Latvia
Eleventh Place	Norway
Twelfth Place	Ukraine
Thirteenth Place	Denmark
Fourteenth Place	Italy
Fifteenth Place	Kazakhstan
Sixteenth Place	Slovenia

April 24–May 10, 2007

Moscow/Mytischi, Russia

GOLD MEDAL	Canada
SILVER MEDAL	Finland
BRONZE MEDAL	Russia
Fourth Place	Sweden

Fifth Place	United States
Sixth Place	Slovakia
Seventh Place	Czech Republic
Eighth Place	Switzerland
Ninth Place	Germany
Tenth Place	Denmark
Eleventh Place	Belarus
Twelfth Place	Italy
Thirteenth Place	Latvia
Fourteenth Place	Norway
Fifteenth Place	Austria
Sixteenth Place	Ukraine

May 2–May 18, 2008

Halifax/Quebec City, Canada

GOLD MEDAL	Russia
SILVER MEDAL	Canada
BRONZE MEDAL	Finland
Fourth Place	Sweden
Fifth Place	Czech Republic
Sixth Place	United States
Seventh Place	Switzerland
Eighth Place	Norway
Ninth Place	Belarus
Tenth Place	Germany
Eleventh Place	Latvia
Twelfth Place	Denmark
Thirteenth Place	Slovakia
Fourteenth Place	France
Fifteenth Place	Slovenia
Sixteenth Place	Italy

December 26, 2008–January 5, 2009

Ottawa, Canada

GOLD MEDAL	Canada
SILVER MEDAL	Sweden
BRONZE MEDAL	Russia
Fourth Place	Slovakia
Fifth Place	United States
Sixth Place	Czech Republic
Seventh Place	Finland
Eighth Place	Latvia
Ninth Place	Germany
Tenth Place	Kazakhstan

WORLD JUNIOR CHAMPIONSHIPS, 1977–2009

ALL MEDAL WINNERS BY CUMULATIVE STANDINGS (1977–2010)

Country	Gold	Silver	Bronze	Total
Canada	15	8	3	26
Soviet Union	9	3	2	14
Russia	3	6	5	14
Finland	2	4	6	12
Sweden	1	9	4	14
Czechoslovakia	0	4	6	10
United States	2	1	3	6
Czech Republic	2	0	2	4
Slovakia	0	0	1	1
Switzerland	0	0	1	1

1977 WORLD JUNIOR CHAMPIONSHIPS

CZECHOSLOVAKIA, DECEMBER 22, 1976–JANUARY 2, 1977

FINAL PLACINGS

GOLD MEDAL	Soviet Union
SILVER MEDAL	Canada
BRONZE MEDAL	Czechoslovakia
Fourth Place	Finland
Fifth Place	Sweden
Sixth Place	West Germany
Seventh Place	United States
Eighth Place	Poland*

* relegated to 'B' pool for 1978

ALL-STAR TEAM

Goal	Alexander Tyznych (Soviet Union)
Defence	Risto Siltanen (Finland)
	Lubos Oslizlo (Czechoslovakia)
Forward	Dale McCourt (Canada)
	Bengt-Ake Gustafsson (Sweden)
	Igor Romasin (Soviet Union)

DIRECTORATE AWARDS

BEST GOALIE	Jan Hrabak (Czechoslovakia)
BEST DEFENCEMAN	Viacheslav Fetisov (Soviet Union)
BEST FORWARD	Dale McCourt (Canada)

1978 WORLD JUNIOR CHAMPIONSHIPS

CANADA, DECEMBER 22, 1977–JANUARY 3, 1978

FINAL PLACINGS

GOLD MEDAL	Soviet Union
SILVER MEDAL	Sweden
BRONZE MEDAL	Canada
Fourth Place	Czechoslovakia
Fifth Place	United States
Sixth Place	Finland
Seventh Place	West Germany
Eighth Place	Switzerland*

* promoted from 'B' pool in 1977; relegated to 'B' pool for 1979

ALL-STAR TEAM

Goal	Alexander Tyznych (Soviet Union)
Defence	Risto Siltanen (Finland)
	Viacheslav Fetisov (Soviet Union)
Forward	Wayne Gretzky (Canada)
	Mats Naslund (Sweden)

Anton Stastny (Czechoslovakia)

DIRECTORATE AWARDS
BEST GOALIE	Alexander Tyzhnych (Soviet Union)
BEST DEFENCEMAN	Viacheslav Fetisov (Soviet Union)
BEST FORWARD	Wayne Gretzky (Canada)

1979 WORLD JUNIOR CHAMPIONSHIPS
SWEDEN, DECEMBER 27, 1978–JANUARY 3, 1979

FINAL PLACINGS
GOLD MEDAL	Soviet Union
SILVER MEDAL	Sweden
BRONZE MEDAL	Czechoslovakia
Fourth Place	Finland
Fifth Place	Canada
Sixth Place	United States
Seventh Place	West Germany
Eighth Place	Norway*

* promoted from 'B' pool in 1978; relegated to 'B' pool for 1980

ALL-STAR TEAM
Goal	Pelle Lindbergh (Sweden)
Defence	Ivan Cerny (Czechoslovakia)
	Alexei Kasatonov (Soviet Union)
Forward	Anatoli Tarasov (Soviet Union)
	Thomas Steen (Sweden)
	Vladimir Krutov (Soviet Union)

DIRECTORATE AWARDS
BEST GOALIE	Pelle Lindbergh (Sweden)
BEST DEFENCEMAN	Alexei Kasatonov (Soviet Union)

BEST FORWARD   Vladimir Krutov (Soviet Union)

1980 WORLD JUNIOR CHAMPIONSHIPS
FINLAND, DECEMBER 27, 1979–JANUARY 2, 1980

FINAL PLACINGS
GOLD MEDAL	Soviet Union
SILVER MEDAL	Finland
BRONZE MEDAL	Sweden
Fourth Place	Czechoslovakia
Fifth Place	Canada
Sixth Place	West Germany
Seventh Place	United States
Eighth Place	Switzerland*

* promoted from 'B' pool in 1979; relegated to 'B' pool for 1981

ALL-STAR TEAM
Goal	Jari Paavola (Finland)
Defence	Reijo Ruotsalainen (Finland)
	Tomas Jonsson (Sweden)
Forward	Hakan Loob (Sweden)
	Igor Larionov (Soviet Union)
	Vladimir Krutov (Soviet Union)

DIRECTORATE AWARDS
BEST GOALIE	Jari Paavola (Finland)
BEST DEFENCEMAN	Reijo Ruotsalainen (Finland)
BEST FORWARD	Vladimir Krutov (Soviet Union)

1981 WORLD JUNIOR CHAMPIONSHIPS

WEST GERMANY, DECEMBER 27, 1980–JANUARY 2, 1981

FINAL PLACINGS

GOLD MEDAL	Sweden
SILVER MEDAL	Finland
BRONZE MEDAL	Soviet Union
Fourth Place	Czechoslovakia
Fifth Place	West Germany
Sixth Place	United States
Seventh Place	Canada
Eighth Place	Austria*

* promoted from 'B' pool in 1980; relegated to 'B' pool for 1982

ALL-STAR TEAM

Goal	Lars Eriksson (Sweden)
Defence	Miloslav Horava (Czechoslovakia)
	Hakan Nordin (Sweden)
Forward	Ari Lahteenmaki (Finland)
	Patrik Sundstrom (Sweden)
	Jan Erixon (Sweden)

DIRECTORATE AWARDS

BEST GOALIE	Lars Eriksson (Sweden)
BEST DEFENCEMAN	Miloslav Horava (Czechoslovakia)
BEST FORWARD	Patrik Sundstrom (Sweden)

1982 WORLD JUNIOR CHAMPIONSHIPS

UNITED STATES, DECEMBER 22, 1981–JANUARY 2, 1982
(some games played in Canada)

FINAL PLACINGS

GOLD MEDAL	Canada
SILVER MEDAL	Czechoslovakia
BRONZE MEDAL	Finland
Fourth Place	Soviet Union
Fifth Place	Sweden
Sixth Place	United States
Seventh Place	West Germany
Eighth Place	Switzerland*

* promoted from 'B' pool in 1981; relegated to 'B' pool for 1983

ALL-STAR TEAM

Goal	Mike Moffat (Canada)
Defence	Gord Kluzak (Canada)
	Ilya Biakin (Soviet Union)
Forward	Mike Moller (Canada)
	Petri Skriko (Finland)
	Vladimir Ruzicka (Czechoslovakia)

DIRECTORATE AWARDS

BEST GOALIE	Mike Moffat (Canada)
BEST DEFENCEMAN	Gord Kluzak (Canada)
BEST FORWARD	Petri Skriko (Finland)

1983 WORLD JUNIOR CHAMPIONSHIPS
SOVIET UNION, DECEMBER 26, 1982–JANUARY 4, 1983

FINAL PLACINGS
GOLD MEDAL	Soviet Union
SILVER MEDAL	Czechoslovakia
BRONZE MEDAL	Canada
Fourth Place	Sweden
Fifth Place	United States
Sixth Place	Finland
Seventh Place	West Germany
Eighth Place	Norway*

* promoted from 'B' pool in 1982; relegated to 'B' pool for 1984

ALL-STAR TEAM
Goal	Matti Rautiainen (Finland)
Defence	Ilya Biakin (Soviet Union)
	Simo Saarinen (Finland)
Forward	Tomas Sandstrom (Sweden)
	Vladimir Ruzicka (Czechoslovakia)
	German Volgin (Soviet Union)

DIRECTORATE AWARDS
BEST GOALIE	Dominik Hasek (Czechoslovakia)
BEST DEFENCEMAN	Ilya Biakin (Soviet Union)
BEST FORWARD	Tomas Sandstrom (Sweden)

1984 WORLD JUNIOR CHAMPIONSHIPS

SWEDEN, DECEMBER 25, 1983–JANUARY 3, 1984

FINAL PLACINGS

GOLD MEDAL	Soviet Union
SILVER MEDAL	Finland
BRONZE MEDAL	Czechoslovakia
Fourth Place	Canada
Fifth Place	Sweden
Sixth Place	United States
Seventh Place	West Germany
Eighth Place	Switzerland*

* promoted from 'B' pool in 1983; relegated to 'B' pool for 1985

ALL-STAR TEAM

Goal	Evgeny Belosheikin (Soviet Union)
Defence	Alexei Gusarov (Soviet Union)
	Frantisek Musil (Czechoslovakia)
Forward	Petr Rosol (Czechoslovakia)
	Raimo Helminen (Finland)
	Nikolai Borschevsky (Soviet Union)

DIRECTORATE AWARDS

BEST GOALIE	Alan Perry (United States)
BEST DEFENCEMAN	Alexei Gusarov (Soviet Union)
BEST FORWARD	Raimo Helminen (Finland)

1985 WORLD JUNIOR CHAMPIONSHIPS

FINLAND, DECEMBER 23, 1984–JANUARY 1, 1985

FINAL PLACINGS

GOLD MEDAL	Canada
SILVER MEDAL	Czechoslovakia

BRONZE MEDAL	Soviet Union
Fourth Place	Finland
Fifth Place	Sweden
Sixth Place	United States
Seventh Place	West Germany
Eighth Place	Poland*

* promoted from 'B' pool in 1984; relegated to 'B' pool for 1986

ALL-STAR TEAM

Goal	Timo Lehkonen (Finland)
Defence	Bobby Dollas (Canada)
	Mikhail Tatarinov (Soviet Union)
Forward	Mikko Makela (Finland)
	Michal Pivonka (Czechoslovakia)
	Esa Tikkanen (Finland)

DIRECTORATE AWARDS

BEST GOALIE	Craig Billington (Canada)
BEST DEFENCEMAN	Vesa Salo (Finland)
BEST FORWARD	Michal Pivonka (Czechoslovakia)

1986 WORLD JUNIOR CHAMPIONSHIPS

CANADA, DECEMBER 26, 1985–JANUARY 4, 1986

FINAL PLACINGS

GOLD MEDAL	Soviet Union
SILVER MEDAL	Canada
BRONZE MEDAL	United States
Fourth Place	Czechoslovakia
Fifth Place	Sweden

Sixth Place	Finland
Seventh Place	Switzerland*
Eighth Place	West Germany**

* promoted from 'B' pool in 1985
** relegated to 'B' pool for 1987

ALL-STAR TEAM

Goal	Evgeny Belosheikin (Soviet Union)
Defence	Sylvain Cote (Canada)
	Mikhail Tatarinov (Soviet Union)
Forward	Shayne Corson (Canada)
	Igor Viazmikin (Soviet Union)
	Michal Pivonka (Czechoslovakia)

DIRECTORATE AWARDS

BEST GOALIE	Evgeny Belosheikin (Soviet Union)
BEST DEFENCEMAN	Mikhail Tatarinov (Soviet Union)
BEST FORWARD	Jim Sandlak (Canada)

1987 WORLD JUNIOR CHAMPIONSHIPS

CZECHOSLOVAKIA, DECEMBER 26, 1986–JANUARY 4, 1987

FINAL PLACINGS

GOLD MEDAL	Finland
SILVER MEDAL	Czechoslovakia
BRONZE MEDAL	Sweden
Fourth Place	United States
Fifth Place	Poland*
Sixth Place	Switzerland**

Canada and the Soviet Union were disqualified

* promoted from 'B' pool in 1986
** relegated to 'B' pool for 1988

ALL-STAR TEAM

Goal	Sam Lindstahl (Sweden)
Defence	Jiri Latal (Czechoslovakia)
	Brian Leetch (United States)
Forward	Ulf Dahlen (Sweden)
	Juraj Jurik (Czechoslovakia)
	Scott Young (United States)

DIRECTORATE AWARDS

BEST GOALIE	Markus Ketterer (Finland)
BEST DEFENCEMAN	Calle Johansson (Sweden)
BEST FORWARD	Robert Kron (Czechoslovakia)

1988 WORLD JUNIOR CHAMPIONSHIPS

RUSSIA, DECEMBER 26, 1987–JANUARY 4, 1988

FINAL PLACINGS

GOLD MEDAL	Canada
SILVER MEDAL	Soviet Union
BRONZE MEDAL	Finland
Fourth Place	Czechsloavkia
Fifth Place	Sweden
Sixth Place	United States
Seventh Place	West Germany*
Eighth Place	Poland**

* promoted from 'B' pool in 1987
** relegated to 'B' pool for 1989

ALL-STAR TEAM

Goal	Jimmy Waite (Canada)
Defence	Greg Hawgood (Canada)
	Teppo Numminen (Finland)

Forward   Theoren Fleury (Canada)
           Alexander Mogilny (Soviet Union)
           Petr Hrbek (Czechoslovakia)

DIRECTORATE AWARDS
BEST GOALIE	Jimmy Waite (Canada)
BEST DEFENCEMAN	Teppo Numminen (Finland)
BEST FORWARD	Alexander Mogilny (Soviet Union)

1989 WORLD JUNIOR CHAMPIONSHIPS

UNITED STATES, DECEMBER 26, 1988–JANUARY 4, 1989

FINAL PLACINGS
GOLD MEDAL	Soviet Union
SILVER MEDAL	Sweden
BRONZE MEDAL	Czechoslovakia
Fourth Place	Canada
Fifth Place	United States
Sixth Place	Finland
Seventh Place	Norway*
Eighth Place	West Germany**

* promoted from 'B' pool in 1988
** relegated to 'B' pool for 1990

ALL-STAR TEAM
Goal	Alexei Ivashkin (Soviet Union)
Defence	Rickard Persson (Sweden)
	Milan Tichy (Czechoslovakia)
Forward	Niklas Eriksson (Sweden)
	Pavel Bure (Soviet Union)
	Jeremy Roenick (United States)

DIRECTORATE AWARDS

BEST GOALIE	Alexei Ivashkin (Soviet Union)
BEST DEFENCEMAN	Rickard Persson (Sweden)
BEST FORWARD	Pavel Bure (Soviet Union)

1990 WORLD JUNIOR CHAMPIONSHIPS

FINLAND, DECEMBER 26, 1989–JANUARY 4, 1990

FINAL PLACINGS

GOLD MEDAL	Canada
SILVER MEDAL	Soviet Union
BRONZE MEDAL	Czechoslovakia
Fourth Place	Finland
Fifth Place	Sweden
Sixth Place	Norway
Seventh Place	United States
Eighth Place	Poland*

* promoted from 'B' pool in 1989; relegated to 'B' pool for 1991

ALL-STAR TEAM

Goal	Stephane Fiset (Canada)
Defence	Alexander Godynyuk (Soviet Union)
	Jiri Slegr (Czechoslovakia)
Forward	Dave Chyzowski (Canada)
	Jaromir Jagr (Czechoslovakia)
	Robert Reichel (Czechoslovakia)

DIRECTORATE AWARDS

BEST GOALIE	Stephane Fiset (Canada)
BEST DEFENCEMAN	Alexander Godynyuk (Soviet Union)
BEST FORWARD	Robert Reichel (Czechoslovakia)

1991 WORLD JUNIOR CHAMPIONSHIPS

CANADA, DECEMBER 26, 1990–JANUARY 4, 1991

FINAL PLACINGS

GOLD MEDAL	Canada
SILVER MEDAL	Soviet Union
BRONZE MEDAL	Czechoslovakia
Fourth Place	United States
Fifth Place	Finland
Sixth Place	Sweden
Seventh Place	Switzerland*
Eighth Place	Norway**

* promoted from 'B' pool in 1990
** relegated to 'B' pool for 1992

ALL-STAR TEAM

Goal	Pauli Jaks (Switzerland)
Defence	Dmitri Yushkevich (Soviet Union)
	Scott Lachance (United States)
Forward	Mike Craig (Canada)
	Eric Lindros (Canada)
	Martin Rucinsky (Czechoslovakia)

DIRECTORATE AWARDS

BEST GOALIE	Pauli Jaks (Switzerland)
BEST DEFENCEMAN	Jiri Slegr (Czechoslovakia)
BEST FORWARD	Eric Lindros (Canada)

1992 WORLD JUNIOR CHAMPIONSHIPS

GERMANY, DECEMBER 26, 1991–JANUARY 4, 1992

FINAL PLACINGS

GOLD MEDAL	Commonwealth of Independent States
SILVER MEDAL	Sweden
BRONZE MEDAL	United States
Fourth Place	Finland
Fifth Place	Czechoslovakia
Sixth Place	Canada
Seventh Place	Germany*
Eighth Place	Switzerland**

* promoted from 'B' pool in 1991
** relegated to 'B' pool for 1993

ALL-STAR TEAM

Goal	Mike Dunham (United States)
Defence	Scott Niedermayer (Canada)
	Janne Gronvall (Finland)
Forward	Alexei Kovalev (CIS)
	Michael Nylander (Sweden)
	Peter Ferraro (United States)

DIRECTORATE AWARDS

BEST GOALIE	Mike Dunham (United States)
BEST DEFENCEMAN	Darius Kasparaitis (CIS)
BEST FORWARD	Michael Nylander (Sweden)

1993 WORLD JUNIOR CHAMPIONSHIPS
SWEDEN, DECEMBER 26, 1992–JANUARY 4, 1993

FINAL PLACINGS
GOLD MEDAL	Canada
SILVER MEDAL	Sweden
BRONZE MEDAL	Czech Republic
Fourth Place	United States
Fifth Place	Finland
Sixth Place	Russia
Seventh Place	Germany
Eighth place	Japan*

* promoted from 'B' pool in 1992; relegated to 'B' pool for 1994

ALL-STAR TEAM
Goal	Manny Legace (Canada)
Defence	Brent Tully (Canada)
	Kenny Jonsson (Sweden)
Forward	Paul Kariya (Canada)
	Markus Naslund (Sweden)
	Peter Forsberg (Sweden)

DIRECTORATE AWARDS
BEST GOALIE	Manny Legace (Canada)
BEST DEFENCEMAN	Janne Gronvall (Finland)
BEST FORWARD	Peter Forsberg (Sweden)

1994 WORLD JUNIOR CHAMPIONSHIPS

CZECH REPUBLIC, DECEMBER 26, 1993–JANUARY 4, 1994

FINAL PLACINGS

GOLD MEDAL	Canada
SILVER MEDAL	Sweden
BRONZE MEDAL	Russia
Fourth Place	Finland
Fifth Place	Czech Republic
Sixth Place	United States
Seventh Place	Germany
Eighth Place	Switzerland*

* promoted from 'B' pool in 1993; relegated to 'B' pool for 1995

ALL-STAR TEAM

Goal	Evgeny Riabchikov (Russia)
Defence	Kenny Jonsson (Sweden)
	Kimmo Timonen (Finland)
Forward	Niklas Sundstrom (Sweden)
	Valeri Bure (Russia)
	David Vyborny (Czech Republic)

DIRECTORATE AWARDS

BEST GOALIE	Jamie Storr (Canada)
BEST DEFENCEMAN	Kenny Jonsson (Sweden)
BEST FORWARD	Niklas Sundstrom (Sweden)

1995 WORLD JUNIOR CHAMPIONSHIPS
CANADA, DECEMBER 26, 1994–JANUARY 4, 1995

FINAL PLACINGS
GOLD MEDAL	Canada
SILVER MEDAL	Russia
BRONZE MEDAL	Sweden
Fourth Place	Finland
Fifth Place	United States
Sixth Place	Czech Republic
Seventh Place	Germany
Eighth Place	Ukraine*

* promoted from 'B' pool in 1994

Note: no team was relegated to 'B' pool from this year's tournament because in 1996 the 'A' pool expanded to ten teams and a new round-robin format

ALL-STAR TEAM
Goal	Igor Karpenko (Ukraine)
Defence	Bryan McCabe (Canada)
	Anders Eriksson (Sweden)
Forward	Jason Allison (Canada)
	Eric Daze (Canada)
	Marty Murray (Canada)

DIRECTORATE AWARDS
BEST GOALIE	Evgeny Tarasov (Russia)
BEST DEFENCEMAN	Bryan McCabe (Canada)
BEST FORWARD	Marty Murray (Canada)

1996 WORLD JUNIOR CHAMPIONSHIPS

UNITED STATES, DECEMBER 26, 1995–JANUARY 4, 1996

FINAL PLACINGS

GOLD MEDAL	Canada
SILVER MEDAL	Sweden
BRONZE MEDAL	Russia
Fourth Place	Czech Republic
Fifth Place	United States
Sixth Place	Finland
Seventh Place	Slovakia*
Eighth Place	Germany
Ninth Place	Switzerland*
Tenth Place	Ukraine**

* promoted from 'B' pool in 1995
** relegated to 'B' pool for 1997

ALL-STAR TEAM

Goal	Jose Theodore (Canada)
Defence	Nolan Baumgartner (Canada)
	Mattias Ohlund (Sweden)
Forward	Jarome Iginla (Canada)
	Johan Davidsson (Sweden)
	Alexei Morozov (Russia)

DIRECTORATE AWARDS

BEST GOALIE	Jose Theodore (Canada)
BEST DEFENCEMAN	Mattias Ohlund (Sweden)
BEST FORWARD	Jarome Iginla (Canada)

1997 WORLD JUNIOR CHAMPIONSHIPS

SWITZERLAND, DECEMBER 26, 1996–JANUARY 4, 1997

FINAL PLACINGS

GOLD MEDAL	Canada
SILVER MEDAL	United States
BRONZE MEDAL	Russia
Fourth Place	Czech Republic
Fifth Place	Finland
Sixth Place	Slovakia
Seventh Place	Switzerland
Eighth Place	Sweden
Ninth Place	Germany
Tenth Place	Poland*

* promoted from 'B' pool in 1996; relegated to 'B' pool for 1998

ALL-STAR TEAM

Goal	Brian Boucher (United States)
Defence	Chris Phillips (Canada)
	Mark Streit (Switzerland)
Forward	Christian Dube (Canada)
	Sergei Samsonov (Russia)
	Michael York (United States)

DIRECTORATE AWARDS

BEST GOALIE	Marc Denis (Canada)
BEST DEFENCEMAN	Joseph Corvo (United States)
BEST FORWARD	Alexei Morozov (Russia)

1998 WORLD JUNIOR CHAMPIONSHIPS

FINLAND, DECEMBER 25, 1997–JANUARY 3, 1998

FINAL PLACINGS

GOLD MEDAL	Finland
SILVER MEDAL	Russia
BRONZE MEDAL	Switzerland
Fourth Place	Czech Republic
Fifth Place	United States
Sixth Place	Sweden
Seventh Place	Kazakhstan*
Eighth Place	Canada
Ninth Place	Slovakia
Tenth Place	Germany**

* promoted from 'B' pool in 1997
** relegated to 'B' pool for 1999

ALL-STAR TEAM

Goal	David Aebischer (Switzerland)
Defence	Pierre Hedin (Sweden)
	Andrei Markov (Russia)
Forward	Olli Jokinen (Finland)
	Eero Somervuori (Finland)
	Maxim Balmochnykh (Russia)

DIRECTORATE AWARDS

BEST GOALIE	David Aebischer (Switzerland)
BEST DEFENCEMAN	Pavel Skrbek (Czech Republic)
BEST FORWARD	Olli Jokinen (Finland)

1999 WORLD JUNIOR CHAMPIONSHIPS
CANADA, DECEMBER 26, 1998–JANUARY 5, 1999

FINAL PLACINGS
GOLD MEDAL	Russia
SILVER MEDAL	Canada
BRONZE MEDAL	Slovakia
Fourth Place	Sweden
Fifth Place	Finland
Sixth Place	Kazakhstan
Seventh Place	Czech Republic
Eighth Place	United States
Ninth Place	Switzerland
Tenth Place	Belarus*

* promoted from 'B' pool in 1998; relegated to 'B' pool for 2000

ALL-STAR TEAM
Goal	Roberto Luongo (Canada)
Defence	Vitali Vishnevsky (Russia)
	Brian Campbell (Canada)
Forward	Daniel Tkachuk (Canada)
	Brian Gionta (United States)
	Maxim Balmochnykh (Russia)

DIRECTORATE AWARDS
BEST GOALIE	Roberto Luongo (Canada)
BEST DEFENCEMAN	Maxim Afinigenov (Russia)
BEST FORWARD	Vitali Vishnevski (Russia)

2000 WORLD JUNIOR CHAMPIONSHIPS
SWEDEN, DECEMBER 25, 1999–JANUARY 4, 2000

FINAL PLACINGS
GOLD MEDAL	Czech Republic
SILVER MEDAL	Russia
BRONZE MEDAL	Canada
Fourth Place	United States
Fifth Place	Sweden
Sixth Place	Switzerland
Seventh Place	Finland
Eighth Place	Kazakhstan
Ninth Place	Slovakia
Tenth Place	Ukraine*

* promoted from 'B' pool in 1999; demoted to 'B' pool for 2001

ALL-STAR TEAM
Goal	Rick DiPietro (United States)
Defence	Mathieu Biron (Canada)
	Alexander Rjasantsev (Russia)
Forward	Milan Kraft (Czech Republic)
	Alexei Tereschenko (Russia)
	Evgeny Muratov (Russia)

DIRECTORATE AWARDS
BEST GOALIE	Rick DiPietro (United States)
BEST DEFENCEMAN	Alexander Rjasantsev (Russia)
BEST FORWARD	Milan Kraft (Czech Republic)

2001 WORLD JUNIOR CHAMPIONSHIPS

RUSSIA, DECEMBER 26, 2000–JANUARY 5, 2001

FINAL PLACINGS

GOLD MEDAL	Czech Republic
SILVER MEDAL	Finland
BRONZE MEDAL	Canada
Fourth Place	Sweden
Fifth Place	United States
Sixth Place	Switzerland
Seventh Place	Russia
Eighth Place	Slovakia
Ninth Place	Belarus*
Tenth Place	Kazakhstan**

* promoted from 'B' pool in 2000
** demoted to 'B' pool for 2002

ALL-STAR TEAM

Goal	Ari Ahonen (Finland)
Defence	Rostislav Klesla (Czech Republic)
	Tuukka Mantyla (Finland)
Forward	Jason Spezza (Canada)
	Jani Rita (Finland)
	Pavel Brendl (Czech Republic)

DIRECTORATE AWARDS

BEST GOALIE	Tomas Duba (Czech Republic)
BEST DEFENCEMAN	Rostislav Klesla (Czech Republic)
BEST FORWARD	Pavel Brendl (Czech Republic)

2002 WORLD JUNIOR CHAMPIONSHIPS
CZECH REPUBLIC, DECEMBER 25, 2001–JUANUARY 4, 2002

FINAL PLACINGS
GOLD MEDAL	Russia
SILVER MEDAL	Canada
BRONZE MEDAL	Finland
Fourth Place	Switzerland
Fifth Place	United States
Sixth Place	Sweden
Seventh Place	Czech Republic
Eighth Place	Slovakia
Ninth Place	Belarus
Tenth Place	France*

* promoted from 2001; demoted for 2003

ALL-STAR TEAM
Goal	Pascal Leclaire (Canada)
Defence	Jay Bouwmeester (Canada)
	Igor Knyazev (Russia)
Forward	Mike Cammalleri (Canada)
	Marek Svatos (Slovakia)
	Stanislav Chistov (Russia)

DIRECTORATE AWARDS
BEST GOALIE	Kari Lehtonen (Finland)
BEST DEFENCEMAN	Igor Knyazev (Russia)
BEST FORWARD	Mike Cammalleri (Canada)

2003 WORLD JUNIOR CHAMPIONSHIPS
CANADA, DECEMBER 26, 2002–JANUARY 5, 2003

FINAL PLACINGS
GOLD MEDAL	Russia
SILVER MEDAL	Canada
BRONZE MEDAL	Finland
Fourth Place	United States
Fifth Place	Slovakia
Sixth Place	Czech Republic
Seventh Place	Switzerland
Eighth Place	Sweden
Ninth Place	Germany*
Tenth Place	Belarus**

* promoted from 2002
** demoted for 2004

ALL-STAR TEAM
Goal	Marc-Andre Fleury (Canada)
Defence	Carlo Colaiacovo (Canada)
	Joni Pitkanen (Finland)
Forward	Scottie Upshall (Canada)
	Igor Grigorenko (Russia)
	Yuri Trubachev (Russia)

DIRECTORATE AWARDS
BEST GOALIE	Marc-Andre Fleury (Canada)
BEST DEFENCEMAN	Joni Pitkanen (Finland)
BEST FORWARD	Igor Grigorenko (Russia)

2004 WORLD JUNIOR CHAMPIONSHIPS

FINLAND, DECEMBER 26, 2003–JANUARY 6, 2004

FINAL PLACINGS

GOLD MEDAL	United States
SILVER MEDAL	Canada
BRONZE MEDAL	Finland
Fourth Place	Czech Republic
Fifth Place	Russia
Sixth Place	Slovakia
Seventh Place	Sweden
Eighth Place	Switzerland
Ninth Place	Austria*
Tenth Place	Ukraine**

* promoted from 2003
** demoted for 2005

ALL-STAR TEAM

Goal	Al Montoya (United States)
Defence	Dion Phaneuf (Canada)
	Sami Lepisto (Finland)
Forward	Jeff Carter (Canada)
	Valtteri Filppula (Finland)
	Zach Parise (United States)

DIRECTORATE AWARDS

BEST GOALIE	Al Montoya (United States)
BEST DEFENCEMAN	Sami Lepisto (Finland)
BEST FORWARD	Zach Parise (United States)

2005 WORLD JUNIOR CHAMPIONSHIP

UNITED STATES, December 25, 2004–January 4, 2005

FINAL PLACINGS

GOLD MEDAL	Canada
SILVER MEDAL	Russia
BRONZE MEDAL	Czech Republic
Fourth Place	United States
Fifth Place	Finland
Sixth Place	Sweden
Seventh Place	Slovakia
Eighth Place	Switzerland
Ninth Place	Germany*
Tenth Place	Belarus*

* promoted from 2004; demoted for 2006

ALL-STAR TEAM

Goal	Marek Schwarz (Czech Republic)
Defence	Dion Phaneuf (Canada)
	Gary Suter (United States)
Forward	Patrice Bergeron (Canada)
	Jeff Carter (Canada)
	Alexander Ovechkin (Russia)

DIRECTORATE AWARDS

BEST GOALIE	Marek Schwarz (Czech Republic)
BEST DEFENCEMAN	Dion Phaneuf (Canada)
BEST FORWARD	Alexander Ovechkin (Russia)

2006 WORLD JUNIOR CHAMPIONSHIP

CANADA, December 26, 2005–January 5, 2006

FINAL PLACINGS

GOLD MEDAL	Canada
SILVER MEDAL	Russia
BRONZE MEDAL	Finland
Fourth Place	United States
Fifth Place	Sweden
Sixth Place	Czech Republic
Seventh Place	Switzerland
Eighth Place	Slovakia
Ninth Place	Latvia*
Tenth Place	Norway*

* promoted from 2005; demoted for 2007

ALL-STAR TEAM

Goal	Tuukka Rask (Finland)
Defence	Luc Bourdon (Canada)
	Jack Johnson (United States)
Forward	Steve Downie (Canada)
	Evgeni Malkin (Russia)
	Lauri Tukonen (Finland)

DIRECTORATE AWARDS

BEST GOALIE	Tuukka Rask (Finland)
BEST DEFENCEMAN	Marc Staal (Canada)
BEST FORWARD	Evgeni Malkin (Russia)

2007 WORLD JUNIOR CHAMPIONSHIP

SWEDEN, December 26, 2006–January 5, 2007

FINAL PLACINGS

GOLD MEDAL	Canada
SILVER MEDAL	Russia
BRONZE MEDAL	United States
Fourth Place	Sweden
Fifth Place	Czech Republic
Sixth Place	Finland
Seventh Place	Switzerland
Eighth Place	Slovakia
Ninth Place	Germany*
Tenth Place	Belarus*

*promoted from 2006; demoted for 2008

ALL-STAR TEAM

Goal	Carey Price (Canada)
Defence	Kristopher Letang (Canada)
	Erik Johnson (United States)
Forward	Jonathan Toews (Canada)
	Alexei Cherepanov (Russia)
	Patrick Kane (United States)

DIRECTORATE AWARDS

BEST GOALIE	Carey Price (Canada)
BEST DEFENCEMAN	Erik Johnson (United States)
BEST FORWARD	Alexei Cherepanov (Russia)
TOURNAMENT MVP	Carey Price (Canada)

2008 WORLD JUNIOR CHAMPIONSHIP

CZECH REPUBLIC, December 26, 2007–January 5, 2008

FINAL PLACINGS

GOLD MEDAL	Canada
SILVER MEDAL	Sweden
BRONZE MEDAL	Russia
Fourth Place	United States
Fifth Place	Czech Republic
Sixth Place	Finland
Seventh Place	Slovakia
Eighth Place	Kazakhstan*
Ninth Place	Switzerland†
Tenth Place	Denmark*†

*promoted from 2006; † demoted for 2009

ALL-STAR TEAM

Goal	Steve Mason (Canada)
Defence	Drew Doughty (Canada)
	Victor Hedman (Sweden)
Forward	Viktor Tikhonov (Russia)
	Patrik Berglund (Sweden)
	James van Riemsdyk (United States)

DIRECTORATE AWARDS

BEST GOALIE	Steve Mason (Canada)
BEST DEFENCEMAN	Drew Doughty (Canada)
BEST FORWARD	Viktor Tikhonov (Russia)
TOURNAMENT MVP	Steve Mason (Canada)

2009 WORLD JUNIOR CHAMPIONSHIP

Ottawa, CANADA, December 26, 2008–January 5, 2009

FINAL PLACINGS

GOLD MEDAL	Canada
SILVER MEDAL	Sweden
BRONZE MEDAL	Russia
Fourth Place	Slovakia
Fifth Place	United States
Sixth Place	Czech Republic
Seventh Place	Finland
Eighth Place	Latvia*
Ninth Place	Germany*†
Tenth Place	Kazakhstan†

*promoted from 2008; † demoted for 2010

All-Star Team

Goal	Jaroslav Janus (SVK)
Defence	P.K. Subban (CAN), Erik Karlsson (SWE)
Forward	John Tavares (CAN), Cody Hodgson (CAN), Nikita Filatov (RUS)

Directorate Awards

BEST GOALIE	Jacob Markstrom (SWE)
BEST DEFENCEMAN	Erik Karlsson (SWE)
BEST FORWARD	John Tavares (CAN)
TOURNAMENT MVP	John Tavares (CAN)

WORLD WOMEN'S CHAMPIONSHIPS, 1990–2009

1990 World Women's Championship

CANADA, March 19–25, 1990

FINAL PLACINGS

GOLD MEDAL	Canada
SILVER MEDAL	United States
BRONZE MEDAL	Finland
Fourth Place	Sweden
Fifth Place	Switzerland
Sixth Place	Norway
Seventh Place	Germany
Eighth Place	Japan

1992 World Women's Championship

FINLAND, April 20–26, 1992

FINAL PLACINGS

GOLD MEDAL	Canada
SILVER MEDAL	United States
BRONZE MEDAL	Finland
Fourth Place	Sweden
Fifth Place	China
Sixth Place	Norway
Seventh Place	Denmark
Eighth Place	Switzerland

DIRECTORATE AWARDS

BEST GOALIE	Annica Ahlen (Sweden)
BEST DEFENCEMAN	Geraldine Heaney (Canada)
BEST FORWARD	Cammi Granato (United States)

1994 World Women's Championship

UNITED STATES, April 11–17, 1994

FINAL PLACINGS

GOLD MEDAL	Canada
SILVER MEDAL	United States
BRONZE MEDAL	Finland
Fourth Place	China
Fifth Place	Sweden
Sixth Place	Norway
Seventh Place	Switzerland
Eighth Place	Germany

DIRECTORATE AWARDS

BEST GOALIE	Erin Whitten (United States)
BEST DEFENCEMAN	Geraldine Heaney (Canada)
BEST FORWARD	Riikka Nieminen (Finland)

1997 World Women's Championship

CANADA, March 31–April 6, 1997

FINAL PLACINGS

GOLD MEDAL	Canada
SILVER MEDAL	United States
BRONZE MEDAL	Finland
Fourth Place	China
Fifth Place	Sweden
Sixth Place	Russia
Seventh Place	Switzerland
Eighth Place	Norway

DIRECTORATE AWARDS

None awarded

1999 World Women's Championship

FINLAND, March 8–14, 1999

FINAL PLACINGS

GOLD MEDAL	Canada
SILVER MEDAL	United States
BRONZE MEDAL	Finland
Fourth Place	Sweden
Fifth Place	China
Sixth Place	Russia
Seventh Place	Germany
Eighth Place	Switzerland

DIRECTORATE AWARDS

BEST GOALIE	Sami Jo Small (Canada)
BEST DEFENCEMAN	Kirsi Hanninen (Finland)
BEST FORWARD	Jenny Schmidgall (United States)

2000 World Women's Championship

CANADA, April 3–9, 2000

FINAL PLACINGS

GOLD MEDAL	Canada
SILVER MEDAL	United States
BRONZE MEDAL	Finland
Fourth Place	Sweden
Fifth Place	Russia
Sixth Place	China
Seventh Place	Germany
Eighth Place	Japan

DIRECTORATE AWARDS

BEST GOALIE	Sami Jo Small (Canada)
BEST DEFENCEMAN	Angela Ruggiero (United States)
BEST FORWARD	Katja Riipi (Finland)

2001 World Women's Championship

UNITED STATES, April 2–8, 2001

FINAL PLACINGS

GOLD MEDAL	Canada
SILVER MEDAL	United States
BRONZE MEDAL	Russia
Fourth Place	Finland
Fifth Place	Sweden
Sixth Place	Germany
Seventh Place	China
Eighth Place	Kazakhstan

DIRECTORATE AWARDS

BEST GOALIE	Kim St. Pierre (Canada)
BEST DEFENCEMAN	Karyn Bye (United States)
BEST FORWARD	Jennifer Botterill (Canada)
MVP	Jennifer Botterill (Canada)

2003 World Women's Championship

CHINA, April 3–9, 2003

CANCELLED DUE TO SARS OUTBREAK

2004 World Women's Championship

CANADA, March 30–April 6, 2004

FINAL PLACINGS

GOLD MEDAL	Canada
SILVER MEDAL	United States
BRONZE MEDAL	Finland
Fourth Place	Sweden
Fifth Place	Russia

Sixth Place   Germany
Seventh Place   China
Eighth Place   Switzerland
Ninth Place   Japan

DIRECTORATE AWARDS

BEST GOALIE	Kim St. Pierre (Canada)
BEST DEFENCEMAN	Angela Ruggiero (United States)
BEST FORWARD	Jayna Hefford (Canada)
MVP	Jennifer Botterill (Canada)

ALL-STAR TEAM

Goal	Pam Dreyer (United States)
Defence	Gunilla Andersson (Sweden), Angela Ruggiero (United States)
Forward	Jayna Hefford (Canada), Jennifer Botterill (Canada), Natalie Darwitz (United States)

2005 World Women's Championship

SWEDEN, April 2–9, 2005

FINAL PLACINGS

GOLD MEDAL	United States
SILVER MEDAL	Canada
BRONZE MEDAL	Sweden
Fourth Place	Finland
Fifth Place	Germany
Sixth Place	China
Seventh Place	Kazakhstan
Eighth Place	Russia

DIRECTORATE AWARDS

BEST GOALIE	Chanda Gunn (United States)
BEST DEFENCEMAN	Angela Ruggiero (United States)

BEST FORWARD	Jayna Hefford (Canada)
MVP	Krissy Wendell (United States)

ALL-STAR TEAM

Goalie	Natalya Turnova (Kazakhstan)
Defence	Cheryl Pounder (Canada)
	Angela Ruggiero (United States)
Forward	Hayley Wickenheiser (Canada)
	Maria Rooth (Sweden)
	Krissy Wendell (United States)

2007 World Women's Championship

CANADA, April 3–10, 2007

FINAL PLACINGS

GOLD MEDAL	Canada
SILVER MEDAL	United States
BRONZE MEDAL	Sweden
Fourth Place	Finland
Fifth Place	Switzerland
Sixth Place	China
Seventh Place	Russia
Eighth Place	Germany
Ninth Place	Kazakhstan

DIRECTORATE AWARDS

BEST GOALIE	Noora Raty (Finland)
BEST DEFENCEMAN	Molly Engstrom (United States)
BEST FORWARD	Hayley Wickenheiser (Canada)
MVP	Hayley Wickenheiser (Canada)

ALL-STAR TEAM

Goalie	Kim St. Pierre (Canada)

Defence   Delaney Collins (Canada)
              Angela Ruggiero (United States)
Forward   Natalie Darwitz (United States)
              Krissy Wendell (United States)
              Hayley Wickenheiser (Canada)

2008 World Women's Championship

CHINA, April 4–12, 2008

FINAL PLACINGS

GOLD	United States
SILVER	Canada
BRONZE	Finland
Fourth Place	Switzerland
Fifth Place	Sweden
Sixth Place	Russia
Seventh Place	Japan
Eighth Place	China
Ninth Place	Germany

ALL-STAR TEAM

Goalie   Noora Raty (Finland)
Defence   Emma Laaksonen (Finland)
              Julie Chu (United States)
Forward   Hayley Wickenheiser (Canada)
              Natalie Darwitz (United States)
              Jayne Hefford (Canada)

DIRECTORATE AWARDS

BEST GOALIE	Noora Raty (Finland)
BEST DEFENCEMAN	Angela Ruggiero (United States)
BEST FORWARD	Natalie Darwitz (United States)
MVP	Noora Raty (Finland)

2009 World Women's Championship

Hameenlinna, FINLAND, April 4–12, 2009

FINAL PLACINGS

GOLD	United States
SILVER	Canada
BRONZE	Finland
Fourth Place	Sweden
Fifth Place	Russia
Sixth Place	Kazakhstan
Seventh Place	Switzerland
Eighth Place	Japan
Ninth Place	China

All-Star Team

Goalie	Jesse Vetter (USA)
Defence	Carla MacLeod (Canada)
	Angela Ruggiero (USA)
Forward	Michelle Karvinen (Finland)
	Julie Chu (USA)
	Natalie Darwitz (USA)

DIRECTORATE AWARDS

BEST GOALIE	Charline Labonte (Canada)
BEST DEFENCEMAN	Jenni Hiirikoski (Finland)
BEST FORWARD	Hayley Wickenheiser (Canada)
MVP	Carla MacLeod (Canada)

NATIONAL & CANADIAN WOMEN'S HOCKEY LEAGUES, 1999–2008

ALL-TIME STANDINGS

1999–2000
Eastern Division

	GP	W	L	T	GF	GA	P
Sainte Julie Pantheres	35	20	8	7	109	68	47
Montreal Wingstar	35	18	7	10	116	62	46
Ottawa Raiders	35	9	20	6	61	109	24
Laval Le Mistral	35	7	23	5	78	177	19

Western Division

	GP	W	L	T	GF	GA	P
Beatrice Aeros	40	35	3	2	217	37	72
Brampton Thunder	40	29	5	6	208	64	64
Mississauga Chiefs	40	21	13	6	133	79	48
Clearnet Lightning	40	4	33	3	44	249	11
Scarborough Sting	40	3	34	3	49	170	9

CHAMPIONSHIP FINALS
March 18   Sainte Julie Pantheres 2/Beatrice Aeros 2
March 19   Beatrice Aeros 1/Sainte Julie Pantheres 0
Beatrice wins championship 3–1 in points

2000–01
Eastern Division

	GP	W	L	T	GF	GA	P
Montreal Wingstar	40	30	6	4	163	63	64
Sainte Julie Pantheres	40	22	15	3	168	102	47
Ottawa Raiders	40	11	25	4	78	150	26
Laval Le Mistral	40	5	33	2	68	261	12

Western Division

Beatrice Aeros	40	35	2	3	222	46	73
Brampton Thunder	40	30	7	3	223	82	63
Mississauga Ice Bears	40	21	16	3	107	97	45
Toronto Sting	40	8	29	3	82	168	19
Clearnet Lightning	40	5	34	1	77	219	11
Vancouver Griffins	18	14	4	0	91	43	28

CHAMPIONSHIP FINALS

Beatrice Aeros 2/Sainte Julie Pantheres 2
Beatrice Aeros 8/Sainte Julie Pantheres 1
Beatrice wins championship 3–1 in points

2001–02

Eastern Division

	GP	W	L	T	GF	GA	P
Ottawa Raiders	30	14	10	6	71	72	34
Montreal Wingstar	30	11	14	5	66	78	27
Le Cheyenne de la Metropol	30	11	15	4	73	85	26

Western Division

Beatrice Aeros	30	23	2	5	149	39	51
Mississauga Ice Bears	30	12	10	8	82	81	32
Brampton Thunder	30	8	14	8	73	97	24
Telus Lightning	30	4	18	8	59	120	16

Pacific Division

Vancouver Griffins	31	27	4	0	84	14	54

CHAMPIONSHIP FINALS

Beatrice Aeros 3/Brampton Thunder 2 (OT)

2002–03
Eastern Division

	GP	W	L	T	OTL	GF	GA	P
Montreal Wingstar	36	18	15	3	0	83	81	39
Ottawa Raiders	36	13	20	1	2	96	122	29
Quebec Avalanche	36	10	20	5	1	87	120	26

Central Division

	GP	W	L	T	OTL	GF	GA	P
Beatrice Aeros	36	32	3	1	0	201	54	65
Brampton Thunder	36	27	9	0	0	152	71	54
Mississauga Ice Bears	36	19	13	3	1	122	111	42
Telus Lightning	36	0	34	1	1	54	236	2

Western Division

	GP	W	L	T	OTL	GF	GA	P
Calgary X-Treme	24	23	1	0	0	144	37	46
Vancouver Griffins	24	10	13	0	1	82	92	21
Edmonton Chimos	24	3	20	0	1	35	132	7

CHAMPIONSHIP FINALS
Calgary X-Treme 3/Beatrice Aeros 0

2003–04
Eastern Division

	G	W	L	T	OTL	GF	GA	P
Montreal Axion	36	20	10	5	1	113	84	46
Ottawa Raiders	36	9	23	4	0	85	144	22
Quebec Avalanche	36	4	28	2	2	65	163	12

Central Division

	G	W	L	T	OTL	GF	GA	P
Toronto Aeros	36	33	2	1	0	197	42	67
Brampton Thunder	36	28	6	2	0	190	72	58
Oakville Ice	36	17	17	2	0	118	99	36
Telus Lightning	36	8	28	0	0	66	224	16

Western Division

Calgary X-Treme	12	11	1	0	0	64	9	22
Edmonton Chimos	12	1	11	0	0	9	64	2

CHAMPIONSHIP FINALS
Calgary X-Treme 5/Brampton Thunder 4 (OT/SO)

2004–05
Eastern Division

	G	W	L	T	OTL	GF	GA	P
Montreal Axion	36	24	9	2	1	140	85	51
Ottawa Raiders	36	14	19	2	1	101	128	31
Quebec Avalanche	36	5	25	4	2	53	132	16

Central Division

	G	W	L	T	OTL	GF	GA	P
Brampton Thunder	36	30	3	2	1	165	70	63
Toronto Aeros	36	24	6	4	2	142	68	54
Oakville Ice	36	13	15	6	2	97	99	34
Telus Lightning	36	4	28	4	0	72	189	12

CHAMPIONSHIP FINALS
Toronto Aeros 5/Montreal Axion 4 (OT)

2005–06
Eastern Division

	G	W	L	T	OTL	GF	GA	P
Ottawa Raiders	36	21	8	4	3	122	77	49
Montreal Axion	36	14	17	3	2	100	122	33
Quebec Avalanche	36	4	28	2	2	58	135	12

Central Division

	G	W	L	T	OTL	GF	GA	P
Durham Lightning	36	23	6	5	2	107	74	53
Brampton Thunder	36	19	12	5	0	113	97	43
Oakville Ice	36	20	14	1	1	118	100	42
Toronto Aeros	36	13	17	4	2	114	127	32

CHAMPIONSHIP FINALS

April 15   Montreal Axion 1/Brampton Thunder 0

2006–07

	G	W	L	T	OTL	GF	GA	P
Etobicoke Dolphins	20	15	1	2	2	87	66	64
Mississauga Aeros	21	15	5	0	1	107	51	31
Brampton Thunder	16	8	8	0	0	71	66	16
Oakville Ice	17	6	8	1	2	40	53	15
Montreal Axion	13	6	6	0	0	66	56	13
Quebec Avalanche	12	2	8	2	0	41	91	6
Ottawa Raiders	11	2	8	0	0	25	54	5

CHAMPIONSHIP FINALS

April 14   Brampton Thunder 4/Montreal Axion 0

Note: the NWHL was replaced by the CWHL in 2007

2007–08

Central Division

	GP	W	L	OT	GF	GA	P
Brampton Canadette-Thunder	30	22	7	1	111	59	45
Mississauga Chiefs	30	21	8	1	115	61	43
Vaughan Flames	30	12	16	2	69	101	26
Burlington Barracudas	30	11	18	1	76	98	23

Eastern Division

	GP	W	L	OT	GF	GA	P
Montreal Stars	28	21	6	1	112	55	43
Ottawa Capital-Canucks	28	8	17	3	58	102	19
Quebec Phoenix	28	8	21	1	56	121	17

PLAYOFFS

Burlington 2 at Ottawa 1
(Burlington advanced)

Mississauga 6 at Vaughan 2
Mississauga 6 at Vaughan 2

Mississauga 4 at Montreal 3
Mississauga 1 at Montreal 4
(Mississauga won tie-breaker)

Burlington 2 at Brampton 5
Burlington 3 at Brampton 3
(Brampton advanced)

CHAMPIONSHIP FINALS

Mississauga Chiefs 3/Brampton Canadette-Thunder 2 (OT)

CANADIAN & WESTERN WOMEN'S HOCKEY LEAGUES, 2008–09

CWHL Regular-Season Standings

	GP	W	L	P
Montreal Stars	28	24	3	49
Brampton Thunder	26	19	6	39
Mississauga Chiefs	26	16	8	34
Burlington Barracudas	25	10	13	22
Vaughan Flames	25	4	19	10
Ottawa Senators	24	4	20	8

League Playoffs

(best-of-two plus sudden-death OT in case of tie)

March 14 Brampton 3/Mississauga 2
March 15 Mississauga 4/Brampton 1
OT tie-breaker: Brampton, Jayna Hefford
Brampton Thunder advance to Clarkson Cup finals

March 14 Montreal 6/Burlington 1
March 15 Burlington 3/Montreal 1
OT tie-breaker: Montreal, Noemie Marin
Montreal Stars advance to Clarkson Cup finals

WWHL Regular-Season Standings

	GP	W	L	OTL	P
Calgary Oval X-Treme	23	20	2	1	42
Minnesota Whitecaps	22	18	3	1	38
Edmonton Chimos	24	14	10	0	28
Strathmore Rockies	23	6	16	1	13
B.C. Breakers	24	0	22	2	2

League Playoffs
Semifinals
March 7   Calgary 9/Strathmore 0
March 7   Minnesota 4/Edmonton 0

Finals
March 8   Minnesota 2/Calgary 0

Both finalists advance to Clarkson Cup finals

CLARKSON CUP FINALS
Kingston, Ontario

Round Robin
March 19   Minnesota 4/Montreal 3
March 19   Brampton 4/Calgary 3

Semifinals
March 20   Montreal 4/Brampton 1
March 20   Minnesota 2/Calgary 1

Finals
March 21   Montreal 3 Minnesota 1

CANADIAN & WESTERN WOMEN'S HOCKEY LEAGUES, 2009–10

CWHL Regular-Season Standings

	GP	W	L	OTL	GF	GA	Pts
*Montreal Stars	30	23	5	2	122	70	48
*Mississauga Chiefs	30	21	8	1	94	60	43
Burlington Barracudas	30	19	8	3	94	80	41
Brampton Thunder	29	12	14	3	76	78	27
Vaughan Flames	29	9	19	1	77	111	19
Ottawa Senators	30	5	23	2	61	125	12

*advanced to Clarkson Cup as top two teams

Playoffs (winner advances to Clarkson Cup)

March 20   Brampton 4/Vaughan 1
March 20   Burlington 4/Ottawa 3 (OT)
March 21   Brampton 2/Burlington 1

WWHL Regular Season Standings, 2009–10

	GP	W	L	T	OTL	GF	GA	Pts
*Minnesota Whitecaps	12	10	2	0	0	44	24	20
Edmonton Chimos	18	7	7	0	4	40	48	18
Strathmore Rockies	18	7	10	0	1	43	55	15
Calgary Oval X-Treme	0	0	0	0	0	0	0	0
British Columbia Breakers			DID NOT PLAY					

*advanced to Clarkson Cup for finishing in first place

Clarkson Cup
Richmond Hill, Ontario

Semifinals
March 27   Brampton 3/Montreal 2
March 27   Minnesota 3/Mississauga 1

Finals
March 28   Minnesota 4/Brampton 0

HOCKEY POOL NOTES

HOCKEY POOL NOTES

HOCKEY POOL NOTES

HOCKEY POOL NOTES